TAUNTON'S

FOR PROS BY PROS

ROOFING

WITH ASPHALT SHINGLES

MIKE GUERTIN

The Taunton Press

The Taunton Press, Inc., 63 South Main Street, PO Box 5506, Newtown, CT 06470-5506
e-mail: tp@taunton.com

Editor: David Schiff
Jacket/Cover design: Cathy Cassidy
Interior design and layout: Jeff Potter/Potter Publishing Studio
Illustrator: Mario Ferro
Photographer: Mike Guertin unless otherwise noted

Library of Congress Cataloging-in-Publication Data

Guertin, Mike.
Roofing with asphalt shingles / Mike Guertin.
p. cm. -- (Taunton's for pros/by pros)
Includes index.
ISBN 1-56158-531-9
1. Shingles--Handbooks, manuals, etc. 2. Roofing,
Bituminous--Handbooks, manuals, etc. I. Title. II. For pros, by pros.
TH2441 .G84 2002
695--dc21 2002010453

Printed in the United States of America

10 9 8 7 6 5 4 3 2

About Your Safety: Homebuilding is inherently dangerous. From accidents with power tools or hand tools to falls from ladders, scaffolds, and roofs, builders and homeowners risk serious injury and even death. We try to promote safe work practices throughout this book, but what is safe for one builder or homeowner under certain circumstances may not be safe for you under different circumstances. So don't try anything you learn about here (or elsewhere) unless you're certain that it's safe for you. If something doesn't feel right, don't do it. Look for another way. Please keep safety foremost in your mind whenever you're working.

In memory of my father, Ray Guertin, who passed away shortly after I finished writing this manuscript. He always told me I could accomplish anything I put my mind to. He never imagined this mediocre student would ever try writing books. I miss him every day.

ACKNOWLEDGMENTS

Until I wrote my first book, *Precision Framing,* I didn't realize that the author is only one small part of the team that gets a book out on the shelves. Without a doubt, I'd have to say the single most important individual to pull the pieces together and polish what I started is freelance editor David Schiff. Although I'll admit he drove me crazy with umpteen questions, pleas for additional photography and drawings, and requests for more description, what you'll learn from this book is far more comprehensive and clear than it would have been without his aid.

I also thank Stefanie Ramp, who received a half-baked project and had the dirty and thankless job of bugging me and David to keep us on some sort of schedule right down to the bitter end.

This book would have been pitifully brief if not for the command decisions of Peter Chapman, who let us expand the page count by 80 percent and allowed us to double the number of photographs and triple the number of drawings. He was patient and supportive, leaving the dirty work for Stefanie.

I thank my brother Bruce, who did for me what he swore he'd never do again—roof a house. You'll see him (or his hands) throughout the photographs, which he was so patient to pose for while I snapped off more than 1,400 exposures.

Then there are the magic people in the production department who take a pile of unformatted text and boxes of numbered slides and photographs, and breathe life into them on the pages you'll see within: Paula Schlosser, Wendi Mijal, and their staff. And thanks to Mario Ferro, who took my cheesy sketches and sorted out all the perspective, so the drawings you see say more than my words.

I must thank those friends outside the book loop for their support: Rick Arnold, who taught me what little he knew at the time (22 years ago) about roofing and together we figured out how to keep the water from leaking inside; Gary Katz, with whom I've traded many a late night e-mail of commiserations; and *Fine Homebuilding* Managing Editor Roe Osborn, from whom I still keep learning how to write, edit, and photograph (as well as dine at nice restaurants).

Contents

Introduction

About 80 percent of North American residential roofs are covered with asphalt roof shingles. These shingles have been around since the turn of the 20th century and owe their popularity to low cost, ease of installation, good performance, and adaptability to most roof designs.

When the homebuilding business in my area was slow in the early 1980s, my crew and I did a lot of roofing. Soon we were introduced to pneumatic roof staplers and our production doubled. From the start, we decided to be fussy about the appearance of our roof installations. The slots in three-tab shingles had to be straight, as well as the horizontal course lines. After all, it doesn't take much more time to do a nice job than it does to hack things up.

Layovers, strip-offs and reroofs, and new homes: We did (and still do) it all. We learned some of the details of a well-installed shingle job simply by reading the wrapper on a bundle of roof shingles. Every bundle has the installation instruction right there on it as well as warranty information. Most manufacturers' instructions are similar if not identical. From time to time, I read the instructions on a new bundle just to see if anything has changed.

The bundle wrapper is a good place to start, but of course it doesn't have the room for detailed information about all the situations you will encounter when shingling a roof and, just as important, when preparing a roof to be shingled. From installing drip edge to capping ridges, you'll find all the details you need in this book to install a roof that will fulfill its two important and distinct functions: To enhance the beauty of the home and to remain watertight for many years.

The individual skills you need to install a roof are among the easiest in the building trades to acquire, and you don't need a lot of specialized tools to get started. Creating a beautiful and waterproof roof does take diligence, however, and I have tried to instill that diligence throughout this book. Also, to be a good roofer you need to know more than just the right detail procedures. You need to understand how the roof works as a system. This is why, for example, you'll find a chapter devoted to ventilation.

As with any trade, it is quite possible to be a superb and diligent roofing

mechanic and lose money on every job. To make a good living, you need to know how to size up a job and create a strategy for attacking it efficiently. It's not enough to know the procedures for how to do the racking pattern or the pyramid pattern or even shingle from the top down. The trick is to know when each approach is most efficient, and this book is designed to arm you with the knowledge to make those decisions. Of course if you are a do-it-yourselfer, your livelihood won't depend on an efficient plan, but having one will help ensure that roofing your own house or garage doesn't become a career.

My crew and I find it's pretty rare for people to compliment us on our roof jobs. I guess most people just don't give the roof much thought. Of course when water leaks into the house, no matter what the source, you know who they call first. But that's okay. When we step back for a final look before getting into our trucks, we know we're looking at a job we can be proud of.

CHAPTER 1

Shingles and Other Materials

ASPHALT ROOFING has been around for more than a century. It's beyond me how anyone conceived of producing a roofing material from a gooey, sticky flammable petroleum product that oozed out of the earth. Yet the results are amazing.

Weighing about 2 to 3 pounds per square foot (psf), asphalt shingles are lightweight compared with slate or tiles made of concrete or clay. Asphalt shingles have good fire resistance; many have a class A rating, especially those built around a fiberglass base material. They last 20 to 40 years depending on the product, the quality of installation, and the climate, whereas wood, tile, slate, plastic, rubber, and steel are all more durable, with life spans ranging from 30 to 80 years. Yet asphalt shingles are less expensive in the long run because material and labor costs are so much less than the other products. Once installed, asphalt roof shingles need little or no maintenance and are easy to repair if damaged.

You'll find asphalt roof shingles used on nearly every style of home. You can install them on roof pitches as low as 2 in 12 and on slopes all the way up to vertical walls (see an explanation of roof pitches on p. 98). Asphalt roof shingles are easy to install, so anyone in reason-

This house was roofed with laminated shingles, which are also referred to as architectural or dimensional shingles. They are made by bonding two layers of shingle material.

Anatomy of an Organic Felt Shingle

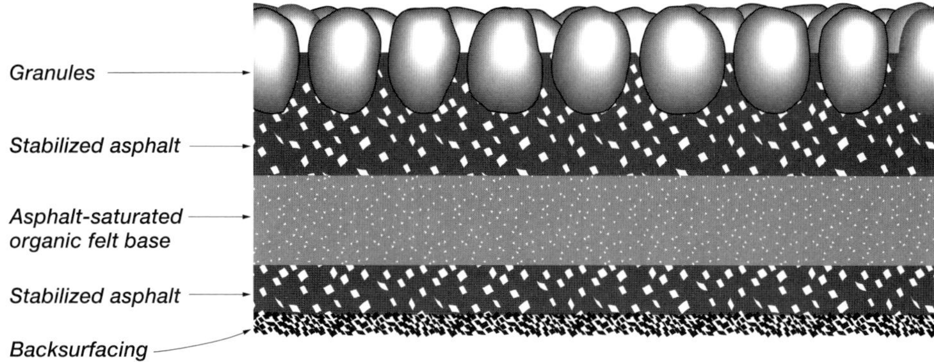

able physical condition who doesn't suffer from vertigo and is handy with simple tools can roof a house.

There are a tremendous number of shingle products available for a new roof or a replacement roof. Knowing what asphalt shingles are made from and how they are put together will help you choose the best shingles for a particular roof. The product you choose can have a direct effect on how long the roof will last. Later in this chapter, I'll explain manufacturer warranties and discuss materials you'll need in addition to the shingles.

Anatomy of an Asphalt Shingle

Although there have been various designs and many improvements over the years, basic shingle composition remains the same. Asphalt shingles are constructed in layers, each serving a particular function. The backbone of the shingle is the base material. Surrounding and impregnating the base is specially formulated asphalt. The face is coated with colored granules, and the bottom is coated with finely crushed minerals.

Base materials

The base material gives shingles strength to resist tearing during handling, installation, and in windy conditions. Asphalt shingles have a base of either organic felt or fiberglass. Organic felt was the base for the first asphalt material developed in the late 1890s, but fiberglass-based shingles, introduced around 1960, are lighter and less expensive to manufacture. By the late 1970s, fiberglass was more commonly used than organic felt.

ORGANIC FELT The original asphalt shingles used an organic felt fabric made from a combination of cellulose and fiber from cotton and wool rags. Since the 1940s, organic felt has been made exclusively from cellulose from wood fiber, recycled paper, and cardboard. Today's organic felt shingles typically are thicker and heavier than fiberglass shingles.

Organic felt shingles are prone to three aging problems that detract from a roof's appearance: clawing, curling, and fishmouthing. The problems occur when the cellulose fibers in the base material dry out and the asphalt becomes brittle. When clawing occurs, shingle tabs rise in the middle while the exposed edges curl downward (see the top photo on p. 6).

■ WORK SAFE
■ WORK SMART
■ THINKING AHEAD

Organic felt shingles often have a class C fire-resistance rating, which means that the roofing can resist only light exposure to fire. This is important when selecting shingles in fire-prone areas. Some local building codes and zoning ordinances prohibit class C roofing.

Some signs of age deterioration include clawing (top), curling (center), and fishmouthing (bottom). Organic felt-based shingles are more prone to these problems than shingles with a fiberglass base.

The result looks like a bear's paw, puffed in the middle and rounded along the edges. Curling is the opposite; the centers of the tabs remain flat on the roof and the edges curl up as shown in the center photo at left. With fishmouthing, the butt edges of the shingle tabs lift in the middle while the corners stay down (see the bottom photo at left). All three problems are signs that the shingles are old or defective and need to be replaced.

The major advantage of organic felt-based shingles is that they resist tearing better than fiberglass-based shingles. This means that organic felt can withstand more punishment during installation and in windy conditions without ripping and breaking apart.

Today, more companies produce fiberglass shingles than organic. Still you may find that organic shingles are more commonly used in your area, perhaps because organic shingles may be produced locally, which makes them less expensive than fiberglass. Or it may be due to roofer or homeowner preference.

INORGANIC FIBERGLASS Fiberglass-based shingles suffered from a bad reputation when first introduced because many early models weren't durable; they tore easily and wind blew them off roofs. Even today, many old-timers swear by felt because of these early problems. While it is true that fiberglass shingles

Anatomy of a Fiberglass Shingle

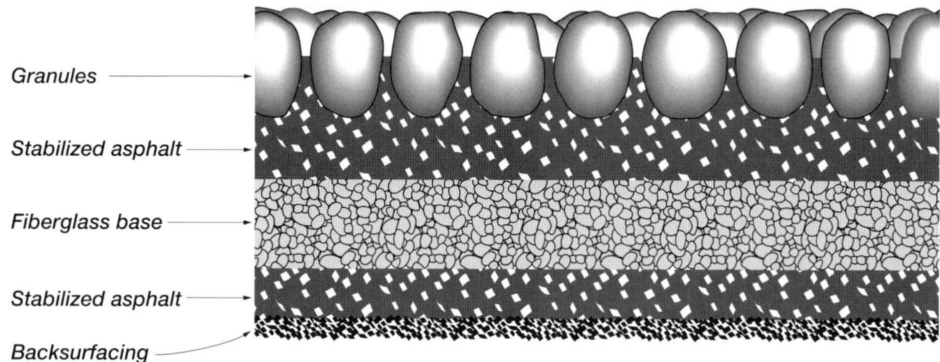

tear more easily during installation, once in place they are just as durable as felt.

Clawing, curling, and fishmouthing can occur with fiberglass, but it is much less common than with felt. Fiberglass has another problem of its own called thermal splitting. As the shingles age, they become less flexible. As a result, the expansion and contraction caused by daily and seasonal temperature changes can cause older shingles to split. The splits can run vertically through successive courses (horizontal rows) of shingles or horizontally along a shingle as shown in the photo at right. Thermal splitting occurs on shingles that are very securely self-sealed (see p. 10), with the splits often going all the way through individual shingles and continuing through the shingles beneath. Thermal splitting can lead to serious roof leaks. Heavier-weight fiberglass shingles are less prone to this problem.

Asphalt

Asphalt gives shingles their resistance to water and makes them tough. The asphalt used in shingles is formulated to provide long-term stable service in the microclimatic extremes of temperature, sunlight, wind, and precipitation that roofs endure. In simple terms, the more asphalt in a shingle, the heavier and more durable it will be. But the quality of the asphalt used also plays a big part.

Organic felt shingles contain two types of asphalt. The first is liquid and saturates the cellulose felt. The second, a stabilized asphalt coating, is applied to both faces of the saturated felt and serves as the adhering surface for mineral layers. The stabilized asphalt coatings are modified with fillers that make the shingles tougher and longer lasting. Fiberglass-based shingles don't need liquid asphalt saturation, so they are only coated with stabilized asphalt.

All roof shingles will eventually degrade and fail. Except in cases of extreme weather conditions or events, the longevity of a roof is directly related to the quality of the asphalt and the strength of the heat from the sun. Heat robs asphalt of its oil, causing the shingle to become brittle. Brittle shingles crack and lose their protective granule surface coating, and the degradation process accelerates. When shingles lose patches of their granular surfacing, called spalling or blistering, the countdown to replacement should quicken. The exposed asphalt coating will deteriorate even

Thermal splitting is most likely to occur in fiberglass shingles. The splits frequently penetrate through the shingle overlaps and result in leaks.

■ WORK SAFE
■ WORK SMART
■ THINKING AHEAD

An important advantage of fiberglass is that these shingles can resist severe exposure to fire. This higher class A fire-resistance rating is sometimes required by local building code and insurance policies.

■ WORK SAFE
■ WORK SMART
■ THINKING AHEAD

Department of Energy studies have shown that buildings with light-colored roofs use less energy to cool than buildings with dark-colored roofs. Because attic temperature is directly affected by shingle color, the use of light-colored asphalt roof shingles can help reduce cooling costs for homes in Southern regions where houses use more energy for cooling than for heating.

more rapidly and precipitate further granule loss, which quickly leads to leaks.

Mineral-surface coatings

Both sides of roof shingles receive a coating of granular minerals. The back is surfaced with fine crushed sand, mica, talc, or other mineral material. This coating keeps shingles from sticking to one another during storage and delivery.

The face is covered with decorative granules of crushed stone, crushed slate, crushed limestone, ceramic-coated sand, or other minerals. But these granules do more than just make the roof look good—they shield the asphalt layers against UV sunlight, slowing down the process of degradation, and they also provide fire resistance.

The color of these mineral granules affects how long the shingles will last, especially in hot, sunny climates. The darker the shingle, the more of the sun's heat it will absorb. As a result, dark shingles (and the attic space beneath) get hotter and the asphalt degrades more rapidly.

ALGAECIDE ADDITIVES Roofs that stay damp because of excessive rain, humidity, or shade are subject to unsightly algae. These dark, blotchy, or streaky stains show up on all but the darkest shingle colors. Algae stains have no effect on a roof's performance or life span, but the stains do annoy most homeowners. To resist algae growth, many manufacturers add zinc- or copper oxide-coated granules to the surface coating. In most places, this is enough to quell algae staining, but roofs in very humid areas such as the Southeast and the Pacific Northwest require higher concentrations of zinc or copper oxide. Some companies offer special algae-resistant shingles that have higher concentrations of the coated granules.

Moss and lichens can also take hold and flourish on the rough granular surface of roofs, but unlike algae, moss and lichens can damage shingles. The growths can be retarded by the same treatments as those used for algae.

Algae stains are unsightly but they don't damage the shingles.

Shingle Terms

Following are some common terms you will encounter when doing a shingling job:

- **Butt edge** is the bottom edge of the shingle.
- **Top lap** is the portion of shingle that's covered by the next shingle laid on top. It's typically 7 in. wide.
- **Head lap** is the portion of the top lap that's covered by the next two shingle courses. It's typically 2 in. wide.
- **Exposure** is the part of the shingle exposed to the weather. It's typically 5 in. wide.
- **Cutouts** are slots of shingle material cut out of the exposure of a tabbed strip shingle. It's typically ⅜ in. to ½ in. wide.
- **Tabs** are the portions of the exposure bounded by the cutouts.
- **Self-seal strip** is an adhesive strip or dots on the shingles that bond the butt edge to the shingle beneath when exposed to heat from the sun.
- **Release strip** is a plastic strip applied to the back of shingles to prevent the self-sealing strips from sticking shingles together while bundled.
- **Exposure-gauge notches** are minute cuts that some manufacturers emboss on the side edges of strip shingles to help the installer gauge the proper exposure.
- **Offset-gauge notches** are minute cuts embossed by some manufacturers along the top edge of shingles to help the installer gauge a standard 6-in. offset on three-tab shingles.
- **Fastener location** is the horizontal line where fasteners must be located. This is typically 5⅝ in. above the butt edge. (For more on shingle fastening, see chapter 7.)
- **Shingle course** is a horizontal row of shingles across the roof.

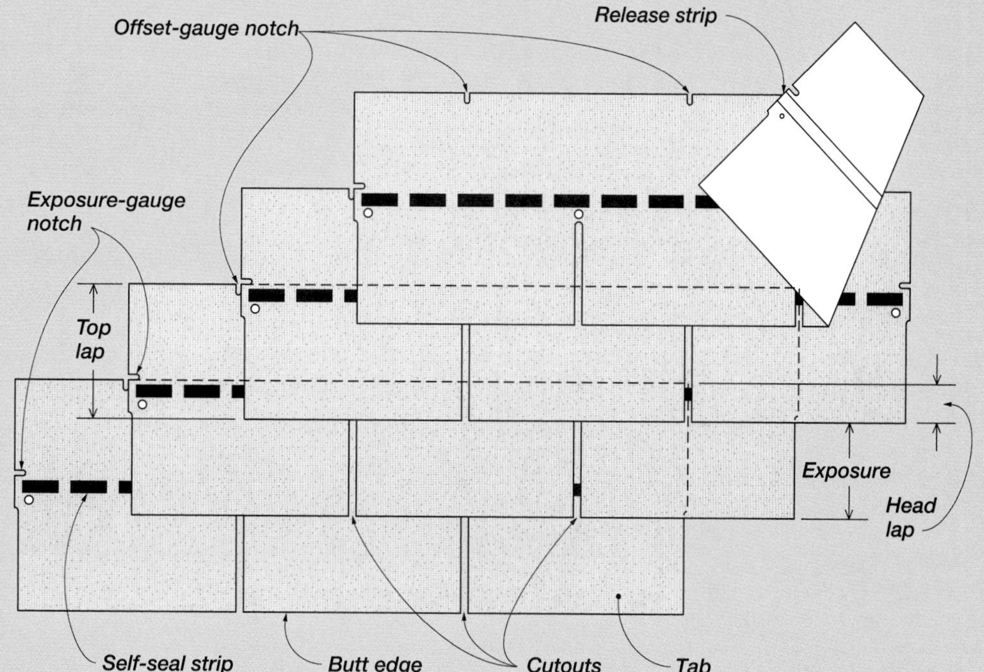

Self-seal strips seal down the lower edge of overlapping shingles. The strip is normally applied along the middle of the shingle on the front (bottom). In the case of some laminated shingles (top), the strip is found on the back bottom edge.

Seal strip and release tape

Nearly every model of asphalt roof shingle has a heat-activated seal strip that seals the shingle tabs to the shingle beneath to reduce the chance of wind uplift and damage. The strip may be a line or dots of sealant on the face of the shingle midway between the top and bottom edges or it may be underneath along the butt edge (see the photo above). The manufacturers select the location of the seal strip to correspond to the shingle product or pattern. The seal strips are activated by the sun's heat, so shingles installed during winter or on a side of the roof that is rarely exposed to the sun will require special installation procedures detailed in chapter 8. The seal strip will activate on winter roof installations during warmer weather, but the special installation procedures prevent shingles from blowing off in the meantime.

Manufacturers also bond a release tape to the back of each shingle to prevent shingles from sticking to each other while they're stored in bundles. The tape is typically made of plastic and positioned to match the seal strip on the shingle beneath. Seal strips may stick a little to the release tape, but the shingles can be gently separated without damage to either. There's no need to remove the tape; many manufacturers print "do not remove" right on the plastic.

Asphalt Shingle Products

Asphalt shingle manufacturers stamp and laminate shingle material into a variety of designs. However, all designs fall into one of two types—strip shingles and interlocking shingles. Each type has specific physical characteristics that affect how the shingles are installed and give the completed roof a distinctive appearance, and each type can be further differentiated by style. Shingle styles are made aesthetically different through the use of cutouts, laminating layers, granule color shading, and shaping.

Manufacturers produce shingles in popular styles that are nearly identical to those of other manufacturers; three-tab strip shingles are the most common example of this. But manufacturers also design and produce shingle styles that are unique to them.

In this section, I'll describe strip shingles and the popular styles within the classification. Then I'll describe the second, less popular group: interlocking shingles.

Strip shingles

In the early 1900s, asphalt roof shingles were plain rectangles that mimicked the size and shape of traditional slate and wood shingles. After World War I, manufacturers began stamping asphalt shingle material into elongated strips with cutouts that formed multiple tabs, hence the name strip shingle. Stamping the material into strips rather than small rectangles made the production more efficient and the installation easier. Instead of handling lots of 8-in.- or 12-in.-wide shingles, roofers had fewer 2-ft.- or 3-ft.-long shingles to handle.

Most of the asphalt shingles manufactured today are strip shingles. The size of strip shingles is fairly standardized at 12 in. tall and 36 in. wide, which is convenient for production, shipping, handling, and installation. And through the use of cutouts and laminating layers, the exposure size and scale is in keeping with the scale of traditional roof-covering materials such as wood, tile, and slate. There are some odd-sized shingles available including metric-sized shingles that measure approximately 13¼ in. by 39⅜ in. Strip shingles come in many styles, but the most common are multi-tab cutout, no cutout, random cutout, and laminated.

MULTI-TAB CUTOUT Among the common styles of strip shingles, multi-tab cutout is by far the most widely used and was one of the first styles developed. Its simple design goes well with most architectural styles, and it mimics the appearance of a slate roof. The exposure portion of the shingle is divided into two, three, or four tabs by stamping cutout slots in the shingle material (see the photo at right). The three-tab model is the most prevalent. The tabs and cutout sizes are equally divided along the strip and display a uniform pattern when installed with regular vertical offsets between courses. Some manufacturers decorate multi-tab shingles by shaping the corners of the tabs or by laminating ribbons of shingle material on top of a basic tabbed shingle for a distinctive look. These variations of cutouts, shaping, and laminations are strictly aesthetic; they don't affect shingle performance or installation.

NO CUTOUT These look like multi-tab shingles without the cutouts. Some manufacturers trim the butt edge of the shingles with either a regular or irregular pattern for a different appearance, but straight butts are the norm (see the top photo on p. 12). Some scientists who study shingle performance believe that no-cutout shingles are more prone to splitting due to thermal shrinkage after the self-seal strips fully adhere than are multi-tab shingles. I think shingles without any cutouts look ugly and the potential for splitting is likely. It makes intuitive sense that the cutouts in tabbed shingles will relieve some of the stresses of expansion and contraction that causes shingle splitting.

RANDOM CUTOUT These are similar to multi-tab shingles except that instead of uniform tabs of the same width and height, random slots are cut from the exposure and the tabs are trimmed at different heights (see the bottom photo on p. 12). The result is a unique look. Roofs covered with random-cutout shingles stand out, especially in neighbor-

■ WORK SAFE ■ WORK SMART ■ THINKING AHEAD

Check the shingle wrapper before you begin laying out a roof to see if you're dealing with English- or metric-sized shingles. The control lines (described in chapter 6) need to be gauged to match the exposure and length of the shingles. Metric shingles are slightly bigger, so if you don't take this into account, you'll use more shingles than you anticipated because you'll be overlapping the shingles further than necessary.

In multi-tab strip shingles, narrow vertical slots are cut out of the exposure portion to create tabs. Three-tab shingles, shown here, are the most common. Two-tab and four-tab shingles are also available.

No-cutout shingles are common in some localities. They are made just like other strip shingles but without the slots cut out of the exposure.

In random-cutout shingles, random slots are cut from the exposure, and the tabs are trimmed at different heights. The look mimics randomly laid hand-split cedar shingles.

hoods where most roofs have three-tabbed shingles. The look mimics that of randomly laid hand-split cedar shingles but costs much less.

LAMINATED The laminated shingle style is also referred to as architectural, dimensional, or multi-thickness shingles. These are made by bonding two layers of shingle material. The top layer is a full-height (approximately 12-in.) shingle with large, random notches of material removed from the exposure portion. The bottom layer is about 7 in. tall and is adhered beneath the notched exposure area of the top layer. The result is a three-dimensional effect with random high and low tabs (see the photo and the illustration on the facing page). Manufacturers often blend different shades of surface granule colors to the top and bottom laminates to enhance the appearance of the roof.

Although laminated shingles are more expensive than single-layer shingles, they are becoming increasingly popular. Many models of laminated shingles have higher wind resistance than multi-tab shingles, and their random design makes them easier to install and results in less waste (for more on this, see chapter 7). Many models of laminated shingles come in thicker versions with longer warranties than multi-tab, random cutout, or no-cutout shingles do. Although the shingles cost more, the installation labor is roughly the same as for the others. So year for year, these premium shingles may actually be more cost effective than basic shingles.

Interlocking shingles

Interlocking shingles aren't nearly as popular as strip shingles. They were much more popular a generation ago, before the advent of self-seal strips, because they are very wind-resistant. Today interlocking shingles are used mostly in coastal and other wind-prone

Laminated shingles, also called architectural or dimensional shingles, are made by bonding two layers of shingle material. They are more expensive than single-layer shingles.

areas. The bottom or side edges of each shingle have tabs that interlock into the course of shingles beneath and/or on either side. The interlocking holds the exposure portion of each shingle down rather than relying on a seal strip.

The shingle shape is not a good indicator of the visual effect on the completed roof. Once these specialty shingles are interlaced, the effect may be a series of hexagons, diamonds, Ts, or other shapes (see the photo on p. 15). Generally, interlocking shingles are more costly than regular strip shingles, both in material and labor.

Construction of a Laminated Shingle

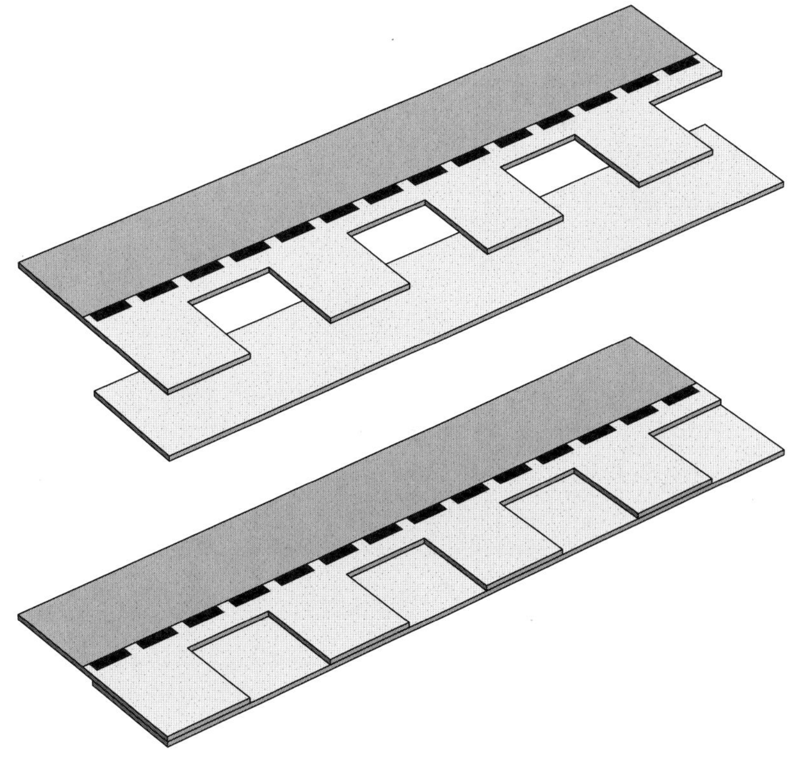

Roof Material Warranties

Asphalt shingle manufacturers offer limited warranties on their products. The key word here is "limited." Most warranties cover only the shingles, not labor, and are usually on a basis that is prorated as the shingles age. Except in the case of catastrophic premature fail-

Mineral-Surface Roll Roofing

Roll roofing is typically used on low-pitch roofs between 1 in 12 and 4 in 12 where shingles won't do the job or have special installation precautions. Roll roofing is also used on utility buildings and on some homes with high-pitch roofs because it is less expensive to purchase and easier to install than strip shingles.

But along with the up-front cost savings comes shorter life expectancy. Because roll roofing is applied in large sheets, it is more prone to damage from the stresses of expansion and contraction. It also is not built up in overlapping layers as shingles are. You can expect a roll roofing installation to last from 10 to 20 years. Patching the roof regularly with roof cement can extend its life.

Roll roofing is made from essentially the same fabrics, asphalt, and minerals as strip shingles. It comes in rolls 36 in. wide and about 36 ft. long in either single- or double-coverage styles. The top surface of single-coverage material is entirely covered with granules, while the double-coverage material is only covered on the bottom half that will be exposed.

In single-coverage applications, the fastener heads are left exposed. Single-coverage roll roofing should only be used on roof pitches greater than 2 in 12. Double-coverage roll roofing is installed using concealed nails and gooey lap cement (a viscous liquid asphalt) to bind the lower exposure half of an overlapping sheet to the upper half of the sheet beneath after it's been nailed down.

Roll roofing is typically used on low-pitch roofs, as shown in the photo above, but also can be used on high-pitch roofs, as shown in the photo below. Roll roofing is made of the same materials as strip shingles, but it comes in rolls 3 ft. wide and 36 ft. long.

Single-coverage roll roofing doesn't give you much protection; it can easily blow off on a windy day and you have to be diligent in watching for damage and wear to prevent water from finding its way in. I'd only relegate animals to live in shelters covered with it. Double-coverage roll roofing is a safer bet for wind resistance and leak resistance. The installation process can be messier than catching a greased pig at the fair, since unlike mud, lap cement doesn't wash off with soap and water. Plan on wearing old shoes, gloves, pants, and shirt and putting them out in the trash when the job is done (see chapter 9 for more on installation procedures).

ure, shingles almost always last their warranted life span. If they do fail a few years early, it's not worth dealing with the manufacturer for the pittance of a prorated materials refund.

When buying shingles, I concentrate on getting the best product for the job at the best price, rather than worrying about warranties. Still, it's important to understand what warranties cover and—just as important—what they do not, in case you do have that rare catastrophic premature failure. Warranty information is available from manufacturers and suppliers and is printed on every bundle of shingles.

Although specific warranties vary from one manufacturer to another, there are certain key points to pay attention to. The most important things to look for in a warranty are:

- Life expectancy
- Wind damage coverage
- Algae and fungus coverage
- Material and/or labor warranty

Life expectancy

Shingles are typically marketed by life span: 20, 25, 30, or 40 years. Given proper installation and average climatic conditions, you can expect a 20-year shingle to remain leak-proof for 20 years. The life span designations are an important consideration when comparing price from one manufacturer to another.

Everything else being equal, roofing on a steep pitch will last longer than roofing on a shallow pitch. Depending on the slope of the roof and how harsh your climate is, a 20-year shingle may only last 18 years or it may last 30 years.

But don't expect a lot from a warranty if a roof fails prematurely. Most manufacturer warranties are prorated for the life span by the year or month and

Before the advent of self-seal strips, interlocking shingles were developed to resist wind. They are still available in many parts of the country.

cover only the shingles, not the labor. Also, if only a few shingles on a roof fail, the manufacturer may only pay to replace those that are defective. This usually leaves the roof with a patchwork look because you can never get an exact color match.

Some manufacturers do offer full material and labor warranties for periods ranging from 3 to 10 years. But even these benefits may be limited to repairs of defective shingles or a layover roof (a second layer of shingles added over the original) rather than full removal and replacement of the defective shingles. In many cases, a manufacturer may also require that the initial installation be completed by an "approved" installer in order for the warranty to be in force.

Of course, to be eligible for coverage under a warranty, there must be a problem with the roof. Warranties typically cover only defects that cause leaks in

▪ WORK SAFE ▪ WORK SMART ▪ THINKING AHEAD

Note whether a warranty is transferable. Some warranties apply only to the homeowner at the time the shingles were installed, whereas other companies extend the warranty to a second owner under certain conditions. Transferability may be an issue if you are installing a roof to make a home more marketable.

the roof, not cosmetic defects. Many things that you may find objectionable such as algae staining, spalling, clawing, or fishmouthing may be considered cosmetic defects.

Wind damage

Warranties have limited wind damage coverage, with most shingles being warranted to a maximum wind speed of 55 or 60 mph. Some shingles are warranted at higher wind speeds, and local building code may require these shingles. If the house is in a coastal or other high-wind area, it pays to install shingles with high-wind ratings. Products are available with wind ratings up to 110 mph.

Installation instructions give specific procedures that must be followed for roofs exposed to consistently high winds. These normally include extra nails and additional sealant between the shingle tabs and the shingle beneath (for more information on installing shingles in high-wind areas, see chapter 8).

Don't count on the self-sealing strips to activate when the roof is installed in the late fall or winter in northern climates. When the strips don't stick the shingles down, shingles can blow off, even without very high wind. The worst case of shingles blowing off I have inspected occurred on a winter shingle installation. One-third of the shingles landed in the front yard, and heavy rains came that evening. Warranties typically don't cover shingles blowing off if the shingles haven't self-sealed.

It's rare for whole roofs or sections to blow off. More often a few shingle tabs snap off on roofs installed in cold weather. This doesn't mean you should only install asphalt roof shingles during the warm weather; just take the extra precaution of hand-sealing shingles installed in winter. Hand-sealing simply involves dabbing a couple of half-dollar-sized spots of asphalt roof cement between the shingle tabs and the top of the shingle beneath (see the sidebar on pp. 228–229). This extra step is usually recommended in shingle manufacturers' instructions for cold weather and high-wind installations.

Shingles are typically marketed by life span—20, 25, 30, or 40 years. The life-span designations are an important consideration when comparing price.

Algae and fungus coverage

Some manufacturers warrant against algae and fungus problems but only on products specifically designed and marketed as resistant to algae and fungus. Even then, the coverage period for resistance may be less than the warranted life of the shingle. For instance, a 25-year algae-resistant shingle may only be covered for 10 years against algae staining.

Material and/or labor warranty

I always give my clients a clean shingle bundle wrapper or warranty card to read. This way, in the event of a claim, they won't be surprised to discover that labor and materials other than the shingles themselves are not covered. Sometimes labor is included if a defect becomes evident during the first few years. If so, these periods should be listed in warranty information. Read the wrapper and the warranty information on marketing materials. If you are installing a roof for a client, make sure they understand what's covered and what's not.

Roofing installers may also provide warranties beyond what is covered by the manufacturer's limited warranty. These need to be evaluated on a case-by-case basis and should always be put in writing. Many roofers back up the manufacturer's warranty with their own warranty that they will provide the necessary labor if shingles fail. Others offer workmanship warranties.

Preserving the warranty

Shingle warranties are under siege from the moment that the product leaves the manufacturer's plant. Wholesalers and retailers can void a warranty by improperly storing shingles, but preserving the warranty is primarily in the hands of the installer.

Installers must pay strict attention to the manufacturer's installation instructions in order for the shingles to perform as expected and to safeguard the warranty. If the roofing fails, contact the installer or shingle manufacturer. A manufacturer's representative will come out to inspect the roof. The inspector may be an independent inspector, a representative of the shingle retailer or wholesale distributor, or an employee of the manufacturer. You can be sure the inspector will scrutinize whether the installer adhered to the instructions. These include everything from roof sheathing and ventilation to underlayment, flashing, and, in particular, proper fastening and tab sealing.

Shingles are rated for maximum wind speed, typically 55 or 60 mph. Manufacturers' warranties won't cover blow-off catastrophes such as this when a severe storm passes through with higher wind speeds.

Other Materials Needed to Install a Roof

Lots of products besides shingles are required to prepare, install, and finish an asphalt-shingled roof. Underlayment and metal drip edges prepare the roof deck. Nails and staples fasten the shingles. Flashing directs water back onto the roof shingles at intersections with chimneys, walls, vents, skylights, and other obstacles. And vents keep air moving beneath the roof deck to help cool it.

Underlayment

Shingle underlayment is a water-resistant or waterproof material that is installed over the roof sheathing before the shingles are installed. Most manufacturers' instructions specify that underlayment be installed beneath their shingles. Omitting the underlayment may void the manufacturer's warranty.

Underlayment was developed to answer practical building concerns. Historically, asphalt-impregnated felt (a type of underlayment also known as tarpaper) was, and still is, installed to temporarily "dry-in" a building before

At a casual glance, all felt underlayment looks similar (see the photo at left), but a closer look reveals the differences. Premium 15# shingle underlayment, shown at top right, has fiberglass fibers that reinforce and resist wrinkling from moisture, whereas 30# underlayment, shown at bottom right, is twice as thick as ordinary 15# shingle underlayment.

the shingles are installed. Tarpaper is water-resistant, so it sheds most rain. This allows construction to continue inside the building during inclement weather before the shingles are installed.

In addition, until plywood and OSB structural panels were commonly used, roofs were sheathed with softwood planks. The wood contained resin pockets that could bleed and degrade the asphalt in the shingles. Underlayment provided a separation between the roof boards and the shingles.

There are two distinct types of underlayment that are used beneath shingles. One is asphalt-impregnated felt and the other is waterproof shingle underlayment.

FELT UNDERLAYMENT Asphalt-impregnated felt underlayment comes in two grades: number 15 and number 30. They are sometimes referred to as 15-pound and 30-pound tarpaper and written as 15# and 30#, respectively. The 15# is for standard duty/thickness and 30# is heavy duty. Traditional felt underlayment tends to wrinkle when it absorbs moisture from rain or condensation. These wrinkles give the wind more opportunity to grab hold and tear off the material. The wrinkles can also telegraph through to the surface of the roof shingles.

Today, there are newer versions of the standard 15# and 30# tarpaper that are fiberglass reinforced. These premium shingle underlayments resist moisture absorption, wrinkling, and wind better than standard tarpaper. They also cost more. No matter which grade or type of tarpaper you use as an underlayment, once the roof shingles are installed with thousands of nails, the water resistance of the underlayment is diminished.

WATERPROOF SHINGLE UNDERLAYMENT Installers refer to this class of products by several names: ice and water barrier, water shield, bituthane, and others. Whereas tarpaper is water-resistant only until you install the shingles, waterproof shingle underlayment is self-healing—it seals around fastener holes. Water that penetrates the shingles won't pass through waterproof underlayment membrane.

Waterproof underlayment is made from polymer-modified asphalt. The underside is self-adhering and covered with a protective release sheet made of plastic or plastic-coated paper. The release sheet is removed during installation. The top surface is overlaid with either a permanent plastic coating or mineral granules similar to those on roof shingles (see the photo on p. 20). Several brands are additionally reinforced with fiberglass.

Their waterproof and self-healing properties make these products useful in critical areas on the roof where leaks are likely. For example, in cold and mixed climates, the eaves are prone to ice dams—thick accumulations of ice that trap melted snow, causing it to back up under the shingles. To avoid this, manufacturers recommend using waterproof underlayment along the first 3 ft. of a roof. Or waterproof underlayment may be installed as a secondary barrier against water penetrating valleys or step flashing where walls and roofs intersect.

In some high-wind areas, roofing installers cover the entire roof with waterproof underlayment for added protection. In case shingles blow off, the underlayment will prevent leaks (for information on underlayment installations, see chapter 5).

Self-healing waterproof underlayment costs roughly 10 times as much as 15# felt and about five times as much as premium fiberglass-reinforced underlayment.

Drip edges

Drip edges are formed from thin-gauge metal (typically aluminum, galvanized steel, or copper) and installed along eaves and rakes. They serve slightly different functions at each edge, but essentially a drip edge helps to shed water as it rolls off the roof and to keep wind-blown water from penetrating under the shingles and down to the roof sheathing. A drip edge bridges the joint between the roof plane and the trim boards of the rake and the fascia (see the top photo on p. 21). You can buy preformed drip edges from roofing-material suppliers or bend your own on site using a sheet-metal brake.

ALONG THE EAVES The most common drip-edge style used along eaves is an "extended" drip edge, so named because it supports the butt edge of shingles where they extend beyond the roof and fascia (see the bottom photo on p. 21).

Fire Resistance of Asphalt Shingles

Roofs are subject to a number of sources of fire ignition: chimney sparks, cinders from woodland fires, or sparks from a nearby burning building. The fire resistance of roof shingles is a major safety concern. Building codes, zoning codes, and fire codes address the issue by adopting fire-resistance standards. One widely accepted standard established by the American Society for Testing and Materials (ASTM) is the "Standard Test Methods for Fire Tests of Roof Coverings" (E-108). This standard classifies the fire resistance of roofing products into three classes:

- Class A—Severe exposure to fire
- Class B—Moderate exposure to fire
- Class C—Light exposure to fire

Asphalt shingle manufacturers present samples of their shingles to laboratories that perform the testing. The tests include resistance to intermittent exposure to flame, flame spread, and material ignition when burning cinders are set atop it.

Most asphalt roof shingles are rated class A, but some (particularly organic-felt shingles) are rated class C. Even a class A rating doesn't mean the material is fire proof; it only means that it passes the fire-resistance test protocol. You can find the fire-resistance rating listed on roof shingle product information and on shingle bundle wrappers.

Preserving Your Shingle Warranty

To get the most from your warranty, keep records of:

- The shingle manufacturer
- Shingle product
- Color
- Date of installation
- The installer's name

Also, save a bundle wrapper and fill out and register a warranty card if the manufacturer provides one.

WORK SAFE ▪ WORK SMART ▪ THINKING AHEAD

Building codes often require underlayment because the roof as a system, not just the shingles themselves, determines the fire-resistance classification of roof material. When underlayment is not used, the roof system may not meet the fire resistance (class A or C) of the shingles used. Some codes specifically state that underlayment must be installed. Others direct the roofing installation to conform to the shingle manufacturer's specifications, which in effect means they require underlayment.

A drip edge also serves an important water-management function. Water flowing down the surface of shingles tends to cling to the shingle surface and roll around the butt edge and up the underside of the shingle. This process is more pronounced during wind-driven storms. A drip edge prevents water from leaking into the roof sheathing and behind the fascia board. In addition, it redirects water back out to the front of the fascia where it can drip off. The top surface of a drip edge ranges from 3 in. to 6 in. wide and attaches directly to the roof sheathing with the underlayment overlapping it.

Before metal drip edges were used, roofers installed an under course of wood shingles, which overhung the fascia by ½ in. to 1 in. Over time, however, the wood shingles rotted away if they weren't protected with primer and paint in damp climates. Some roofers still use wood shingles instead of a drip edge.

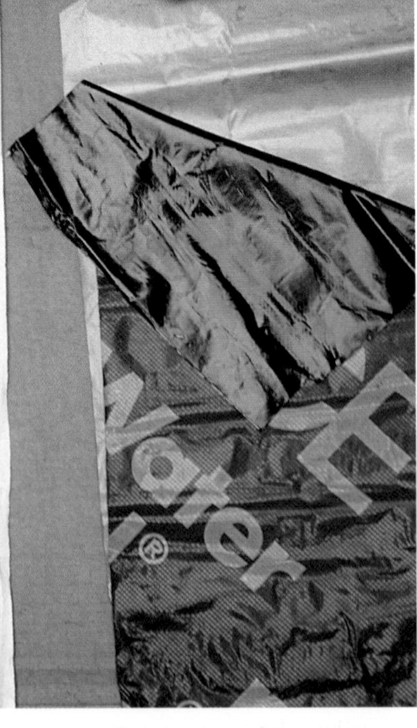

Waterproof shingle underlayment (WSU) has an adhesive backing of rubberized asphalt that self-seals around nail shanks. The surface can be coated with plastic or mineral granules.

ALONG THE RAKES Rake edge flashing should be installed over the underlayment felt. Any wind-driven rain that finds its way between the roof shingles and the rake flashing will be channeled on top of the underlayment, rather than into the joint between the roof and wall sheathing or rake board.

Water that drips over the shingles and onto the flashing is kicked away by the bend at the bottom edge of the flashing. (For more on installation procedures for both eaves and rake flashing, see chapter 5.)

VENTED DRIP EDGE A vented drip edge is a specialized style of eaves drip edge that combines the drip-edge functions with roof ventilation. Its shape is similar to an extended drip edge but with a deeper (2-in.) extension that has louvers embossed on the underside. Vented drip edges can be used for roof ventilation retrofits where vents can't be cut into soffits or on new homes with unique roof designs, such as those with no eaves overhang at all. A gap for airflow is left between the roof sheathing and the fascia. To be rigid enough to span this gap, a vented drip edge is made of a heavier-gauge metal than a standard drip edge (see the bottom right photo on p. 21).

CUSTOM-BENT DRIP EDGE You can fabricate a custom-bent drip edge on site to meet any number of unique eaves or rake details. Sheets or rolls of aluminum, copper, or other thin metal can be purchased from roofing suppliers. You can bend the drip edge using a sheet-metal brake, or you can have it custom-fabricated at a sheet-metal shop. A custom drip edge is normally more expensive than preformed stock models primarily because of the extra labor involved, but when an ordinary stock drip edge won't fit, you have no other option.

Metal drip edges come in several profiles and sizes. Some have an extended edge that projects beyond the fascia or rake trim, while others end flush.

An extended drip edge is the most common profile. The extended nose supports the overhanging shingles above and keeps water from blowing back under the shingles in the wind.

A vented drip edge has louvers on the underside of the extended nose of the profile. While supporting the shingles above, it also permits air to flow into the attic.

Flashing

Wherever roof shingles meet a vertical surface such as a chimney or wall or where a roof plane changes directions, such as a valley, you have potential for leaks if seams aren't carefully sealed. To prevent leaks, you need to install metal or plastic flashing to make weather-resistant connections and transitions.

Flashing is formed in different profiles so it can be lapped and overlapped into the shingle courses unique to each connection. The sidebar on p. 24 describes the most common flashing profiles, metals from which they can be made, and what connection they're used to bridge (for more on installing flashing, see chapter 8).

STEP FLASHING Step flashing is used where the slope of a roof meets a wall, the side of a skylight, or the side of a chimney. Made of metal, step flashing can be purchased as rectangular cards measuring 5 in. by 7 in. or 6 in. by 7 in. or 8 in. You can bend the cards on site or purchase them prebent at 90 degrees. You can also custom-cut and bend your own from sheet or coil metal stock.

Step flashing is interlaced between shingle courses so the flashing pieces overlap one another just as the shingles do. The side of the step flashing fits tightly against the wall and is overlapped by the housewrap and siding (see the bottom photo on p. 22). Alongside a chimney, it's covered by counter, or cap, flashing. Water flowing down the side of a wall or chimney is stopped by the step flashing, channeled out onto the shingle surface, and redirected down the roof plane. Step flashing can be made from lead, copper, or galvanized steel, but aluminum is the most commonly used material.

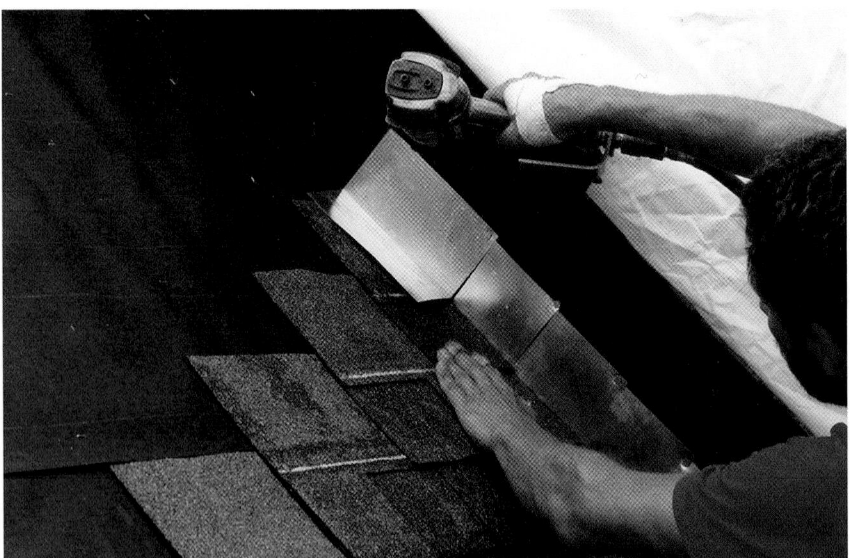

Step flashing is interlaced between shingle courses so the flashing pieces overlap each other just as the shingles do. The side of the step flashing fits tightly against the wall and is overlapped by the housewrap and siding. (Photo by Andy Engel, courtesy *Fine Homebuilding* magazine, © The Taunton Press.)

ROLL AND SHEET-METAL FLASHING Wide sheets or rolls of metal are used to make flashing where the top of a roof plane meets a vertical wall or chimney or to form a valley.

In the case of a vertical wall, the flashing is bent to make the transition from the wall to the pitch of the roof. The housewrap and siding cover the top edge of the flashing, and the bottom edge of the flashing overlaps the top course of roof shingles. Water running down the wall is directed away and on top of the shingles.

Chimney flashing works in a similar way. The counterflashing, which the mason lays into a mortar joint, covers the top of the flashing.

Valley flashing can be installed either as a liner and covered with the roof shingles or left exposed in a valley. Valley liner is bent in a V and installed in the valley over the roof sheathing, continuously from ridge to eaves. It bridges any gaps in the sheathing at the valley and covers rough edges. Water that penetrates the roof shingles is collected and runs out at the eaves edge. Exposed valley flashing is formed in a V or W and also runs from ridge to eaves, but the center is left exposed with roof shingles overlaying 6 in. to 12 in. on each side. Water running down the pitch of the roof is collected by the valley flashing and channeled to the eaves edge.

Fasteners

Asphalt roof shingles, underlayment, flashing, and drip edges all need to be mechanically fastened to the roof sheathing. There are a wide variety of nails and staples available to do the job (see the chart on p. 25). Be sure to select the right fastener for each situation to speed installation, to comply with manufacturers' instructions and building codes, and to ensure compatibility with metal flashing to avoid corrosion.

ROOFING NAILS FOR HAND-NAILING

Essentially everything—underlayment, shingles, and flashing—can be installed using a common roofing nail. Roofing nails have a 12-gauge shank, a head diameter of at least ⅜ in., and come in lengths from ⅞ in. to 3 in. Building code and shingle manufacturer requirements will dictate the length you'll need to use.

In general, the nail needs to penetrate at least ¾ in. into the roof sheathing (if the sheathing is thicker than ¾ in.) after going through the shingles. If the sheath-

Types of Flashing and Their Uses

Flashing	Location Used	How Formed	Typical Material
Step	Wall/roof (parallel to roof slope)	Preformed or formed on site from roll	Aluminum, galvanized steel, copper, lead-coated copper
Wall/roof	Wall/roof (perpendicular to roof slope)	Formed on site from roll	Aluminum, galvanized steel, copper, lead, lead-coated copper
Valley flashing	Valley	Formed on site from roll, sheet, or fabricated at sheet-metal shop	Aluminum, galvanized steel, copper, lead, lead-coated copper
Chimney flashing	Around chimney	Formed on site from roll or sheet	Aluminum, galvanized steel, copper, lead, lead-coated copper
Skylight	Head and bottom skylight	Preformed by skylight manufacturer	Coated aluminum or copper
Vented boot	Vent pipes	Preformed	Plastic or aluminum flange and rubber collar

Roll and sheet metal can be custom-bent, soldered, and hammered to fit any possible roof intersection that needs flashing. Typical places you'll use these flashing pieces are along the bottom edge of dormers (top left), around chimneys (bottom left), and to line valleys (above). (Photo above by Andy Engel, courtesy *Fine Homebuilding* magazine, © The Taunton Press.)

Metals for Flashing

- **Galvanized steel** is the least expensive flashing material, but over time the galvanization can wear off and rust will appear, especially in coastal areas. The cut edges of the steel will rust quickly. Some galvanized coatings do "self-heal" or "creep" to cover scratches and cuts that penetrate the coating.
- **Aluminum** is often used as a valley liner that is covered by roof shingles. It can also be exposed along wall intersections, but the shiny mill finish detracts from the roof's appearance. Painted aluminum looks better. Thin aluminum won't last long on seaside homes, so select thicker-gauge aluminum or a different metal.
- **Enameled steel or aluminum** is durable because of the baked-on finish, which is similar to the paint on automobiles. Pieces are best purchased preformed rather than bending them yourself. The bends you make can crack the enamel finish and corrosion can take hold.
- **Lead** is soft and easy to form by hand without using a metal brake. It is thick and durable and weathers to a dull gray. Once pressed onto the roof surface, lead lays flat without nails, which is a bonus, since aluminum, steel, and copper often lift up when they expand on hot days. Lead comes in rolls and stands up well in coastal areas. Although lead doesn't rust as steel will, it will eventually corrode through, usually lasting two shingle lifetimes.

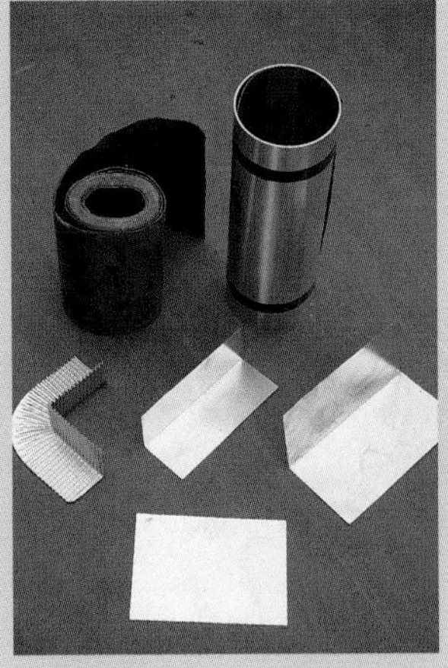

Metal flashing can be custom-bent from rolls such as the lead (left) and aluminum rolls shown here, or from sheets such as the one shown at the bottom. It can also be purchased in preformed shapes.

- **Copper** is a premium material that lasts a long time. Unfinished copper will eventually turn brown and then shift to a pale green patina that many people find attractive. Alternatively, lead-coated copper turns dull gray, like lead flashing. You can buy either type in sheets or rolls. Copper is somewhat malleable so it's easy to work with. Exposed valleys are usually flashed with copper, and it works just as well where roofs meet walls. It stands up well to salt water so it's good in coastal areas. If you want to achieve the green patina faster, there are accelerating washes available. There are also coatings to maintain the shiny, mill finish.

ing is ¾ in. thick or less, the nail must penetrate completely through the sheathing. But meeting code may not be your only consideration; if you have thick fingers like I do, then you'll have a hard time starting a 1-in. nail even though it may meet the penetration requirement. Nails that are 1¼ in. or 1½ in. long are most commonly used and readily available. Longer 1¾-in. or 2-in. nails may be needed when you install hip and ridge-cap shingles because of the extra layers of shingle material and ridge vent.

Roofing nails are made from a combination of metals. Galvanized steel nails are the most prevalent, but there are differences between galvanized coatings. Electroplated nails have a relatively thin galvanized coating. Although the nails are covered by the shingle course above, they will encounter some moisture during a rainstorm. Over time the coating may deteriorate and the nails can rust. This is most likely to occur in coastal areas where salt in the air accelerates the process.

Hot-dipped galvanized coatings are thicker and usually more durable. I say usually because low-quality coatings can chip off when you're hammering the nails in and corrosion will quickly follow. High-quality "double-dipped" galvanized roofing nails don't cost much more and have the best resistance to rust.

Electrolysis can be a problem if you fasten metal accessories with a nail of a different metal. Flashing is typically aluminum, lead, or copper, so if you use galvanized roofing nails to install flashing, it may corrode around the nail heads.

The more moisture that reaches the fastener, the faster the deterioration; salt air accelerates the process even more. On most roofs this isn't a big issue because the deterioration may be so slow that the roof shingles will need replacing long before the flashing corrodes around the nail heads. Copper and aluminum roofing nails are available if you need them. They are much more costly than galvanized roofing nails, but you won't need many just to install the flashing. They should always be used in cases where the nail heads will be exposed to the weather or if the home is close to salt water.

COLLATED ROOFING NAILS FOR PNEUMATIC NAILERS Pneumatic tools speed shingle installation dramatically. They use compressed air to drive a piston within the nailer that in turn drives fasteners (nails or staples) faster than you can blink your eye (see chapter 2 for a further description of pneumatic equipment). I think a nailer pays for itself on the second or third roof job. Collated roofing nails—the nails that pneumatic nails drive—are the same size as those available for hand-nailing. The nails are collated on thin wire threads and rolled into a coil, which rests in a basket, then nails automatically advance to the nose of the nailer. Common nail lengths range from 1 in. to 1¾ in. (For more on pneumatic nailer safety, use, and concerns, see chapter 2.)

WIDE-CROWN STAPLES FOR PNEUMATIC STAPLERS Most manufacturers permit the use of wide-crown staples to

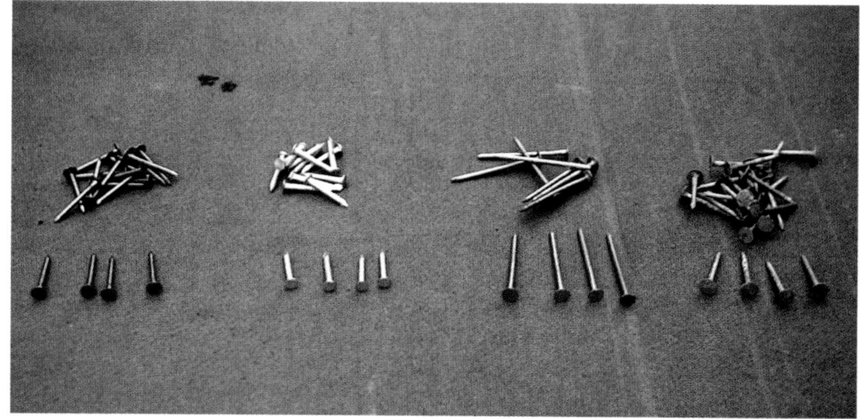

Roofing nails made of copper (left) and aluminum (second from left) are used with copper and aluminum flashing to prevent corrosive galvanic reactions. For shingling, hot-dipped or electroplated galvanized-coated steel nails are used. These nails come in lengths from ⅞ in. to 2 in. and longer (right and second from right).

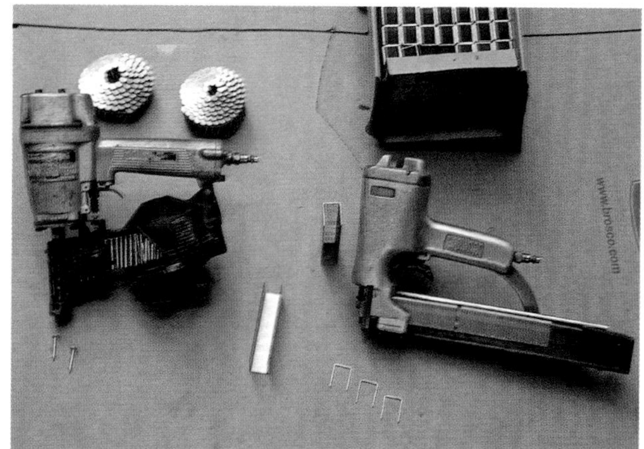

Pneumatic nailers drive nails that are collated into coils on thin wires, whereas pneumatic staplers drive staples with 1-in.-wide crowns.

Fasteners for Roofing

Fastener	Purpose	Typical Material
Roofing nails	Fasten shingles, underlayment, flashing, and drip edge	Galvanized steel, aluminum, copper
Collated pneumatic roofing nails	Fasten shingles, underlayment, flashing, and drip edge	Galvanized steel
Collated pneumatic roofing staples	Fasten shingles, underlayment, flashing, and drip edge	Galvanized steel
Roof tins/tin caps	Used with nails or staples to hold underlayment	Aluminum, steel
Plastic or metal cap nails	Fasten underlayment when left exposed to weather	Plastic, galvanized steel
Staples	For mechanical stapler; used to temporarily hold underlayment flashing or drip edge in place	Steel, galvanized steel

Special Preformed Flashing

Specialized flashing is available for specific locations, such as vent pipes and the tops and bottoms of manufactured skylights. Although you could make custom flashing for each case, it's probably not worth the time or the expense.

Vent pipe flashing is made from an embossed metal or formed plastic flange with a rubber collar that seals around the pipe. The flat portion of the flange laps between courses of shingles to shed water. Sizes are available based on vent pipe diameter.

Skylight flashing is usually supplied preformed by the skylight manufacturer. The head flashing slips under the roof shingles above the skylight and directs water around it to the step flashing and shingles along the sides of the unit. The skylight's bottom flashing overlaps the top of the shingles beneath to keep water flowing down the roof.

Boot flashing has a rubber collar that grips the vent pipe tightly to prevent leaks, while the wide bottom flange interlaces into the shingle courses to shed the roof water around the base of the pipe.

Skylights usually come with their own specialized flashing kits.

Plastic cap nails (right) and tin caps applied with separate nails are used to secure felt underlayment in windy conditions or for extended periods of time.

install roof shingles, although their literature typically encourages you to use nails. Some building codes, however, forbid the use of staples. The concern people have with roofing staples is that the thin crown wire can cut through the roof shingle and leave the shingles prone to blowing off. Personally, I've had very good success using them and think they're fine as long as they are installed properly (for information on correct stapler use, see chapter 7).

Staples need to be no thinner than 16 gauge and have a 15⁄16-in. crown (nominally an inch). The legs range from 7⁄8 in. to 1 3⁄4 in., but you'll usually only find 1 1⁄4 in. and 1 1⁄2 in. stocked. Don't confuse

Metal or plastic roof vents are installed near the ridge of the roof to ventilate the attic.

wide-crown pneumatic staples with ordinary staples described next. As you can see in the bottom photo on p. 25, these roofing staples are much larger. The staplers are lighter, less expensive, and hold more fasteners per load than pneumatic nails. Staples are subject to the same sheathing penetration requirements as nails. Watch the quality of the galvanized finish too; thin electroplated staples can corrode rapidly.

STAPLES FOR MECHANICAL STAPLERS Ordinary staples can make short work of installing step flashing and underlayment that will be quickly covered by shingles. You drive in these 3⁄8-in. to 1⁄2-in. crowned thin-gauge staples with simple spring-actuated squeeze or hammer staplers. They are similar to the staples you find in a desktop paper stapler. The crowns are too thin to resist pulling through underlayment under windy conditions, but if you're just laying out a couple of courses immediately ahead of roof shingling, ordinary staples are all you need.

ROOF TINS Also known as tin caps, roof tins are thin, 2-in.-dia. disks of aluminum, steel, or galvanized steel. They are used to increase the surface area of nail heads or staples that hold down tarpaper underlayment. Although not usually necessary, they are a useful precaution against fasteners pulling through when conditions are windy or when a long time will pass before shingles are installed.

METAL OR PLASTIC ROUND-TOP NAILS These nails have wide metal or plastic caps already attached to serve the same function as roof tins. You may find it easier to use these rather than fumbling with roof tins and separate nails, especially when the wind is blowing underlayment into your face.

There's a version of the plastic round-top nail that's designed to work with a pneumatic nailer. In this system, which really speeds production, a standard pneumatic coil roofing nailer is outfitted with a plastic cap feeder. The caps come in a separate coil and feed under the nail at the nose of the nailer. When the nailer is fired, the nail drives through the broad plastic cap and into the underlayment.

Roof-venting equipment

To meet ventilation requirements, you may need to install roof vents, which allow air to move freely through the attic space or rafter cavity. The moving air keeps the underside of the roof sheathing

Flash vents are used to vent a shed roof where it meets a vertical wall.

cool so the shingles don't overheat and it carries away moisture vapor (see chapter 4 for a complete description of roof ventilation and how the process works). Some vents, such as turbine vents and surface-mounted roof vents, install on the plane of the roof; others install on the roof ridge. The most common types are:

- Surface-mounted roof vents
- Roof turbines
- Cupolas
- Ridge vents
- Flash vents (for more on installation, see chapter 7)

SURFACE-MOUNTED ROOF VENTS

These go by many names: pot vents, mushroom vents, roof louvers, domed vents, among others. Standard passive roof vents are basically a covered hole in the roof. A hole is cut in the roof sheathing and the air flows out through the vent covering it. The shroud over the vent prevents rain from entering, and a screen or louver baffles keep insects and other varmints out. Roof vents are made of plastic or metal and come in various shapes and sizes with a flange flashing formed at the bottom. Some models also

Some ridge vents are made of metal that forms the vent and the cap all in one, as shown at left in the photo above. Other types shown in the photo above are made of plastic and come in rolls or rigid 4-ft. sections. Plastic ridge vents are covered with cap shingles as shown in the center photo above.

come with an electric fan that increases air movement.

Some of these vents are downright ugly but they serve the function. Look through your supplier's inventory to see what models are in stock, and choose a color that matches your roof shingles as closely as possible. The aluminum models may take paint so you can conceal them by painting.

ROOF TURBINES Turbines are unsightly on the front of a house. They are about 2 ft. tall and 1 ft. or more in diameter and there's no way to conceal them, so avoid them altogether or at least locate them at the rear of the house. The passive turbine blades spin and create a negative pressure in the attic when the wind blows, drawing air out. They can be effective at evacuating hot, moist air from attics provided breezes are consistent. Adjustable base flanges allow installation on a range of roof pitches.

CUPOLAS These are decorative vents that straddle the ridge of a roof. They come in a variety of sizes and are installed over a hole in the roof sheathing at the ridge. Cupolas have their own roof, trim, and siding, and screen-covered louvered sides to permit airflow. Today, this traditional type of roof vent is often installed only as a decorative feature, but if you are installing cupolas, there's no reason not to use them as working roof vents. Suppliers don't often stock cupolas, but they can order them. They come with bases that can be trimmed or adjusted so you can fit them to the roof pitch on site.

The problem with cupolas is that they require a lot of maintenance. Homeowners often aren't keen on climbing up on a roof to scrape and paint cupolas every few years. Because of the heat radiating from the roof shingles on sunny days, the paint on cupolas never seems to last as long as on the siding of the house. Also, birds, bats, and squirrels sometimes break through the screen inside the louvers and get into the attic.

Though often used for decoration, cupolas were originally used for roof ventilation. Many stock models are available with bases that can be cut to match most roof pitches.

RIDGE VENTS Ridge vents cover a space left or cut in the sheathing along the ridge of a roof (see the center photo on the facing page). Warm air rising in the attic or rafter air space passes through the cut in the sheathing and through the ridge vent to the exterior. They come in several styles; some provide the weather cap on the ridge and others are covered by roof shingles and are virtually invisible from the ground.

Variable-pitch metal ridge vents have protected slots along both edges that permit airflow. They cover the ridge and cap it in one piece. There's no need to install shingles over this style as with other ridge vents because it is a finish piece of trim itself. Several colors are available, although they typically won't

Collated roofing nails typically come electroplated. Look for premium brand nails with durable electroplated coatings because many generic nails have thin electroplating that will rust quickly.

Roof cement comes in different consistencies for different uses. Thick cement is troweled on, liquid cement is spread between roll roofing sheets, and cement in a tube keeps mess to a minimum for spot applications.

match the roof shingle color perfectly, making them noticeable from the ground. They are simple to install but can be easily bent or dented during installation, which will be visible.

Available from several manufacturers, roll ridge vents consist of a matrix of plastic or fiberglass material about 1 in. thick, and some are wrapped with a filter fabric to keep out blowing snow. Air flows from the slot in the sheathing, through the vent matrix, and exits at the edges of the vent. They're easy to install on any roof pitch and are covered by roof cap shingles, for which manufacturers include long nails to install. Some of the nails have 1-in.-long plastic collars around the base of the nail shanks that prevent you from driving the nail too far (overdriving crushes the vent and reduces airflow).

Rigid-plastic ridge vents come in different styles; some look like thick, corrugated cardboard and others have external baffles and look similar to metal ridge vents. Like roll ridge vents, these adjust to a variety of roof pitches and are covered with cap shingles.

FLASH VENTS Flash vents are specially designed to be used where the top edge of a shed roof meets a wall (see the top photo on p. 28). Often shed roofs that terminate into a wall are left unvented or are vented with unsightly mushroom roof vents. Flash vents are a good alternative that also flashes the transition between roofs and wall. The top flange fastens to the wall and is covered by the siding. The bottom flange covers the top of the roof shingles. A slot left in the roof sheathing permits air to flow up and into the vent where it escapes through louvers.

Asphalt roof cement

It's a rare roof job that can be completed without asphalt roof cement, also called roof tar, flashing cement, or roofing cement. Roof cement is used for a number of reasons:

WORK SAFE
WORK SMART
THINKING AHEAD

Although the net free ventilation area (the amount of air space each vent provides per linear foot or per unit measured in square inches or square feet) is roughly the same for externally baffled vents as for roll-type vents, the externally baffled vents typically enable better airflow.

- To seal shingle tabs down
- To seal the edges of shingles along an open metal valley
- To cover exposed nail heads
- To patch leaks
- To seal laps in roll roofing

There are a variety of roof cements formulated to bond well to roof materials and maintain a leak-proof seal through a wide temperature range. Many are even formulated to bond to both wet and dry shingles, which is great for patching leaks or finishing a job in the rain.

A thinner type of roof cement, lap cement, is formulated to bond overlapping layers of underlayment or roll roofing. Quick-setting cement has a volatile solvent base that evaporates fast, which is useful when you want something to stick and set quickly.

The various products come in large pails, small cans, and in caulk gun tubes for easy dispensing.

Rain diverters

Rain diverters are simple metal channels that direct rainwater. They are used on roofs without gutters to keep entryways dry or to channel water into a gutter. Since diverters are slipped beneath a course of shingles, they can be added any time after shingling is complete.

Rain diverters shed water away from doorways and entrances. A wide roof flange slides beneath a row of shingle tabs, and the upright leg directs the water away to the sides.

CHAPTER 2

Tools, Equipment, and Safety

Roofing can be a tricky and dangerous job, but if you have the right tools and safety equipment, you can get the job done right with minimal hassle and little risk of injury. (Photo by Andy Engel, courtesy *Fine Homebuilding* magazine, © The Taunton Press.)

YOU CAN EQUIP YOURSELF to shingle a simple roof for less than $50. All you really need is a canvas nail pouch, hammer, tape measure, utility knife, chalkline, and a pencil. But investing in more specialized tools and equipment will make the job faster and safer.

I'll begin this chapter by reviewing basic hand tools and production-oriented pneumatic equipment, then I'll look at tools and equipment used to remove and repair roof shingles. I'll wrap up by discussing the staging equipment needed to safely get up on the roof and stay there as well as other safety equipment that's common on today's construction sites.

Hand Tools

You probably already have many of these tools if you're in the construction business. If you're an avid do-it-yourselfer, they are probably kicking around your basement or garage. Unless you're a real tool hound, don't bother going out and reoutfitting yourself. Make do with the

You can drive roofing nails with any type of hammer or roofing hatchet. The author prefers a light, short-handled hammer like the one at left.

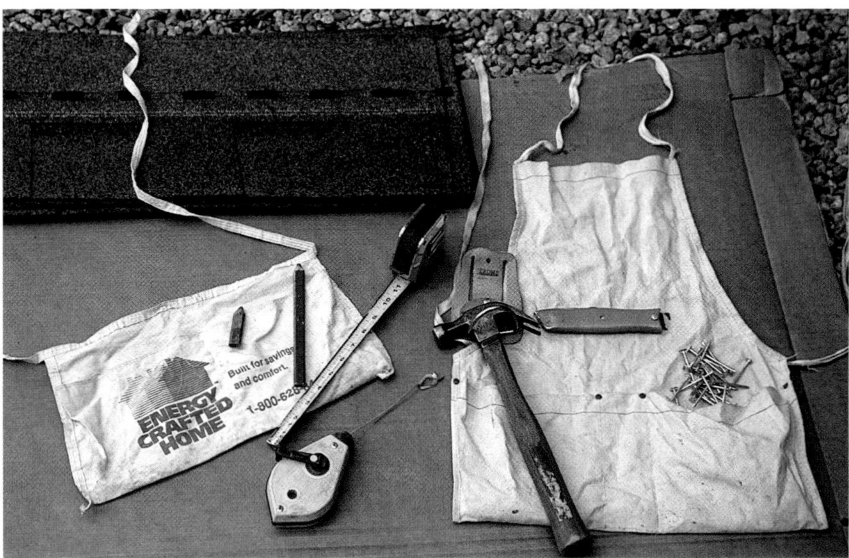

Shingling requires only the most basic tools (a hammer, a utility knife, a chalkline, a tape measure, a pencil, and a nail pouch), but other tools make a pro's job faster and easier.

tools you have unless you think you'll be doing lots of roof shingling.

Hammers and hatchets

You can use just about any hammer to drive roofing nails. Select one that's comfortable to use and to carry on your tool belt. For roofing, I prefer a 16-oz. curved claw hammer rather than my 28-oz. long-handled rip-claw framing hammer. Driving short roofing nails is much different from driving 16d spikes. Rather than using your whole arm to swing the hammer, you'll use a shorter stroke with a wrist snap. This action favors lightweight driving tools.

Some roofers like a hammer with a serrated face, whereas others like a smooth face. Although a serrated face won't slip off the nail head, it is more likely to break the galvanized coating and invite rust.

A roofing hatchet is designed to install wood roof shingles—it has a square head on one end and a hatchet for splitting shingles on the other. Some asphalt-shingle roofers like to use hatchets because the blade has several holes in it. You can put a peg in one of the holes to gauge shingle exposure, but I'll describe another more accurate way of gauging exposures in chapter 6. I'm kind of clumsy at times, so the last thing I want to be swinging near my head is the sharp end of a hatchet.

Although designed for installing wooden shingles, roofing hatchets have gauge notes or pins that can be handy for setting exposures on asphalt shingles. (Photo by Jefferson Kolle, courtesy *Fine Homebuilding* magazine, © The Taunton Press.)

Utility knives

Utility knives are used to cut through roof shingles. Often you'll only need to scribe partway through the shingle and bend it to separate the pieces, but other times you'll have to draw the knife over the line several times to cut all the way through. The fillers in the asphalt and the mineral coatings on the top and bottom of the shingles are very abrasive and wear knife blades rapidly. Knives are available that let you open the body

WORK SAFE ■ WORK SMART ■ THINKING AHEAD

If you're going to hand-nail roof shingles regularly, you may want to consider getting a hammer or hatchet with a wood handle. The wrist-snap technique of driving roof nails favors a short handle in addition to a light driving head. You can easily shorten the handle on a wooden hammer, if you like.

WORK SAFE ▪ WORK SMART ▪ THINKING AHEAD

There are several styles of utility knives, but most important is to get one with a retractable blade. The fixed-blade models work fine, but you'll wish the blade retracted the first time you jam your hand into your tool pouch and come up with the sharp end.

quickly without a screwdriver—a great feature for roofers who need to change blades often.

Choose a model that feels good in your hand. I like small and simple straight knives, but you may prefer a large-grip angled knife. Be wary of those that have blade-storage compartments with flimsy doors. The doors seem to open up frequently and dump the extra blades.

You'll use two types of utility-knife blades for roofing. Since the knives are small, consider carrying two, one for each blade type. The two kinds of blades are straight blades and hooked blades. Both are double-ended so you get two cutting edges on each blade. Straight blades are used for sharpening pencils, scribing, and snapping shingles from the backside. They are easy to control along a straightedge and are used to cut starter shingles for the eaves or crosscut shingles that butt into a chimney or wall.

Hook blades are used to trim shingles once they are installed. The hook wraps all the way through the thickness of a shingle, so it's easy to cut the excess shingle overhang along rakes and trim out cut valleys with one pass.

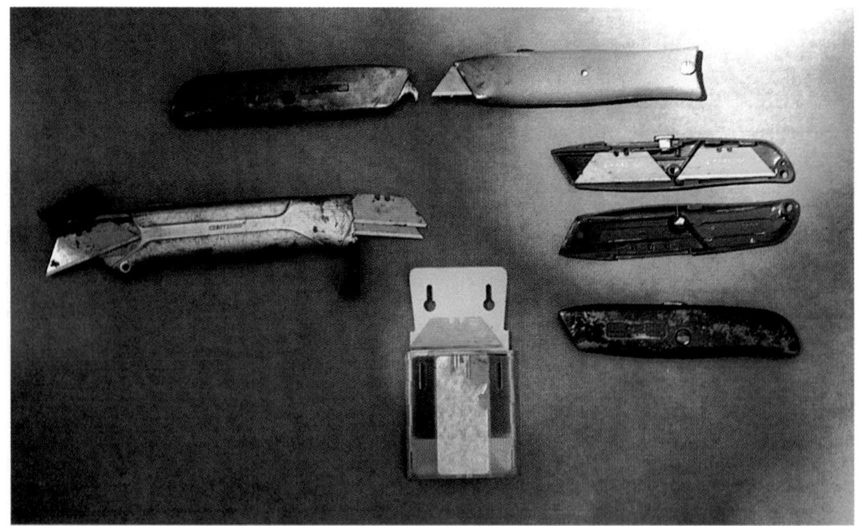

Utility knives have replaceable blades that are retractable on most models. Some models need to be unscrewed to change blades (right) and others have a toolless quick-change feature (left). The blade profiles used for roofing are the straight blade (upper right) and the hook blade (upper left).

There are mechanical shingle shear tables that cut shingles like a super heavy-duty paper cutter. A pivot base allows you to cut shingles lengthwise, crosscut at 90 degrees, and cut any angle in between. The cutting shear produces straight, clean cuts, but with a price tag of up to $500, this is a tool for production roofers.

Chalklines

Chalklines are also called chalk boxes or chalk reels. Today's chalklines should not to be confused with my grandfather's chalkline; his was a string wound on a stick and drawn out over a solid block of chalk each time he had to strike a line. Now chalklines are spools of string wound inside a teardrop-shaped plastic or metal box that's filled with powdered chalk. The string is automatically rechalked every time it's withdrawn from the box.

Several models are available. The newer speed-wind types reel up the string rapidly for quick rechalks. But be wary of cheaper speed-wind models; their plastic gearing can strip out with heavy use. Models without speed-wind take longer to rewind but rarely seem to jam or strip out since there are no gears inside, just a direct-drive shaft.

Look for models with winding handles that fold up or can be disengaged when the string is pulled out. Models without this feature become annoying when the spinning handle catches your hand or clothes. Also look for one with a chalk refill cap at the end of the box that twists on and off. The caps are more reliable than sliding doors that wear out and can open at inopportune times, either filling your tool pouch with chalk or spilling out onto a nearly complete roof job.

CHALK Powdered chalk comes in several colors. Be conscious of whether the color you choose is indelible. I prefer to use white or blue chalk because both wash off easily. Red, yellow, and orange are nice and bright but may stay on the roof shingles weeks or months after you have a spill.

If you're going to do a lot of roofing, save money by buying chalk in gallon containers, then transferring the chalk into smaller bottles that fit in your pouch. Keep the chalk containers dry because any moisture will make the chalk clump up. The clumps will plug the spout on your chalk bottle when you try to pour it out.

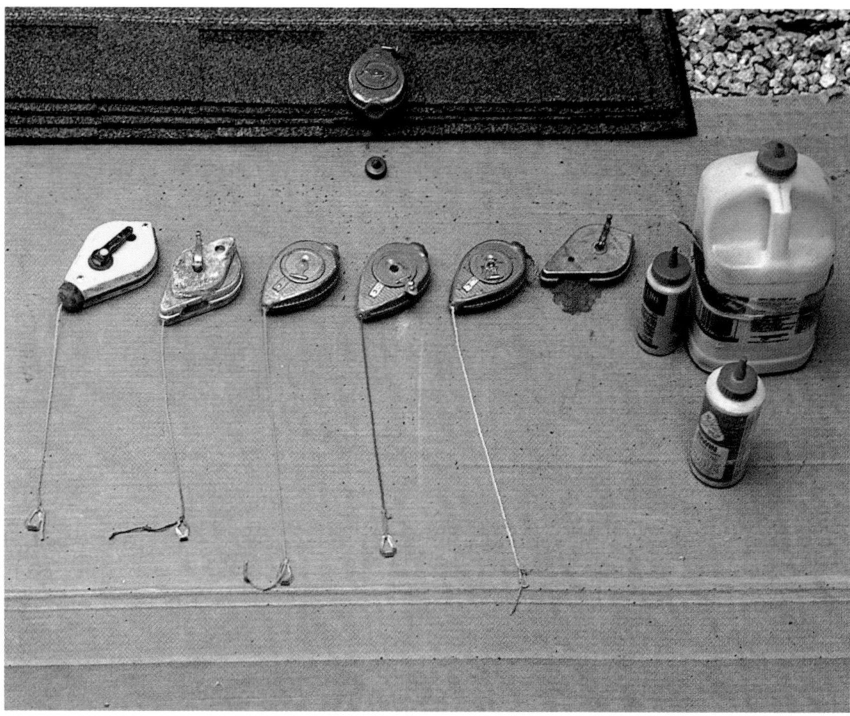

Chalklines come in several styles including popular quick-reel models like the yellow one shown here. Chalk comes in several colors. Blue and white chalk washes away in the rain, whereas red, orange, and yellow chalk are indelible.

Tape measures

Tape measures are steel or fiberglass rulers that roll up into a box either automatically or manually with a winding lever. You may need a couple of tape measures

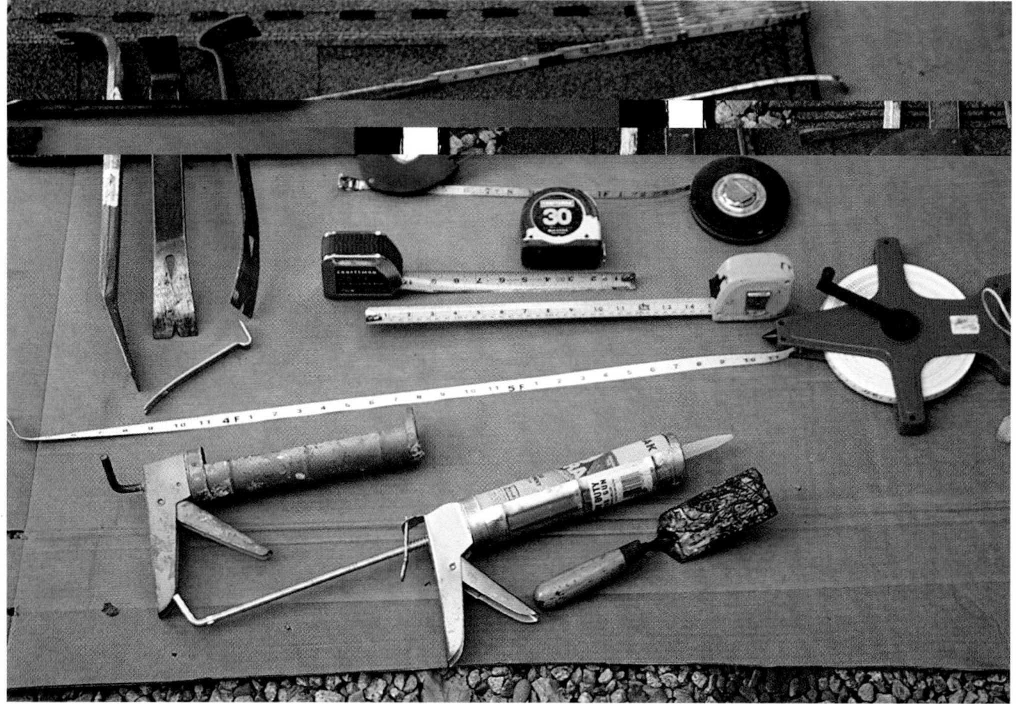

There's a wide array of tools you will find useful on roofing jobs. Several tape measures of lengths from 25 ft. to 100 ft. will handle most residential roofs. Flat bars are great for stripping shingles as well as for making repairs. You'll need a caulking gun and a trowel to dispense roof cement.

■ WORK SAFE ■ WORK SMART ■ THINKING AHEAD

Keep a couple of chalklines in your pouch, each with different-colored chalk. Sometimes the control lines that guide shingle placement need to be readjusted. The extra color makes it clear which are the new lines.

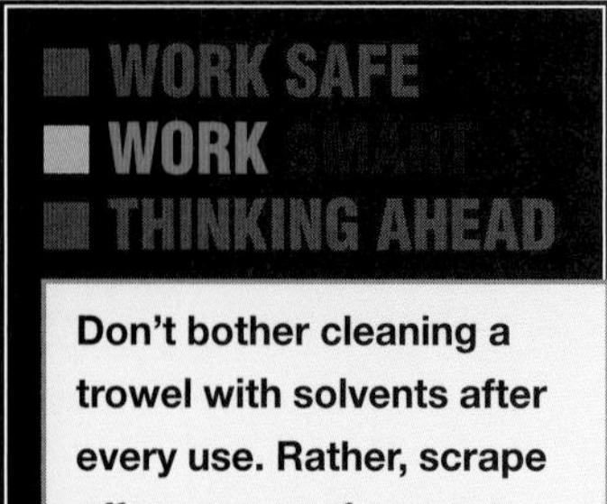

Don't bother cleaning a trowel with solvents after every use. Rather, scrape off excess roof cement onto scraps of shingles and wrap the trowel in double plastic bags until your next project.

for different purposes, but the one you use the most should be a self-retracting 25-ft. or 30-ft. tape with a stiff 1-in. blade. You'll need the stiff blade to extend the tape up to the ridge or down to the eaves edge to measure out control lines. Narrow-blade tapes are hard to control in a breeze, and you'll find yourself walking up and down the roof plane every time you need to take a measurement.

Having two tapes up on the roof with you can be handy. You can stretch one out at each gable end to measure out horizontal course lines and leave them in place. Then you can snap chalklines between the tape measures without having to spend the time drawing marks. And you will inevitably drop one; having two will enable you to keep working without playing fetch.

The other type of tape you'll need is a 50-ft. or 100-ft. narrow-blade steel tape. Don't bother getting one that's self-retracting; they're too bulky and unreliable. A long tape is necessary on large roofs to check dimensions and establish vertical control lines. There's no need to make room in your tool pouch for this heavy tape; just keep it with other incidental tools in a box on the roof.

Caulk guns

On nearly every roof job, you'll need to dispense some roof cement. Roof cement in a tube is much easier to control than out of a can. You can use any type of caulk gun, but I prefer a mid-priced model with a solid frame and handle.

Trowels

For bulk applications of roof cement, you may find that troweling it on from a can is faster and more cost effective than using caulk-gun tubes. I like to use a small rectangular trowel rather than a mason's triangular trowel. This gives a 1-in. end and 4-in. edges to spread narrow or wide swaths of cement. Also, this trowel makes it easy to dig the tar from the container.

Flat bars

Flat bars come in many shapes and sizes. They're ordinarily used for framing and demolition work, but they come in handy for roofing too. Most have a wide, flat end with a slight bend and a hook and claw on the other end for increased leverage. I like a flat steel bar rather than a crowbar and ripping bar that have round shanks. You won't need a flat bar much on a new roof installation, but they're good for popping up misplaced nails and for separating shingles that have sealed down before you have a chance to position them.

Nail thieves

Nail thieves have hooks at the end for grabbing nail shanks between shingles. The thin blade easily slides between shingle layers, then by hammering on the upright leg of the thief near the handle, the hooks draw out the nails. Although you won't need a nail thief regularly, it is good for pulling nails out of shingles from inaccessible places such as under dormer soffits that meet a roof.

Staplers

Not to be confused with pneumatic roofing staplers, these staplers are mechanically activated and drive narrow-crown, short-leg staples similar to those used in desktop staplers. They're handy for quickly tacking underlayment felt to the roof sheathing and step flashing to a wall. There are two types that differ by operation: hammer staplers and spring-actuated squeeze.

Hammer staplers eject a staple upon impact with a solid surface. They make fast work of attaching underlayment, but they are limited by your swinging aim to accurately place a staple.

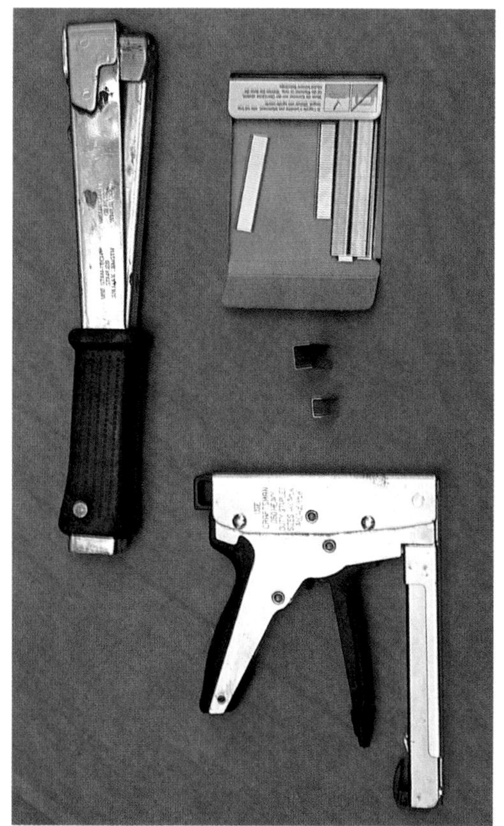

Hammer staplers (top left) make fast work of jobs such as installing underlayment. Spring-actuated staplers are slower but better for accurate fastener placement.

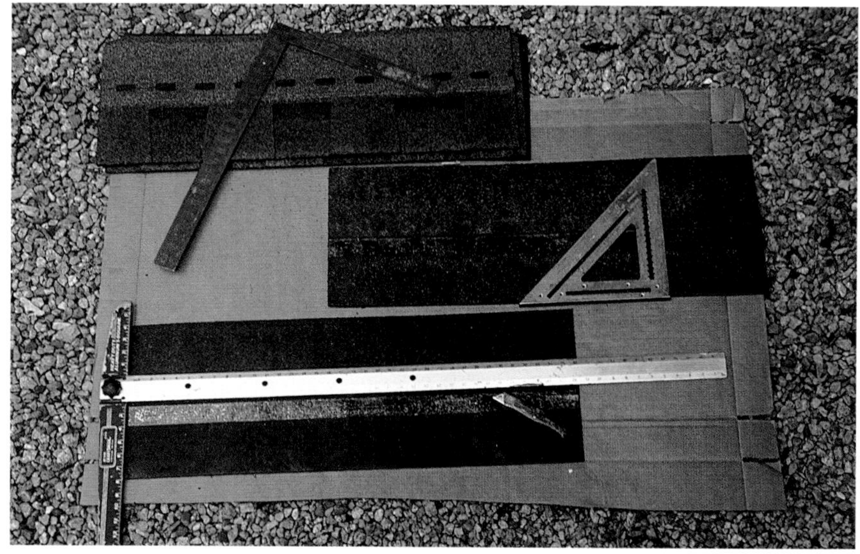

Squares and straightedges guide shingle cutting.

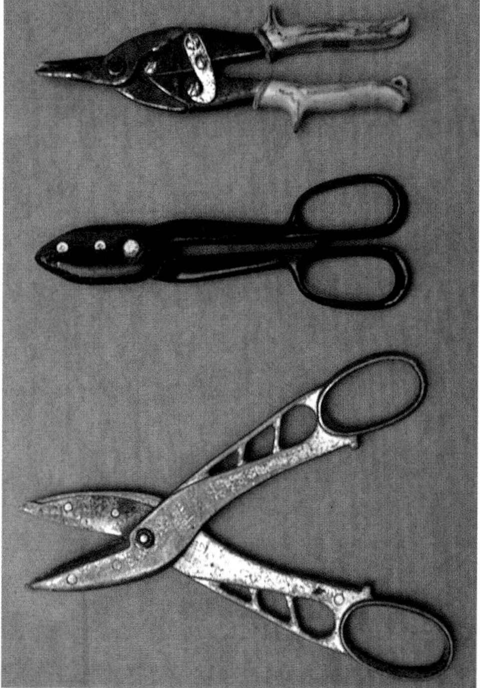

Metal shears are needed to cut metal flashing and can also be used to trim shingles.

Squeeze staplers are slower to operate than hammer staplers, but they allow you to place a staple precisely where you want it. To operate, hold the stapler's nose where you want to eject a staple and squeeze the trigger handle. I use a squeeze stapler to tack the upper corner of step flashing to a wall.

Squares and straightedges

You'll need to trim shingles throughout the roofing process, so to make accurate cuts use squares and straightedges.

Shingles are typically 12 in. tall and 36 in. long. Use a large try square or a framing square to make accurate 90-degree crosscuts. To make cuts along the length of a shingle, you can use a drywall T square or, as I prefer, the top edge of another shingle.

Metal snips

You can use metal snips to cut both metal flashing and roof shingles. Drip edges, valley flashing, and roll flashing will need to be trimmed to length. Although you could use your utility knife to scribe and snap the metal, metal snips give a much cleaner and accurate cut. Some roofers like the control they get from metal snips to trim shingles along rakes and in valleys rather than

■ WORK SAFE
■ WORK SMART
■ THINKING AHEAD

It's not practical to carry large squares or straightedges around with you while you're on the roof, so make as many cuts as you can on the ground. Plan a series of cuts and keep the tools near a bundle of shingles ready to guide your knife.

The nail stripper hangs from a string around your neck and holds and dispenses loose nails for hammering. The coil caddy hangs on your tool belt and holds several coils of pneumatic roof nails.

using a knife. The shingles' surface granules will quickly dull the snips, so you may want to have one pair for shingles and another for cutting metal.

Tool belts and pouches

It's tough to choose from all the belts and pouches available. The system you choose will depend to some extent on your roofing style. Some roofers sit on one hip while applying shingles, some kneel, and others stand. If you sit, you'll be limited to a single tool pouch on one side rather than double pouches that a roofer who stands or kneels can use.

A basic belt with a hammer loop or hook is a good start. The size and style of pouches will depend on the nail-storage capacity you'll need and how many tools you want to have with you at all times.

I tend to stand while I roof, so I prefer two leather pouches with a belt that feeds through each pouch. This setup allows me to shift the pouches and hammer hook to different positions on the belt for comfort. A simple pair of canvas pouches works for other roofers; the choice is purely personal. I find that lighter is better. Don't overfill your tool pouches with nails and tools or you'll limit your mobility. Keep extra tools in a box up on the roof.

Nail strippers

A nail stripper isn't what it sounds like; you don't use it to strip roofs. Nail strippers are small metal boxes that hang around your neck and hold roofing nails (see the photo at left). If you're going to hand-nail roof shingles, you'll want one of these to speed production. Its unique design orients the nails with the points down into slots at its base. You extract nails from the box by sliding them along the slot and out a spring door at the side. By grabbing a group of nails between your index and middle finger, you're prepared to nail off a shingle or two without reloading. Nail strippers are sold as right- or left-handed models.

Coil nail holders

These gadgets thread through your belt and are great for loading up with several coils of nails for a pneumatic nailer. You could just pack a couple rolls into your tool pouch, but they are likely to get bent. Even small bends in the collating wire of coil nails can cause irritating nail-feed malfunctions. The holders are rigid and keep the coils of nails from being deformed. You can also make up a holder yourself from a piece of PVC pipe with an end cap. Do this by cutting a couple of small slots in the back to feed a belt through and a wide slot in the front to slide coils up (see the photo above left).

Gloves

Work gloves are almost essential unless you have leather skin. After a couple of days roofing barehanded, the roof shingles wear through several layers of skin on my fingers and leave them tender. The problem is worse in wet and cold weather. Of course, gloves can be cumbersome, which slows production.

What works for me is a pair of thin leather or synthetic leather framing-style gloves that leave the fingertips exposed. I wrap my fingertips with just a couple of layers of cloth athletic tape. The gloves give my palms protection, and the tape protects my fingertips without causing loss of dexterity. The tape is easy to replace when it wears out.

Rubber gloves are useful to keep your hands clean while troweling on roof cement. Regular leather or cloth gloves work, but the tar may pass through. Save gooey gloves in a plastic bag or just discard them after a couple of messy uses.

Fingerless gloves protect your hands without sacrificing dexterity. Adhesive athletic tape protects fingertips.

Pneumatic Equipment

It would be tough to compete in the asphalt shingle roofing trade without using pneumatic equipment to increase production. Pneumatic nailers and staplers drive fasteners much faster than you can by hand. Some people insist that shingles installed with pneumatically driven fasteners are more prone to failure than shingles fastened with hand-driven nails. They claim that nailers drive fasteners too deep or not deep enough and that haphazard pneumatic users drive fasteners in the wrong location on the shingles.

The bottom line is that pneumatic nailers and staplers (and hammers for that matter) are only as good as the installer handling them; as you'll see in chapter 7, there can be installation problems when pneumatic-tool operators don't use prudence. Regardless, some municipalities have adopted building codes that don't permit shingles to be installed with pneumatically driven fasteners.

Other components of a pneumatic nailing system include a compressor to pump and store air at high pressure, a regulator to keep the air pressure within operation range, an automatic oiler to lubricate the tools, and hoses with special fittings to deliver the compressed air to the nailers and staplers.

Compressors

Compressed air is an efficient way to provide power to pneumatic nailers and staplers, allowing the tools to be smaller and lighter than if they were electrically powered. Although air compressors come in a variety of sizes and configurations, they all have three main parts: a motor, an air pump, and a tank. The motor, which can be electric or gasoline, drives an air pump that stores compressed air

The heart of a pneumatic-tool system is a pressure-regulated compressor. Rubber and plastic air hoses get the compressed air to the tools and metal fittings connect everything together.

in a tank. Some air pumps have oil reservoirs for lubrication and others are oilless. Tanks come in several sizes and shapes as well. Gas compressors are great if there's no electric power available, but the constant drone of the engine is annoying. As long as you perform routine maintenance on an oil or oilless pump, either can last a long time before needing professional service.

Make sure you use a compressor that meets or exceeds the air requirements of the pneumatic tool or tools you'll be using. Since pneumatic roofing tools don't require a lot of air capacity compared with framing nailers, you can get by with just about any compressor to operate one or two nailers. To operate three or four nailers or staplers, look for a compressor with a larger (15- to 20-gallon) tank and higher cubic feet per minute (cfm) output.

Pressure regulators

The air pressure entering a nailer or stapler has a direct effect on how well and consistently it drives fasteners. Too much pressure will drive fasteners too deeply, whereas low pressure won't drive them deep enough. Pressure regulators keep the output of an air compressor within a certain range and maintain the hose pressure even more precisely.

Compressors have a built-in regulator that turns the motor on and off and maintains a tank pressure range of about 80 pounds per square inch (psi) to 120 psi. When the air in the tank is depleted below 80 psi, the compressor motor kicks in and circulates the pump to replenish the air. When the pressure reaches 120 psi, the compressor motor stops. But this oscillation in the air pressure may cause the tool to underdrive fasteners at the low-pressure end of the cycle and overdrive at the high end. Additional air-pressure regulators can remedy the problem.

One type of regulator fastens to the air outlet of the compressor tank or is included on the compressor. It emits a consistent pressure of air into the air hoses. This eliminates most of the oscillation in pressure that comes from the compressor pump regulator. But if you are operating several nailers or staplers on the same compressor, you may find that different brands or types of pneumatic roofing tools may need different pressures to operate optimally. Also, older tools may need more pressure to operate well.

Using inline air-pressure regulators can control the air pressure reaching each specific tool. They can be inserted anywhere along the lengths of air hose that deliver air to each tool or be connected right to the tool itself. Many models are small and easy to connect using quick-disconnect fittings.

Automatic oilers

Pneumatic tools need lubricating oil to keep the internal pistons and seals from seizing up. You can put several drops of pneumatic lubricating oil into the tool a couple of times a day or you can use an automatic oiler. Automatic oilers fasten to the air outlet on the compressor tank and continuously feed minute amounts of lubrication into the airstream. This ensures that each tool being powered by the compressor receives adequate lubrication and prevents oil from dripping out of the nose of the tools as sometimes happens when lubricating manually.

The drawback to oilers is that the hoses collect oil and can be messy. Also, they hang onto the side of the compressor and can break off when handled frequently.

Air hoses and fittings

Air hoses deliver the compressed air from the compressor tank to the nailers and staplers. They are made from various types of rubber and plastic and they come in several diameters. Air hoses can be flexible or rigid and heavy or light depending on the rubber or plastic of which they're made.

Roofers have different preferences for their hose arrangements. I prefer large-diameter flexible rubber hoses as the main feed line between the compressor and an air T that provides connections for two or more hoses. The large inside diameter (ID) main hose provides plenty of air volume to supply several tools at once. From the T to each tool, I like to use small ID, lightweight plastic hoses. These somewhat rigid hoses don't put a drag on the installer like heavy rubber hoses can when moving around on the roof.

Hoses and tools can be outfitted with male and female quick-disconnect fittings so you can assemble exactly the hose lengths and accessories you need. Fittings come in a couple of diameters and types. Outfit all your equipment with fittings of the same type and diameter, but keep other styles and sizes on hand to make conversions for specific purposes or if you have to link to someone else's equipment.

Connectors with ⅜-in. ID permit air volume for long runs from the compressor to a T, while smaller ¼-in. ID connectors provide plenty of air to individual tools operating off the common T. However you decide to set up your hoses, start at the compressor tank and always end the pressure side of each connection with a female fitting. Female fittings have rubber O rings that seat an internal plug to cut off airflow when the male end of a hose length is disconnected. Without this arrangement and the sealing feature, any hose termination not connected to a tool would leak air constantly. Outfit all your pneumatic tools with a male fitting, and be careful not to install male or female fittings backwards.

Roofing coil nailers

All roofing nailers are similar in design and operation. A basket holds the coil of roofing nails and adjusts for different nail

> **WORK SAFE ■ WORK SMART ■ THINKING AHEAD**
>
> If you incorrectly install a female fitting on a nailer or stapler, the tool can hold a charge of air capable of firing once. This would be every bit as dangerous as carrying around a gun with one bullet in the chamber, thinking it was empty.

Coil nailers (left) and staplers (right) pay for themselves after just a couple of roof jobs. They drive fasteners faster than you ever could by hand.

WORK SAFE
WORK SMART
THINKING AHEAD

Many professional tool shops have demonstration models of pneumatic nailers and staplers that they'll loan out in hopes that you'll purchase one once you see how well they perform. If you're thinking of buying one but aren't sure, it's a great way to try before you buy.

lengths. The nails automatically advance one at a time into the firing chamber. When the nailer is actuated, an internal piston pushes a hardened steel driver through the firing chamber and drives the nail. The sequence is initiated by squeezing a trigger while the safety contact tip at the nose of the nailer is depressed on the roof shingle.

There are two operation modes for pneumatic tools: bump fire (also called contact trip or bounce fire) and sequential fire (also called trigger or restrictive fire). Most nailers are outfitted with triggers that permit bump-fire operation. When the trigger is squeezed constantly, the operator fires the nailer by bumping the safety contact tip onto the shingle. A nail is driven each time the nose of the nailer makes contact. This operation mode is the fastest for installing shingles, but the accuracy of nail placement is compromised. You can easily shoot a nail too high or low on the shingle, or the nailer can be tilted and drive a cockeyed nail. I'll examine the problems with improperly driven nails in chapter 7.

You can trigger-fire a nailer set up with a bump-fire trigger by first placing the nose firmly to the shingle and then squeezing the trigger. But this can cause you to unintentionally shoot two nails because the nailer recoils and your arm may instantaneously push the nose back to the work surface.

The alternative operating system (sequential fire) is safer. Nailers with sequential-fire triggers can't be bump fired. You must follow a precise sequence to initiate a fire. First the nose must be placed on the shingle and then the trigger squeezed. After the nail is driven, the nose must be released and reset before the trigger will initiate another fire. Since you are forced to set the nose with a sequential-triggering system before firing, accurate placement and orientation of the nail is almost ensured. But of course, it's a little slower process than bump firing.

Some nailers have features that make them superior for roofing. Newer models make it easy to fine-tune how deeply the nails are set. Others have articulating nose assemblies that automatically orient the nail square to the shingle even when you tilt the nailer a little. This feature ensures a precisely set nail every time you fire. A built-in air filter is a good feature that keeps debris from entering through the air fitting and wearing the internal nailer parts.

Roofing staplers

Pneumatic staplers operate in much the same way as roofing nailers. Rather than holding nails in a basket, staplers have a track that guides a series of glued-together staples to the firing chamber. Since the crown of the staples is about 1 in. wide, you have to hold the stapler perpendicular to the shingle. Otherwise, the staples will go in tilted, and one side of the crown of the staple will protrude above the shingle surface and cause problems, which I'll take a closer look at in chapter 7.

Staplers are lighter than nailers so they're easier to handle, and staples are cheaper and easier to load than nails. Staplers also cost less than nailers, but you won't find them used as frequently on job sites. Although most shingle manufacturers permit staples to be used as fasteners, the packages typically state that nails are the preferred fasteners. Because the surface area of a staple crown is smaller than the surface area of a roofing nail, shingles will tear through staples easier than through nails in a high wind. Some municipalities prohibit staples for fastening roof shingles.

Stripping and Repair Tools and Equipment

Unless you install shingles exclusively on new homes, you will find yourself tearing off old layers of shingles before installing new shingles. There are specialized and not-so-specialized tools and equipment to remove and collect the old shingles, protect the building and surrounding area, and expedite cleanup. There are also simple tools you'll need to replace existing shingles that are sealed down and become brittle.

Stripping shovels

Before specialized shingle-stripping shovels (also called stripping tools) became available, roofers used ordinary flat shovels or pitchforks to pry the old shingles off of the roof sheathing. I still use a flat shovel I borrowed from my father 20 years ago. I modified the shovel to increase leverage by bolting a 2×3 to the heel of the blade, and my father hasn't seen it since.

There are many versions of stripping shovels. Some look like ordinary flat shovels and others look like something from another world. Some common features on specialized stripping shovels include notches along the blade edge to grab nails as well as bent handles and fulcrum bars for extra leverage. Stripping shovels cost $30 to $50 each, but they pay for themselves quickly.

Everyone has a different way they like to strip a roof. Top down, sideways, or bottom up, they all get the job done (see chapter 4 for a complete description of roof stripping). Some roofers like to sit while stripping and others prefer to stand. How you like to strip a roof will be a factor in which stripping shovel works best for you, but the only way to decide on which type is to try them out.

Stripping shovels can be specialized tools with teeth. The mini shovel is for tight places, but you can also use an ordinary flat shovel. Old tarps catch the debris, while sawhorses and A-frames protect small bushes from being crushed.

I borrowed a couple from friends and tried them out before settling on one to purchase.

MINI STRIPPING SHOVELS Some of these look like miniature versions of full-sized stripping shovels and others have a unique appearance. With handles about 18 in. to 24 in. long and narrower blades, these tools are great for getting into tight spots where you need more control. For example, a mini shovel is great for peeling up shingles around step flashing and also works well for popping out stubborn nails that the full-sized shovels missed. Think about how often you'll use a mini shovel before you lay out the cash, though. For pros, they're a must, but carpenters and do-it-yourselfers who only occasionally tackle a roof can generally get by with a multipurpose flat bar.

■ WORK SAFE
■ WORK SMART
■ THINKING AHEAD

Lumber yards often use large tarps to cover shipments, so if you're a regular customer they'll probably save some for you. The tarps generally have holes from use and abuse, but they're fine for protecting plants, covering the sides of a house, and collecting shingle debris.

Tarps

Tarps serve a variety of functions on a roofing project. On jobs that will be stripped and reroofed, you'll want to have a couple of tarps in good condition large enough to cover the roof. Even with today's improved weather forecasting, it's not worth taking a chance. Ordinary plastic sheets will work in a pinch but they tear easily, especially in windy weather. Reinforced woven polyethylene tarps are lightweight and durable. You can use canvas tarps that are more durable than poly, but they are two to three times heavier, bulky, and hard to handle.

After a few uses as a temporary roof cover, poly tarps will develop tears and holes, so you won't want to use them for roof protection anymore, but they can still be used to protect the walls of the house from falling shingles or to collect shingle debris on the ground. You can also use old tarps to drag collected shingles to a waste container. I'll discuss this more in chapter 4.

Sawhorses

No job site is complete without sawhorses. On roofing jobs, they're great for protecting small and medium-sized landscaping plants from the deluge of stripped shingles—just set them up to straddle the plants and throw a tarp over the top. They also make a great worktable with a piece of structural panel (plywood or OSB) laid across two horses, which comes in handy when you need to cut a batch of cap or starter singles—not easy to do on a rooftop on your knees.

■ WORK SAFE
■ WORK SMART
■ THINKING AHEAD

Even if you aren't doing a tearoff, shingles will occasionally fall off the roof. When they do, they often fly back toward the side of the house with enough punch to break windows. Be sure to protect windows with tarps. Even if you don't cover an entire wall, take a walk around the house and consider covering vulnerable windows.

Trash pails

You'll need this humble member of the equipment assemblage for collecting debris and hauling. Don't waste your money on a light-duty trash pail. Go for the thick, super-heavy-duty type. Also, don't buy a huge pail. The tendency is to fill whatever receptacle you have at hand, and there's no way you'll be able to move a large trash can full of old shingles.

Roll magnets and bar magnets

The old roofing nails fly everywhere when you tear off roof shingles. Even when you carefully protect the ground and landscaping with tarps, the small nails can fall through tears and holes. The easiest way to locate and pick up errant nails so they don't find their way into the homeowners' feet is to run a large magnet over the ground. Several types are available, the cheapest being a simple 1-ft.- or 2-ft.-long bar magnet dragged with a rope. Other types have wheels and a handle. Several passes may be necessary to gather all the nails, especially in deep lawn.

Staging and Ladders

Ladders are used primarily to get up on a roof. You need staging to create a safe and stable work platform along the perimeter of a roof or on the roof itself if the pitch is too steep to safely work on.

Fall protection is a major safety issue. The Occupational Safety and Health Administration (OSHA) and various state authorities regulate proper staging and ladder use. The following descriptions are merely a survey of what's commonly used. Check with equipment manufacturers for operation instructions and ensure regulatory compliance before using staging or ladders on a work site. This may sound like "lawyer-speak" but it's good advice to heed. I've suffered my share of falls from roofs because I've been too lazy, careless, cheap, or overconfident in my traction. One fall costs more in lost time than taking the time to set up safe ladders and staging in the first place.

Perimeter staging

This type of staging gives you a comfortable work platform along the eaves of the house so you can safely install the first series of shingle courses. Once you have 3 ft. or 4 ft. of roof shingles installed, you'll stand on the roof or roof staging to continue. This is when the staging serves as a safety stop in the event of a fall, as well as provides a place to store and pass up tools and materials.

Pump-jack staging is adjustable, thereby increasing the range you can reach up the roof plane. Other staging, such as A-frames and wall jacks, is stationary and has to be reset to adjust the height, which can be time-consuming.

PUMP JACKS Pump-jack staging is probably the most versatile type because the height can be adjusted without removing the planks or staging itself. The jacks ride vertically on 4×4 wooden or metal posts and operate with a foot lever to raise and a crank to lower. Braces fastened to the roof or wall framing hold the top of the poles away from the wall. There are supplemental brackets available to hold guardrails and a platform for tools and materials. These brackets slide on the post above the jacks.

Another type of pump-jack system uses integrated metal poles. When used with metal staging planks, the metal poles can be placed farther apart than 4x4s supporting wooden planks. Pump-jack systems are expensive but if you do a lot of roofing, they're worth it. Rental shops usually have pump jacks available as well.

A-FRAMES These homemade contraptions serve a couple of purposes. As staging, A-frames support planks to create an efficient work level for ranch-height roofs (8 ft. to 12 ft. off the ground). Staging planks are set on horizontal cross members of the A-frames so they can only be adjusted to predetermined heights. You can also use A-frames to protect tall landscape plants in much the same way as

Pump-jack staging systems are the most versatile. Jacks hold planks and ride up and down on wooden or aluminum poles.

A-frame staging is a simple way to gain access to eaves. Simple to make, it can also be used to protect tall plants that sawhorses can't cover.

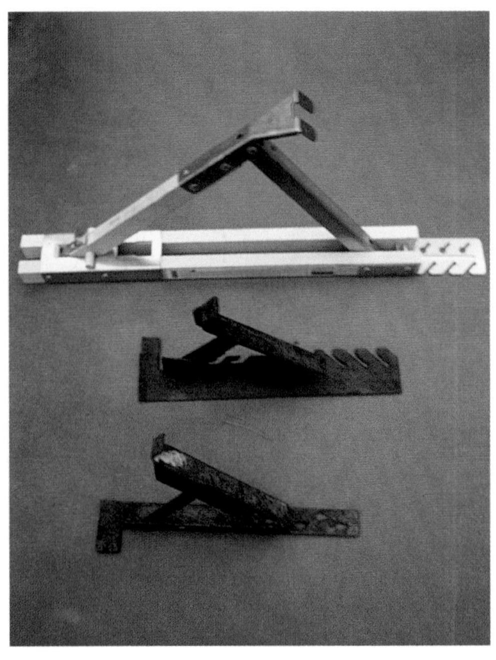

Roof jacks come in several sizes and styles, as shown in the photo at right. The bottom leg is nailed into the roof framing and planks set across the top leg to provide horizontal work levels on the roof deck. (Photo above by Andy Engel, courtesy *Fine Homebuilding* magazine, ©The Taunton Press.)

When you need solid staging at only one level on a new construction job, you can install through-wall jacks in a reasonable amount of time.

sawhorses by straddling the plants and covering with a tarp.

WALL JACKS Wall jacks bolt through the exterior wall of a house and support staging planks. Usually they are set about waist height to the fascia so you can reach and install roof shingles several feet up the roof. The fastening bolt extends through the width of the wall and is supported by a horizontal block spanning across the face of two or more studs. Wall jacks are typically used on new construction only because the bolt would require drilling holes through the interior finish of inhabited homes. To reset wall-jack staging height, you must slide off the staging planks, remove the jacks, drill new holes, and set up the jacks again—a time-consuming process.

LADDER JACKS You can turn your ladders into staging by hooking ladder jacks onto the upper rungs. The jacks create a horizontal cradle to support staging planks between ladders. You can adjust the height of ladder jacks, but you first have to remove the staging planks.

Special hooks turn a conventional ladder into a roof ladder you can hang over the ridge.

You can make up simple roof ladders from 18-in.-wide strips of sheathing and 1×2 cleats nailed about a foot apart. These ladders protect the shingles from foot traffic and give you extra traction on steep pitches (left). They also provide support for the end of planks that stage adjacent roofs (below).

You should only use ladder jacks with heavy-duty ladders, and make sure you don't exceed a ladder's load rating.

Roof staging

Once you have several shingle courses installed along an eaves, you'll need roof staging to keep your feet braced while you work your way up steep roof pitches. You can walk on low-pitch roofs without the aid of roof staging, but a "cow catcher" (a row of roof-jack and plank staging along the eaves) can provide extra security.

ROOF JACKS Roof jacks are the most common roof staging and several types are available. Roof jacks are nailed or screwed through the roof sheathing and into solid framing (roof rafters or trusses). The jacks support staging planks or toeholds of 2×4 lumber. Horizontal rows of jacks and planks are spaced at intervals up steep roof pitches that correspond to the limit of your reach; this can be anywhere from 6 ft. to 8 ft. depending on the shortest worker's height. The models that support planks have adjustable brackets so you can set the angle of the plank to the most comfortable position for each roof pitch. The 2×4s on toehold staging are only wide enough to catch your toes on; they aren't as common (or as safe) as plank jacks. I'll look at setting up and working on roof-jack staging in chapter 7.

ROOF LADDERS You can purchase special hooks that attach to a conventional ladder to turn it into a roof ladder (see the top left photo). The hook hangs the ladder over the roof ridge to provide

Aluminum ladders and fiberglass ladders are most common today. Look for ladders rated as heavy-duty type 1 or 1A.

Making a Ridge Box

A ridge box is a simple piece of equipment you make yourself to hold extra tools and fasteners while you're working on a roof. I like one that's about 12 in. wide and 16 in. to 18 in. long with 6-in. sides. Make the box from plywood with extra-long side panels that extend 6 in. below the base of the box. The side panels become legs that straddle the ridge and keep the box stable.

A ridge box with extended or applied legs is a handy spot to keep tools and supplies.

access up a steep roof pitch. Another type of roof ladder is site-built and constructed by nailing wood cleats onto a 12-in.- to 24-in.-wide piece of plywood or OSB. The top of the ladder is nailed through the roof sheathing beneath a shingle tab at the top (see the photos at right on p. 47). Roof ladders are used most often at gable ends and along the intersections of roofs and walls where you have to cut off or cut in shingles and flashing. They also can be used to protect shingles in high-traffic areas from damage during construction.

Staging planks

The lumber planks you lay across A-frames or other staging equipment should be rated for staging-plank use.

Although many people use common dimension lumber as staging planks, it is not intended for that purpose and may fail, resulting in serious injury or death. Look for span ratings on staging planks that indicate the maximum weight loading and maximum support spacing.

Aluminum staging planks are strong, reliable, and can span greater distances than lumber planks. They are also more expensive than lumber planks but they last much longer.

Ladders

Avoid inexpensive extension ladders; instead look for industrial-duty type 1 or 1A ladders made of aluminum or fiberglass. You'll probably want more than one for multiple access points to a roof and perhaps a variety of lengths. Additional equipment is available to increase ladder steadiness, including stabilizers for the top and foot braces for the bottom.

Stabilizers are wide, U-shaped metal extrusions that attach to an upper rung and spread the contact area of the ladder. You can adjust the stabilizer so it rests on the roof deck or the wall of the house so the ladder doesn't rest on the edge of the gutter or drip edge. Foot braces secure the bottom feet of the ladder to the ground and keep them from kicking out.

Shingle lifts

Hauling 20 squares of 90-lb. bundles of shingles up onto a roof is time-consuming, backbreaking, and potentially dangerous work. Any equipment that can ease the burden is an asset. My first preference is to have the roof shingle supplier deliver the bundles to the roof with a boom truck or conveyor system. But delivery timing or limited site access can foil the plan. An alternative is to employ a mechanized shingle lift. Several systems are commercially available or can be rigged up with a little ingenuity. The most common types use an electric motor and cable system to run a small platform up and down the rails of an ordinary ladder. An operator at the base loads the bundles and another on the roof off-loads and spreads them out along the ridge.

Roofing Footwear

You might not think of boots and shoes as equipment, but for roofing they should be carefully selected for traction, ankle support, and their wear effect on the shingles. The soles on many workboots favored by carpenters don't grip well to roof sheathing or to the shingle surface. And although you shouldn't rely on footwear as fall protection, you need stability to be productive.

Some roofers prefer sneakers because of their soft rubber soles and nonaggressive pattern. But sneakers may not provide enough ankle support to work on steeper roof pitches. I prefer lightweight, mid-height hiking boots for their nonskid soles and ankle support. Unfortunately, the aggressive knobbed soles on hiking boots can tear up the granular shingle surface, especially on a hot day, so I use my older pairs of boots with soles worn nearly smooth. They've outlived their usefulness for mountain climbing but work fine on a roof.

Slipover soles provide extra traction on steep or frosty roofs.

You can also get slipover soles that are like sandals for your shoes or boots. There are several models available with sole surfaces that grip. Some soles have small spikes that work well on frosty roof sheathing, and others have durable foam surfaces that give you superior traction without damaging asphalt shingles on a hot day.

Experiment with several types of footwear to find what you feel most comfortable with because in the end that's what really counts.

Roofing in Comfort

To be as comfortable as possible when roofing, consider using some of the following equipment.

Knee Pads

If you like to kneel while you install shingles, you'll want to investigate high-quality knee pads. Cheap knee pads wear out quickly and the band that wraps around the back of your leg can dig in uncomfortably. I've met a few roofers who swear by hockey shin pads.

Hip Pads

These pads are a necessity for roofers who like to sit on one hip while roofing. They keep you from sliding on the roof shingles and protect your pants from wearing through. Commercially available hip pads are hard to locate, but you can make your own out of an old car or truck inner tube. Crosscut a 16-in. section of inner tube and make an elongated U cut on the inside edge, leaving a 3-in. to 4-in. segment at the bottom of the U. Punch two holes at the top corners of the tube where you started and ended the U cut so you can tie a strap through. Step into the pad with the rubber on the outside over your hip and the U on the inside of your leg, then tie a strap of inner tube rubber or rope around your waist and through the two holes in the top of the pad.

Roof Pads

Another way to sit (or kneel) on the roof in comfort is on a foam or plastic pad. There are commercial models available, but you can easily make one out of a piece of polyurethane foam from an old mattress. You can also buy pieces of foam from fabric and craft stores. Foam grips the shingle surface and prevents you from sliding, and it protects the shingles too, especially on hot days when the surface is soft.

Reinforced Pants

These pants have leather- or synthetic leather-reinforced panels at the knees and hips. Reinforced pants cost more than ordinary workpants but they last far longer. Ordinary pants will wear out quickly at the knees or hips if you kneel or sit while roofing.

Homemade hip pads cut from an old rubber inner tube are a must if you like to sit on one hip while roofing. The pad protects your pants from wearing out and also helps you resist sliding down the roof.

Roof pads are nothing more than pieces of urethane foam. You can cut them from old foam bed mattresses or purchase commercial versions. (Photo by Andy Engel, courtesy *Fine Homebuilding* magazine, © The Taunton Press.)

For complete fall protection, nothing beats a full-body harness. These are available from shops specializing in safety equipment and from some tool stores.

Safety Equipment

OSHA is the national agency that regulates workplace safety. Many states have workplace regulatory agencies as well. When your workplace is the roof of a house, you need to pay special attention to safety, not only to comply with regulations but also to protect yourself and those who work with you.

Fall protection

OSHA has put a lot of effort into workplace fall protection. In some jurisdictions, they have worked closely with local homebuilders associations to develop safety programs that suit residential contractors. There are both performance and prescriptive regulations that govern fall protection safety. Contact your state or regional OSHA office for current information since regulations are updated from time to time.

Fall-protection devices common in commercial construction have been adopted and adapted for use in residential construction. For roofing work, body harnesses and lanyards are the most versatile fall-protection equipment.

HARNESSES In the old days, roofers who insisted on wearing fall protection wrapped wide leather belts around their waists and tied heavy ropes from the belts to anchor points along the ridge. Enough slack in the ropes permitted them to move freely around the roof. This system saved some lives but also caused some serious injury and deaths. Because of the excess slack in the rope, a roofer could fall several feet before being jolted to a halt. The jolt concentrated around his waist, frequently causing serious internal organ damage, a broken back, or both.

Today's full-body harnesses and connection systems minimize the length

General Safety Notes

It takes more than a good fall-protection system to create a safe job site. You have to establish practices and systems to protect the building, your clients, your employees, and yourself.

Client Safety

The homeowners need safe access points into and out of the house, so designate primary and secondary access doors that are out of harm's way. Cordon off entryways that may be in the line of falling debris. If falling debris is a possibility at all entryways, consider creating covered pathways using tarps and A-frame staging. This is just as important if you are working on a new house where other tradespeople are coming and going while you are working.

Client safety doesn't end at the end of the day. Make sure that there are no loose shingles or tools on the roof that can fall or blow off after you leave. Pick up stripped shingles and shingle debris before leaving and place them in a container. You never know who may be in the yard and step on nails embedded in small pieces of debris. Limit access to staging where children are likely to play.

Personnel and Personal Safety

According to the federal Department of Labor, you are responsible for appropriate safety training for your employees, so establish and enforce minimum safety practices for tool and equipment use. Inspect staging and safety equipment regularly and keep it in good working order. Keep records of your safety training sessions, inspections, instructions, and any injuries sustained. Be sure to keep a first-aid kit on hand for the inevitable cuts, scrapes, and punctures. And lead by example—follow your own work and safety rules.

Tool Safety

Pneumatic nailers and staplers can be dangerous if not kept in good working order and handled safely. Read all safety instructions that come with the tools and train employees in their proper use. Take extra precautions using pneumatics when homeowners are present—errant nails can travel pretty far.

Eye and Hearing Protection

Everyone working with or near anyone using pneumatic tools should wear safety glasses and hearing protection. Be sure to use only OSHA-compliant equipment. Have employees try on and choose glasses and ear plugs (or ear muffs) that feel comfortable because comfortable safety equipment is more likely to be worn.

of the freefall and cushion the shock of a fall by spreading the harness support system over a greater area of the body than a belt alone. Look for these safety systems in contractor tool shops or industrial safety equipment shops. Since there are a number of styles available, review several before choosing one that suits your roofing habits.

GUARDRAILS Guardrail systems are available that attach to the roof much like roof jacks. Vertical posts have a flat steel plate at the bottom that slips between shingle courses so the fasteners aren't driven through shingle exposures. The upright posts have brackets to which you attach two horizontal 2×4 guardrails and a toe rail. When you set up a guardrail system around the edges of a roof, you have full freedom of movement without wearing a harness or pulling around a tether line that can get in the way while you're shingling. I prefer a harness system for most roofs, though. I think they're a little more versatile than guardrails and take much less time to set up.

Whatever you do, use some sort of fall protection. Do this to comply with OSHA rules, but more important do it for your own safety.

CHAPTER 3

Material Planning and Ordering

IN THIS CHAPTER, you'll learn how to calculate the quantity of shingles and all the other materials you'll need for a roofing job. I'll describe two methods for determining the area of a roof and how to gauge the number of extra shingles you'll need for waste, overlaps, and starter shingles. I'll discuss what you should be aware of when ordering shingles so you have enough to complete the job and how to make sure the shingles you receive are of good quality.

Allow yourself plenty of time to calculate the quantity of shingles, underlayment, flashings, and other materials needed to roof a house. The more accurate your count, the less time you'll waste waiting for material deliveries during the project.

Calculating the Shingle Quantity

Roof shingles are sold by both the bundle and by the square. A square of shingles is the quantity needed to cover 100 sq. ft. of roof. Shingles are packaged in paper- or plastic-wrapped bundles designed to be light enough for a person to carry, so heavier shingles require more bundles per

Estimating a Roof from the Ground

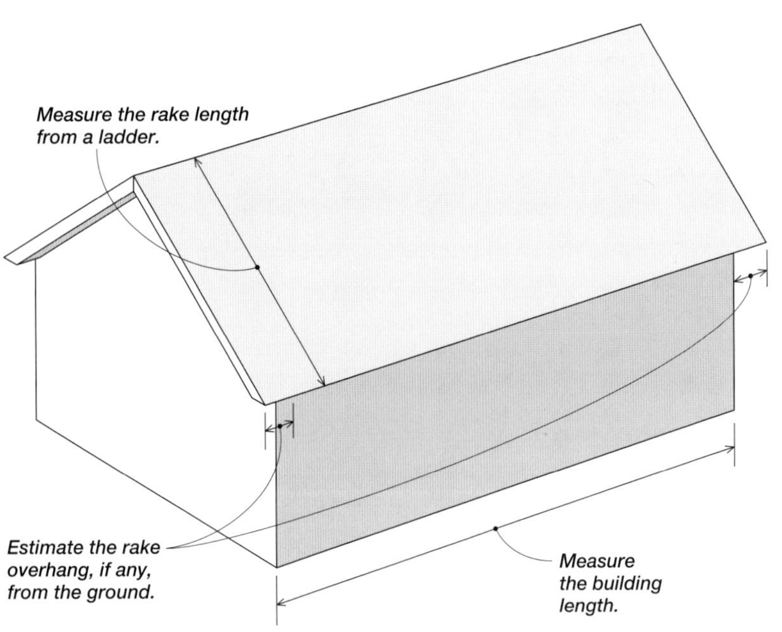

square. Three bundles to a square is most common, which applies to most three-tab strip shingles and some lightweight laminated shingles. Heavier three-tabbed shingles and laminated shingles require four, or sometimes five, bundles to cover a square. When shingles come three bundles to the square, there are 29 standard-sized shingles (12 in. by 36 in.) in each bundle.

Figuring out the roof area is the first step to determine how many bundles you'll need to order. There are two ways to size up a new or freshly stripped roof: the measurement method and the sheet-count method. There's a third method for calculating bundles when you'll be laying new shingles over old or if the old roof is still in place.

Once you have a bundle or square count for the main roof area, you'll add additional shingles to account for waste, starter shingles, and extra shingles for hip and ridge caps.

Measurement method

The most accurate way to determine how many bundles of shingles you'll need is to hop up on a roof and measure each roof plane. If all the roof planes are rectangles, all you have to do is multiply the length times the width of each plane to get the square footage and then add up the square footage of each plane (for more complicated roofs, see the sidebar on pp. 56–57).

Often the roof is too steep to walk on without safety equipment, so you need to do the estimate from the ground. In that case, measure the length of the building at the ground level and estimate any rake-edge overhangs. Then, from a ladder, use a stiff, wide-blade measuring tape to measure from the eaves edge to the ridge (see the drawing at left).

Sheet-count method

When the sheathing is still exposed, I'm more inclined to use the sheet-count method than the measurement method. It's fast and you can usually complete it from the ground. Of course, you can use this method only on roofs sheathed with 4-ft. by 8-ft. structural panels.

Each structural panel is 32 sq. ft., and you can easily count the full panels from the ground. You can also tally them up by gauging the relative size of ripped and crosscut sheets along the edges of the roof to the size of a full sheet. Diagonally cut sheets along hips and valleys are a little more difficult to size, but you can usually assign them a relative size such as half or quarter of a full sheet and be close enough (see the drawing on the facing page).

If the shingles you are using come three bundles to a square, calculating the number of bundles you'll need is simple. Each bundle covers 33.3 sq. ft. of roof area—close enough to the 32 sq. ft. a sheet covers. So just order one bundle for each sheet of roof sheathing.

For other bundle counts per square, divide the number of sheets of sheathing by three and you'll have the total number of squares needed to cover the roof. This works because three sheets of sheathing equal roughly 100 sq. ft. (one square).

This may sound like a crude measurement method, but you have to be realistic about how accurate you really need to be. The 1.3-sq.-ft. difference per sheet is a good margin to allow for waste along gable or hip edges. I'll look at calculating waste further in the next section.

Shingle-count method

This method makes it easy to size up most roofs if the old shingles haven't been stripped off yet or if you'll be doing a layover, that is, shingling over existing shingles.

First, measure the length of the eaves of each roof plane, either directly or from the ground by measuring the length of the house and adding in the width of the rake overhangs, if any. Alternately, if the existing shingles are standard three-tab, you can get the eaves' length by counting the number of tabs along the ridges and eaves to determine the length in feet (one tab is equal to 1 ft.).

Now, to get the length of the rakes, count the existing courses of shingles from eaves to ridge. The exposure on each course of shingles is 5 in., so you can multiply the number of courses by 5 in. and then divide by 12 to get the length of the rakes. Just be sure to check that the existing shingles are standard 12-in. by 36-in. shingles and not metric size. Multiply the length of the eaves by the length of the rake and you have the area in square feet.

Additional shingles

If you order shingles based solely on the area of the roof, you won't have enough. You'll need shingles for starter courses along the eaves and sometimes at rakes, and you'll need shingles to cap hips and ridges. Cutting shingles also generates waste. In some places, including at the rakes, against walls and chimneys, and at valleys, you'll need to cut shingles. Some of the cutoffs will be big enough to use as starter shingles or in other areas where cut shingles are needed, but smaller cutoffs will be waste.

WASTE FACTOR The only roof that will generate no waste from cutting is that rare simple gable whose roof length is divisible by the 3-ft. length of a shingle.

Sizing up Roofs Using the Sheet-Count Method

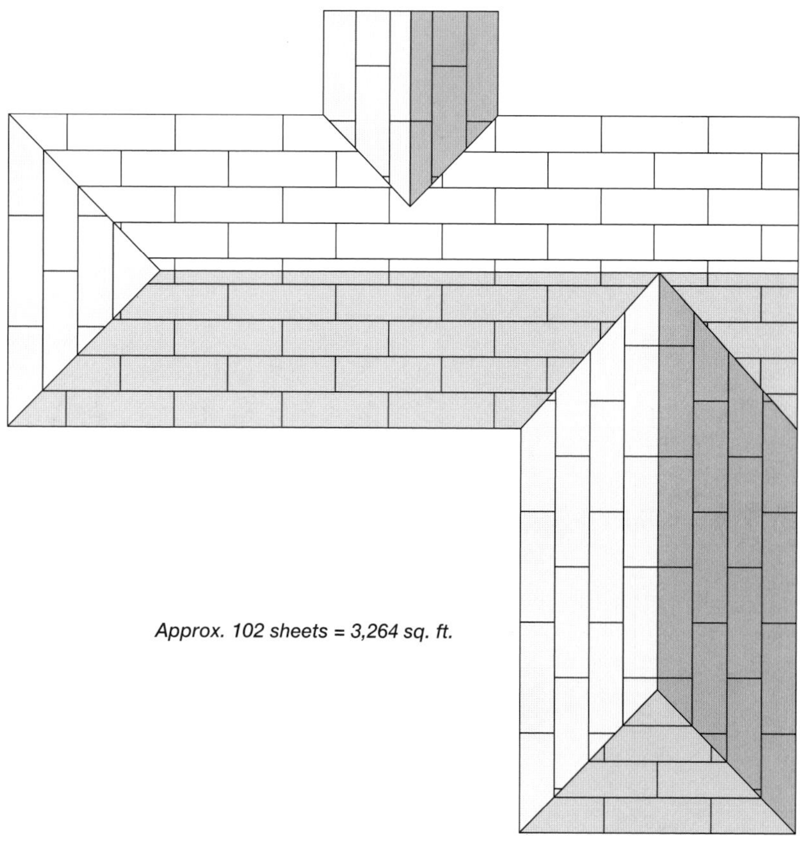

Calculating the Area of a Complex Roof

Areas of complex roofs with multiple hips and valleys take the most time to calculate. Start by making a rough sketch of the roof. To simplify the calculation, break down the sketch into rectangles and right triangles (triangles with one 90-degree corner), then take as many measurements of the roof as you can to match the sides of the rectangles and triangles on the sketch.

Use visual cues from the existing roof shingles or roof sheathing to determine square lines off eaves edges or ridges. These cues will help you measure the lengths of the sides of the rectangles and triangles. For instance, the cutout slots on shingled roofs run perpendicular (90 degrees) to the eaves, and nail rows in sheathing are pretty close to square also. It is difficult sometimes to get accurate measurements. Don't get too concerned though; just round lengths to the nearest 6 in.

With the sketch filled in with measurements, you can determine the size of the roof area. The area of a rectangle is length multiplied by width, whereas the area of a right triangle is the length of the two sides that meet at the 90-degree corner multiplied together and divided by two (this works because a right triangle is half a rectangle).

Tally the square footages of all the rectangles and triangles, which will give you the total square footage for the roof. The example here shows the calculation for a roof with two hips.

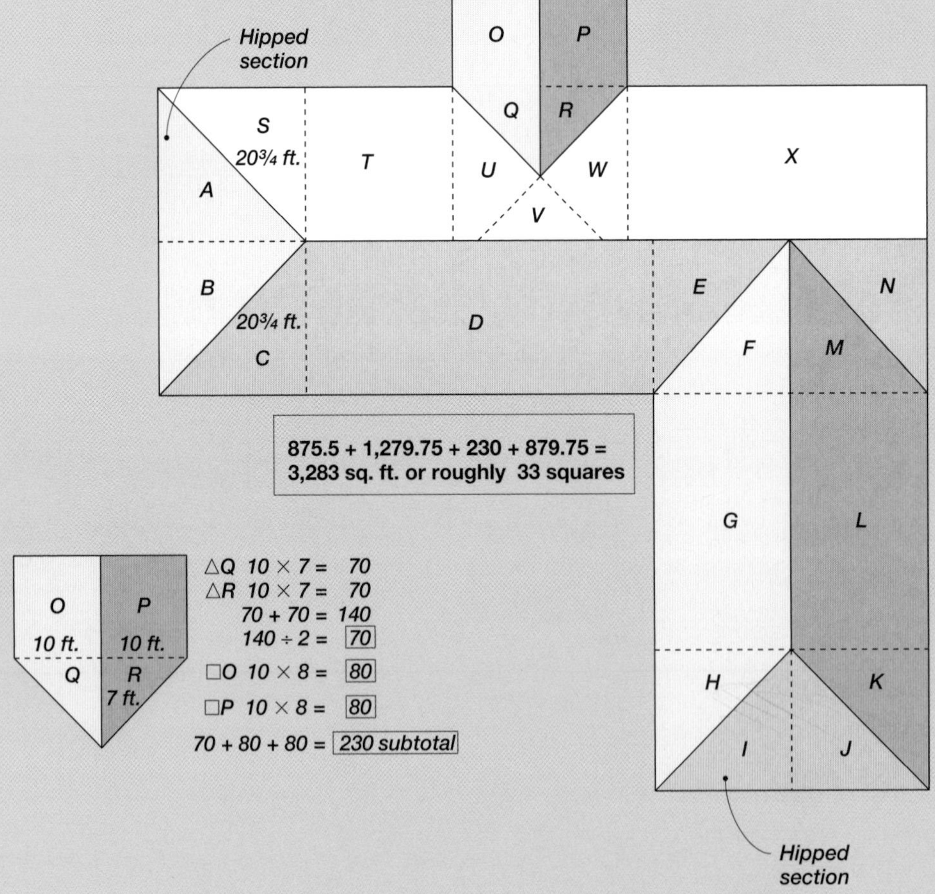

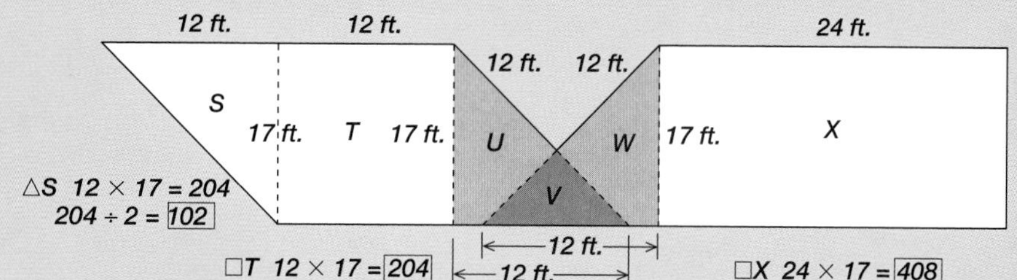

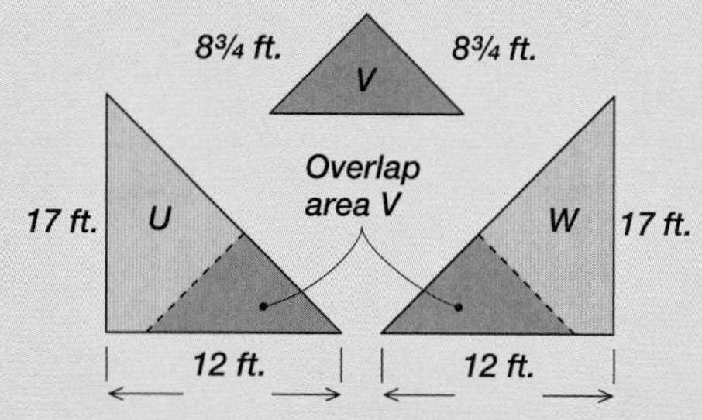

Areas 'U' and 'W' are odd because they have an overlapping section 'V'. Rather than reconfiguring to establish several smaller right triangles, it's easier to subtract out the overlap ('V') from the total areas of 'U' and 'W'.

△U 12 × 17 = 204
△W 12 × 17 = 204
408

Subtract overlap
△V 8.75 × 8.75 = 76.5
331.5

331.5 ÷ 2 = 165.75

102 + 204 + 165.75 + 408 =
879.75 subtotal

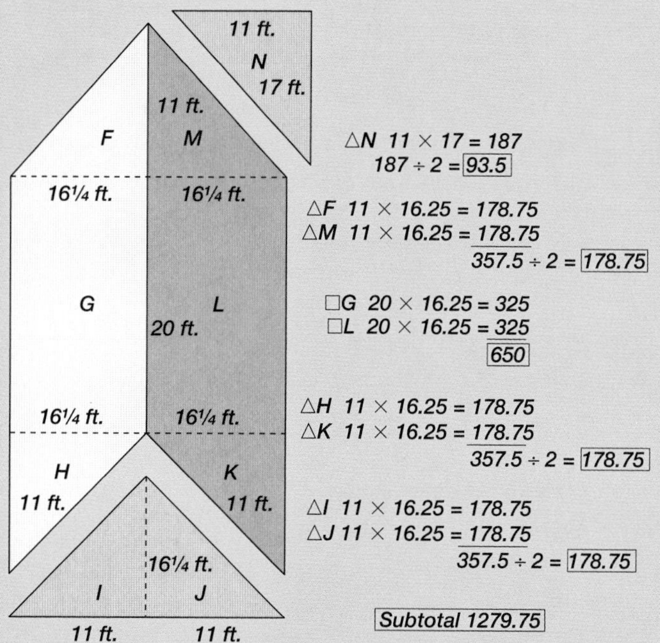

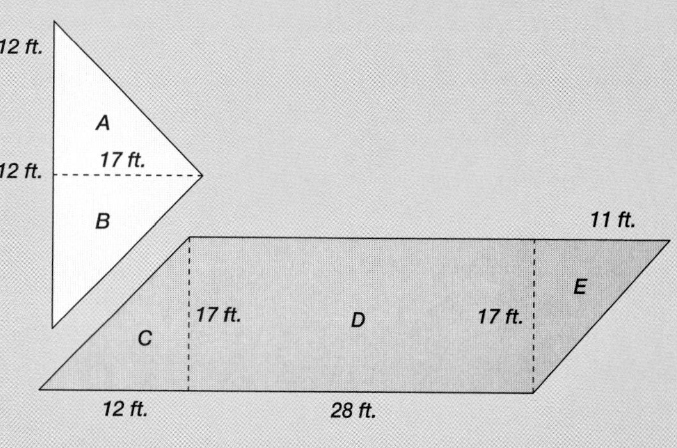

△A 17 × 12 = 204
△B 17 × 12 = 204
408
408 ÷ 2 = 204

△C 17 × 12 = 204
204 ÷ 2 = 102

□D 28 × 17 = 476

△E 17 × 11 = 187
187 ÷ 2 = 93.5

Subtotal 875.5

Waste is generated at numerous places on a project. Fall-off pieces along a gable end, trimmings along valleys, and damaged shingles can add up to 5 percent of the total shingles needed to roof a house. (Photos by Andy Engel, courtesy *Fine Homebuilding* magazine, © The Taunton Press.)

WORK SAFE ▪ WORK SMART ▪ THINKING AHEAD

Laminated shingles typically generate less waste than three-tab shingles do because you don't have to maintain a cutout pattern, but it's tricky to determine exactly how many square feet of shingles you will be able to salvage. It's best to plan your order using the same waste factor that you would use for three-tab shingles—at worst you'll just have a couple of bundles to return.

Other simple gable roofs will require cut shingles at the rakes. From there, the waste factor increases with every obstruction, such as a chimney, and with every hip or valley.

For a simple roof, I generally figure 1 percent as a waste factor. On a complex roof with open valleys, I add 5 percent and sometimes more. There's no calculation you can use to determine the extra shingles you'll need for waste. With experience estimating jobs, you'll get a feel for how many extra shingles to order.

Waste is also generated when shingles are damaged, which is inevitable when you're moving shingles around a steep roof slope and some will slide off. You may be able to salvage part of the damaged shingle, but don't count on it. You can also waste shingles when you nail them improperly and have to remove them. You may drive nails too low in the exposure or fasten one off a control line.

If you have a crew that tends to be sloppy and damage shingles, you'll probably need a couple of extra bundles per job. If your crew is conscientious, one extra bundle should be enough for most jobs.

EXTRA VALLEY MATERIAL Valleys are either woven or cut; both methods require about the same number of shingles (see p. 210). On a woven valley, each course of shingles is extended beyond the valley crease and at least 12 in. onto the adjacent roof plane. You'll use 2 ft. of extra shingle material for each pair of woven courses. In the case of cut valleys, the shingles from the first roof plane that's shingled also extend onto the adjacent roof plane at least 12 in. just like woven valleys. Shingles from the next roof plane are cut just up from the valley line, and the cutoff pieces usually aren't big enough to use elsewhere on the roof. Order two extra shingles per linear foot of valley to account for the overlaps and cutoffs. On a 16-ft. valley, you would need 32 shingles or roughly one extra bundle.

It may take several extra bundles of shingles to provide starter shingles along the eaves and rake edges on a large roof.

STARTER SHINGLES Starters are shingles with the exposure portion trimmed off, leaving just the self-seal strip and top lap. They are fastened along the eaves edges to seal down the first course of shingles and provide coverage material beneath the tab cutouts just like the top lap of each successive course.

When you're using laminated shingles to roof a house, you can save a little money by ordering cheaper three-tab shingles for the starters or better yet, use shingles left over from a previous job. Since laminated shingles have no cutouts, all you really need the starter strip to do is seal the shingles down and shed any water that passes through the joints between shingles.

RAKE-EDGE STARTER SHINGLES You don't need to install starters along the rake, but some roofers do it to create a neater-looking edge where shingles extend past rakes. To install, you can cut the exposure off as you would for eaves starters, or, if you are using three-tab shingles, you can just install the shingles along the rake. Don't use full laminated shingles for rake starters; the exposure portion is too thick. Determine the number of shingles to order for starters by measuring the length of the eaves and rakes, then round up to the nearest foot and divide by three (the length of a shingle).

HIP AND RIDGE CAP SHINGLES Hips and ridges are covered with cap shingles, which are 1-ft. shingle squares that wrap over the hip or ridge. Like regular shingles, they overlap for a 5-in. exposure.

On roofs shingled with three-tab or no-cutout shingles, you simply cut standard shingles into caps. You can cap about 35 lin. ft. of ridge or hips with each bundle of three-tab shingles that come three bundles to the square. You can also

You can cap 35 lin. ft. of ridges and hips with each bundle of shingles. (Photo by Andy Engel, courtesy *Fine Homebuilding* magazine, ©The Taunton Press.)

Waterproof shingle underlayment helps weatherproof critical areas of the roof including eaves, valleys, and roof/wall intersections.

salvage waste shingle pieces and portions of damaged shingles for use as caps.

For roofs shingled with laminated shingles, multi-cutout shingles, and other patterned shingles, you'll have to order hip-and-ridge shingles that are manufactured as companions to the specific shingle product you are using. They're sold by the bundle and usually cap 35 lin. ft., but check with your supplier because some products vary. Just measure the length of the ridges and hips and divide by 35 to determine how many bundles of regular or hip-and-ridge shingles you'll need.

Other Materials

There are so many other items you'll need to complete a roofing job, it's easy to overlook something when you order materials. To prevent this, I made a standard checklist of every type of material I might need. Of course, I don't need everything on the list for every job, but the list is a good way to make sure you don't forget anything (see the checklist on the facing page).

Underlayment

You may need both felt underlayment and waterproof shingle underlayment depending on the shingle manufacturer's underlayment requirements, your preferred practices, and your local building code.

The standard minimum felt underlayment used is 15# and each 3-ft.-wide roll covers approximately four squares of roof area (400 sq. ft.). The improved fiberglass shingle underlayment has about the same weight and coverage as the 15#. The thicker 30# underlayment also comes in 3-ft.-wide rolls but only covers roughly two squares.

Waterproof shingle underlayment comes in 36-in.-wide rolls of three

Roof-Order Checklist

Job address:

Shingle manufacturer: | **Shingle model:** | **Color:**

Shingles	**Bundles**
Shingle quantity (main house)	
Shingle quantity (garage)	
Shingle quantity (other)	
Total bundles of shingles	
Starter shingles	
Rake starters	
Total bundles of starters	

Hip and ridge shingles (if required)

Flashing	**Metal**	**Quantity**
Step flashing (6 in. by 8 in.)		
Step flashing (6 in. by 8 in.)		
Roll flashing (8 in.)		
Roll flashing (8 in.)		
Roll flashing (8 in.)		
Roll flashing (12 in.)		
Roll flashing (12 in.)		
Sheet-metal stock (3 ft. by 8 ft.)		
Boot flashing ($1\frac{1}{2}$ in.)		
Boot flashing (2 in.)		
Boot flashing (3 in.)		
Boot flashing (4 in.)		

Pneumatic fasteners	**Cases**
Coil ($1\frac{1}{4}$ in.)	
Coil ($1\frac{1}{2}$ in.)	
Coil ($1\frac{3}{4}$ in.)	
Staples ($1\frac{1}{4}$ in.)	
Staples ($1\frac{1}{2}$ in.)	

Underlayment	**Rolls**
15# underlayment	
30# underlayment	
Fiberglass underlayment	
Waterproof underlayment	

Drip edges	**Color**	**Quantity**
Drip edge (10 ft.)		
Rake edge (10 ft.)		
Venting drip edge (8 ft.)		

Ventilation	**Type**	**Mfg.**	**Quantity**
Ridge vent			
Ridge vent			
Ridge vent			
Roof vent			
Roof vent			
Roof turbine			
Flash vent			
Exhaust hood			
Exhaust hood			

Hand nails	**Metal**	**Quantity**
$1\frac{1}{4}$ in.		
$1\frac{1}{4}$ in.		
$1\frac{1}{4}$ in.		
$1\frac{1}{2}$ in.		
$1\frac{1}{2}$ in.		
$1\frac{3}{4}$ in.		
$1\frac{3}{4}$ in.		
2 in.		

Other	**Quantity**
Roof cement (gallon)	
Roof cement (tube)	
Tin caps/roof tins	
Staples (¼ in.)	
Staples (⅜ in.)	

Other	**Quantity**

Other	**Quantity**

WORK SAFE ▪ WORK SMART ▪ THINKING AHEAD

Remember to deduct the number of squares of waterproof underlayment from the amount of felt underlayment you'll need—and of course you don't need underlayment at all if you are laying a new roof over old shingles.

lengths—75 ft. to cover two squares, 50 ft. to cover one and a half squares, and 36 ft. to cover one square. Some manufacturers don't make all three lengths.

Even if I use felt underlayment elsewhere, I generally run full-width waterproof underlayment along the eaves and valleys, where rain runoff is concentrated. I split the roll to 18 in. wide to cover the connections where the roof meets a wall.

Fasteners

It's difficult to calculate exactly how many fasteners you'll need for a single roof job. Of course, if you roof all the time, this won't be a problem because you can use the leftovers on the next job. On average, you'll need about 2 lb. of nails per square. If you are using six nails per shingle, order 3 lb. per square.

Roofing nails for hand-nailing are typically sold in 5-lb. and 50-lb. boxes. Some suppliers open kegs and sell nails by the pound, but this is becoming less common. The larger the nail carton you order, the better the value for your dollar. If you use pneumatic tools to do the bulk of your fastening, you'll probably only use hand nails to install flashing and to nail cut-in shingles along rakes, walls, and around chimneys. I order a 50-lb. box, dump it into an empty joint-compound pail, and use it up over half a dozen jobs.

On most new roofs, you can use 1¼-in. nails to meet the penetration requirements, but 1½-in. nails may be more comfortable to hold and drive, especially if you have thick fingers like I do.

Pneumatic coil nails and staples come in cases. Coil nails typically have 60 rolls per box with 120 nails per coil (7,200 nails per box). Staples have from 6,000 to 10,000 staples per box depending on manufacturer and box size. I usually figure a box of nails or staples will fasten 18 squares of shingles with four fasteners per shingle or 12 squares with six fasteners per shingle. This rule of thumb leaves me enough extra fasteners for cap shingles, flashings, and some underlayment fastening.

If you're laying underlayment under windy conditions, you'll want to have a few pounds of roof tins (tin caps) handy. Buy them by the 5-lb. box and keep them in your inventory.

The only other fasteners you'll need are staples to tack down underlayment and perhaps flashing. They come in boxes of 1,250 to 10,000 staples, and you'll go through these faster than you think. I keep 5,000 to 10,000 on hand. Use ¼ in. to ⅜ in. for roofing purposes; longer staples are hard to drive into roof sheathing.

Ventilation

I've seen some roofers complete entire roofs and then go back and cut in vents afterwards, not because they like to do it that way but because they forgot to order the vents. When you measure up a roof, determine what type and how many vents you'll install on the roof. In chapter 4, I'll describe how to calculate the number of roof vents you'll need for a given roof.

Surface-mounted roof vents and roof turbines are sold by the piece, so once you know how many you need it's easy to place an order. The same goes for dryer and bathroom exhaust vent caps.

Ridge vent is sold by length, by the carton, or by the roll depending on the style you choose. Metal ridge vent typically comes in 8-ft. and 10-ft. lengths. Rigid-plastic ridge vents designed to be covered with shingles normally come in 4-ft. lengths, but suppliers may sell them by the carton only; this gives you a minimum purchase of 36 lin. ft. to 48 lin. ft. Flexible-plastic ridge vent comes in rolls of 20 ft. to 50 ft.

WORK SAFE ▪ WORK SMART ▪ THINKING AHEAD

I prefer to overlap the horizontal joints of underlayment by 5 in. rather than the usual 2 in. if I'm drying-in a roof. The underlayment sheds most of the rain until you can install the shingles, thereby keeping everyone inside dry. Order 10 percent more underlayment if you plan to increase the overlap.

Remember to order ridge vents and other ventilation accessories far enough in advance.

Measure the length of ridge you will be venting and order lengths of vents accordingly. Vents that are designed to be capped with shingles typically end 2 ft. to 3 ft. from the rakes or hips, so you can deduct that footage from your order.

Most manufacturers of these shingle-over vents supply 2-in. to 2½-in. roofing nails so you can nail cap shingles through the vents and into the sheathing. The small bags of nails can fall out of the roll or box, though, so it's prudent to have some long nails of your own just in case. Also order the end caps or end plugs if your style of ridge vent requires one or the other.

Drip edge and flashing

In the Northeast, where I live, it is customary to use an extended drip edge for both the eaves and the rakes. But in some parts of the country, it's common to use a different, nonextended profile for the rakes. Drip edge and rake edge come in 10-ft. lengths and three or four stock colors. Just measure your linear footage and figure about 4 in. for overlaps between pieces.

Vent pipe boots are sold individually for standard-sized pipes (1½ in., 2 in., 3 in., and 4 in.), and some universal models are available with embossed rings in the rubber gasket so you peel out sections to match the pipe diameter. If the plumber hasn't cut in the vent pipes on a new house before you shingle it, someone will have to install the boot flashing later.

You'll need step flashing where the roof slope meets a wall, such as on a dormer. To calculate how many pieces of flashing you'll need, measure the length in inches of the roof alongside the wall and divide by 5 (the length of the shingle exposure), then add a few extra pieces.

When the roof calls for an open valley, you can flash it with sheet metal or roll roofing. You can have a metal shop bend a metal valley flashing or you can order the sheet stock and bend it yourself. The sheets should be a minimum of 36 in. wide so 18 in. extend up each side of the valley. Plan to leave an 8-in. to 12-in. overlap between sections when you calculate how many lengths of flashing you'll need for each valley.

If you plan to use roll roofing to form an open valley, just measure the length of the valleys. Use rolls of single-coverage roll roofing, which has the granular mineral coating over most of the surface. Rolls are typically 36 in. wide and 36 ft. long and come in a narrow range of colors, usually just white and black.

When a roof ends at a wall, such as where a porch roof meets the house, it will also require roll flashing. It could be lead, copper, or aluminum. Suppliers

WORK SAFE ▪ WORK SMART ▪ THINKING AHEAD

Check with your supplier on availability and lengths of specialized vents such as filter vents and venting drip edge. Some suppliers don't stock these items, and you'll need to give them advance notice for special orders.

WORK SAFE ▪ WORK SMART ▪ THINKING AHEAD

Order new boot flashing when you are replacing a roof or installing new shingles over old; it's not worth the trouble to reuse old flashing.

often sell lead and copper by the pound, so you'll have to find out from them what the weight-to-length ratio is for a given width. Aluminum is commonly sold in rolls of 25 ft. to 50 ft.

Cements and sealants

If you install and repair roofs on a regular basis, it's a good idea to keep a gallon can of asphalt roof cement on hand. You may only use a trowel-scoop or two on any single roof, but you can go through a lot on an emergency repair. The alternative is to buy cement in caulk-gun tubes. I get at least one tube for every roofing job and always have a can in inventory.

Sometimes you'll need another sealant such as silicone or butyl caulk. Normally you won't need them until the end of the job, so you can always pick up a tube as needed rather than ordering ahead of time.

Ordering Shingles

The most important part of ordering roof shingles is selecting a reliable supplier, preferably one who specializes in roofing materials. Many big-box building-material suppliers carry roof shingles, but when they come up 10 bundles short on an order, you're the one left waiting.

Look for dealers who keep shingles in stock. They'll have the best selection, and if you suddenly discover you are 10 bundles short, they'll get them to you in a day or two. Also look for a dealer that adheres to proper storage standards, which I'll discuss on the facing page.

Ask about a dealer's delivery equipment and practices, too. Boom trucks and shingle lifts are preferable to tailgate delivery. For a nominal fee, professional suppliers will deliver the shingles up to the roof, saving you time and money.

Order enough

It's annoying to get close to wrapping up a roof and discover you are a couple of bundles of shingles short. Try to order enough shingles to complete the project and have a bundle or two left over, then leave the extra bundles for the client. They'll come in handy when a tree branch damages the roof or a hurricane blows off a few tabs. Or you can hang on to extra three-tab shingles to cut into starter shingles on another project. Also, check your supplier's return policy. Good suppliers will take returns on full bundles provided you've stored them in a protected area.

Special orders

High-end specialty designer shingles and those with uncommon colors are not stocked by suppliers because the suppliers don't sell enough to justify keeping the inventory. The supplier will have to special-order the shingles from the manufacturer or a regional wholesaler. Before placing an order, have your supplier check on the availability of the total quantity of shingles you'll need and the delivery date. When a manufacturer is out of stock, you may have to wait weeks or even months until the next production run for that model or color of shingle.

Also check the return policy on special-order shingles because many suppliers won't accept returns on shingles they don't ordinarily stock. You'll have to be very accurate on your order calculation to ensure you have enough without grossly overordering. Of course, it's always better to have a few extra bundles than not enough. The last thing you want is to wait a month for a few bundles of special-order shingles, and on top of that, you'll

WORK SAFE ▪ WORK SMART ▪ THINKING AHEAD

Flashing for skylights is best ordered from the skylight manufacturer. You can also reuse the flashing from skylights on reroof and layover jobs; just take extra care removing them.

WORK SAFE ▪ WORK SMART ▪ THINKING AHEAD

Different suppliers carry different brands of shingles. You may want to develop relationships with two or three local dealers so you can offer your customers a wider range of products, especially in the higher end "designer" shingles.

WORK SAFE ▪ WORK SMART ▪ THINKING AHEAD

Don't accept a partial delivery with a promise that the balance will be forthcoming shortly. You don't want to begin a roof only to find out that there will be a delay in filling the balance of the order.

end up with a different lot number. It's best to explain this to your clients and let them know your price includes a few "insurance bundles." If the homeowner doesn't want to keep any extra shingles, you can always roof a friend's utility shed or your dog's house.

Age of shingles

Shingles age while they're sitting in a supplier's warehouse or yard, and as they do, their quality becomes compromised. Manufacturers often don't print the date the shingles were made on the bundle, so you have to trust the supplier's assurance that the shingles are fresh. Reputable suppliers will rotate their stock so you don't end up with old shingles.

If shingles do sit for too long, a number of problems arise. As shingles age, the asphalt begins to dry and the shingles become more brittle, which makes them harder to install. The surface granules on shingles can become discolored due to dissolved asphalt leaching from the underside of the shingles stacked above it, which happens more readily if the bundles are exposed to moisture. And because some parts of a laminated shingle are thicker than other parts, they can become seriously deformed if they are stored for too long.

The deformation combined with the increased brittleness from age can prevent the shingles from flattening out on the roof for months or years after installation. Not only may this result in a poor-looking roof but also may prevent the self-sealing strips from activating and bonding to the shingles above.

Storage

Check a supplier's shingle-storage system. There are three important things to note: Are the shingles protected from weather? Are they shaded from sunlight? How are bundles stacked on the pallets

Avoiding Shingle-Color Variations

Shingle manufacturers blend different color granules to surface shingles. Each manufacturing run, or lot, may have different shading in the granule blend. If you place shingles from different lots next to one another on a roof, the variation in shading may show up and detract from the roof's appearance. Manufacturers typically stamp lot numbers or production dates on the bundle wrappers along with the color name to help you keep lots separate.

Ask your supplier to deliver a single lot number to your job site when you call in the order. If there aren't enough bundles of that lot number, have the supplier keep the different lots on separate pallets. Avoid mixing lots on the same roof plane unless no one can see the roof from the ground. Color variations between lots aren't usually significant enough to be evident when the shingles are installed on different roof facets but can be when the shingles are interlaced together on one plane.

Manufacturers normally do not warrant shingles for variations in shingle color, only for performance. Many manufacturers' printed instructions warn against mixing lot numbers on a roof. Some manufacturers claim to have perfected their blending equipment to avoid color variations, so they no longer stamp lot numbers on their bundle wrappers. I'd still be wary and call the manufacturer's representative if you do discover distinguishable color variations in shingles without lot numbers.

This roof shows what can happen if you mix shingles from different lot numbers even if the manufacturer and the designated color are the same.

Some suppliers ignore manufacturers' storage requirements, which can void the warranty before you even get the shingles. Here shingles are improperly stored outside in direct sunlight.

and how many pallets are stacked atop one another?

Shingles should be kept dry during storage. Climate-controlled warehouses are best, but many suppliers use open-sided sheds, which are okay. Suppliers who store shingles out in the open expose them to rain, snow, and sunlight, all of which accelerate the deformation process and aging of the shingles. Sunlight superheats the top bundles on a pallet, which can cause discoloration of surface granules especially when moisture is present. Don't count on plastic bundle wrappers to keep the shingles dry inside; they merely retain the water that gets in through holes. In addition, the thin plastic pallet wraps are usually riddled with holes, so they offer little protection.

Manufacturers limit how many bundles of shingles can be stacked atop one another. Although the limit varies by company, it is typically around 16 bundle layers high per pallet. Manufacturers also limit the number of pallets that can be stacked to two. Shingles are heavy and the ones in the bundles at the bottom of a pallet deform quickly, especially if pallets are incorrectly stacked several high. Make sure your supplier follows these guidelines because those who use poor storage practices may void the manufacturer's warranty even before you receive the shingles.

CHAPTER 4

Roof Ventilation and Roof-Deck Preparation

ROOF VENTILATION requires air-intake vents at the bottom of the roof and exhaust vents at the top. As the sun heats the attic, the warm air rises through the top vents, drawing cooler air through the lower vents. This prolongs shingle life by cooling the underside of the sheathing. The flowing air also carries away moisture vapor that might otherwise condense and rot sheathing and even rafters.

When you are preparing to shingle a house, you have an opportunity to evaluate the roof-ventilation system and correct any shortcomings. To help you understand how roof ventilation works, I'll first describe the benefits and mechanics of good ventilation. I'll look at examples of what can happen to a roof that is ventilated inadequately or not at all. Then I'll explain how to calculate the minimum ventilation requirements and plan a passive roof-ventilation system that works for most homes. Some new

Roof ventilation is something to think about before you even start shingling a roof. Without adequate ventilation, the entire roof assembly, not just the shingles, may be in jeopardy.

In addition to the big moisture and air-leak offenders (bath vents, dryers, and recessed light cans), there can be literally dozens of small leaks made by plumbers or electricians when they drill holes. You can easily seal these gaps with foam sealant or acoustical caulk.

homes have roof-framing systems that make it difficult to incorporate ventilation, so I'll describe how these unvented roofs work and ways to build in or retrofit venting spaces.

In the second part of the chapter, I will discuss preparing old roofs for new shingles, from removing the existing shingles to evaluating the roof deck. You'll see how to strip old shingles, repair or replace sheathing, and size up the roof for new shingles.

Roof and Attic Ventilation

When attics and houses were drafty and without insulation and roofing materials such as slate, clay tiles, and cedar shingles were forgiving of temperature extremes, nobody worried about roof ventilation. However, with modern asphalt shingles and tightly constructed houses, the effectiveness of the ventilation system directly affects how long the roof shingles, sheathing, and framing will last.

Although shingle manufacturers and building codes have minimum roof-ventilation requirements, many home-builders, remodelers, and roofers don't understand how roof ventilation works and don't take it seriously. As a result, we are seeing the damaging effects of inadequate roof ventilation even in relatively new construction because ventilation standards aren't met or are defeated by the poor building practices of builders and unknowing homeowners.

Benefits and mechanics of roof ventilation

When the sun shines on a roof, the shingles absorb the heat and conduct some of it through the sheathing and into the attic. The temperature in an unvented attic can reach 100°F to 140°F (40°C to 60°C) on a sunny day. Shingle manufacturers' research has shown that excess heat shortens the life of shingles, so they require that a minimum area of vent space be installed on roofs. The minimum requirement is based on the ceiling area that each roof covers.

Moisture finds its way into the attic from the living space primarily by piggybacking on air that leaks through holes in the ceiling but also by vapor diffusion through the ceiling material. Air leaks through the holes that trade contractors drill in wall plates for wires and pipes, around chimney air spaces, around electric boxes, and through recessed light fixtures. Insulation doesn't stop air from moving through these holes; it just slows it down a little. Roof ventilation moves this excess moisture out into the atmosphere so it can't condense on attic surfaces where it will cause rot and mold.

VENTILATION MECHANICS Roof ventilation starts with intake vents along the lower portion of the roof, normally in the soffits. Intake vents can be rectangular or round soffit vents, continuous-strip soffit vents, or venting drip edge (see p. 19). Fresh air enters the intake vents and exits through exhaust vents set high on the roof. Exhaust vents can be mushroomlike roof vents, gable-end vents, roof turbines, or any of the variety of ridge vents.

Two natural forces control the ventilation airflow. The first and most consistent force is the "stack effect." Warm air is lighter and more buoyant than cool air, thus as the air in an attic warms it rises and escapes through the exhaust vents. This creates a negative pressure within the attic and draws in cooler air through the soffit vents. This process works even in cold weather because the air inside the attic is still warmer than the air outside.

The other force moving air in the attic is wind. When wind blows across the exhaust vents, particularly ridge vents, it creates a negative pressure much like air moving over the top of an airplane wing. This negative pressure draws air out of the exhaust vents and in turn draws air in through the intake vents creating airflow in the attic. Some ridge-vent designs, especially those with external baffles, have been shown in research to be more effective than others at taking advantage of the negative pressure created by wind.

Exhaust Vents

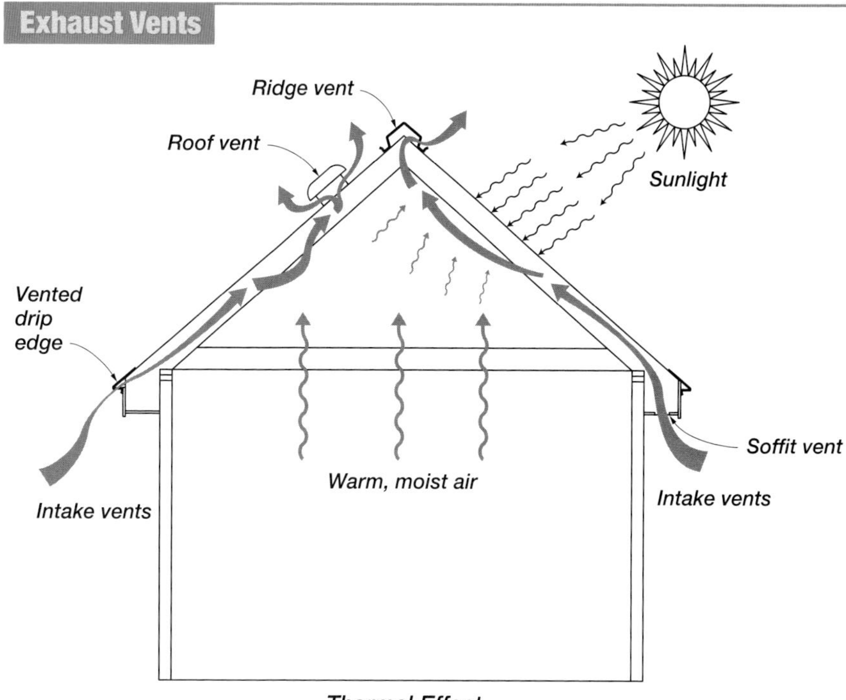

Thermal Effect

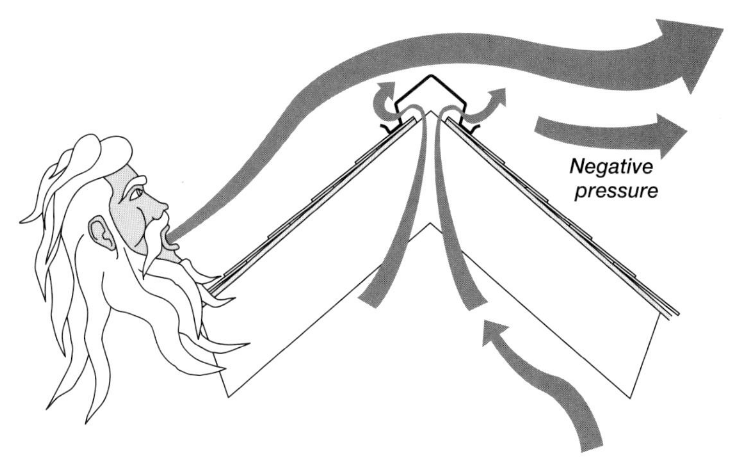

Wind/Air-Pressure Effect

Inadequate roof ventilation

Inadequate roof ventilation and the problems it creates can result from a lack of understanding of the importance of ventilation, poor ventilation planning, or bad installations.

The series of energy crises during the 1970s and early 1980s sparked an interest in improving the energy efficiency of existing and new homes. One of the easiest energy upgrades undertaken by homeowners was installing attic-floor insulation in homes that never had insulation before.

The old houses typically didn't have attic ventilation, aside from the occasional gable vent and gaps in the eaves trim, attic windows, and roof planking. But this was enough to ventilate the attic because the air and heat escaping into the uninsulated attic through the ceiling below accelerated the ventilation process. Also, the escaping heat from the house kept the attic relatively warm and dry during the winter.

Insulating the attic floor reduced the heat loss into the attic so it became cooler. The insulation also filled the space between the underside of the roof planking and the exterior wall plate near the eaves, reducing what little airflow there was. The moisture vapor that piggybacked on air leaks into the attic cooled and condensed on the roof framing and caused problems including rot and mold infestations.

New homes built at that time had insulation but often didn't include attic ventilation. The need for ventilation wasn't identified by builders and not always addressed by building codes. Plywood roof sheathing and soffits made the attics tighter than board sheathing

Mold and rot can quickly take hold in an attic that is poorly or inadequately ventilated. (Photo by Steve Culpepper, courtesy *Fine Homebuilding* magazine, © The Taunton Press.)

and soffits on old homes. These practices reduced or eliminated attic ventilation and caused latent problems that weren't noticed for several years.

Today's building codes have minimum standards for attic ventilation in new homes. But sometimes building designers and builders don't plan the ventilation system properly, so the ventilation doesn't work as well as it should or it doesn't work at all. Other times, improper installation of attic insulation and ventilation diminishes the effectiveness of the system.

PROBLEMS WITH POOR VENTILATION

The most common problem with inadequate roof ventilation is shortened shingle life. Most people don't even know this is happening until leaks are discovered because the shingles deteriorate so slowly. A 25-year roof may start losing the granules from its surface rapidly and start splitting and leaking when it's only 17 years old.

In addition to hastening shingle deterioration, excess attic heat increases cooling costs. Even with insulation, high attic heat during the summer will move toward the inside of the house and require the cooling equipment to run longer and work harder.

Roof sheathing and roof shingles can deform over a hot attic especially when the moisture level increases. The lower veneers in plywood can swell due to the excess heat and moisture and cause the sheets to sag between rafters or trusses. This is especially pronounced in thinner sheets of plywood or those made with fewer veneers.

Inadequate ventilation also increases the likelihood that ice dams will form on the roof. Ice dams occur on cold, sunny days when the sun melts snow on the roof, then the melted snow freezes when it passes over the eaves overhangs. This happens because any heat inside the attic makes the shingles on the main part of the roof warmer than the shingles on the overhangs. On sunny days in winter, heat can build up in poorly ventilated roofs and start the thaw/freeze cycle. Good attic ventilation keeps the roof cooler and reduces the likelihood of ice dams forming.

When moisture vapor is trapped in a poorly ventilated attic during the winter, it can condense on cold surfaces such as the roof framing and sheathing. Liquid water in the attic can cause several problems. It can deform the roof sheathing, facilitate rot or drip, and saturate the insulation thus reducing its effectiveness. It also fosters mold growth.

Calculating and Planning Ventilation

New homes normally have roof ventilation planned and partially installed before the roof is ready for shingling, but many older homes will need to have ventilation equipment retrofitted. Reroofing is a good time to do the work. The first steps are calculating how much venting is necessary and planning where to install ventilators.

Latent Ventilation Problems Can Go Unseen

I helped a friend reroof his house that was barely 20 years old. Built in the 1970s, there were no roof vents installed and the insulation was sandwiched tightly between the vaulted ceiling and the underside of the roof sheathing. We found that the plywood sheathing was mostly rotted away when we began stripping off the shingles. The only thing keeping us from falling through into the ceiling beneath were the shingles themselves. Over the years, the moisture vapor that passed through the ceiling and into the rafter cavities had condensed, causing sheathing rot that wasn't detected until we walked on the roof. Luckily the roof rafters hadn't begun to decay significantly.

Poor or nonexistent roof ventilation can promote mold growth. Mold will grow on the wood in the attic when the moisture level is high. The spores and chemicals produced by the mold can irritate the lungs of the home's occupants, especially young children. In some cases mold can cause serious health problems. And once mold infests a house, it is nearly impossible to eliminate.

(Photo © Lynn Grandpre.)

Venting Dryers and Bathrooms

More and more new homes are being built with washing machines and clothes dryers installed on the top floor to be near bedrooms. Some builders vent the dryer exhaust into the attic because it is easy to do. But pouring air that contains dozens of gallons of water into the attic every month, especially during the winter, is a stupid idea. There's no way for a fixed, passive roof-ventilation system to exhaust all that moisture before it condenses and causes problems.

Bathroom exhaust fans carry moist air from baths and showers and so must be treated exactly as dryer exhaust vents. Additionally, many inexpensive bathroom exhaust fans have leaky housings and fittings. You'll need to seal these leaks to keep excess moisture out of the attic.

Running the dryer or bathroom exhaust pipe through the attic floor and terminating it next to a soffit vent won't help. Warm, moist air will rise into the attic no matter how much the installer hopes it will be sucked out a soffit vent. Also, don't cut a separate 4-in.-dia. vent into the soffit for the exhaust pipe because then the moist air will indeed be sucked through nearby soffit vents—right back into the attic.

There are two choices for venting dryer or bath exhaust. One option is to duct the exhaust into a roof-mounted exhaust hood, which you can install when you install the roof shingles. The other way is to vent the exhaust through the exterior wall of the house. If you vent through a wall, make sure the exhaust vent is at least 6 ft. below any vented soffit area to prevent the moisture vapor from being drawn into the attic.

Terminating bathroom- or dryer-vent ducts into the attic or soffit is asking for moisture trouble. Properly vented ducts must be connected to roof-vent hoods or wall vents that discharge the excess moisture out of the house and prevent it from entering the attic.

Minimum ventilation requirements

The generally accepted minimum roof ventilation requirements are 1 sq. ft. of vent opening for every 300 sq. ft. of ceiling area when the vent opening areas are distributed equally between the soffit and the ridge, or 1 sq. ft. of vent opening for every 150 sq. ft. of ceiling area when the ventilators are installed anywhere (soffit, roof, or ridge) and aren't equally distributed.

Most building codes and shingle manufacturers use these standards. There are other formulas that reduce the minimum ventilation by taking into consideration air barriers and vapor diffusion retarders installed as part of the ceiling. But it is unlikely these are present in older homes and ascertaining if they are can be difficult, so it's probably safest to stick with the minimum standards. Also, in most situations, overventilation is not a problem, so when in doubt, add extra vents.

Planning vent locations

Where you plan to install ventilators directly affects how much vent area you'll need. You'll need less ventilation on a roof when you choose to (and can) install half of the vents along the soffit and half at the ridge (the 1:300-sq.-ft. formula). The vents low on the roof can be rectangular or round soffit vents, but the preferred ventilators are continuous soffit vents or venting drip edge because they spread the vent area equally along the eaves. The vents high on the roof can be roof vents installed close to the ridge or preferably continuous ridge vent (see the photo on the facing page).

Sometimes you can't install the vents equally between the soffit and ridge and will have to resort to the second calculation that permits you to install ventila-

The best arrangement for roof vents is to have half of them located low on the roof along the eaves edge or soffit and the other half located high on the roof, such as this ridge vent. (Photo © Rick Arnold.)

tion equipment anywhere in the attic (1:150 sq. ft.). This is the case on hip roofs when the house is nearly square and the ridge is short.

Even though building codes and shingle manufacturers permit random-ventilator installation, I don't recommend it. In order to take advantage of the two natural forces that drive the ventilation process, vents need to be located in high and low positions on the roof. If you put all the vents in the soffit or low on the roof, you may not be adequately venting an attic even though you have met the standard. When at all possible, attempt to install at least some of the vents high on the roof or gable end to encourage more thorough venting.

Calculating vent area

There are three steps in calculating how many vents you will need. First you'll determine the square footage, then you'll calculate the vent area, and finally you'll match the vent area to the vents you want to use.

1. Measure the interior finished ceiling square footage. For flat ceilings, measure from exterior wall to exte-

Sealing Recessed Lights

There are new recessed light cans that are airtight. They have no holes in the housing and when installed with a gasket to seal the rim to the drywall, they won't leak air.

But most recessed light cans have lots of holes that allow moist air to travel freely between the living space and the attic. Recessed cans in bathrooms and laundry rooms pose the biggest problem because of the higher moisture levels there.

The holes in IC-rated thermally protected recessed-fixture models can be sealed with HVAC mastic, but models rated non-IC will need to be covered with a sealed box made of rigid-foam insulation. The box solution can also be used for IC-rated fixtures. The rating is marked on all recessed fixtures.

To box in a recessed fixture, begin by removing the insulation from around recess lights. Make a five-sided box from a rigid-foam insulation that is at least 1 in. thick, and make it big enough to leave about 5 in. or 6 in. of air space between the sides and the can itself. Seal all the joints in the boxes with acrylic adhesive sealing tape intended for air sealing (don't use ordinary duct tape) or use spray foam sealant. Bond each box to the ceiling plaster or drywall with expanding foam sealant, then seal up the holes in the box you have to make for wires or hanger wires.

A similar air-leakage threat exists in homes with whole-house fans that are used in the summer to draw fresh cooler air into the home by blowing warmer air from the ceiling level into the attic. The louvers on these units don't seal very well and leak warm, moist air into the attic during the winter. You should seal these up and insulate them when not in use.

Calculating Vent Area for a Complex Roof

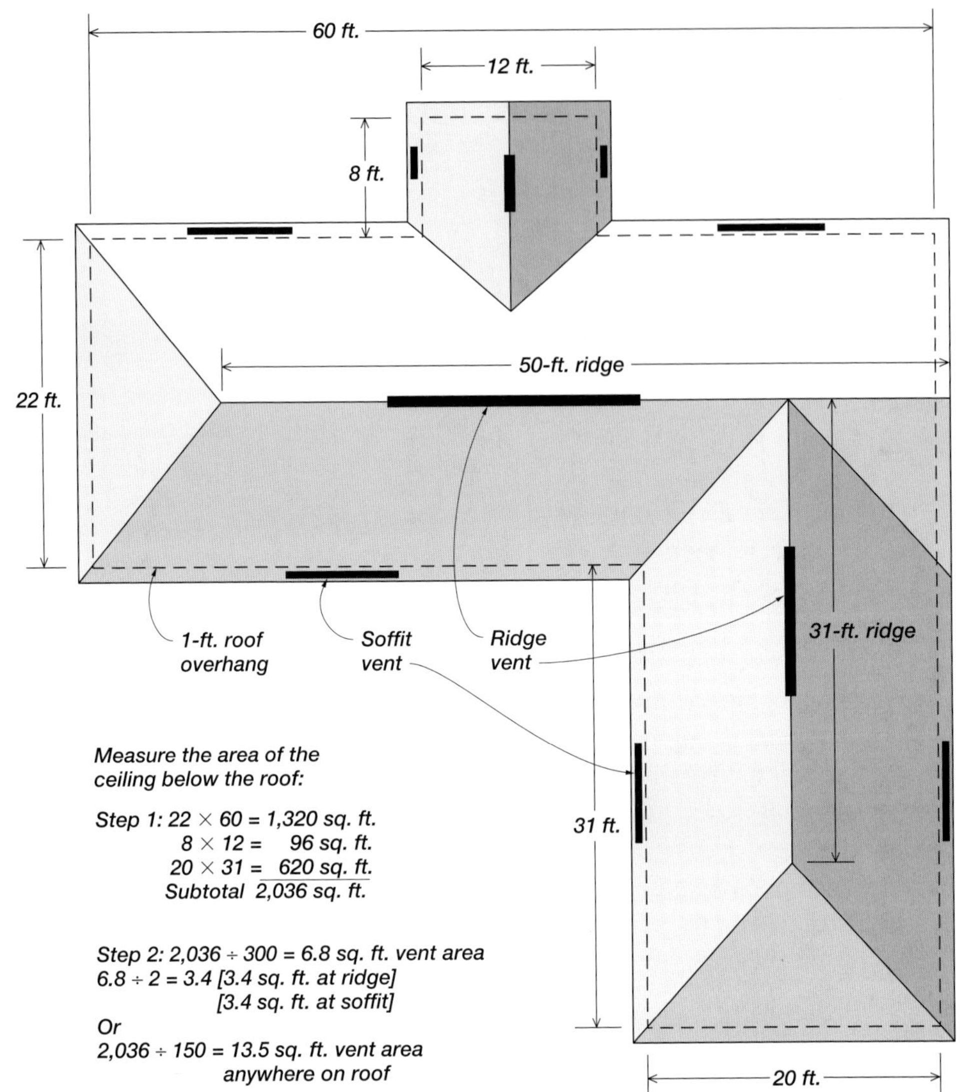

rior wall; there's no need to include fascia or rake overhangs in your calculation. The area of a vaulted or cathedral ceiling needs to be calculated based on the actual surface area of the interior finished ceiling.

Getting accurate measurements can be difficult, especially on homes with multifaceted roofs and varying ceiling styles. When in doubt, overestimate the ceiling area. Complex roofs are more likely to have excess air leaks into attics, so a little extra ventilation can be a good thing. The total ceiling area for the example in the illustration above is 2,036 sq. ft.

2. Calculate the vent area. If your vent areas will be equally distributed between the top and bottom of the roof, divide the total square footage of the ceiling by 300. This will give you the total number of square feet of open vent area needed to ventilate the roof. In the example, you'd need 6.8 sq. ft. of vent area. Otherwise, divide the square footage by 150. This would require 13.5 sq. ft. of vent area for the example roof.
3. Match the calculation to the equipment. Each piece of ventilation equipment is rated for net free vent area (NFVA). The NFVA of vents may be measured in square feet or square inches, so be careful. Vents rated in square inches will have to be converted to square feet. Remember that one square foot equals 144 square inches, not 12 square inches! So, if you determined in step 2 that the roof needs 6.8 sq. ft. of vent area divided between the ridge and soffit, you'd need to install enough vents to meet 980 sq. in. of NFVA.

   Ridge vents and continuous soffit vents are commonly rated by the linear foot of vent. So, for the example roof, you would need 27.2 ft. of ridge vent rated at 0.125 sq. ft. per lin. ft. and 54.4 ft. of soffit vent rated at 0.0625 sq. ft. per lin. ft. (See the chart at right for NFVAs of common vent styles.)

There's usually no problem if you overventilate a roof. On newly constructed homes, roofers often install ridge vents along the full length of the ridge and builders install continuous soffit vents. The minimum ridge- and soffit-vent sections are depicted on the sample roof drawing. You can see how installing vents along the entire soffit and ridge would exceed the calculated minimum and adequately ventilate the roof.

Maintaining ventilation pathways

You can make the effort to calculate, plan, and install the necessary venting equipment for a roof only to have someone else block the airflow and defeat the purpose of the vents. This often happens when attic insulation is installed haphazardly, blocking the free flow of air from the soffit vents or venting drip edge. The insulation installer or builder should insert air chutes where the soffit meets the roof. These corrugated plastic or foam-plastic baffles create a space between the insulation and the sheathing to permit free airflow. The vent channel space needs to be wide enough to work: Current studies show you

Net Free Vent Area of Common Vents

Type of Vent	Approximate Net Free Vent Area (in square feet)
EXHAUST VENTS	
Ridge vent (metal, roll, rigid)	0.125 per lin. ft.
Roof vent (mushroom-type vent)	0.35 each
Roof turbine (12 in. dia.)	0.75 each
Gable vents (rectangular)	
12 in. by 12 in.	0.39 each
12 in. by 18 in.	0.57 each
18 in. by 24 in.	1.04 each
24 in. by 30 in.	2.25 each
INTAKE VENTS	
Soffit vents (rectangular)	
4 in. by 16 in.	0.2 each
6 in. by 16 in.	0.3 each
8 in. by 16 in.	0.39 each
Soffit vents (round)	See manufacturer's specifications
Continuous-strip soffit vent	0.0625 per lin. ft.
Vented drip edge	0.0625 per lin. ft.
Perforated vinyl or aluminum soffit material	0.1 per sq. ft.

To work properly, allow at least 1 in. of space on both sides of the ridge board.

Power vents use an electric fan to discharge air from an attic. They can be useful to ventilate a roof, but the vent system must be designed properly and the unit must be maintained.

need at least 1½ in. to 2 in. of space between insulation and sheathing to ensure the free flow of air.

The vents themselves may not perform to their potential when they aren't installed properly. To maximize the effectiveness of ridge vents, you need a slot that is at least 1 in. wide at both sides of the peak. If a ridge board is present, you'll need to cut away more plywood to give you 1 in. on both sides of the ridge board. Roll-type vents are soft, so you need to be careful not to crush them when you cover them with cap shingles.

Power vents

Electrically powered roof vents can be an effective way to move air through the attic. These vents, typically mounted on the roof, have electric fans that force air out. They look like oversized roof vents (see the photo at right above).

For power vents to work properly, you must also install an adequate amount of intake venting, and the intakes must be located only along the soffit. If other vents are located at the ridge or in the gables, the power vent will suck air from the closest hole. As a result, the lower portion of the roof won't get vented. You can defeat a perfectly adequate passive venting system by installing a power vent.

A second problem can develop with power vents. When they stop working because of a motor failure or electrical problem, the roof isn't ventilated. The homeowner may not realize the power vent has stopped working until the next time the roof needs replacement. And of course, power fans cost money to run. In my opinion, powered vents should only be installed when specifically designed as part of a ventilation system by a qualified building engineer.

WORK SAFE
WORK SMART
THINKING AHEAD

Even if you're roofing a new home, it's still worth checking the sheathing to make sure it is properly installed and structurally sound because even small defects can telegraph through the new shingles and make the roofing job look bad.

Unvented Roofs

There are some roof systems that are specifically designed to eliminate the need for ventilation. These unvented roofs are sometimes called compact roofs or hot roofs. Here I will look at how these roofs work, how they can fail, and how they can be ventilated if necessary.

Unvented roof configurations

Hot roofs can be built on site in a variety of ways; the illustration below shows one common design. An alternative to site building is to use structural insulated panels (SIPs), also referred to as stress-skin panels. SIPs are sandwiches of rigid foam with a skin of OSB or plywood on both faces.

All unvented roof systems have rigid-foam insulation and an airflow retarder or barrier such as paint or a plastic sheet behind a tongue-and-groove wood ceiling. The airflow retarder prevents moisture vapor from entering and moving through the assembly. The rigid insulation keeps the dew point temperature of the first condensing surface high enough so condensation won't take place within the roof assembly when it's cold outside.

Problems with unvented roofs

Improperly designed or constructed unvented roofs are prone to failure. Moisture vapor can enter the system, condense, and rot structural framing. And because these roof assemblies have

Unvented Roofs

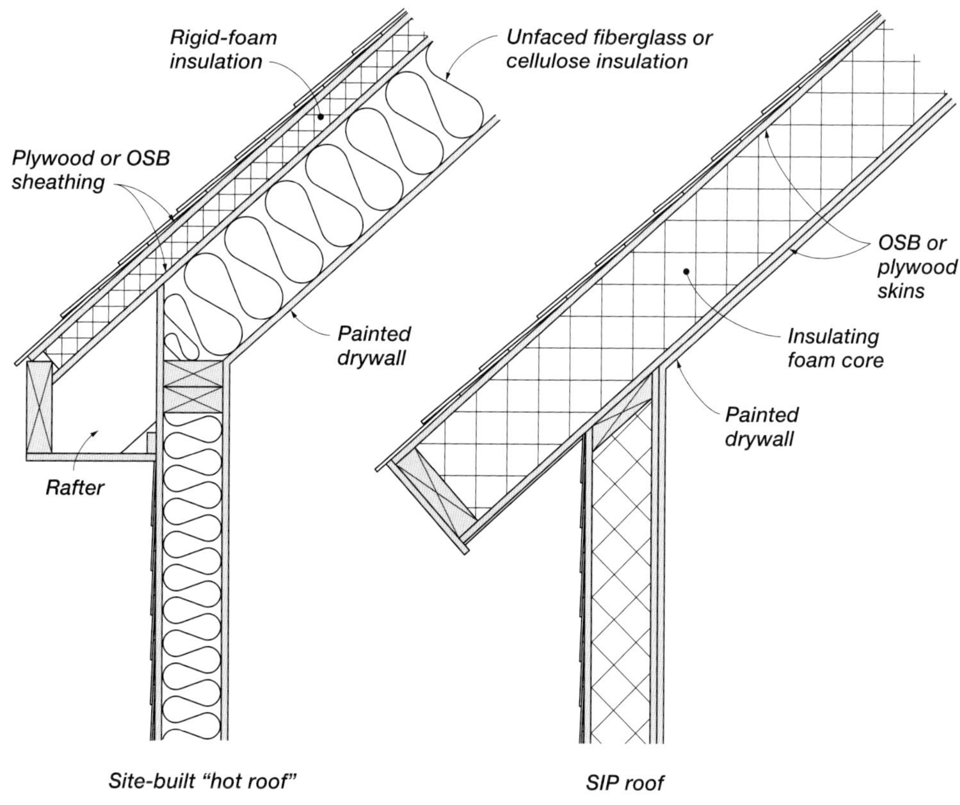

no inspection area as an open attic does, the damage can develop unnoticed.

Unvented roofs also have no channel to carry heated air away from the underside of the sheathing, and the insulation only helps retain the sun's heat. As a result, the surface temperature of the roof shingles can reach 150°F or greater on a sunny summer day. This can cause shingles to age rapidly and fail prematurely.

SHINGLE WARRANTY AND BUILDING CODES Most shingle manufacturers will not warrant their shingles for installation over unvented roofs. Other companies reduce their warranty periods for unvented installations. Homeowners should understand the facts about shingle warranties before shingling their unvented roofs.

Local building codes may prohibit unvented roof construction too, although

Venting an Unvented Roof

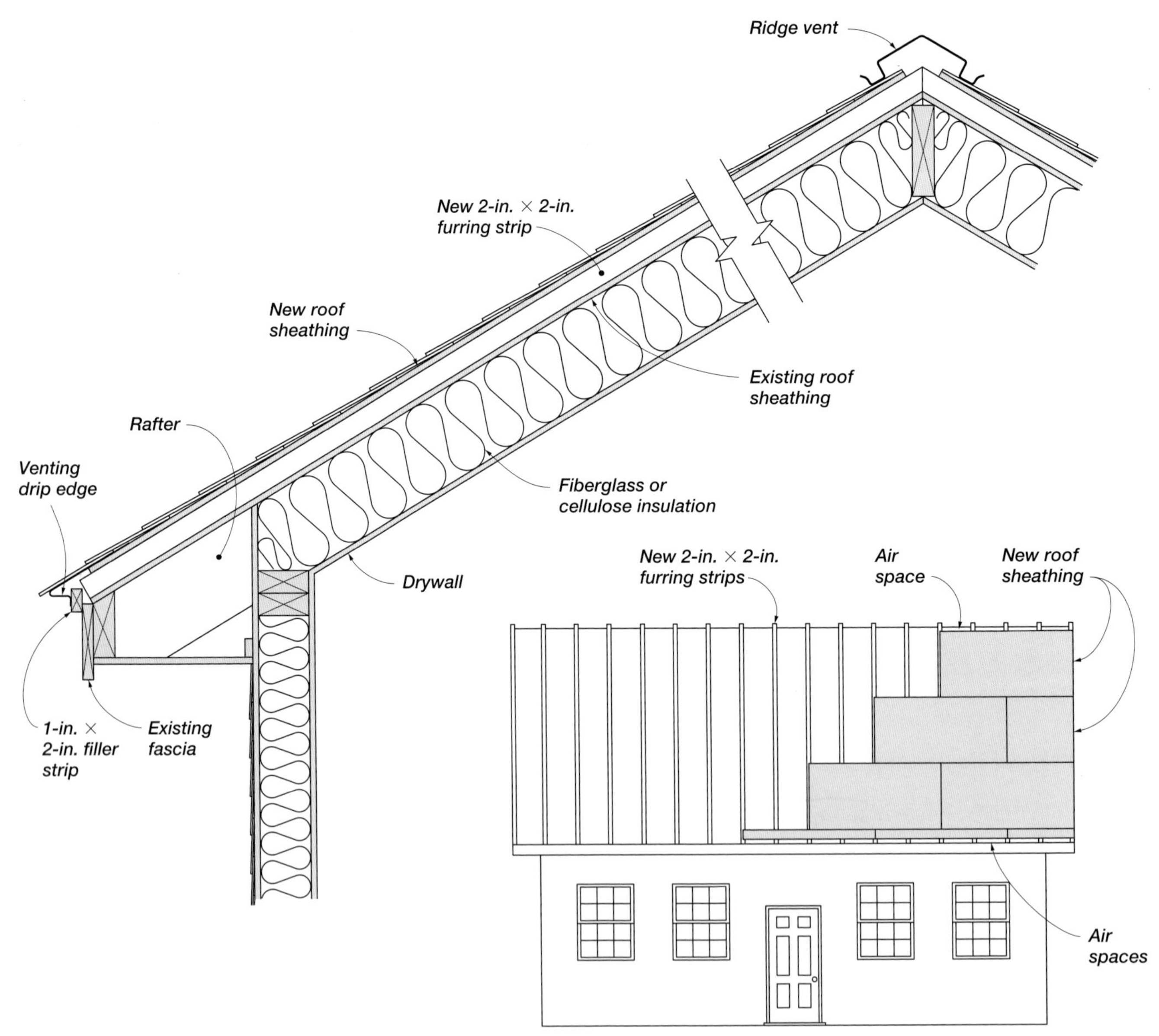

that doesn't always prevent builders from seeking special permission to use an unvented design or from ignoring the building code.

Ventilating unvented roofs

There are ways to ventilate an unvented roof. The simplest way I've found is to overlay a vent space and an additional layer of roof sheathing over the existing roof framing (see the drawing on the facing page). First remove the existing roof shingles from the roof, then fasten 1½-in.- or 2-in.-thick furring strips from eaves to ridge over the existing roof sheathing above each rafter or roof truss position—the strips provide the channels for ventilation.

Using a hole saw, bore 2-in. to 4-in. holes at 1-ft. intervals through the existing roof sheathing to permit moisture from the unvented portion of the roof to escape. Sheath over the furring strips with new structural panels. The easiest way to vent the channels is to use venting drip edge along the eaves edge and ridge vent at the top.

You will have to add extra pieces of trim along the rake edges to cover the edge of the furring strips and may have to add extra trim at the fascias. Once the trim details are complete, the additional layered vent system won't be evident.

Preparing Old Roofs

More than 50 million single-family homes and about 10 million two- to four-family homes in the United States are roofed with asphalt shingles. A vast majority of these homes are at least 20 years old. Since most asphalt shingle roofs last 15 to 20 years, that means that every year, there are lots of homes that need new shingles. Shingle manufacturers and

This old roof was already overloaded with three separate shingle layers. When the top layer began to fail prematurely, all the layers had to be removed before new shingles were installed.

building codes permit one layover asphalt shingle roof over an old roof but when it's time for the third roof, the shingles must be stripped off before new roof shingles are installed (see the photo above).

I recommend stripping even a single layer off before reroofing. New shingles lay flatter, look better, and last longer when installed directly over the roof sheathing than shingles installed over a layer of old shingles.

Stripping existing roof shingles

Stripping shingles from a roof isn't complicated but it is a messy, dirty job. With a little planning and care when tearing off the shingles, you can control the mess and reduce the time it takes to clean up.

PROTECT THE SURROUNDING AREA, SHRUBS, AND HOUSE Old asphalt shingles are brittle and break into pieces when you tear them off the roof, scattering all over the yard. Picking up the small

Old shingles are brittle and break up into lots of small pieces when being stripped off a roof. It's best to plan how you're going to control and clean up the mess before pushing the pieces off the edge of the roof.

Old tarps laid on the ground make cleanup easy. Tarps draped over sawhorses and A-frames protect landscaping plants from damage.

shingle bits and nails from the lawn and landscaping around a house is a time-consuming nuisance. Instead of letting the old shingles fall on the ground, contain the mess and protect the landscaping by spreading tarps to catch the falling shingles.

Cover the ground around the house with tarps sized from 30 sq. ft. to 80 sq. ft. to cover the ground. Overlap the edges about a foot or two. These tarps are small enough to drag easily when they are loaded with shingles.

Straddle bushes and trees with sawhorses and A-frames to protect them from falling shingles (see the bottom photo at left). Cover the equipment with structural panels or tarps to deflect and collect the waste. Without the structural support from the horses and staging, plants may be crushed under the weight of the fallen shingles.

You can control where most of the stripped shingles land by setting up roof-jack staging along the eaves. The planks will catch the shingles as they slide down the roof. You can carry or push the shingles to a specific drop point or throw them right into a trash container from the roof if it's close enough.

It's also wise to drape tarps over the face of the house to protect windows and siding from falling shingles. This is a good use for old torn tarps—little waste will find its way through the holes.

PROTECT THE ATTIC FLOOR Before you start a tearoff, look inside the attic to see if the roof is sheathed with sawn boards or structural panels. With sawn boards, small pieces of broken shingles, nails, and loose surface granules will easily fall through the spaces, making a mess on the attic floor. Belongings stored in the attic will also need to be protected. Spread tarps or if you're running short, a 6-mil polyethylene plastic sheet over the

Cover stored belongings and exposed insulation in the attic with tarps or plastic sheets before stripping a plank-sheathed roof like this.

Use a flat bar to carefully separate shingles from flashing along sidewalls, chimneys, and vents so the flashing can be reused. (Photo by Rich Ziegner, courtesy *Fine Homebuilding* magazine, © The Taunton Press.)

attic floor and its contents. Since there won't be a lot of debris, you don't have to worry about overloading the protective sheet.

Roofs sheathed with structural panels will only have a few horizontal joints that debris can fall through. Except for protecting belongings, there may be little benefit from covering the entire attic floor in these cases.

REMOVE SHINGLES The easiest way to tear off old shingles is to use specially designed stripping shovels. The blade slips between the roof sheathing and the bottom of the shingles. Pressing down on the handle lifts the shingles free by either tearing them from the nails or pulling them up along with the nails. In a pinch, pitchforks and flat-blade shovels work too but not as aggressively as stripping shovels.

Drive the stripping shovel under the shingles, and press down on the handle just far enough to pop the nails free from the sheathing, not far enough to break through the old shingles. Pull the shovel out and drive it under the shingles again. Use several drives to the left, right, and deeper under the shingles until you detach 4 sq. ft. to 10 sq. ft. of shingles (you could loosen sections of shingles larger than 10 sq. ft., but they become too cumbersome to handle and dump off the roof).

Next, lift the loosened section of shingles up until it breaks free. You can do this by pushing the shovel handle all the way down until the blade tears through the shingle, or you can lift the handle up and fold the loose shingles over until the leading edge breaks.

It's easier to strip shingles from roofs sheathed with structural panels than it is from plank-sheathed roofs. The horizontal seams between planks catch the teeth of the ripping shovel and slow the process. One way to avoid

WORK SAFE
WORK SMART
THINKING AHEAD

Keep a push broom on the roof to sweep the sheathing free of shingle granules and small chips as you work. The granules and debris make the roof very slippery, and even though you may be wearing a safety harness, a short fall can be very unnerving.

this problem is to attack the shingles using the sideways ripping method. Moving the shovel in the direction of the seams, you are less likely to be stumped by them. Only occasionally will you lock into the butt joints between boards.

Be careful when stripping away shingles from flashing along walls, chimneys, and skylights. Flashing that is still in good shape can be reused, saving you the time and effort it takes to strip back siding or cut into mortar to install new flashing. Rather than attack the shingles around flashing using a stripping shovel, use a flat bar. You can control a flat bar better and unlace the shingles and flashing from one another without causing damage.

You'll often encounter flashing that has been adhered with tar, which will make removing the old shingles very difficult. Try using an electric heat gun to soften the roof cement but don't use a torch—the fire risk is too great. Even when using a heat gun, have a bucket of water nearby. The time you spend cleaning up the old flashing will be a lot less than you would spend replacing it.

Maintaining sure footing on roofs is important when stripping shingles. Loose shingles and granules make even medium roof pitches slippery and dangerous. Nail a 2×4 cleat along the lower limit of the stripped shingles or install roof jacks with planks to lock your heels into to give you a stable workstation from which to strip shingles. But don't rely solely on these footholds to provide fall protection. When cleats and planks get cluttered with shingle debris, they too pose a hazard. Use a safety harness system for fall protection, but remember not to use the safety harness to hold your body weight.

REMOVE NAILS AND REMAINING PIECES Tearing off shingles using stripping shovels removes 95 percent of the old roofing and fasteners. The remaining 5 percent will be pieces of shingle held fast by stubborn nails. You'll have to remove all the pieces of shingle before reroofing—don't cover over the pieces with the new shingles because small

On steep pitches where sliding on debris makes it hard to keep a sure footing, nail a 2×4 cleat to brace your feet against (above) or use roof jacks with planks set across. (Photos by Rich Ziegner, courtesy *Fine Homebuilding* magazine, ©The Taunton Press.)

1. Special shingle-stripping shovels make tearing off old shingle layers fairly easy. The author likes to start at the ridge and clear a space to work as shown here.

2. Slide the shovel along the roof sheathing and drive it under the shingles. Press down on the shingle handle a little to pop the nails holding the shingles.

3. Work the shovel deeper under the loosened shingles until a 4-ft. to 10-ft. area is lifted.

4. Fold the loose section of shingles over to break it free.

5. Push the shingles off the roof and onto the tarps below.

Different Approaches to Shingle Stripping

Roofers have different ways they like to attack a tear-off job. Some like to rip shingles off from the top down, some from the bottom up, and others like to work their way across the roof. Sometimes the location of the waste container determines the method.

Working from the bottom is efficient for low-pitch roofs where the shingles won't slide down the roof slope. On steeper pitches, the shingles would keep sliding under your feet and increase the danger of falling.

Working from the bottom up can save you work when the trash container is on the opposite side of the house. You can move the shingles you strip up and over the ridge and down the side where the container is. This is usually less work than tossing them down and then carrying them around the house to the container.

Stripping from the top down is probably the most popular technique. Even on low-pitch roofs, gravity assists you by pulling the shingles down the roof slope and out of the way.

Sideways stripping works on low- and medium-pitch roofs where you want to move shingles toward one end of a roof to make waste collection easier. Push the shingles ahead of you as with the bottom-up method and off the gable end or off the eaves edge farther down along the roof. Install roof jacks and planks along the eaves to catch shingles and keep them from falling.

Wherever you start stripping the roof, break through the old shingles and clear a section about 4 ft. around yourself. When you begin prying up old shingles, you'll end up breaking off small chunks, but after you clear an area of sheathing to stand on, you can pry up bigger sections of shingles.

lumps will telegraph through the finished roof and increase the shingle wear at these spots. It's best to remove as many nails as possible rather than pounding them in. Although it is easier to drive them flush with the sheathing surface, they may work their way out over time and puncture through the new roof. Inevitably you'll have to drive some nail heads down; just keep it to a minimum.

Instead of using a stripping shovel to remove the stubborn nails, you can try a pry bar or flat bar or a small shingle stripping tool. You may have better luck getting the smaller tools under individual nail heads than you do using a shovel.

CLEAN UP Picking up the stripped shingles is easy if you covered the ground with tarps first. Just fold up the edges of the tarp and drag the shingles to the container. While you are tearing off the shingles, keep an eye on where they are falling to make sure the tarps are catching all the shingles. Drag and dump your tarps before they get overloaded, or lay another tarp on top of the accumulated scrap and keep on stripping. Later you can haul away each tarp layer without having to divide up a tarp load that's too heavy to drag.

Nails always seem to fall through or off the tarps and hide in the lawn. To pick them up, make a few passes around the house with a wide bar magnet or a commercial nail magnet on wheels.

SHINGLE DISPOSAL Check with your local or state waste-disposal agencies to find out what regulations, if any, exist that stipulate the disposal of asphalt shingles. You might be required to dispose of the shingles at a special facility, not the local landfill.

Most roofers contract with a trash-hauling company to supply and remove large waste containers. When you order a container, let the waste company know you'll be filling it with roof shingles. Some companies limit the weight you can load into their containers or they charge extra if you exceed the normal maximum. Shingles weigh 200 lb. to 300 lb. per square, so you can estimate how much weight you'll be loading.

Have the waste container placed as close to the building as possible to minimize how far you have to haul the waste. Just be aware that when containers are unloaded from and loaded onto trucks they can damage driveway surfaces and lawns. You can lay scrap plywood under the container wheels or skids as protection.

Evaluating and Repairing the Roof Deck

When you strip shingles, you may be the first person to have a look at the roof sheathing since the house was built. Older homes with plank sheathing often have rotted, split, and warped boards (see the top right photo below). Even newer homes sheathed with plywood or OSB structural panels may be damaged from roof leaks or inadequate roof ventilation as shown in the bottom photo below. Problems with the sheathing need to be remedied before you cover it with new roof shingles because any defects such as dips or humps and even wide gaps in the roof sheathing of old or new homes can telegraph through the new shingles and make the roof look bad.

Solving problems with old planks

Solid-wood plank sheathing was used exclusively until the 1950s when plywood became readily available. Plank sheathing continued to be used through

■ WORK SAFE ■ WORK SMART ■ THINKING AHEAD

Check out shingle-recycling facilities. Some asphalt-driveway formulations use ground-up roof shingles as part of the filler material. See if there are local recycling companies or asphalt suppliers that accept shingles for this purpose. You'll be reusing waste and may even save some of the cost of dumping.

After stripping off the old roof shingles, evaluate the condition of the roof sheathing before installing new shingles. As shown in the photo above, old plank roofs often have narrow warped or cracked boards that will telegraph defects through the new roof. Where plywood sheathing was used, the sheathing may be rotted or delaminated, as shown in the photo at right, due to leaks or ventilation problems.

Even if you covered the ground with tarps, it's a good idea to sweep the perimeter of the house with a wide bar magnet to collect any nails that fell off. (Photo by Rich Ziegner, courtesy *Fine Homebuilding* magazine, ©The Taunton Press.)

WORK SAFE
WORK SMART
THINKING AHEAD

Even If the roof boards are in fairly good shape and you just plan to shingle over them, be sure to check the nails fastening them to the framing. Over time, wood framing can lose its grip on nails or nails can rust away. Reset loose nails and add additional ones to ensure the boards are secure.

the 1970s, but it is rare to find it used now in new construction because a couple of inherent qualities of wood planks can cause premature failure of asphalt shingles. (However, plank roofs are preferable for wood shingles or shake-roof shingles.)

Solid-wood planks swell and shrink through the seasons as humidity levels change. Shrinking and swelling roof boards can move enough to cause asphalt roof shingles to split, especially as the asphalt shingles age and become brittle. The only remedy for this problem is to cover wood planks with plywood or OSB structural panels. The panels don't have to be thick—⅜ in. or ½ in. is adequate when attached over solid-lumber planks.

Another shortcoming of plank sheathing is the horizontal gaps between boards. Inevitably the proper nailing position for some courses of shingles will fall right on top of a gap. You have a few choices when this happens. You can ignore the problem as many roofers do and just drive a row of loose nails, you can nail too high and risk a blow-off or voiding of the warranty, or you can nail too low on the course and install the next course at a short exposure to cover the nail heads. None of these are great solutions.

REPAIRING WOOD-PLANK SHEATHING

The best solution is to resheath the roof with structural panels. If you choose to work with the existing roof planks rather than resheath with plywood or OSB, you'll have to replace rotted and warped areas with boards of the same thickness.

Cut out damaged sections over the center of the rafters, which will give you half the rafter thickness to nail the patch to. Begin by removing any nails, then make the cuts with an old carbide blade in your circular saw. You're bound to hit some buried nails, so be sure to wear safety glasses to protect your eyes from flying metal chips.

You'll need to match the thickness of the old planks, which can vary widely. You can use either new plank sheathing or pieces of plywood or OSB panels for patches. If you do choose planks, use only kiln-dried boards; boards that are not thoroughly dry could shrink below the plane of the old planks. Structural panels are stable, so they won't shrink. In either case, you can shim between the rafter and sheathing patch to bring the patch into the same plane as the old planks.

When it looks like you'll need extensive patches, consider laying structural-panel sheathing over the entire roof. It will probably make the work easier and faster, and it will definitely result in a better job.

Structural-panel roof sheathing

Plywood and OSB are easier and faster to install, more stable, and less expensive than lumber sheathing. The big concern when evaluating panel sheathing is determining whether it's thick enough for the rafter or roof-truss spacing. Building codes permit sheathing as thin as 5⁄16 in. for spans up to 16 in. on center and ⅜ in. for spans up to 24 in. on center depending on the grade. The trouble is these standards aren't enough. Sheathing this thin will sag between the framing members, causing the roof to look like a series of waves or humps (see the photo on the facing page). In addition, you won't feel safe standing on such thin sheathing.

A better standard for roof sheathing is to use a 7⁄16-in. or ½-in. minimum thickness for roof framing that is 16 in. on center and 19⁄32-in. or ⅝-in. sheathing for 24-in. on-center framing. You will feel more stable walking on the roof, and there will be little if any sagging between rafters or trusses.

To ensure a good-looking, quality shingling job, make sure the sheathing is properly nailed down. Check along each rafter or truss location to see that the minimum nail spacing is followed. Along panel edges look for nails spaced a maximum of 4 in. to 6 in. apart and 8 in. to 12 in. apart in the middle of the sheets. Also look for nails that aren't set flush with the sheathing surface and drive them in.

Check the roof for square

During the initial evaluation of a roofing job, you checked the roof at a few points to determine how many shingles to order, but you may not have checked whether the roof is square. Roofs that are out of square can make the slots between shingle tabs look cockeyed.

To determine if a roof is square, measure from the eaves to the ridge at several points along the roof to see how parallel they run. Do the same from one gable end to the other to determine parallel and also measure the roof diagonally.

Use your eye or a taut string to check how straight the roof edges are—some adjustments can be made with the shingles to overcome crooked edges so the roof looks even.

If the roof isn't square, you can give the illusion that it is by tweaking how you position the shingles. Make a sketch of the roof and note your findings. This will help you decide how to correct the errors when you lay out for the roof shingles. I'll take a closer look at how to make shingle adjustments in chapters 5 and 7.

Thin roof sheathing may meet the building-code requirements, but it can sag between roof-framing members. These sags and humps telegraph through and detract from the finished roof.

Annotated Roof-Dimension Plan

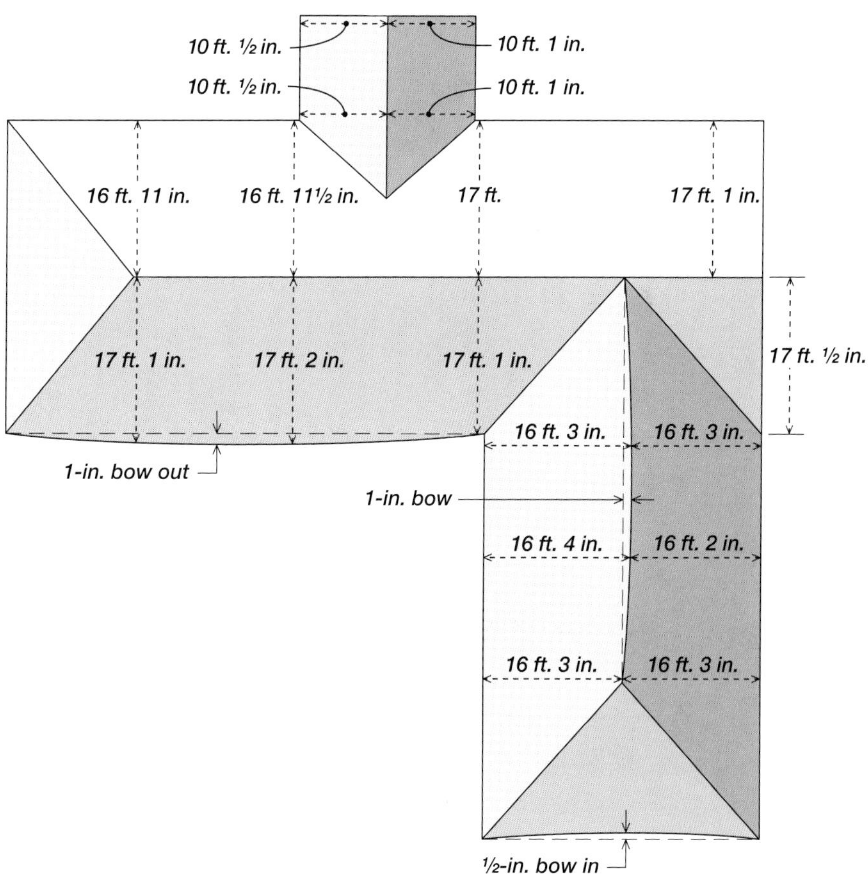

CHAPTER 5

Preparing the Roof for Shingling

Before you can start roofing, you need to erect staging, set drip edges, and roll out underlayment.

THERE'S A LOT of work to do before you can start nailing shingles to a roof. For starters, you need to set up safe staging at a comfortable level along the eaves. It's possible to shingle the lower courses by standing on the roof and working backwards, but it's not a good idea on roof pitches greater than 5 in 12. Standing on the edge of a sloping roof facing the ground 20 ft. below isn't a prescription for a feeling of security.

Then of course, you'll need to get all of the heavy roof shingles and underlayment onto the roof. Carrying bundles of shingles up a ladder one at a time is backbreaking and time-consuming. Automation is the way to go and there are several options I'll investigate.

When you strip off the old shingles, chances are you'll uncover old plank roof sheathing that needs repair or upgrading before you can shingle over it. Even on new roofs, you need to check the sheathing to be sure it's adequate and properly installed.

Then you have to set the drip edges, prepare the valleys to make them more water-resistant, roll out underlayment over the roof sheathing, and install waterproof shingle membrane at critical locations that require extra leak protection. I will cover all of this in this chapter before moving on to establishing shingle control lines in chapter 6.

Staging the Roof Edge

Staging is set up below the eaves of a house to give you a stable place to stand at a comfortable height when you start roofing a house. For every roofing situation, there is a staging that works best. A-frame staging works well for short eaves on ranch houses and Cape Cod-style homes, but it can't get you up to second-story roofs. For those roofs you'll need through-wall jacks or pump jacks. Through-wall jacks are limited to new-construction roofs, whereas pump jacks work under just about all conditions for any style of house but they take longer to set up.

Site-built staging and ladder jacks are okay for limited work on low roof edges but aren't as effective or safe as the other systems for long eaves and heavy use. The equipment involved in each type of staging is described on pp. 45–47. In this chapter, I'll tell you which staging is best for each situation and how to set it up along the house eaves. There's no need to set up staging along the rake on gable ends of a house because you'll be able to work your way up the rakes by working off of the roof and roof staging.

Choosing and setting up staging

When choosing the right staging for the job, you need to think about the height of the eaves, obstacles such as plantings, and whether the house is still rough-framed or finished. Also consider how long it will take to set up and break down a staging system. Sometimes the simplest staging is the most economical. You'll also need to think about the ground slope because some systems won't work well on uneven or steep grades.

The staging should put you at a comfortable working height. Waist height usually feels the best, but you can set up staging from mid-chest to ankle level depending on how much adjustment it has. You may need to tackle other operations such as installing soffit vents while up on the staging, so you can choose a middle level and save the time of resetting or adjusting the equipment.

A-FRAMES This is the easiest staging system to put up. I use A-frames that are 7 ft. to the top crossbar with other crossbars set about 18 in. apart. That gives an effective comfortable working range for eaves that are 7 ft. to about 12 ft. above grade. A-frames don't work well on steep or very uneven terrain, however. Each pair of legs must be set level and the dif-

A-frame staging is the simplest way to set up along eaves that are 12 ft. or shorter.

ference between the pairs can't be more than 1 ft. because the staging will be unstable. You can straddle small and medium-sized bushes with A-frames but not hedgelike plantings that are close to the house.

You should space A-frames about 8 ft. to 14 ft. apart depending on the span range of the staging planks you have. I usually use two layers of 16-ft.-long rough-cut spruce planks that are a full 2 in. thick. I space the A-frames 12 ft. to 14 ft. apart. You can set up a guardrail system by nailing 2×4 upright posts along the A-frame legs and attaching 2×4 rails between them.

SITE-BUILT STAGING You can construct secure staging from 2×4s. Site-built systems are typically nailed into the house for structural support, so they are best used on new construction projects where the siding and windows haven't been installed yet. For safety, limit site-built staging to eaves no higher than 10 ft.

The easiest way to make staging is to fasten a horizontal 2× crossbar between the house and a 2× post. Good attachment points on the house are outside corners, window-rough openings, and door-rough openings. Make sure the post is on solid ground or set on a wide block of wood for stability. After you nail on the crossbar, nail a 2×4 support block beneath the bar at both the house and post. Nail the staging planks to the crossbars to give lateral support to the posts, and tie a couple of diagonal braces back to the building. If you want to incorporate guardrails into the staging, use 2×4 posts that extend at least 3 ft. above the crossbar, then nail 2×4 guardrails between the posts.

PUMP-JACK STAGING Pump jacks are the most versatile staging system for roofing. They can be set up on uneven terrain, they fit easily around landscape plantings, and they can be adjusted to any height from ground level to eaves. If you are using a pump jack that rides on wooden posts, follow the manufacturer's directions on how to assemble the posts, how far they should be spaced, and the maximum post height.

1. **Attach the post brace.** At each post location, measure from the ground to the top of the fascia, then attach a post brace (a metal bracket with a diagonal brace that comes with the pump-jack system) at the top of each post to match the eaves height at the locations you're putting the pump jacks. Slide the pump jack on the bottom of the post before you tilt it up. Also slide on pump-jack accessories like guardrail or workbench attachments if you like.

Site-built staging works in a pinch. Here some 2×4s are nailed together to form an outrigger and support post to hold a plank. A 2× cleat nailed to the wall supports the end of the plank.

2. **Raise the posts.** This is the trickiest part. You can set up the posts by yourself if they aren't too tall, but long posts will take two people to handle. I like to put the base of the post against the foundation so there's no chance it will kick out when lifting the other end. You could have someone else hold the base of the post, but if he loses hold of it, you'll have a hard time controlling the pole. Start lifting the pole at the top end and push it upward as you walk toward the base. Once the pole is upright, move the base away from the house and lean the top against the eaves.
3. **Attach the post braces to the house.** Set a ladder alongside the post so you can fasten the brace at the top of the post to the house. Choose the attachment point for the brace carefully, and make sure your nails or screws go through the sheathing into solid framing. Also, you have to protect existing siding and trim. Fastening to the roof may seem like the obvious choice, but the brace will get in the way and need to be removed and reinstalled a couple of times while you shingle. The soffit or wall may be better choices provided you can locate the framing.

   The nailing plates on the braces will rub against whatever you fasten them to, so put a pad of plywood or a wood shingle between each nailing plate and any finished surface to prevent the plates from scratching the paint and bruising the siding or trim when you walk along the staging planks and make the posts wiggle. Drive nails or screws long enough to penetrate through the holes in the brace plate, the block, and the siding or trim, and into the framing beneath by at least 2 in. You will create holes in the trim or siding that you'll need to caulk and touch up after you take down the staging.
4. **Support the bottom of the post.** Each post must be set on a base to prevent it from sinking into the earth. Some manufacturers make base attachments. Alternately, you can use a cutoff from a wood plank or a couple of pieces of plywood about 10 in. by 10 in. or bigger. You also need to attach the bottom to the

Pump-jack staging takes a little longer to set up than other types of staging but it's more versatile. The jacks ride up and down on poles so they can be adjusted to any height.

The top of the pole is braced with a standoff bracket that's nailed to the building. Protect siding by inserting a wood cushion between the brace and the siding.

The bottom of the pump-jack pole needs a base support to keep it from sinking into the ground. Commercially available models have a peg that sticks into the ground to keep the pole from shifting, a cup to receive the pole, and a wide foot to spread the load.

Through-wall jacks work on new-construction jobs. The top bolt sticks through the wall and is supported by a block spread between the wall studs. Planks rest on the top leg, and posts with guardrails can be set up for fall protection.

house or otherwise secure it to keep it from moving. You can use a regular brace attached to the house for this purpose. Tall posts need intermediate bracing. Check the manufacturer's requirements; often they're spaced every 8 ft. to 10 ft. up the pole.

5. **Put the planks in place.** Lay staging planks across the pump jacks while they're close to the ground, and make sure they overlap the jacks by at least 8 in. at each end. Creep the jacks equally up the poles a couple of feet at a time. If you raise one jack too high relative to the jacks on either side of it, you will have trouble operating the jacks and may put too much lateral stress on the poles. When you reach your working level, lock the pump jacks according to the manufacturer's instructions and set up the guardrails.

Before hopping up on the staging each day, give it a visual check. Look to see that the planks have the minimum overlap, that the braces are still securely attached, and that the pump jacks are still in the locked position. Also check to see that the post bases aren't sinking into the soil and that the post is straight.

THROUGH-WALL STAGING The house alone supports through-wall jack staging with no posts set on the ground. This allows you to use the staging at any height without worrying about obstacles or uneven grade below. However, you can only use through-wall staging on new-construction or gut-rehab projects where the sheathing and framing are exposed. Through-wall jacks are supported by bolts that go through the sheathing to 2× blocks attached to the inside of the framing (see the photo at left).

As with A-frames and site-built staging, you can't adjust through-wall jack staging without removing the planks and resetting the jack height, so choose a comfortable working level that won't require time-consuming resets. Also, choose jack locations that are within 2 ft. of window- or door-rough openings. Otherwise you'll need two people to set up the jacks: one on a ladder to hold the jack and one inside to slip a cross block in place and install the retaining nut. Here's how to set up through-wall jack staging.

1. **Predrill blocks and sheathing.** Predrill a hole through each 2× block that will span the face of the studs on the inside of the building. Use 2×4 blocks when studs are spaced 16 in. apart and 2×6 blocks for 19.2-in.- and 24-in.-spaced studs. Be sure to select blocks without knots or other defects. For extra safety if the wall studs are spaced 24 in. or farther apart, use double blocks. From the inside, drill holes through the sheathing where the blocks will go.
2. **Install the bracket and blocks.** Pass the bracket bolt through the hole

in the sheathing, then slip on the wood block and spin on the nut/handle. If the jack set didn't come with large-diameter washers to put under the nuts, add some yourself for safety. Orient the block across the studs so that the bolt is level. Attach the block to the studs using common nails no shorter than 10d, then tighten the nut until the jack is snug to the sheathing.

3. **Install pads to support the bracket.** The bottom of the jack bracket rests against the sheathing and needs to be supported and fastened. Use pads made of 12-in. squares (roughly) of sheathing scraps to spread the concentrated force on the bottom of the jacks. If you rest the base directly on the sheathing, it may puncture and send you tumbling. Drive a nail or screw through the hole in the bottom of the jack through the block and into the sheathing to keep the bottom from rotating.
4. **Install the planks.** Spread your staging planks across the jacks, making sure that the ends overlap the jacks by at least 8 in. Set up guardrails, midrails, and toeguards when working above 6 ft. off the ground to meet OSHA fall-protection standards or use safety harnesses.

LADDER JACKS Pump jacks and through-wall stagings are worth the time and effort it takes to install them on long eaves where you'll be working for a while. But ladder jacks are much quicker to set up and are adequate for eaves up to 12 ft. long.

To set up, lean two ladders against the house. The top of each ladder must extend above the eaves but must not rest on it. Attach ladder stabilizers to rest against the wall a couple of feet below

Ladder jacks hook onto ordinary ladders and have outriggers that support staging planks. They are practical for use along short eaves such as the one on this bay roof.

the eaves, then screw a tether rope to the wall and tie it to the ladder to keep the ladder from sliding sideways.

Hook the ladder jacks to the rails and rungs of each ladder at the same height, and adjust the jacks so the bottoms where the staging planks rest are level. Set up staging planks across the jacks, making sure you dig the bases of the ladders into the ground or tie them to the building to prevent them from kicking out.

Access to staging

Ladders are the most obvious and usually the best way to get to your staging, but don't set ladders against the staging or staging planks. It's better to lean the ladder against the building where it will be more stable. Use a ladder stabilizer to give you wider bracing and to stand the ladder off the building. Depending on the type of staging and how high it's set, you can either rest the ladder against the wall or on the roof. Since the ladder isn't part of the staging, you can move it out of the way when you shingle through the area where it rests.

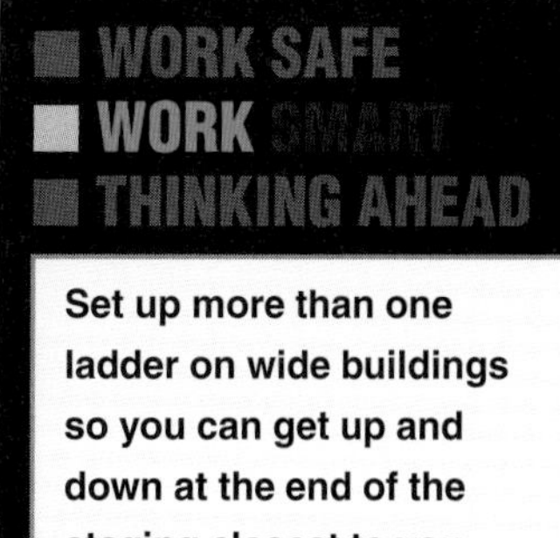

Set up more than one ladder on wide buildings so you can get up and down at the end of the staging closest to you. Store your material (drip edge, nails, etc.) near the bottom of the ladders to save time.

If you are working on a building that's under construction, you may not even need a ladder to access the staging; you can slip in and out of a window-rough opening. This works great for passing shingle bundles and other materials onto the staging. You can carry all your materials up to the second floor and pass them out the window opening. Even if the windows are installed you can still gain access to the staging provided you protect the window jamb. Remove the window sashes and wrap the jamb with scrap pieces of carpeting or heavy-duty tarps so you don't scrape them when moving in and out.

Loading the Roof

A 2,400-sq.-ft. two-story home with a two-car garage will use about 20 squares of roof shingles. That's about 2½ tons to 3 tons of shingles and materials—a lot of weight to handle and get up on the roof. There are several ways you can move the materials up. Then once you have them on the roof, you have to store them until you're ready to install them.

Getting shingles to the roof

Let machinery do the heavy lifting; there's no point in carrying bundles of shingles up a ladder unless you're roofing just a small cottage. Most professional supply companies have delivery equipment that's specially outfitted to lift shingles to the roof and may even supply the labor to load the bundles onto the roof for a small fee. Whatever the price, it's worth it. There are also shingle lifts you can buy or rent that will do a lion's share of the work.

BOOM TRUCK DELIVERY Boom trucks can lift full pallets of shingles to the eaves of one-story roofs but can't reach most second-story roofs. A boom is like a small crane mounted against the back of the cab on a truck. Have the operator lift each pallet of shingles as far up the roof pitch as possible and lower it until it just touches the roof. This stabilizes the pallet so you can unload it safely. Even when a boom can't reach the second-story roof, it may be able to reach a second-story window. You can unload a pallet and stack the shingles near the window. Later, you can pass bundles onto the staging and up to the roof as you need them.

SHINGLE CONVEYORS Conveyors are a pair of motor-driven fabric belts or drive chains with metal legs attached at regular intervals. An operator, usually the driver, loads one bundle at a time onto the conveyor. The metal legs grab the bundles and slide them up the conveyor, then you unload the bundles at the top of the conveyor.

Shingle conveyors are great for getting shingle bundles to a tall roof. They are typically mounted on the back of the delivery truck bed and can extend to most second-story roofs. If you are working on a new house with window openings that are still rough, you can position the staging level with the bottom of a rough opening and just stack the bundles on the second floor as when using the boom-truck method. Suppliers may charge $1 to $5 per square for lifting shingles to the roof with their equipment.

To use a conveyor, the delivery truck needs clear access to an eaves. Have the operator extend the conveyor up as high onto the roof as possible to reduce the amount of walking needed to stack shingles on the roof. The conveyor must be perpendicular to the eaves so that the stabilizer at the top of the conveyor rests level across the roof; otherwise, the shingle bundles may slide off the rails on the way up.

Many building-materials suppliers have boom trucks or shingle lifts that they will use to send shingle bundles to the roof for a nominal charge.

The conveyor can operate intermittently, which is safest, or continuously, which is fastest. The mode you choose depends on your experience with conveyors and how many people you have available to unload.

In the intermittent mode, the operator doesn't turn on the conveyor motor until he has a bundle loaded, then he runs the conveyor until the bundle reaches the top and shuts it off. You pick the bundle off the conveyor and stack it on the roof as the operator loads another bundle of shingles. This method is slow but safe and requires only one person to unload on the roof.

In continuous mode, the operator leaves the conveyor spinning and loads a bundle of shingles on every other or every third set of metal legs as the belts climb up the rails. You have to be careful when lifting bundles off the conveyor and you have to do it quickly. Because the bundles are moving, you have to lift them toward you and up at the same time. If you're too slow or wait too long before lifting a bundle, the metal legs will grab the edge of the bundle. This is dangerous because the bundle can be pulled from your grip and fall, the metal legs can tear into the bundle and damage shingles, the metal legs can grab your arm and try to rip your hand off, and the metal legs may snap off the belts.

You'll need several people unloading to keep up with a conveyor spinning at top speed. I suggest practicing using the intermittent conveyor mode and work your way into the continuous mode by having the operator load one bundle every third or forth set of metal legs and running the belts at slow rotation. After you get the knack for unloading, try speeding up the process.

LADDER LIFTS Like a conveyor system, ladder lifts use a motor to move the shingles to the roof. But instead of a continuous conveyor, ladder lifts run a platform up and down a conventional

An on-site construction lift can raise the shingles while you are roofing. Not only do they do the heavy lifting but they also double as staging.

or proprietary ladder. An operator at the base places two to four bundles of shingles at a time on the platform and operates the controls. Good lifts have a limit switch that senses when the platform reaches the top and automatically stops the motor. You unload the bundles at the top, and the operator returns the platform to the bottom.

Ladder lifts use gasoline or electric motors. You can buy one for $1,200 to $2,000 or you can rent one. Some suppliers loan or rent ladder lifts when you purchase shingles from them. They drop off the lift when they deliver the shingles, and you have a day or two to use the lift before you are required to return it.

HYDRAULIC CONSTRUCTION LIFTS

Large-scale builders often have hydraulic construction lifts for moving and loading construction materials around and between houses being built. They're like front-end loaders outfitted with forks. They can lift entire pallets of shingles and move them around the building. Some of these lifts won't reach the roof of a two-story house, but they may get the shingles to a second-story window. Many large, full-service roofing companies that concentrate on commercial projects have construction lifts, but the lifts are too expensive for most smaller-scale residential roofers.

HAND CARRYING When all other plans fail, you may find yourself carrying bundles to the roof by hand. On new construction projects, you can carry the

WORK SAFE
WORK SMART
THINKING AHEAD

Cranes are frequently used to lift roof trusses on new houses, and you can often make arrangements to have the crane do some of your shingle lifting. Just remember to order the roofing materials early enough so that they're on hand when the crane arrives.

If a crane is on site, it can lift pallets of shingles to a second-floor deck during the framing stage. Later, bundles will be passed to the roof through a window opening. (Photo by Roe Osborn, courtesy *Fine Homebuilding* magazine, ©The Taunton Press.)

shingles into the house and up the stairs to the second floor (or third floor if you are really unlucky) and then pass them out a window onto staging.

If you don't have access to a stairway, you'll have to carry the shingles up a ladder. Have the supplier drop the shingles as near as possible to where you plan to put the ladder. Carry the bundles on your shoulder so you have one hand free to hold the ladder rungs. Using a heavy-duty ladder with a stabilizer bar at the top, rest the stabilizer on the roof sheathing and let the ladder extend about 3 ft. higher than the roof. This makes it easier to step off of the ladder and onto the roof with a bundle of shingles.

Stacking bundles on the roof

Don't try to stack 2½ tons to 3 tons of shingles in one area of the roof; it may not hold. Spread the shingles out. Most roofers like to load the shingles along the ridge, which keeps them out of the way while shingling most of the roof. By the time you shingle your way to the ridge, there are only a few bundles left to move around.

You can stack shingle bundles on roof pitches of 5 or less and not worry about them sliding off (see the sidebar on p. 98). To keep shingles on steeper pitches, you'll need to nail cleats to the roof framing. As long as the bundle wrappers are still intact you can rest bundles against a 2×4 cleat nailed flat against the roof sheathing.

If the wrappers are damaged, you can toenail the cleat on edge so the shingles at the top of the bundle are supported. Set a cleat about 2 ft. down from both sides of the ridge and set two rows of shingles parallel to the ridge. Or you can set the cleats 3 ft. down and set one row of bundles perpendicular to the ridge.

Don't drop the bundles onto the roof; it may damage the shingles or the roof sheathing. Place them in position carefully, and spread the bundles equally along the ridge. If you run out of room, which is likely on a hip roof with a short ridge, nail another cleat 2½ ft. or 3½ ft. below the previous cleat and spread out more bundles.

WORK SAFE
WORK SMART
THINKING AHEAD

If you have to hand-carry shingles up a ladder, it is safest and easiest to make it a two-person job. Have a helper take the bundles from you at the top of the ladder and stack them on the roof.

WORK SAFE
WORK SMART
THINKING AHEAD

Even though many roofers do it, it's not a good idea to lay bundles across the ridge unless you will be using the shingles within a few hours. The shingles will bend and may be more difficult to work with—especially when it's cold and they're too stiff to bend back flat.

Nail a 2×4 cleat about 3 ft. or 4 ft. down from the ridge. Stack shingle bundles on the cleat when they're delivered. Be sure to leave a space in the middle so you can mark your layout and snap chalklines.

Roof Pitches

The slope, or incline, of a roof plane is commonly referred to as the pitch. Roof pitches are described in terms of how many inches the roof rises for every 12 in. it runs. Since the run is always 12 in., it's usually dropped in the description, so when a roofer talks about a "3 pitch" he means a rise of 3 in. in 12 in. of run. You may come across roof pitches stated in fractions. This really gets confusing and is probably best avoided. Stick with standard pitch designations based on a run of 12, since it's the most universally accepted method and the one I use throughout this book.

Asphalt-shingle manufacturers divide roof pitches into four categories—flat roofs, low-slope roof pitches, high-slope roof pitches, and steep-slope roof pitches. Flat roofs are those below a 2 pitch and should not be covered with shingles. Low-slope roof pitches are those from 2 to 4, high-slope roof pitches are those from 4 to 21, and steep-slope roof pitches exceed 21.

Installation requirements for underlayment and shingles differ for the various pitch ranges. For instance, water flows off low-pitch roofs more slowly and the roof may be more prone to backups and leaks. To prevent these problems, a double coverage of underlayment is installed, and the shingle exposure may be reduced. On steep-roof pitches, the self-sealing adhesive strip may not be effective, requiring the shingles to be hand-sealed. I'll describe variations to the standard installation techniques for low- and steep-pitch roofs in chapter 9.

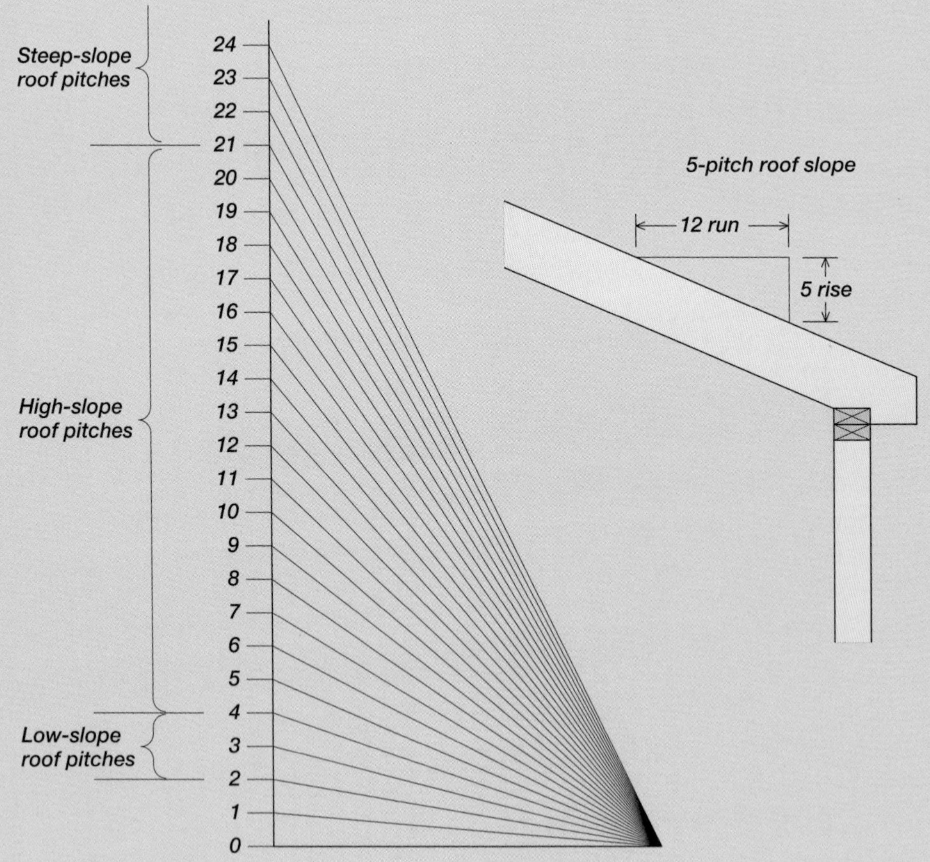

Preparing the Roof Deck

Water runs downhill. The entire sequence of a roofing job is driven by this fact because everything is overlapped to shed water. The first part to go on is the drip edge along the eaves, then you'll prepare the valleys and wall intersections. Underlayment is installed next, and then drip edge is installed over the underlayment at the rake edge. In this section, I'll describe these jobs in the order you'll do them.

Setting drip edge along the eaves

The most popular metal drip edge is the extended style (see p. 19 for more on drip edge styles). When you install the drip edge, you can either line up the sections by eye or you can snap a chalkline as a guide. The method you choose is really a matter of personal preference: Snapping a chalkline can save you time on long roofs because you don't have to keep tacking and eyeballing to make sure the drip edge is straight.

INSTALLING DRIP EDGE BY EYE

Preformed drip edges typically come in 10-ft. sections or sometimes 8 ft. The bends in the sheet metal keep it fairly stiff and straight. Since the drip edge gets nailed to the roof only, not to the fascia, you can keep the drip edge straight and install it by eye as long as you use equal pressure when you press the lower leg against the fascia as you drive fasteners into the top.

You can fasten drip edges with roofing nails or with staples. Be careful using pneumatic equipment though; sometimes the driver will overset the fastener and crinkle the metal. I like to use a hammer stapler to quickly tack down the drip edge and then go back later to secure it with nails. Just be careful not to nail or staple near the extended edge—there's nothing there to attach to and you'll ruin the drip edge. The following steps outline the process of installing drip edge by eye.

1. **Tack-nail the drip edge in place.** Position the first piece of drip edge so that it extends ½ in. beyond the rake board. Tack-nail each end and then one spot in the middle to the roof sheathing. Step back and eye how straight the extended edge is, and make adjustments as necessary by removing the partially driven tack nails and resetting.
2. **Complete the nailing.** Once you're satisfied that the drip edge is straight, drive nails every 12 in. to 16 in. apart and about 1 in. to 2 in. from the top edge.
3. **Install additional drip edge.** Put the next piece of drip edge in place so that it overlaps the first piece by 2 in. to 3 in. You'll have to wiggle the pieces together to get the

WORK SAFE ■ WORK SMART ■ THINKING AHEAD

Paper bundle wrappers won't last long when exposed to the weather. Once the wrappers come loose, wind can lift shingles out of the bundles and send them tumbling down. Plan to load the shingles on the roof just prior to installation. If that's not possible, cover them with a tarp.

The eaves drip edge goes on nice and straight when you snap a chalkline to follow. But you can also install the drip edge by eye with practice.

extended edge of the second piece to fit over the first piece. Cut off the last piece in place, leaving ½ in. extending over the rake board as you did for the first piece.

4. **Miter the valley and hip corners.** When you reach inside corners at valleys and outside corners at hips, trim miters where the extended portions meet, as shown in the photos on the facing page. Let the roof legs of the flanges extend through the valley or over the hip so they overlap as shown.
5. **Trim the rake ends.** Use metal shears or a utility knife to cut the fascia leg flush with the rake board, leaving the top nailing flange to overhang the rake by ½ in. As shown in the illustration at left, this overhang will interlock with the ½-in. extension of the drip edge you'll install on the rake. If you'll be using a rake-edge flashing that doesn't have an extension, just end the eaves drip edge flush with the rake edge.

Interlocking Rake Overhang and Drip Edge

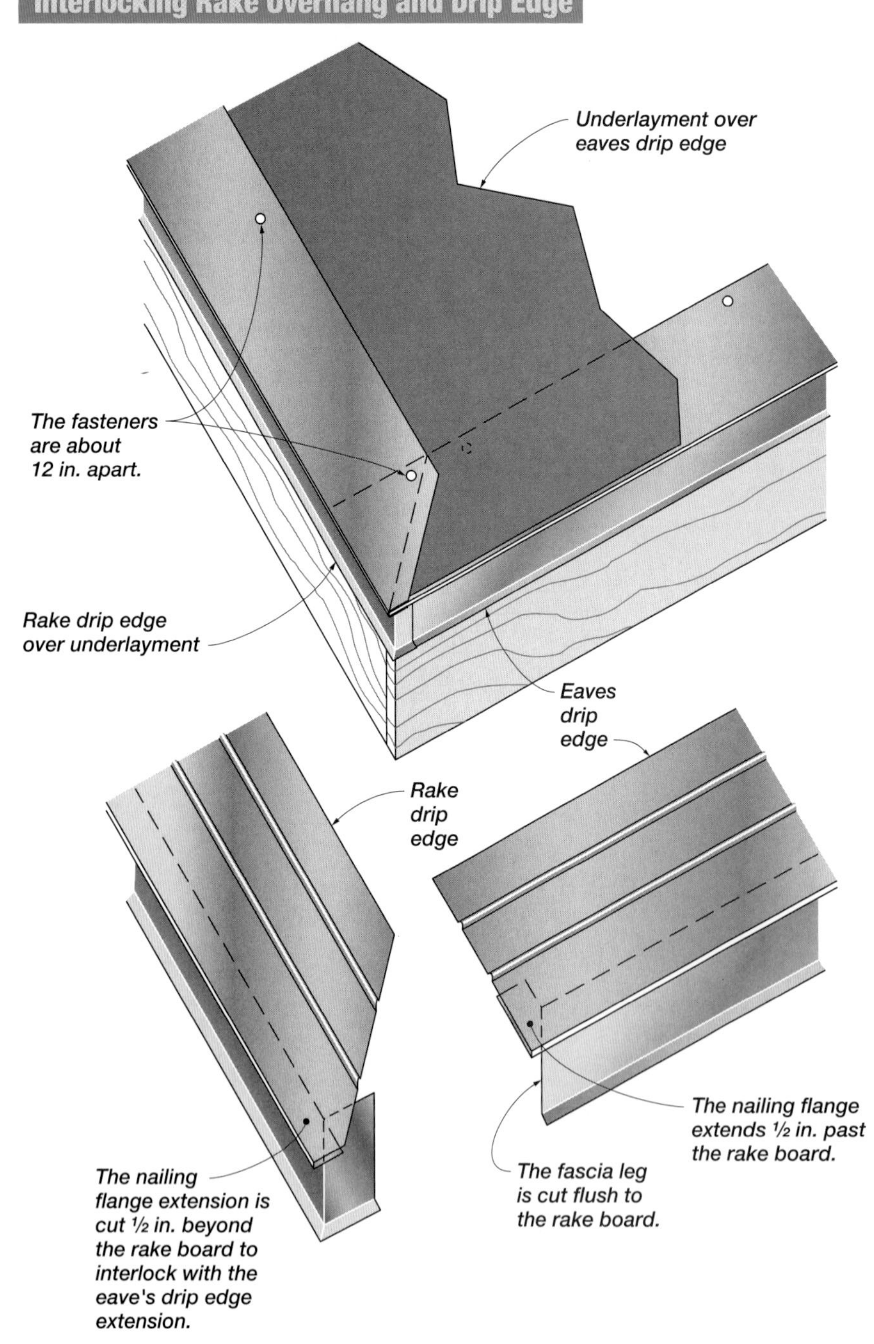

Installing drip edge using a guideline

A chalkline will give you an accurate guide to keep the drip edge straight, and you won't need to tack and eye the edge before nailing it in place. Measure the drip edge from the bend that touches the fascia to the top edge. Different manufacturers have slightly different distances between bends. Common measurements are 3 in. for 5-in. drip edge and 6 in. for 8-in. drip edge, but measure the stock you have to be sure.

Measure up from the fascia at each end of the eaves edge, and make marks to correspond to the width of the top of your drip edge. Snap a chalkline between the marks to guide the installation, then align the top of the drip edge to the chalkline and nail it down as you go. The procedure is the same beginning with step 3 of "Installing Drip Edge by Eye" on p. 99.

Installing venting drip edge

If you decide to use venting drip edge as part of the roof-ventilation system, you can install it in much the same way as regular drip edge. First you must prepare the vent space between the roof sheathing

Venting Drip Edge

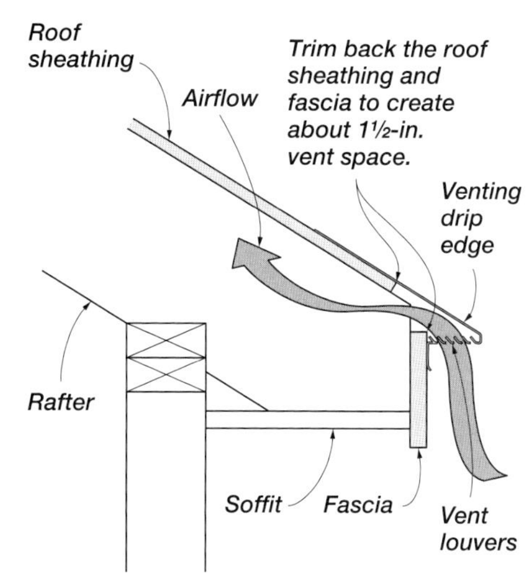

When drip edges meet at the end of hips (left) and valleys (right), miter the corners for a clean look. Whereas the bottom legs and extensions of the edges meet at a miter, the top legs overlap one another.

and the fascia. New houses may already be framed with an air slot, but you'll have to cut a slot on older homes. Hold a piece of drip edge in place to see how much of the sheathing or fascia you'll have to remove to create the air space.

Mark the ends of the roof and snap a chalkline to guide the cut. Pull all the nails out within ¼ in. of the chalkline, or cut through them with an old carbide blade in your circular saw. Be sure to wear safety glasses when cutting because you may have missed removing a nail or two and the metal projectiles are more dangerous than wood chips. Renail the top edge of the fascia and the bottom edge of the sheathing after the rip. Install the venting drip edge in the same way as regular drip edge, either by eye or by snapping a chalkline.

Preparing intersections of roof and walls

Where the roof slope meets a sidewall, you will interlace step flashing with the shingle courses to prevent water from penetrating the intersection. Still, there is a chance that storm-driven water will find its way under standard-sized step flashing. To prevent leaks in case this happens, install self-adhering waterproof shingle underlayment over the intersection (see "Working with Waterproof Shingle Underlayment" on p. 113).

Where the sidewall continues past or ends at the eaves edge, install the bottom of the waterproof shingle underlayment directly over the drip edge and trim it flush to the outer edge. If the sidewall ends before the eaves edge, lap the end of the waterproof shingle underlayment over the top lap of the next closest shingle course. These treatments will direct water away.

CUT THE UNDERLAYMENT TO LENGTH Measure the length of the roof-to-sidewall intersection. Roll out the waterproof membrane on a flat surface, and cut it lengthwise with a utility knife, adding about 1 ft. for the water-shedding overlap at the bottom. There's no need to

Straightening a Crooked Edge

On old houses and on some poorly built new homes, the eaves edge may not be straight. If the eaves edge is no more than ¾ in. out of whack, you can make it appear straight by keeping the top nailing flange straight and bending the fascia leg to accommodate the error. The following steps outline this process.

1. **Snap a reference line.** The idea here is to find the drip-edge position that averages the ins and outs of the fascia. Start by making a mark on each end of the roof, 1 in. up from the eaves edge, and snap a chalkline between these two marks.
2. **Determine the average variation.** Measure the distance between the eaves edge and the reference chalkline at several points until you find the greatest distance and the shortest distance, then average the two distances and subtract 1 in. For example, if the greatest distance is 1⅞ in. and the shortest is 1¼ in., your average variation is ⅝ in.
3. **Snap the guideline.** Add half the average variation to the normal drip-edge overlap measurement. For example, if the drip edge is designed to overlap the roof 3 in., mark each end of the roof 3⁵⁄₁₆ in. from the eaves edge. Snap the guide chalkline between these points.
4. **Bend the fascia legs.** Place each drip-edge section against the fascia, and press gently until the top edge meets the guide chalkline. Look underneath for gaps between the drip edge and the fascia, and mark those areas on the drip edge. It's helpful to have two people conduct this procedure, one to hold the drip edge in place and one to check and mark. Remove the drip edge and bend the leg inward at the marked areas, being careful not to kink the drip lip. Use a ¾-in. by 4-in. block of wood to press against the leg equally if you think pressing with your fingers will cause a kink.
5. **Install the drip edge.** Put the drip edge back in place on the roof and check the bends. Adjust as necessary. You may not always be able to get out all the gaps, but as long as you can close most of them it won't be evident from the ground, especially if gutters are installed.

In chapter 6, I'll review some ways you can compensate for bowed or crooked fascia when you lay out the shingles.

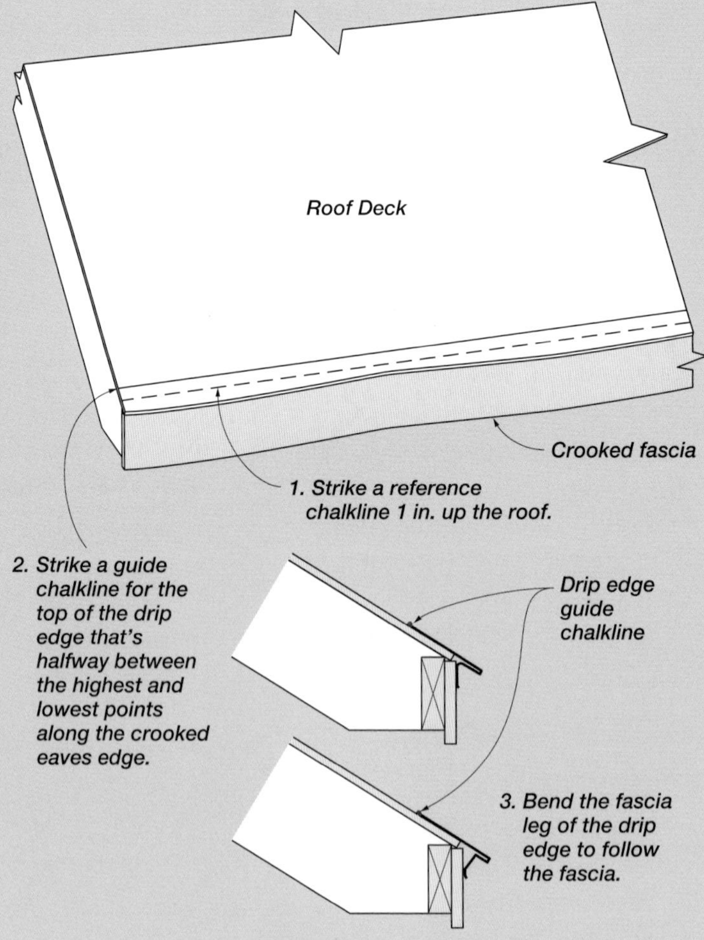

Sidewalls and Vertical Walls

In roofing terms, a sidewall is any wall that meets the slope of a roof and requires step flashing. A vertical wall meets the roof straight across its slope and requires roll flashing. The illustration shows the most common sidewall and vertical wall situations.

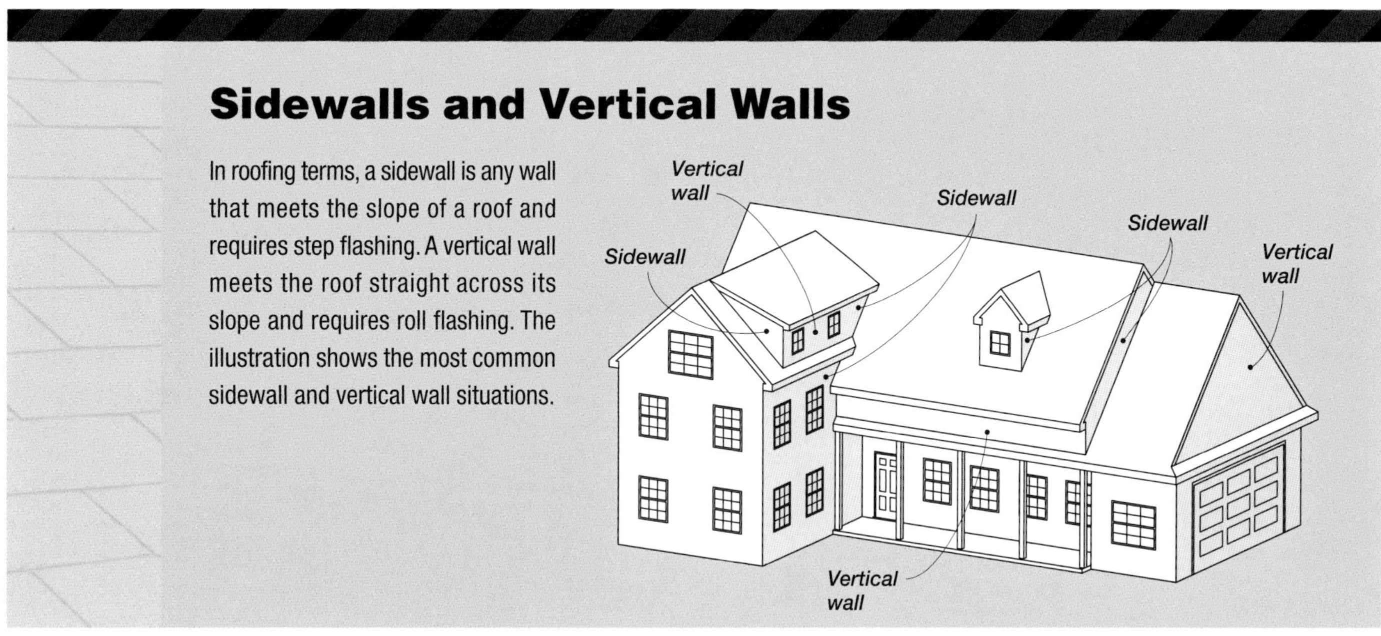

use the full 36-in. width of the membrane. You can cut the sheet down to an 18-in.-wide strip and lay 9 in. of material on the roof and 9 in. on the wall. Fold the sheet in half lengthwise to form a crease that will make it easier to press the material into the corner.

INSTALL THE UNDERLAYMENT Snap a chalkline on the wall 9 in. up from the roof plane as a guide to install the membrane. Peel the release paper back to the center crease, and tack the sticky face to the wall sheathing along the chalkline. Next, press the sheet into the corner at the crease. Pat the membrane into the wall to ensure contact, then lift the bottom edge to remove the remaining release paper. Carefully lay the bottom half of the sheet on the roof sheathing and press to make contact. Using roofing nails, tack along the edge every 2 ft., especially in cold weather when the adhesive doesn't bond well to the sheathing.

Preparing valleys

Where the bottom of two roof slopes meet, a valley is created. Water draining down each of the slopes is concentrated in the valley, making it vulnerable to leaks. Therefore, it's important to design the valley covering with redundant protection and take special care when installing the components.

There are two ways to shingle a valley, both of which I discuss in chapter 8. For a closed valley, you run the shingles through the valley, whereas for an open valley, you stop the shingles several

Install waterproof shingle underlayment to all roof/wall intersections as backup protection for the flashings. Here a half sheet of underlayment is applied to the sidewall. The bottom end extends down over the drip edge.

Anatomy of a Mineral-Surface Open Valley

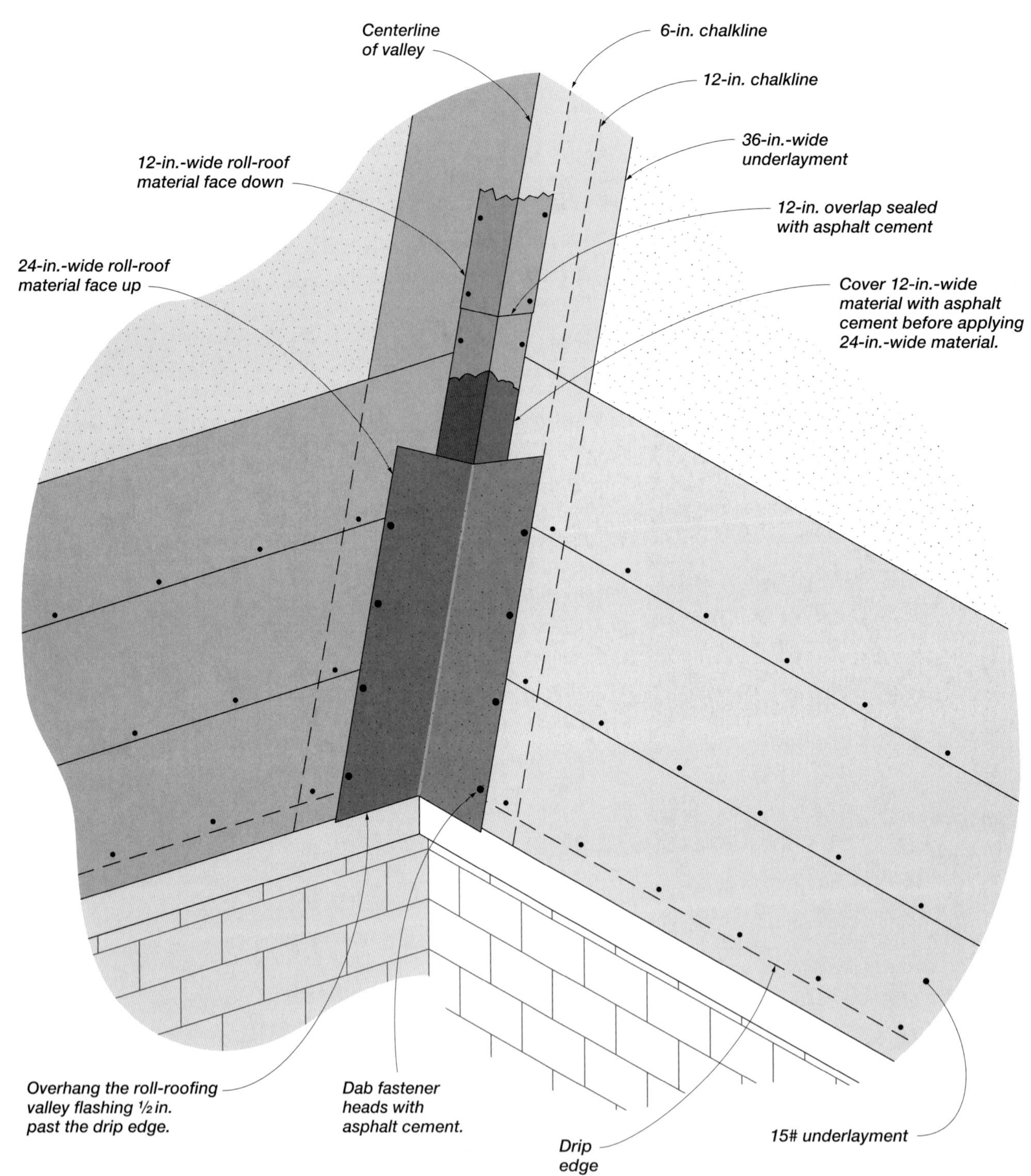

inches from the valley crease, leaving the flashing exposed. The method you choose will affect how you prepare the valley covering.

Review your local building code and the shingle manufacturer's requirements before installing the valley flashing because they may differ from those described below. Before you begin installing any of the valley components, check that the roof sheathing is fastened securely and that none of the nails are sticking up. Even a slightly raised nail head can puncture your valley materials and lead to a leak over time.

Mineral-surface open valley

There are two options for covering open valleys: mineral-surface roll roofing and metal. Mineral-surface roll roofing is constructed in three layers. The first layer is underlayment, which can be asphalt-impregnated felt (tarpaper) or for better protection, self-adhering waterproof membrane (see p. 113). The second layer is a 12-in.-wide strip of roll roofing installed face down, and the third layer is a 24-in.-wide strip of roll roofing installed face up (see the illustration on the facing page). The following steps outline the process of constructing a mineral-surface covering.

1. **Install underlayment.** Start by installing underlayment down the center of the valley, laying it so that no less than 10 in. extends to each side of the valley. Overlap any joints in the felt underlayment by 12 in., and apply asphalt cement between the joints. (Waterproof membrane will only need overlapping—don't apply the cement.) Lay the underlayment over the top of the drip edge at the bottom of the valley and trim it flush. Secure one side with a row of nails 1 in. from the edge, then press the underlayment tightly into the valley crease. Don't use any additional nails.
2. **Cut the roll roofing.** Measure the length of the valley and roll out single-coverage mineral-surface roll roofing onto a flat surface for cutting. Cut a piece the length of the valley plus an extra 2 ft. to trim into a dovetail at the bottom of the valley and to wrap the ridge at the top. Snap a chalkline 12 in. in from one edge of the roll roofing and cut the sheet into two strips, one 12 in. wide and one 24 in. wide
3. **Install the 12-in. strip.** Snap a chalkline on the underlayment 6 in. to one side of the valley centerline as a guide for the first sheet. With the mineral surface down, align one edge of the 12-in. strip to the chalkline and lay it into the valley. Slide the strip down until the outside corners overlap the drip edge by ½ in., then fasten with a row of nails spaced 12 in. apart and 1 in. in from the edge. Make sure the material fits snugly into the valley crease, then fasten the other edge of the strip. Trim the bottom edge for an even ½-in. overlap over the drip edge.
4. **Install the 24-in. strip.** Snap another chalkline 12 in. to one side of the valley centerline to guide the wider valley strip. Cover the surface of the 12-in. sheet, including the nail heads, with asphalt cement. Lay the 24-in. strip face up along the chalkline and into the valley, then slide it down until the lower corners overlap the drip edge by ½ in. and nail along the chalkline edge. Press the sheet into the cement and work out the air bubbles toward the other side of the valley (a block of 2×8 or 2×10 works well to press the surface flat).

WORK SAFE ■ WORK SMART ■ THINKING AHEAD

Don't use asphalt roof cement or solvents on waterproof shingle underlayment. They can deteriorate the modified asphalt that is the heart of the product. For caulking and sealing, use urethane or polymer-modified cements.

Anatomy of a Metal Open Valley

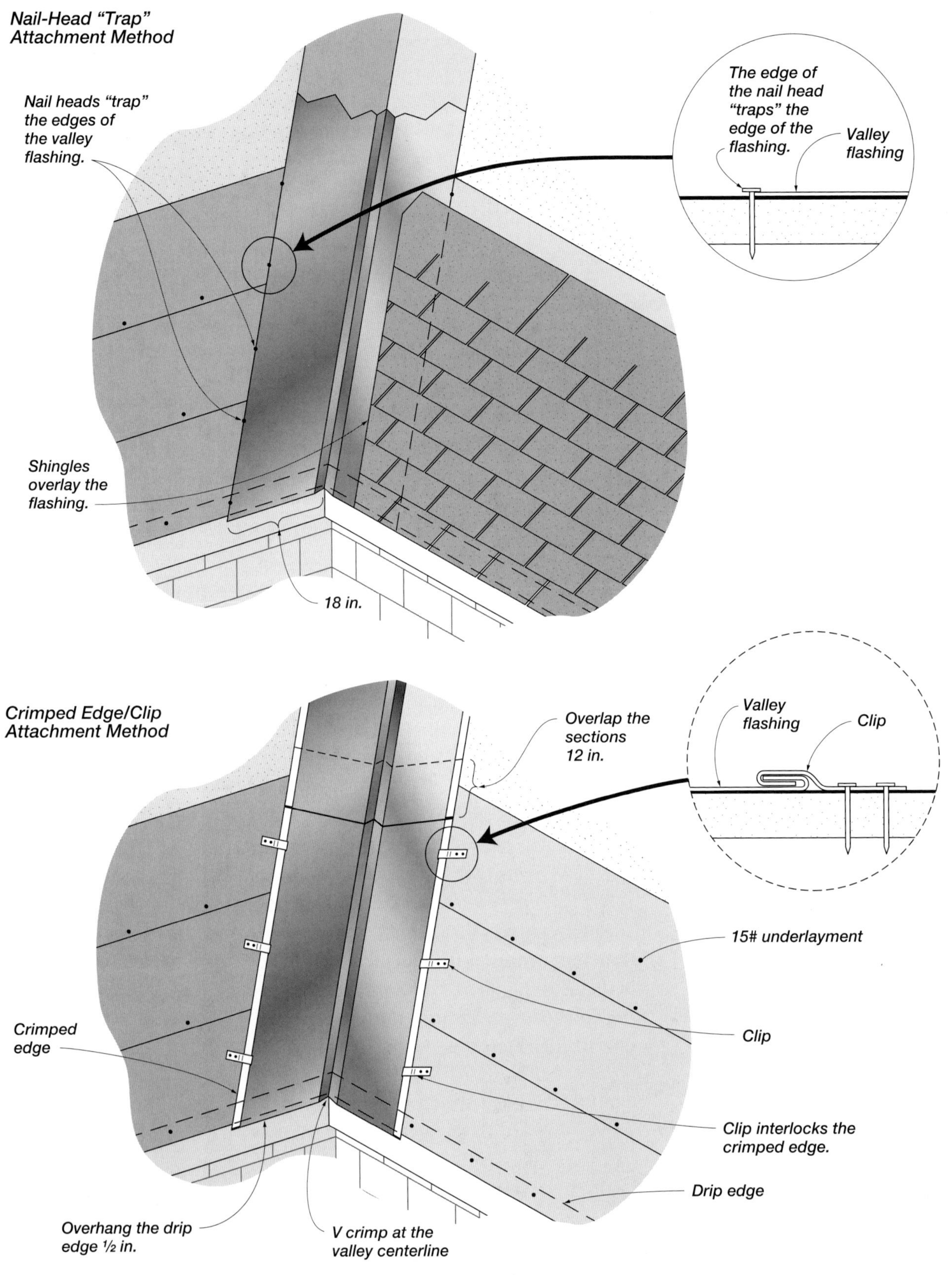

Once you have the sheet tight into the valley, nail the other edge and trim the bottom edge flush with the bottom of the 12-in. strip so it also hangs H in. past the drip edge. (When you have to use multiple pieces of roll roofing along the valley length, overlap the strips by 12 in. and cement the joint.)

Metal open valley

You can install underlayment for metal open valleys the same way as for mineral-surface open valleys. I prefer to use 30# roof felt or better yet, waterproof membrane to isolate the back of the metal from sheathing and to provide a cushion and secondary barrier to leaks.

METAL SELECTION AND SPECIFICATIONS Many people like to use copper for exposed valleys because it weathers first to a medium-brown color and then develops a green patina. But you can also use galvanized steel, stainless steel, aluminum, or other corrosion-resistant metal. If you're roofing near salt water, the flashing will last longer if you use heavy-gauge copper or stainless steel rather than aluminum or regular steel.

The metal should be a minimum of 26 gauge and 24 in. wide. Of course, thicker and wider is better. Limit the length of flashing sections to 8 ft. or 10 ft. because longer pieces are hard to bend and handle and will expand and contract more than shorter sections.

You can bend the metal yourself if you have a metal brake, or you can have the pieces made at a local sheet-metal shop. Use a piece of cardboard to make a template of the valley angle that you or the metal shop can use to check the bends. You can form the metal into a simple V or make the valley a little more water-resistant by bending it as a W with the center inverted V about 1 in. to 2 in. high. This added rib helps prevent the water rushing down one roof pitch from flowing through the bottom of the valley and up under the shingles on the adjacent roof. The inverted V also absorbs horizontal expansion of the metal so it won't buckle on a hot, sunny day.

INSTALLATION Start installing sections of metal valley flashing from the bottom. You can install the first section in two ways. The metal can lay over a woven first course of shingles along the eaves, leaving the end cut square. Or you can cut the lower edge flush with the drip edge and lay the first course over the valley flashing. Overlap additional sections at least 12 in. Some roofers spread roof cement between the lap, but don't use too much if you do; the cement may become liquid on a hot day and flow out of the joint, making a mess on the metal.

One way to fasten the valley flashing is to drive nails through the metal, but this can cause the metal to buckle when it expands. A better way is to trap the edges of the metal under the heads of roofing nails spaced 16 in. apart along each edge of the flashing. Just drive the shank of the nail into the sheathing alongside the metal's edge and hammer the head down until it just touches the flashing. This will allow the flashing to move as it expands so it won't buckle. Drive two nails through the top end of the flashing to prevent it from sliding down.

Another way to secure the valley flashing without the risk of buckling is to use clips that lock into crimped edges on the flashing. When you bend the flashing, fold over 1 in. of the metal onto the top surface of the flashing but don't crimp it closed; leave about 1⁄16 in. of space to accept the clips.

Cut and form 1-in. by 3-in. clips from scrap pieces of the flashing, then fold over 1 in. of the clip and leave the crimp open 1⁄16 in. to interlock into the valley flashing. Drive two nails at the top to hold the flashing, and interlock the clips about every 16 in. to 24 in. along both edges. Center the flashing in the valley, and fasten the clips with two nails through the 1-in. portion that wasn't folded over. Always use nails or clips made of the same metal as the flashing or of stainless steel to prevent corrosion.

When open-valley flashing ends where a fascia from one roof plane dies into another roof plane, as on gable-roof dormers, you have to overlay the end of the valley flashing so it drains out onto the shingle surface of the main roof. If you don't overlap the flashing onto the top of the shingles, water will be directed beneath the shingles and may cause leaks.

Open valleys are often lined with sheet copper. The valley is first lined with 30# underlayment or waterproof shingle underlayment. (Photo by Andy Engel, courtesy *Fine Homebuilding* magazine, © The Taunton Press.)

Closed valley

Building codes and manufacturers usually recommend laying a strip of 30# roofing felt directly on the sheathing from bottom to top of the valley. Then you can either run the regular underlayment through the valley right over the 30# felt, or you can stop the regular underlayment, overlapping the 30# felt 8 in. from the center of the valley. If you stop the underlayment, nail it along the cut edge. Many roofers use roll roofing in place of the 30# roof felt. It doesn't matter if the roll roofing is right side up or upside down.

I don't like to use felt or roll roofing. Both of these materials are subject to damage when you're installing the roof shingles, especially in cold weather when the materials are stiff and brittle. Your heel can easily crack the underlayment or roll roofing. If this happens, you won't have backup drainage if water gets past the valley shingles. I prefer to maximize the valley leakage protection by installing self-adhering waterproof membrane instead. The membrane is much more resilient to traffic during shingle installation and will seal around the shanks of any fasteners inadvertently installed too close to the centerline of the valley. It's cheap insurance against leaks.

Installing felt underlayment

Many people who install roofing don't take shingle underlayment seriously, and they may not install it at all. But it's absolutely crucial for the performance and appearance of the finished roof—it pays to spend the time to install underlayment properly and safely.

In addition, most shingle manufacturers recognize that underlayment is a component of the fire-rating designation for asphalt-shingle roofing systems, and it's necessary to meet code requirements;

Waterproof shingle underlayment is laid in the bottom of the valley as a secondary water barrier in the event the shingles that wrap through the valley leak. Once the membrane is floated in place, fold it halfway back to one side so you can remove the release sheet. After you've adhered one side to the roof sheathing, remove the release sheet from the other side.

check your local building code and shingle manufacturers' instructions for minimum underlayment requirements on specific jobs.

Before you start rolling out underlayment, check the roof sheathing one last time. Make sure there are no missing rows of nails or nail heads that stick up above the sheathing surface. Thoroughly sweep the roof just before you install the underlayment. Anything left on the roof—sawdust, leaves, loose nails, bits of shingles, or surface granules from a tearoff—may telegraph a lump through the shingle surface or may puncture through the underlayment when you walk on it. Make sure the sheathing is dry and frost free. Moisture trapped beneath the underlayment may stay there long enough to cause rot.

OVERLAPPING EDGES Overlap courses of underlayment at least 2 in. on roof pitches greater than 4. For roof pitches from 2 to 4, overlap 19 in., which gives you double coverage. There are typically four guidelines printed on the face of underlayment. The lines are spaced to gauge 2 in. from either edge or 19 in. from either edge.

When a roll of underlayment runs out before you reach the other end of a roof plane, you can overlap the next piece vertically and continue. The minimum end overlap is 4 in.

You don't have to keep underlayment courses aligned precisely. If courses drift up or down a little and aren't perfectly parallel to the eaves edge, don't worry. The point is to maintain a minimum 2-in. overlap and roll the sheets without

Felt underlayment will expand and bubble if it's rained on or if it collects dew when exposed at night. The bubbles can telegraph through the shingles applied over them.

■ WORK SAFE
■ WORK SMART
■ THINKING AHEAD

To give underlayment a chance to relax and acclimate to temperature and humidity, unroll and cut it roughly to length before hauling it up on the roof. This will help reduce wrinkling, especially if you can relax sheets for several hours or, better yet, overnight. The best place to relax underlayment is in an open room (on a new-construction project) or inside a garage. Driveways and sidewalks are acceptable, but don't leave the sheets out overnight.

bubbles or waves. Shingles will be aligned to chalklines you'll snap, not by the lines printed on the underlayment.

ROLLING OUT UNDERLAYMENT

If underlayment is exposed to moisture, it will swell and wrinkle up, preventing shingles from lying flat. This can cause the wrinkle to telegraph through the finished surface of the shingles.

Unless you live in a dry climate, install only as much underlayment as you can cover in a day. Underlayment left exposed overnight is likely to absorb dew or humidity that will make it wrinkle. Fiberglass-reinforced water-resistant underlayment is less likely to wrinkle than ordinary felt underlayment, but it's not immune.

You can roll out underlayment either from the top down or from the bottom up. In either case, it is important to have upper courses overlap the course beneath so the underlayment will shed any water that reaches its surface.

If the roof is steep enough to require roof staging, the best approach is to roll out as much underlayment as you can reach from the staging, shingle that area, then move the staging up to repeat the process.

For lower pitches, you can cover an entire roof plane starting at the bottom and working up. The disadvantage here is that you'll be walking on the underlayment as you work. Even well-nailed underlayment can tear and send you flying, especially when covering roof pitches greater than 7.

Rolling out and precutting felt underlayment makes it easier to handle up on the roof.

Installing underlayment from the top down eliminates this problem, but you have to leave the lower edge of each sheet loose in order to slip the top of the next sheet beneath it. This isn't a problem with two people installing on a calm day, but doing it alone or on a windy day is challenging.

However you choose to install underlayment, the job is easier with two people; one rolling the underlayment out and the other fastening it to the sheathing. If you have to work alone or if conditions are windy, it's a good idea to cut underlayment courses to length before you bring them up to the roof. Roll out and measure underlayment on a sidewalk or other flat, dry surface, and cut it a little longer than the length of the roof—handling a smaller roll on the roof is much easier than a full roll.

TACKING AND TRIMMING UNDERLAYMENT Tack the starting end of the underlayment in the upper corner flush with the rake edge or overlap hips and valleys by 1 ft. Roll out 10 ft. to 12 ft., and adjust the edge up or down to line up with the sheet beneath (or above with the top-down method) or the drip edge. Drive a vertical row of three or four fasteners into the underlayment along the edge of the roll.

Continue stretching out 10-ft. to 12-ft. sections, straightening and fastening until you reach the other end of the roof. Trim the end of the underlayment flush with the gable end or overlap hips and valleys by 1 ft. to 2 ft. In windy conditions, roll the underlayment in the same direction as the wind and fasten as you roll it out rather than straighten it; otherwise the wind is likely to catch the sheet.

Whether you choose to roll out the underlayment from the bottom up or top down, it's important that the first course along the eaves edge overlap the drip edge. Any water flowing on the underlayment will be directed over the drip edge and off the roof. If any of the underlayment happens to drop below the end of the drip edge, just trim it off.

FASTENING UNDERLAYMENT You can fasten the underlayment with nails or staples. The number of fasteners you'll need depends on how long the underlayment will be exposed and how much you will walk on it. When you're rolling out one underlayment course at a time, not walking on it, and covering it with shingles promptly, there's no need to drive lots of fasteners. The shingles will hold the sheets when you cover them. For quick installation, use a hammer stapler to drive a row of staples along the top edge, the bottom edge, and in the middle spaced about 16 in. to 24 in. apart.

When covering an entire roof plane, you can use the same hammer-stapler method to rapidly attach the courses of underlayment. After you roll out several

WORK SAFE
WORK SMART
THINKING AHEAD

Cut out the underlayment for any skylight or roof-vent openings as you roll over them—holes in the roof that are concealed by underlayment are a major safety hazard.

A hammer stapler makes short work of attaching felt underlayment. One person can easily roll out and staple down if it's precut to length.

courses, drive roof nails or pneumatic staples along the top and bottom edges spaced about 6 in. apart and two rows in the middle staggered about 12 in. apart. This pattern will hold down the underlayment in mild winds. Drive the nails or staples through roof tins or use plastic-capped nails for better tear resistance in windy weather.

Adjust pneumatic nailers or staplers so the fasteners don't tear through the underlayment. Fasteners that break through the surface of the underlayment won't hold. Here again, roof tins and plastic-capped nails help; fasteners are unlikely to tear through with the added protection.

DRYING-IN A ROOF Felt underlayment is sometimes installed to cover the roof sheathing and keep the weather out of a building for a short time before roof shingles are installed. This protects the inside of the house on a reroof project and keeps workers dry on a new-construction job.

You can temporarily dry-in a roof by installing felt underlayment over all the sheathing. Furring strips or nails and tin caps protect the underlayment from blowing off. (Photo by Kevin Ireton, courtesy *Fine Homebuilding* magazine, ©The Taunton Press.)

When you will be drying-in, I recommend increasing the underlayment-course overlaps to 5 in. to 6 in. to help keep out wind-driven rain. When a roll runs out, increase the vertical overlap to 8 in. to 12 in. Overlap hips, valleys, and ridges (even when ridge vent will be installed later) to provide extra protection at these critical points.

When there's any chance of high winds, use roof tins or plastic-capped nails to prevent fasteners from tearing through. You can also nail 1×3 furring strips or 2×4s over underlayment to hold it down better (see the photo at left). Along rakes, install rake-edge flashing over the underlayment to keep the wind from catching the edge.

For drying-in, use water-resistant fiberglass-reinforced shingle underlayment rather than ordinary felt to minimize the chance of wrinkles. If the underlayment does wrinkle before you have a chance to lay the shingles, you will have to tear off the affected sheets and reinstall underlayment. Or if there are just a few wrinkles, you can cut the center of them, nail down the edges flat, and install a 12-in. underlayment patch over the cut.

WORK SAFE
WORK SMART
THINKING AHEAD

Even a well-installed dry-in won't guarantee a leakproof cover. Water can easily get in around fastener shanks and small holes in the underlayment. Consider covering the roof with a polypropylene tarp, which will also keep frost and snow from accumulating on the underlayment in the winter.

Setting rake-edge flashing

The final step in preparing a roof deck is installing the rake-edge flashing after the underlayment is in place. Overlap the ends of the underlayment courses with the rake edge and nail it down every 12 in. to 16 in. Any wind-blown rain that gets between the rake edge and the roof shingles will be directed on top of the underlayment where it can drain out. If the rake edge went beneath the underlayment, the water would get to the roof sheathing.

If you cover the roof with waterproof shingle underlayment or run a strip up the rake edges, the rake drip edge can go under or over the material. But check with the underlayment manufacturer for its specific guidelines because they may differ.

You can install the drip edge by eye or use the chalkline-guide method as described on p. 99. If the rake is slightly crooked or bowed, you can use the drip edge to make it appear straight using the method described in the sidebar on p. 102.

Cut back the top nailing flange of the rake drip edge at about a 45-degree angle as shown in the illustration on p. 102, and interlock the end of the rake edge.

As you'll see in the next chapter, you will need to install, or at least temporarily install, the rake edge in order to lay out the vertical control lines that guide shingle installation. When you know you'll have enough time to shingle an entire roof section in one day, install the underlayment and the drip edge along the rakes. If you won't finish or want to roll out just one course of underlayment as you shingle, tack-nail the metal rake edge in a couple of spots but leave the nail heads sticking up. Loosen the nails and slip the underlayment underneath the drip edge as you work your way up the roof.

Rake drip edge always goes over the felt underlayment. Tack the drip edge in place to a chalkline guide and then lift sections to slip the underlayment beneath.

Working with Waterproof Shingle Underlayment

I've already mentioned using waterproof shingle underlayment in addition to or instead of regular felt underlayment in valleys and at the intersections of roofs with walls. There are a couple of other places to consider using waterproof underlayment. It can protect against leakage from ice dams and can waterproof low-pitch roofs where the chance of water backup is greater than on high-pitch roofs.

There are also a few methods for installing waterproof underlayment that are worth examining and a few precautions. I use different methods for removing the release paper and fastening the material depending on the application, wind conditions, and how much help I have.

Ice-dam protection

In cold climates, there is a risk of ice dams that can cause melt water on a snow-covered roof to back up under shingles and leak into the house. Ice dams are most likely to occur along the eaves and in valleys. You can reduce the chance of ice dams forming by following the roof-ventilation recommendations on p. 72.

As backup protection in ice-dam-prone climates, it's a good idea to install waterproof shingle underlayment. This material self-seals around nail shanks so

▪ WORK SAFE ▪ WORK SMART ▪ THINKING AHEAD

Some waterproof underlayment brands are plastic coated and others are granule coated. Neither can be left exposed for long periods of time because both are subject to UV degradation.

Wrapping Odd Intersections

You're bound to encounter odd intersections where multiple roof planes intersect with walls or other building features. Water rushing down from several angles and the possibility of debris collecting and causing backups make these areas vulnerable to leaks. For this reason, I like to install waterproof shingle underlayment in these areas as an extra precaution. To do so, layer pieces of the underlayment starting at the lowest point of the odd intersection. Wrap the pieces up at least 12 in. out of any small valley areas, lapping higher pieces (pieces farther up the roof or wall plane) over lower pieces. There's no harm in being overly cautious and applying multiple layers or covering wide areas that you're concerned may be prone to leaking.

Layer pieces at the lowest point.

Wrap pieces up at least 12 in.

Lap higher pieces over lower pieces.

water can't penetrate as easily as it can through ordinary felt underlayment.

On roofs with pitches greater than 4, waterproof shingle underlayment should extend up the roof to a point at least 2 ft. inside the exterior wall. It may take one or two courses of material to reach this point. For roofs with pitches from 2 to 4, consider covering the entire surface with waterproof membrane for extra protection, as shown in the top illustration on the facing page. Overlap the first course over the drip edge and follow the manufacturer's recommendations for overlapping additional courses.

Roofs with gutters may experience even worse ice damming when the gutters are plugged with debris or ice. The ice dam can form in the gutter and water can back up beneath the lower edge of the drip edge. Some waterproof-underlayment manufacturers recommend applying the underlayment before installing the drip edge and running it over the front of the fascia and behind the gutter as shown in the bottom illustration on the facing page. The drip edge covers the waterproof shingle underlayment, and you can apply an optional second layer of underlayment over the drip edge and seal it with a bead of urethane caulk.

Working alone with waterproof shingle underlayment

Working alone with waterproof shingle underlayment is tricky because the product is self-adhering. On sunny, warm days, the asphalt is so sticky that you only have one chance to get it in place accurately. If the material folds onto itself with the release sheet removed, you'll never get it apart.

When working alone, the best approach is to roll out, measure, and cut each piece while on the ground. On the roof, roll out the material with the release sheet intact. Using a hammer stapler loaded with ¼-in. staples, tack the upper edge as you roll out the course along the eaves. Space staples about 2 ft. to 3 ft. apart and ½ in. to 1 in. from the top edge. The staples are only there to hold the underlayment until you can remove the release sheet and bond the sticky side of the underlayment to the sheathing.

There are two ways to remove the release sheet. Both methods take advantage of the fact that the release sheet is split down the center so the pieces can be removed separately. The first way is the safest. Lift and tack the lower half of the underlayment over the top, using half-driven roofing nails to hold the folded sheet up. Pull the bottom strip of release sheet off the lower half of the underlayment along its entire length, then fold the underlayment down, starting at one end and working toward the other. Work the underlayment flat as you go so you don't catch any bubbles of air or wrinkle the material.

After you have the lower half of the waterproof underlayment bonded to the sheathing, pull the staples out of the top half and fold it down. Peel off the upper strip of release sheet and fold the underlayment back up. Again, watch out for wrinkles and air bubbles as you stick the upper half to the sheathing.

The second way takes a little practice because you peel half the release sheet and press the underlayment down in one action. Grab the lower strip of the release sheet at the center where the two halves overlap. Draw the release sheet toward the bottom edge of the underlayment, then pull the release sheet down at an angle while the underlayment is still lying flat on the roof. At the same time you are pulling the release sheet off with one hand, use the

Covering the Eaves Edge with Waterproof Underlayment

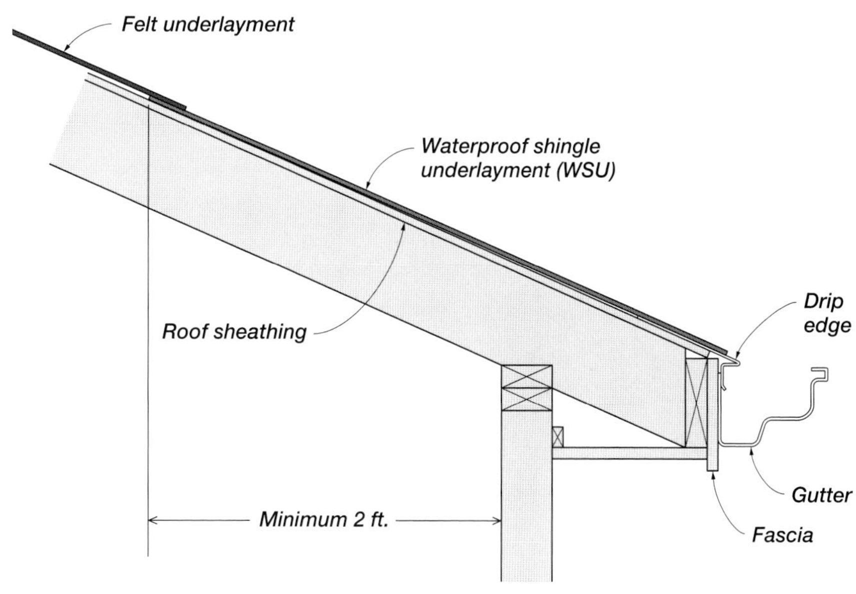

Installing Underlayment Behind the Gutter

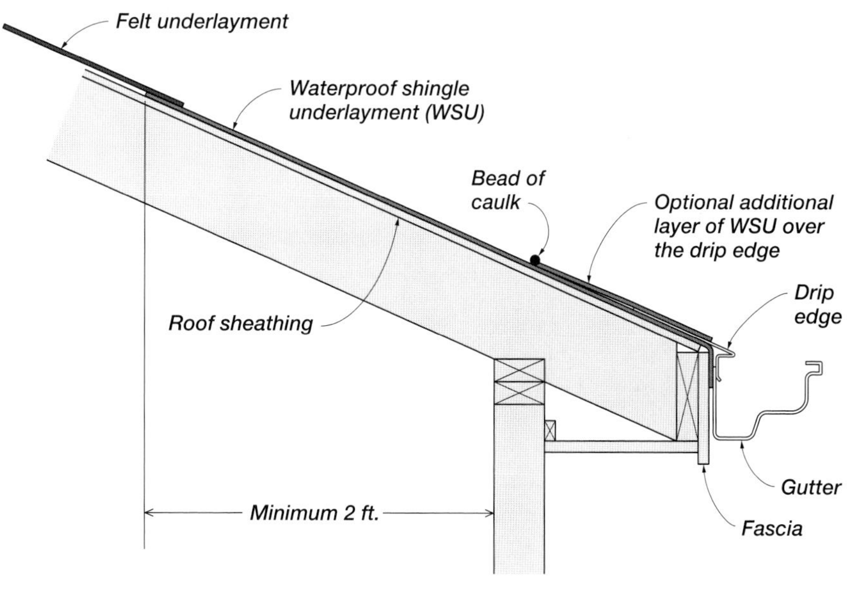

Alternate Ways to Prevent Ice-Dam Leakage

You can resort to older methods to provide secondary ice-dam protection if you don't want to use or can't get waterproof shingle underlayment. One way is to install roll roofing as the first course of underlayment along the eaves. The roll roofing material isn't self-sealing around nails like waterproof membrane is, but it's more water-resistant than ordinary felt underlayment and will shed most of the water.

Another solution is to cement together two layers of felt underlayment. After the first sheet of underlayment is fastened in place, completely coat it with asphalt roof cement. Roll another layer of underlayment over the first and drive nails 16 in. to 24 in. around the perimeter; the roof cement will stick the sheet in place, but the nails keep it from sliding when you step on it. Overlap additional underlayment courses from that point up the roof in the standard fashion. The roof cement will seal around nails where they penetrate the underlayment.

On low-pitch roofs, those from 2 to 4, the layering and cementing process is a little different. Cut and install a 19-in.-wide strip of underlayment as the first course along the eaves. Coat the surface with asphalt cement and overlay with a full-width (36-in.) course of underlayment, then coat the top 19 in. of the second layer with asphalt cement and overlay a third course of underlayment. Continue coating the top half of each course of underlayment and overlapping the next layer at 19-in. intervals until you reach a point at least 2 ft. beyond the inside edge of the exterior wall. Then continue overlaying underlayment courses by 19 in. without the layer of asphalt cement (see the illustration on p. 232).

Layering underlayment and coating with cement is a messy and time-consuming process. When you calculate the cost of materials and time it takes to install each of the ice-dam-protection systems, you'll probably find that using waterproof shingle underlayment gives you the most bang for the buck.

other to smooth out the underlayment and press it onto the roof sheathing. Once you have the bottom half of the underlayment pressed down, adhere the top half just as you would for the first method.

In cool weather, the asphalt may not stick to the sheathing. When this happens, you will have to fasten the waterproof underlayment down with nails. Don't worry when the material doesn't stick immediately; you can install roof shingles right over it. The membrane will stick down to the roof sheathing on the next warm day even when covered with shingles, and the self-sealing feature won't be compromised.

Installing waterproof shingle underlayment with help

Installing waterproof underlayment with two people is faster and easier than doing it alone. There are two methods you can use when you have help—the roll-out method and the drop-in method. In both cases, cutting a piece of underlayment to length will make the process easier.

Start the roll-out method by peeling back the release sheets from the first 2 ft. of underlayment. Butt the end of the underlayment with a rake edge or fold it over a hip and line up the bottom edge over the drip edge. Stick the exposed portion down to the roof sheathing and, if it's cold out, drive a few fasteners to hold it in place. Have a helper control the roll of underlayment and keep the bottom edge straight while you pull off the release sheets (see the bottom photo on the facing page). Periodically press the underlayment down to ensure contact with the sheathing or drive a couple of fasteners if it's cold. This process works well on windy days because the waterproof underlayment bonds down to the sheathing just as the release sheet is removed.

The drop-in method is best done on cool, calm days. Cut the waterproof underlayment to length and flip it face down to remove the release sheet. With a worker at each end, lift and hover the membrane over the placement area. Lower your end of the sheet and stick it in place while your helper holds up his

When two people install waterproof shingle underlayment, one can roll and press down the membrane while the other person gathers up the release sheet.

WORK SAFE ■ WORK SMART ■ THINKING AHEAD

Don't apply waterproof shingle underlayment over felt underlayment; it should only be applied over clean, dry roof sheathing.

end. Work your way down the sheet, lowering it in place until you reach the other end. The process sounds simple but it is complicated on windy and warm days. The wind will make it difficult to hold the sheet steady and drop in place, whereas on a warm day, if the underlayment accidentally touches the roof (or itself) you may never get it apart.

If you do get a wrinkle when sticking waterproof underlayment down, just slice and press the edges flat, then cover over the cut with an 8-in.-wide piece of membrane. Air bubbles are fairly easy to get out; simply poke a hole with a nail and bleed out the air. By driving the nail through the hole after the bubble is gone, the underlayment will seal around the shank.

One person can install waterproof shingle underlayment by first tack-stapling the top edge every 2 ft. Starting at one end, grab and pull the release sheet downward and walk toward the other end.

CHAPTER 6

Laying Out the Roof for Shingling

It's crucial to carefully organize and plan shingle installation. There's more than one way to approach layout, and different methods work better than others depending on the job. Here, a roofer is using the racking pattern.

WE'RE HALFWAY through the book and we haven't laid a single shingle yet. Isn't that always the way? The preparation and planning can take more time than installing the shingles. This chapter covers the heart of prep and planning; in the next chapter you'll get to lay shingles.

Before you can start roofing, you need to decide how to organize the shingle installation. You should establish a process that makes production easy and maintains an offset in the joints between the shingles in successive courses to prevent leaks.

There are two patterns you can follow to organize the layout and installation of shingles. I'll describe the advantages and disadvantages of each and how your roofing style may favor one over the other. Then I'll show you how to guide the installation of each pattern using control chalklines snapped on the underlayment and sometimes on the roof sheathing. Without horizontal and vertical control lines, it's likely that the shingles will "drift" as you install them, leaving the vertical and horizontal patterns of the shingles looking crooked.

Of course, many roofs are more complex than a simple gable with two roof planes. You'll have to shingle around obstacles such as dormers and hips. I'll show you easy ways to establish control lines so that shingle courses and joints will align as you shingle around these obstacles. You'll also see how to mark a line perpendicular to the eaves on roofs without rake edges.

Other situations aren't as easy to deal with, such as roof edges that are severely crooked or not parallel. These problems require compromise and extra layout time. I'll show you ways to establish control lines that will trick a viewer's eye and help make the roof edges and shingle courses look straight and parallel even when they aren't.

Establishing Control Lines

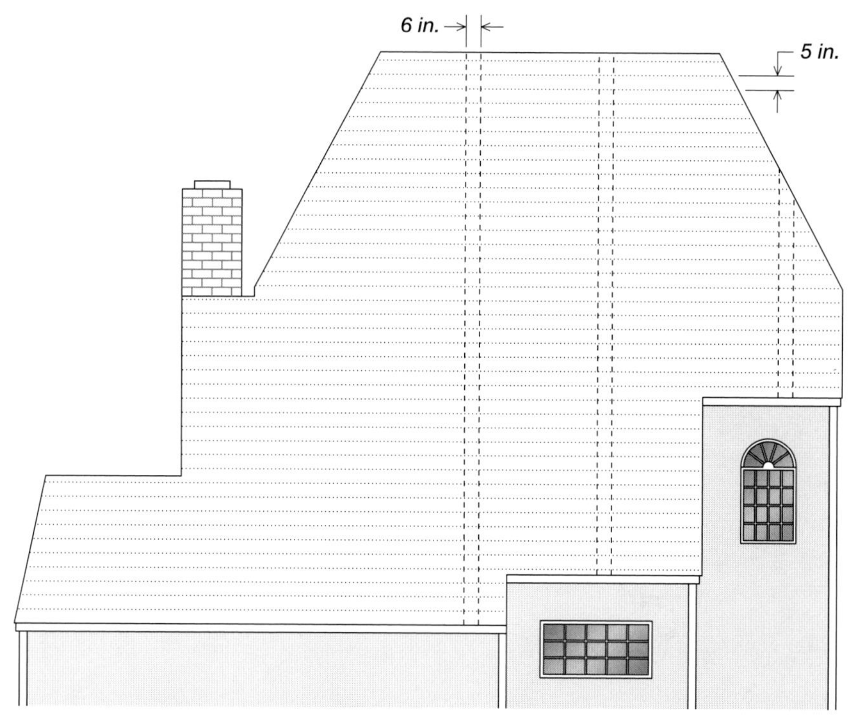

Shingle-Installation Patterns

When I discuss shingle-installation patterns, I'm not talking about creating patterns with roof shingles. Rather, shingle-installation patterns are methods of orienting and interlacing roof-shingle courses to maintain the offset of joints between shingles in successive courses and to speed production by establishing a regular and predictable installation process.

The two most common patterns are the racking pattern and the pyramid pattern. Each pattern has advantages and disadvantages for installation speed and the resulting appearance of the roof. You'll probably find one pattern or the other will work better on certain styles and pitches of roofs or with different types of shingles.

Later in this chapter, I'll describe the vertical control-line layout for each pattern. In chapter 7, I'll look at how to install and fasten the shingles using each pattern.

Racking pattern

The racking pattern is controlled by two or more chalklines running up the roof plane perpendicular to the eaves and ridge. The joints between shingles in successive horizontal courses are offset from one another by a specific measurement, typically 6 in. but 4-in. offsets can also be used. The shingle joints alternate back and forth as the courses go up the roof, hence the name "racking." Because some roofers work from the eaves up to the ridge installing shingles straight up in columns rather than running out courses horizontally, this pattern is sometimes called "straight up" or "column."

Shingle Installation Patterns

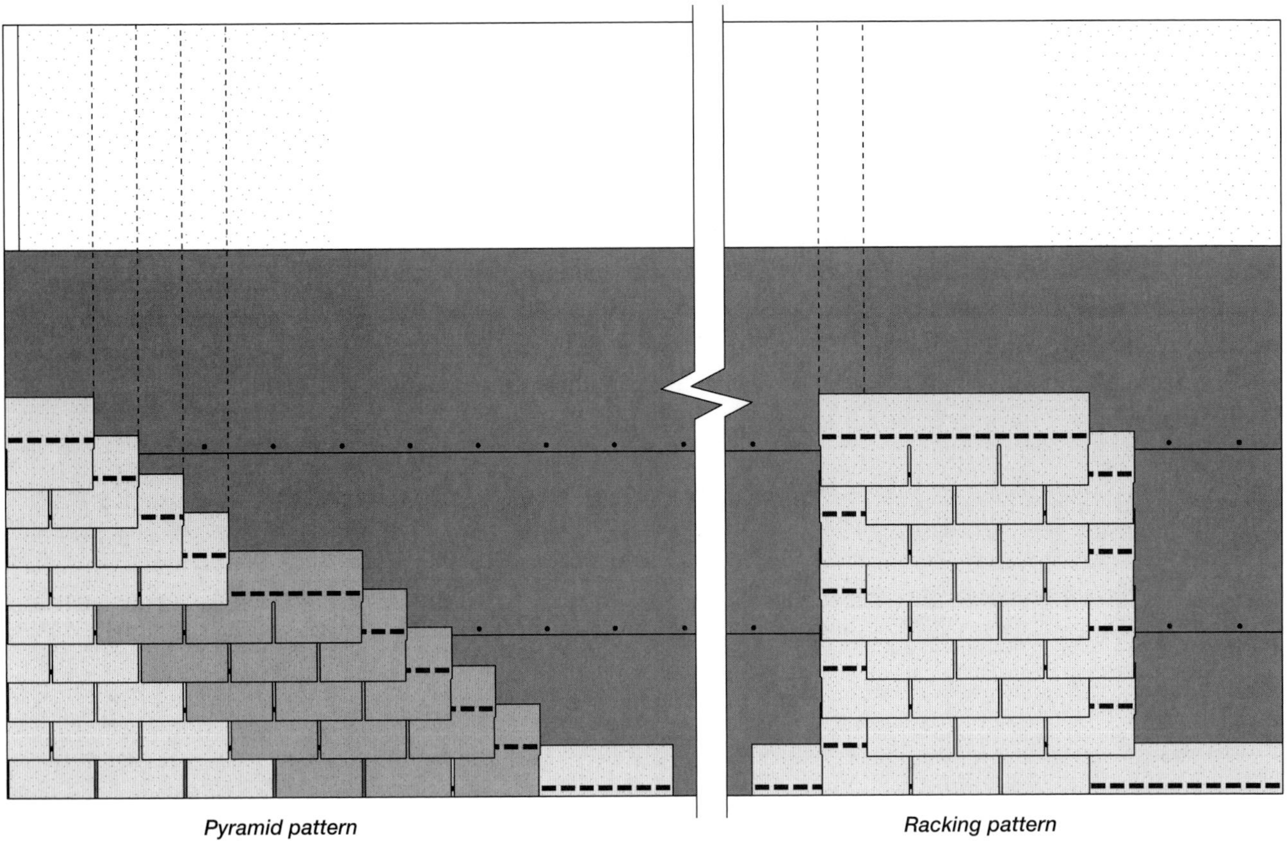

Pyramid pattern *Racking pattern*

WORK SAFE ■ WORK SMART ■ THINKING AHEAD

Always check the shingle manufacturer's instructions. Specialty shingles sometimes require unique installation patterns to create the intended visual effect on the roof or to avoid undesirable effects. In those cases, follow the manufacturer's instructions rather than those described here.

RACKING ADVANTAGES The layout process is fairly easy for the racking pattern. A major advantage is that the racking pattern does a better job of keeping cutout slots in three-tab shingles aligned than the pyramid pattern does. When you install three-tab shingles, you need to keep the cutout slots between the tabs in vertical alignment between successive courses because when the slots drift out of alignment, the roof looks unprofessional.

Roofers often snap vertical control chalklines for the racking pattern in the middle of a roof section. Then after running the first column of shingles up the control lines, workers can install shingles to the left and to the right from the starter column. This enables more workers to coordinate their efforts.

RACKING DISADVANTAGES On the downside, the racking pattern has some annoying installation quirks. Installing shingles vertically from eaves to ridge requires that you skip the last fastener at the end of every other shingle in order to slip the shingles from the next column beneath. As you work your way up each additional column of shingles, you have to lift the loose end of every other shingle in the previous column, slip the end of the new shingle beneath it, and drive a nail (see the top left photo on the facing page). It's hard to hold up the loose end and keep the new shingle from slipping out of position while driving a nail.

Once the loose end is flopped down, you have to drive that skipped fastener at the end of the shingle on the previous column. The whole process slows pro-

One of the disadvantages of the racking pattern comes during installation. The end of every other shingle in a column must be left unnailed and lifted in order to slide the shingle in below it when installing the adjacent column.

When using the racking pattern, alternating shingles are registered against parallel vertical control lines.

duction a bit, and lazy installers often neglect the fastener under the loose shingle end. The bad habit of skipping one fastener on every other shingle is called "cheat nailing," which can lead to shingle drooping (where one end of the shingle slips downward) and blowoffs.

Another disadvantage of racking a roof is the zipper appearance that the pattern can display in the finished roof. The shading of the surface granules on many color-blended shingles is supposed to create a random shading effect across the roof. When individual shingles are offset in a regular pattern from eaves to ridge, the shading randomness can be lost and can actually highlight the back and forth, zigzag look of the pattern (see the photo at right). This frequently happens when shingles from different lot numbers are installed on the same roof plane.

The racking pattern can also be revealed when the cutout slots at the joints between shingles appear wider or narrower than the ones stamped out in the middle of the shingles. As shingles age, they can shrink and the edges curl, especially organic felt shingles. The shrinking makes the slots where the ends of shingles meet appear wider, and the ends may be more likely to curl.

The regular back-and-forth offset of racked shingles can leave an unattractive "zipper" up a roof.

When joints are staggered at regular intervals up the roof, the undesirable zipperlike effect is highlighted. This can

Shingles are installed in a diagonal up the roof in the pyramid pattern. Progressively shorter shingles make up a starter kit and are aligned to several vertical control lines or a rake edge to establish the offset between horizontal shingle courses.

also happen when manufacturers miscut shingles or the installer doesn't butt the shingles tightly together. In any case, the installation pattern is exposed and detracts from the overall appearance of the roof. Some shingle manufacturers advise against using the racking pattern for these reasons.

Laminated shingles and other random shingle styles shouldn't be racked. There is no slot control required, so there is no advantage. And racking will betray a pattern in a style of shingle where you don't want one.

Pyramid pattern

The pyramid pattern is also known as the 45-degree or diagonal pattern. This is because it works up the roof as a diagonal instead of going straight up the roof like the racking pattern. The angle is rarely a true 45 degrees unless you're using a 5-in. shingle offset, but it does appear that way from a distance no matter what the offset. The roof shingles are typically started along one rake edge with ends of shingles in successive courses staggered diagonally to form the appearance of one side of a stepped pyramid.

PYRAMID ADVANTAGES There are several advantages to using the pyramid pattern. Once you get the pyramid started, shingling goes quickly. You can work up a roof at a diagonal or left and right horizontally. Since there are no back-and-forth offsets between courses as with the racking pattern, you don't have to struggle with lifting the ends of shingles and driving fasteners. This speeds production considerably.

The eaves-to-ridge zipper effect is eliminated too. Sometimes a diagonal zipper can develop, but it isn't as obvious as a straight one. The pyramid pattern is the preferred installation pattern for laminated and other random-appearance shingles. Many manufacturers recommend a modified pyramid pattern where the offsets between shingles aren't equal measurements but random themselves. Rather than equal 6-in. offsets, they may recommend an offset of 7 in. for the first course, 9 in. for the next, and then 5 in. This increases the randomness of the roof shingles and reduces the chance a diagonal zipper will show up.

PYRAMID DISADVANTAGE The drawback to the pyramid approach is that it's more difficult to control the vertical orientation of cutout slots in three-tab shingles because you need more vertical control lines. The pyramid-shingle pattern is typically begun along a rake edge and continued across, but it can be started in the middle of the roof too. The diagonal progresses up the roof and moves horizontally with the addition of each horizontal course. If the slots of the initial shingle in a course aren't set precisely, the whole course will be off. To control tab slots on a pyramid pattern accurately, you need to snap six or seven vertical control lines rather than the two needed for the racking method.

There is a way to use the pyramid pattern without vertical control lines. To do this, use a 5-in. offset (sometimes called random) with three-tab shingles. With a 5-in. offset, slots in successive courses only repeat vertically at every twelfth course. That's 5 ft. up the roof, so any deviation in the slots won't be noticeable (see the photo below).

Control-Line Layout

You can shingle a roof without using control lines, but chances are the vertical lines of slots and horizontal lines of butt edges will look crooked. Although this probably won't affect the water-shedding ability of the roof, it will detract from the home's appearance, especially on steep roofs that are a prominent part of the façade.

Vertical control lines keep slots in tab-style shingles aligned, while horizontal control lines keep the butt edges of the shingles in straight courses. Neither is very hard to lay out as long as you keep the shingle overhangs along the rakes and eaves in mind when you establish your primary reference lines. It's important to let the shingles overhang the eaves and the rake drip edges by ¼ in. to ¾ in. to help shed water. Be sure to account for the overhang when you mark for the control lines.

Before you lay out control lines, install the drip edge along the eaves, then roll out at least the first course of underlayment, be it ordinary asphalt-impregnated felt or waterproof shingle underlayment. Also install the drip edge along the rake. If you won't be installing underlayment and drip edge up the entire roof before shingling, tack-nail the drip edge along the rake edges for measurement purposes (see p. 113 for the tack-nailing procedure).

Vertical control lines

Vertical control lines are necessary when you're installing tabbed shingles or other shingle designs with distinct patterns. Without them, the cutout slots or shingle pattern can waver (as shown in the

A 5-in. cutout offset, shown here, eliminates the need for vertical control lines because the pattern repeats only every 12th course, so any deviation in the slots won't be noticeable.

Vertical control lines keep cutout slots aligned straight up the roof. Without vertical control lines, cutout slots will drift as shown in the photo at left. Using lines and good installation technique, the slots look precise from bottom to top as shown in the photo at right.

photo at far left). Laminated and other random-pattern shingles don't need vertical control lines, so you can skip this step in the layout process when you use them. It will be quicker to install random-pattern shingles using the pyramid pattern without control lines. I'll discuss how to do this in chapter 7.

On simple roofs, you can measure and locate vertical control lines from a gable end, provided the roof is relatively square and the rake is straight. The goal is to snap a series of perpendicular chalklines from eaves edge to ridge. You'll set the ends of the shingles up to the chalklines to keep the shingle offset precisely equal and thereby keep the tab slots in line up the roof plane.

There are slightly different methods for arranging chalklines on racking- and pyramid-pattern layouts.

Racking-Pattern Control-Line Layout

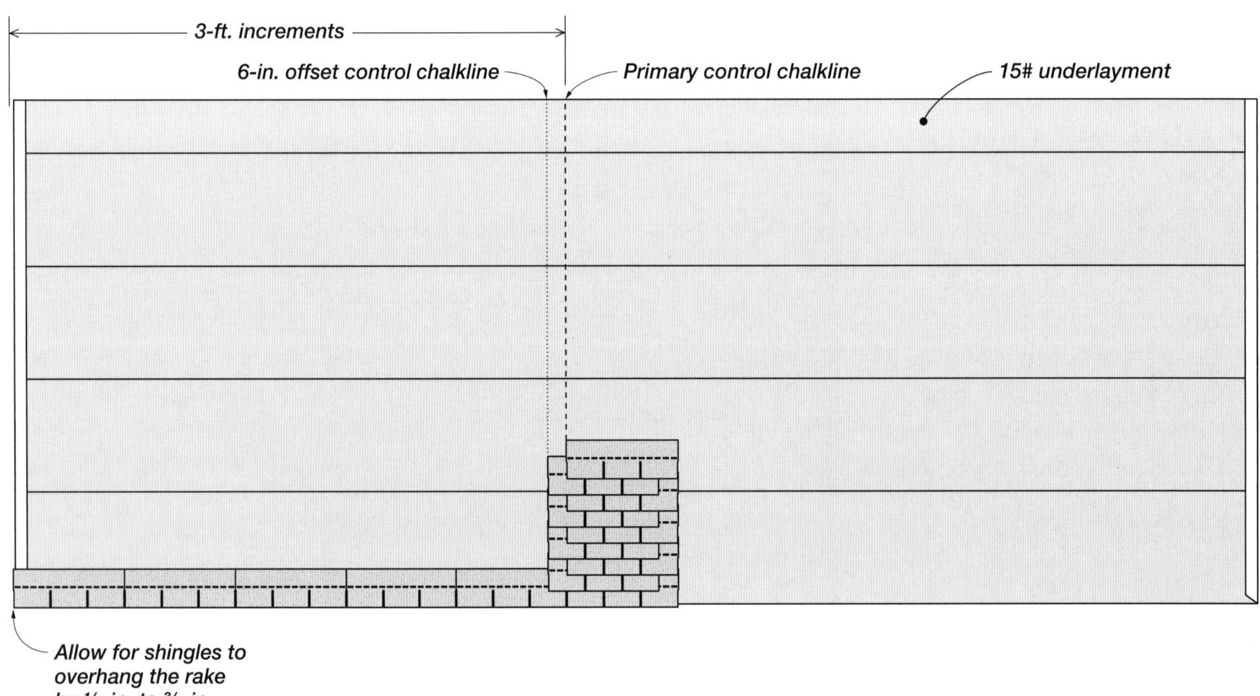

Vertical control lines for a racking-pattern layout

When laying out for common three-tab shingles, you'll need two vertical control chalklines for a 6-in. offset pattern and three chalklines for a 4-in. offset. The cutout slots on roofs shingled with a 6-in. offset will repeat every other shingle course. The slots will repeat every third course when you use a 4-in. offset. Check the manufacturer's instructions when you install shingles with other designs that have a different number of cutout slots or a regular pattern to follow; they may require slightly different procedures than described here.

You want to locate your control lines as close to the vertical center of the roof as possible while saving labor and materials by minimizing the shingle cuts on one side of the roof.

By establishing the chalklines toward the center of the roof, you will minimize the number of shingles that will be installed to either side of the line. This, in turn, minimizes the accumulated error that occurs because of variations in shingle lengths and how tightly you press them together when you install them. The farther a course gets from the line, the more obvious the accumulated error will become as the shingle cutouts drift out of alignment.

Shingle waste and trimming labor are the other issues to consider when choosing the control-line location. You can start your control lines at the precise center of the roof so that the distance between the last row of cutout slots and the rake edge will be equal on the left and right side of the roof, but the benefit may not be worth the cost. In reality, not too many people are going to notice the difference between one side of the roof and the other.

It's important to adjust the vertical control lines to avoid narrow shingle tabs running along a rake edge. They're unprofessional looking, and they can easily break or be blown off in a storm.

You can usually end with full-length shingles along one edge and only have to trim the shingles along the other. This saves time cutting shingles and minimizes waste, provided you don't end up with tabs trimmed down to less than 1½ in. along one rake edge. Short tabs are unsightly and damage easily (see the photo above). I'll describe the control-line layout in optimum circumstances and look at adjustment techniques to use when the shingles or shingle tabs on one rake edge work out to be too narrow.

1. **Check if the rakes are parallel and if the roof is square.** After the drip edges are tacked in place, measure the distance between rake edges along the ridge and along the eaves to see if they deviate from parallel and if so, by how much. To check if the roof is square, measure diagonally from the end of the ridge to the opposite eaves corner, then measure the opposite diagonal. On a large roof plane, even deviations up to 3 in. or 4 in. from square can be accommodated as long as the rake edges are close to parallel.

   When the rakes are out of parallel more than 1 in., the problem will

Adjusting Out-of-Parallel Rake Edges

When a pair of rake edges is out of parallel by up to 1½ in., you can hide the problem by gradually tapering the amount the shingles overhang the drip edge.

First measure the length of the eaves and the length of the ridge. Mark your "proposed" control line as described in step 2 below, but in this case, start by just making the mark on whichever is longer—the ridge or the eaves. Shift the mark as necessary to prevent too-narrow shingle tabs as described in step 3 at right, and allow for a ¼-in. shingle overhang.

Next, measure for the mark at the shorter parallel edge. When doing this, subtract half the difference in the ridge and eaves lengths and then add back in ¼ in. For example, if the rakes are out of parallel by 1¼ in., subtract ⅝ in. and add ¼ in. (the overhang amount you planned at the wide edge) for a total of ⅞ in.

Snap a chalkline between the two marks. This is half the battle—to get the control line established. The second half comes when you install the shingles. You will have to maintain the same cut line up the rake edges, keeping the length of the last shingle in each course equal and letting the shingle overhang vary.

In chapter 7, I'll describe rake starter shingles. These are shingles applied parallel to the rake edge to establish the proper overhang. You can use the starters to guide the shingle-trimming step and help add support to the extra-wide overhanging shingle ends (see p. 148 for details on this process).

be noticeable because the distance from the trimmed edge of the shingles to the slots will change from the bottom to the top of the rake. You can vary the shingle overhang to make adjustments and conceal the error (see the sidebar above).

2. **Mark the "proposed" control line.** Measure along the eaves edge from one of the rake edges to the 3-ft. increment that is closest to the center of the roof and make a mark. When you measure, remember to subtract the shingle overhang of ¼ in. to ¾ in. If you are using a 6-in. offset, the 3-ft. increment will allow you to end every other course along one rake with a full shingle. If you are using a 4-in. offset, every third course on that rake will end with a full shingle (see the illustration on p. 124).
3. **Check that cut tabs will be wide enough.** You want to make sure that all courses end with a tab that's at least 1½ in. wide. That's easy to do because shingle tabs are 1 ft. wide. Measure from the proposed control-line mark to the opposite rake. If the tape reads at least 1½ in. more than a 1-ft. increment, you're in business. If not, you'll need to move the control-line mark toward the rake you measured from in step 1. In this case, you'll have to trim every shingle along both rakes. Fortunately, the odds are you won't have to do this.
4. **Snap the first control line.** Make a mark along the ridge that is the same distance from the rakes as the final mark you made at the eaves. If you planned to use the shingle overhang along the rake to make a minor adjustment for unparallel rakes, be sure to subtract the correct amount when measuring along the ridge. Drive a nail at the mark at the ridge to hold the end of your chalkline, and strike a chalkline down to the mark at the eaves edge. This is your primary vertical control line.
5. **Snap offset control lines.** To establish your offset control lines, measure from the first control line back toward the rake edge you started from. By doing this, the shingles in courses lined up with the offset lines will be trimmed rather than require a narrow inset shingle tab at the end. If your offset will be 6 in., mark and snap one line 6 in. from the first line. If you will be using a 4-in. offset, snap two offset lines—one

4 in. from the first line and one 8 in. from the first line.

Although establishing control lines in the center of the roof minimizes cutout drift, some roofers prefer to work exclusively from left to right or right to left. In this case, you can make your proposed control line just 3 ft. from one rake (remembering to account for the rake overhang). Then measure to the opposite rake edge and make adjustments to prevent ending with a 1½-in. row. Snap the first control line and measure toward the rake for the offset lines.

Vertical control lines for a pyramid-pattern layout

Establishing vertical control lines for the pyramid pattern is typically done along one rake edge but you can start in the middle too. I'll describe the process for starting along one rake edge and then tell you about the modifications necessary to start in the middle. The same concerns about cutout-slot drifting apply to the pyramid pattern as to the racking pattern. The farther you apply shingles from the control lines, the more likely the slots will drift.

ESTABLISH THE PRIMARY VERTICAL CONTROL LINE Assess whether the roof is square and the rakes are parallel (see step 1 on p. 125), and plan the shingle overhang and adjustments if necessary. Make your initial mark along the eaves edge. To locate the mark, subtract the shingle overhang from 3 ft. and then measure in that distance from the rake edge. Measure from that point to the opposite rake edge to see how the final shingles will trim off. If it looks like the last shingle will end up with tabs less than 1½ in. wide, adjust your mark back. Mark the final point for the primary control line along the eaves edge, and duplicate the measurement along the ridge. Strike a chalkline between the marks.

Vertical Control Lines

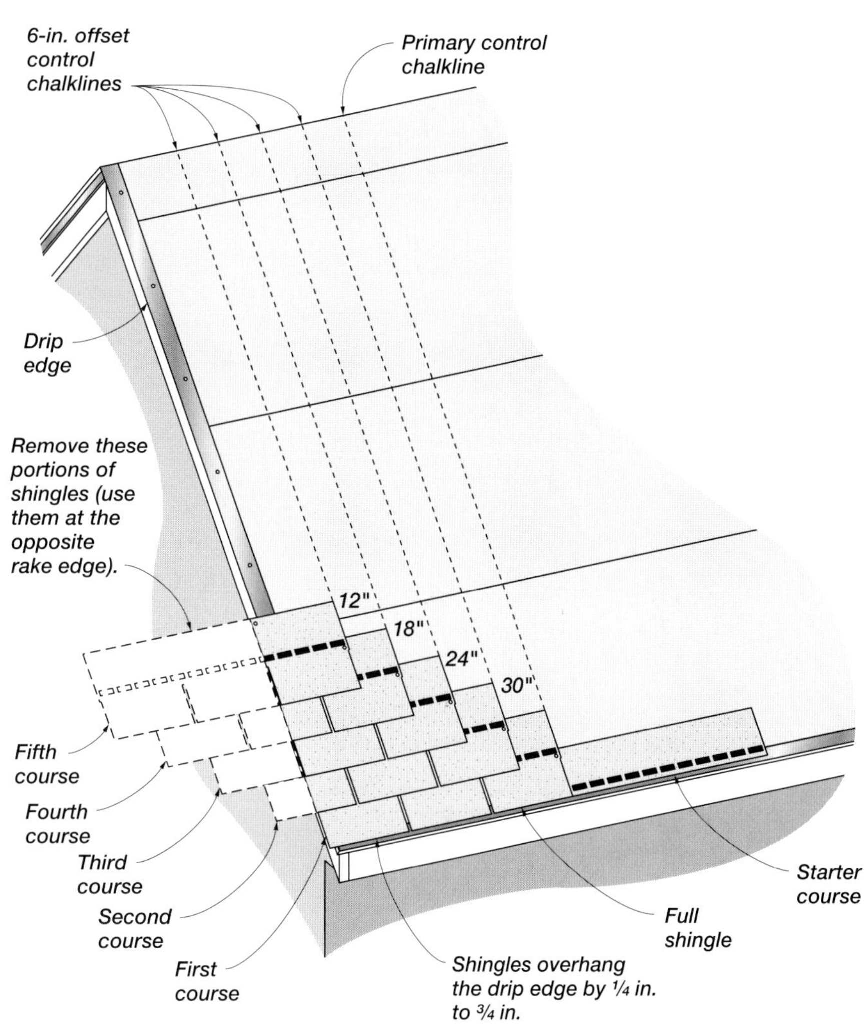

ESTABLISH INCREMENTAL VERTICAL CONTROL LINES Measure back from the primary control chalkline in 6-in. increments for 6-in. offset slots or 4-in. increments for 4-in. offsets. For 6-in. offsets, stop marking when you are about 12 in. from the rake. For 4-in. offsets, stop at about 8 in. This prevents you from using 6-in. or 4-in. shingle pieces at the rake that would be prone to blowing off. In the illustration above, the

Pyramid Pattern Started Mid-Roof

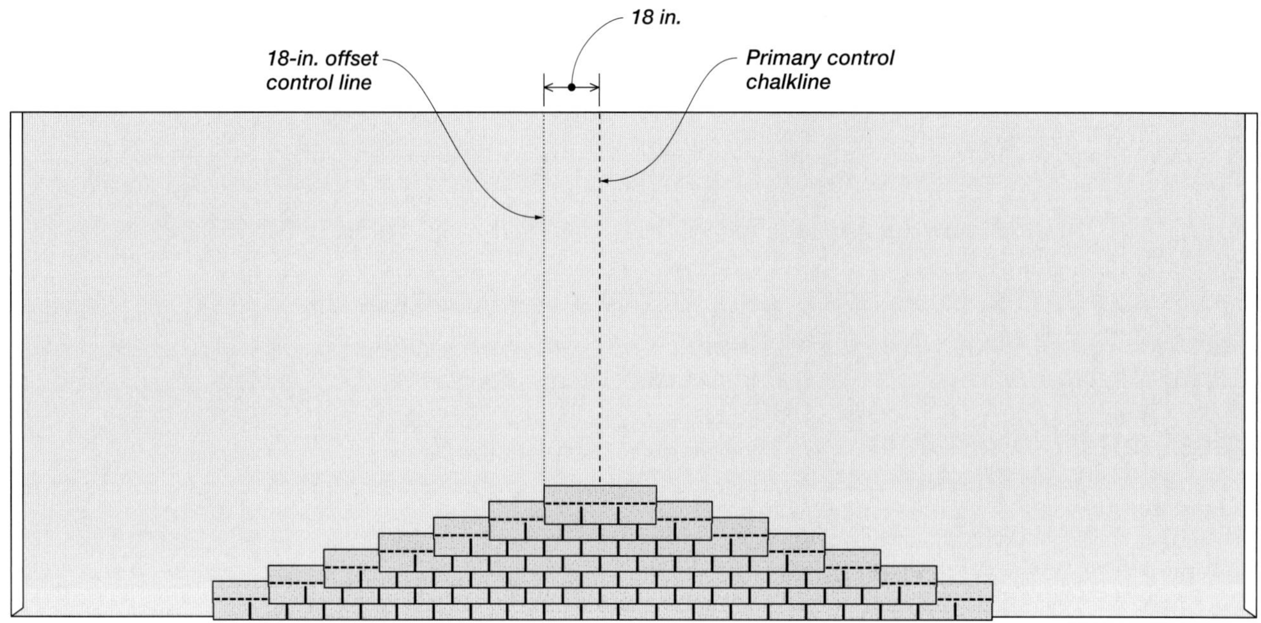

sixth course will start with a 30-in.-long piece to continue the 6-in. cutout offset pattern.

When you start shingling the pyramid, you'll align the factory end of each starting shingle with a control line and trim the excess off the rake-edge end. The starting shingle of each successive course will be indexed to the next control line back toward the rake. When you reach the last control line, start installing full shingles back at the bottom along the eaves edge and work diagonally up the pyramid. You'll reach the point where you'll once again index a series of trimmed shingles to the control lines.

STARTING THE PYRAMID PATTERN MID-ROOF As with the racking pattern, starting the pyramid near the middle of the roof minimizes accumulated error in shingle placement and allows roofers to work both sides of the pattern at one time. Establish mid-roof vertical control lines for the pyramid in the same way as for the racking pattern except for one difference: Instead of snapping the offset control line 6 in. from the primary line, locate it 18 in. away. This way, individual tabs will still be offset by 6 in. but you won't have to cut shingles to create the pyramid. If you want the tabs offset by 4 in., space the lines 16 in. apart.

Horizontal control lines

Horizontal control lines, snapped parallel to the eaves, are used to keep courses straight. Without horizontal control lines, each shingle course is likely to drift up and down a little (see the top photo on the facing page). When your only horizontal reference is the course of shingles below, gauging errors accumulate with each course. You may find your shingles so far off after only five or six courses that you can't correct all the error by snapping

Horizontal control lines help maintain the proper exposure distance. Without them, the butt edge of the shingles can drift up and down along the courses.

and following a single horizontal chalkline. It may take two or three courses to make the adjustment, and breaking your pace to snap corrective chalklines slows production. It's usually more productive to establish horizontal lines while you're laying out vertical control lines. This saves time in the long run and results in a superior shingle installation.

You can strike one horizontal control chalkline for each course of shingles, every other course, every third course, or any combination you feel you need. When you have a line to follow for every course, you merely need to place the top edge of each shingle at the line before you fasten it down. When there's only a line to follow every third or fifth course, you have to judge the shingle courses between the lines using visual cues to the shingle course beneath or by using a gauge on your hatchet or on the base of a pneumatic nailer or stapler. I'll describe how to do this in the next chapter.

Roofers usually develop a preference as to how many horizontal control lines they initially snap in chalk and how many courses of shingles they can lay straight without lines. I find it doesn't take that much longer to snap chalklines for every course as it does for every third, so I just do it.

You don't have to snap all the horizontal control lines up the entire roof all at once. Mark and snap the lines on the underlayment as you roll out courses and work your way up the roof. Register your tape measure to the top of the last course of shingles you installed, and continue marking 5-in. exposures from there.

MARK AND SNAP THE STARTER CHALKLINE The starter course of shingles along the eaves is the first line to establish. Trim off the exposure (lower 5 in. of the shingle) so the self-seal strip will be at the new bottom edge—the right spot to bond to the shingle above. This means the starter course is only 7 in. high. Once the starter course is applied, it is completely covered by the first course of shingles.

When making the 7-in. mark for the starter course and the 12-in. mark for the first course, let the tape measure overhang the drip edge by the amount you want the shingles to overhang.

WORK SAFE
WORK SMART
THINKING AHEAD

On long roofs, have someone press the chalkline down tight to the roof at the midpoint with a finger before you snap the line. This prevents a breeze from causing you to snap a chalkline that isn't straight.

One way to lay out horizontal control lines up the roof is to extend a tape measure along both rakes and snap lines between the tapes.

The starter and first courses have to overhang the drip edge by ¼ in. to ¾ in. You can use the overhang distance to hide minor errors in the straightness of the eaves that you couldn't take out when you installed the drip edge. If the middle of a drip edge bows out ½ in., for instance, you can plan to let the starters overhang ¾ in. at the ends of the roof and the middle only ¼ in. This will allow you to run the starter and first course in a straight line.

Let your tape measure overhang the drip edge by the amount you want the starter course to overhang at one end of the roof. Make two marks on the underlayment; one at 7 in. for the top of the starter course and the other at 12 in. for the first course of full shingles. (Pencil marks are hard to see on black underlayment, so try a light-colored crayon or chalk to make marks.) Do the same at the other end of the roof and snap a chalkline between the marks.

WORK SAFE
WORK SMART
THINKING AHEAD

It's helpful to number your marks so that workers at either end of the building can register the chalkline to the same control mark before snapping the chalkline.

MARK AND SNAP ADDITIONAL CONTROL LINES The rest of the horizontal control lines are referenced to the top of the 12-in. line. Since the exposure of each shingle course is 5 in. (check the manufacturer's instructions for specialty and metric shingles), you only have to mark and snap lines at 5-in. increments from the reference line.

You can mark out for the horizontal lines in one of three ways: You can make marks along the rake edges, you can leave tape measures in place at either end of the roof, or you can use leave-in-place layout tape that gets shingled over.

- **Marking method.** This is probably the most time-consuming method because you're making marks on the underlayment and then revisiting them to snap the chalklines. But snapping lines as you go can be handy on hot days when the underlayment tar absorbs the chalk and makes your lines disappear if you snap them too far in advance.

Set the end of a tape measure on the 12-in. reference line and stretch it out to the ridge along one rake edge. Make marks with a crayon or chalk at the interval you want control lines: every course, every third course, or every fifth course. When the ridge is within ½ in. of parallel to the eaves, make the marks all the way until you reach the ridge. If the ridge isn't parallel, stop making marks about 3 ft. from the ridge. (In a moment, I'll describe how to make adjustments for ridges that aren't parallel.) Duplicate your layout marks at the opposite end of the roof.

- **Two-tape method.** You can avoid the time-consuming process of making the marks to which to register the chalkline by setting up tape measures at both ends of the roof and just snapping chalklines between corresponding measurements. To hold the tape measures in place, drive nails halfway in near the rakes on the 12-in. reference line. Hook the tapes to the nails and extend them along the rakes and over the ridge. Lock the tape measures and let their bodies rest on the opposite roof plane; gravity will keep the tapes taut. With a person at each rake edge, snap chalklines between the tapes (see the photo on the facing page).

  Since both tapes are hooked at the same reference line, all you have to do is call out the measurement to your partner to be sure he's at the same point before snapping. Use the marking method for the last five to seven lines from the top of the roof to adjust an out-of-parallel ridge in ¼-in. increments as described on p. 132).

Problems with Inconsistent Shingle Heights

Horizontal control lines keep the top edges of shingles aligned. Normally, this means the butt edges will be aligned as well. Unfortunately, however, shingles sometimes vary in height; they can vary between brands, lot numbers, and even between shingles from the same bundle. Shingle-height variation between brands isn't an issue because it's rare to mix brands on the same roof, but you may install shingles from different lot numbers on the same roof. Check a few shingles from bundles of different lot numbers for height variations.

The most annoying height variation comes when shingles in the same bundle aren't the same size, as often happens with laminated shingles. In some bundles you'll find two different shingle heights. The manufacturers alternate the two heights within the bundle so they will package tightly. Don't be surprised to find shingle heights that vary by ¼ in.

You can make adjustments if you are aware of the problem. If the height varies between lot numbers, just keep shingles from like-numbered bundles grouped together. This is a good practice anyway to prevent color variations from contrasting. If shingle heights vary within bundles, drop the short shingles down a little from the control chalkline until it aligns with the adjacent shingle. You will probably miss a shingle or two and install them up to the line. Chances are that with laminated shingles the variation won't be evident.

Sometimes shingle heights vary between bundles or even within the same bundle. You can compensate if you are aware of the problem.

You may find that the distance between the horizontal courses and the ridge is different from one end of the roof to the other. To compensate, adjust the last few chalklines by shortening the exposure distance at one end of the roof.

- **Disposable tape method.** The third way to guide the control chalklines is to use "disposable" fabric or plastic measuring tape. These tapes are marked out with simple measurement systems. Some are made specifically for roofing and just have marks every 5 in. Unreel a length from the spool, and staple one end to the 12-in. reference line after lining up a 5-in. mark on the tape. Staple the tape every foot or two along the rake until you reach the ridge. Put a tape along each rake and in the middle of roofs wider than 40 ft. or 30 ft. on windy days. Snap chalklines between registration marks on the tapes. Leaving the tapes in place, install the roof shingles over them. Remember to make adjustments to the last few control lines when the ridge is not parallel.

ADJUSTING FOR RIDGES THAT AREN'T PARALLEL When the ridge is out of parallel to the eaves edge by more than ½ in., you'll have to adjust the layout of the last few courses so that the last shingle course is parallel. If you don't make the correction, the cap shingles will highlight the deviation. Make the adjustment by reducing the exposure measurement at the narrower end of the roof for the last few courses of shingles. Reduce each exposure measurement by ¼ in. in the series of adjustment courses until you make up the discrepancy (see the photo at left). It will take eight courses to make up a 2-in. parallel discrepancy but only two courses for ½ in.

Once you have a pair of marks that are parallel to the ridge, continue making equal 5-in. exposure marks. Don't make the adjustment by expanding the exposure beyond 5 in. at the opposite (wider) end of the roof. Doing so may leave properly placed fasteners or the self-seal strip exposed.

WORK SAFE ▪ WORK SMART ▪ THINKING AHEAD

In cases where you're installing a couple of shingle courses at a time, snap the control lines as you go. If you're using the two-tape method, register it from the top of the last course of shingles installed. If you're using disposable tape, just leave the tape rolls coiled on each section of the roof and continue unrolling and stapling them as you work your way up.

Special Layout Situations

There are several situations that require additional layout control lines to keep the shingles straight. Hip roofs have no rake edges to line vertical control lines up to, so you'll have to establish lines perpendicular to the eaves. When there's an obstacle on a roof plane such as a chimney or dormer, you'll have to snap extra chalklines so the shingles will align above and below. Contemporary-style homes often have broken-up roof planes with multiple eaves, so you'll need to adjust either the width of the starter course or adjust a whole series of course exposures to blend the areas together.

Then there are roofs that are out of square or have edges that are not parallel. These problems can be corrected in layout if they are not too severe.

Preparing vertical lines on hip roofs

Here's how to use the eaves as reference for establishing vertical control lines on a hip roof. Remember, you won't need vertical control lines for laminated shingle roofs; only for tabbed-style and other pattern shingles.

1. **Find a rough center point.** Start by marking and snapping the first two horizontal control chalklines at 7 in. and 12 in. Measure between the hips or between the hip and valley to find the rough center of the eaves.
2. **Find two equidistant points.** Drive a nail into the 7-in. control line at this center point with enough of the head sticking up to hook your tape measure. Measure away from the nail along the control line as far as you conveniently can an equal distance in each direction. Drive a nail at these two points, again leaving the heads up.
3. **Find the perpendicular point.** Hook the end of a tape measure on each of the two outside nails and walk up the roof to the ridge roughly above the center nail. Cross the two tape measures, and shift them left or right until they cross at the same measurement. Make a mark at that point.
4. **Snap the primary vertical control line.** Hook your chalkline on the nail on the 7-in. control line. Extend the line to the ridge, making sure it is covering the mark where the tapes crossed, then snap. This line is perfectly perpendicular to the horizontal control lines.

   Since there is no rake edge on hip roofs at which to end full shingles, you can use this vertical line as your primary vertical control line and snap offset lines from it. Or if you prefer to start elsewhere on the roof, you can use this line to measure, mark, and snap another parallel line as your primary control line.

Establishing a Vertical Control Chalkline Perpendicular to the Eaves Edge

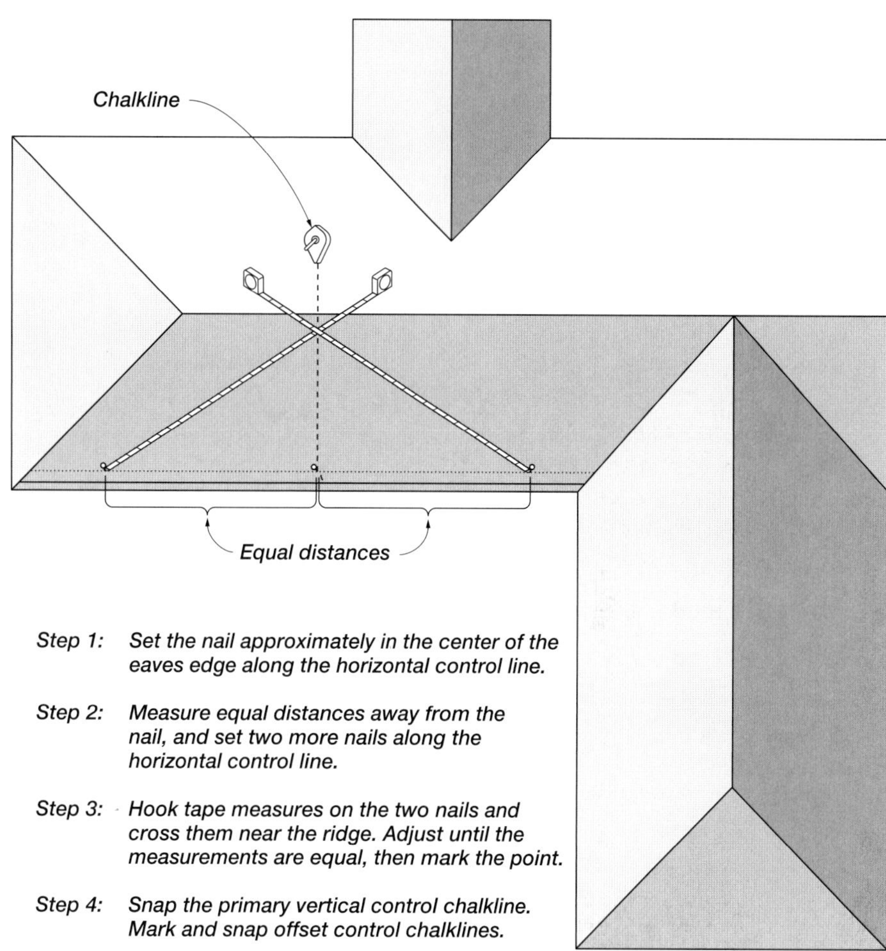

Establishing horizontal control lines around an obstacle

Dormers, chimneys, and other obstacles sticking out of a roof plane require additional horizontal control lines to keep butts aligned on both sides of the obstacle. Tabbed shingles also require addi-

When something interrupts the plane of a roof, like a dormer or a chimney, you need to snap a reference control line above the obstacle. (Photo by Andy Engel, courtesy *Fine Homebuilding* magazine, © The Taunton Press.)

tional vertical control lines to keep the cutouts aligned.

If the obstacle obstructs the middle or upper part of the roof and not the eaves, the horizontal control lines are easy to establish. Start along the eaves edge to mark out and snap the 7-in. and 12-in. control chalklines. Measure up from the 12-in. line in the standard 5-in. exposure increments on both sides of the obstacle. Snap chalklines as you typically would.

When the obstacle interrupts the eaves, you have to establish a horizontal control line above the obstacle and measure backward to the eaves edge.

1. **Establish the control line above the obstacle.** Hook your tape measure on the drip edge, and stretch it up the roof along a rake until you are above the obstacle. Because you will be laying the top edge of a course along this control line, select a point that is divisible by 5 in. and then add 1½. (The difference between two 5-in. exposures and the 12-in. height of a shingle is 2 in. Subtracting another ½ in. for the drip edge gives you 1½ in.) Repeat the process at the opposing rake, then snap a line between the two points (see the illustration below).
2. **Establish starter and first-course lines.** Measure back down toward the eaves edge from the control chalkline above the obstacle, then make marks at the two 5-in. increments that are

Laying Out Horizontal Control Lines around an Obstacle

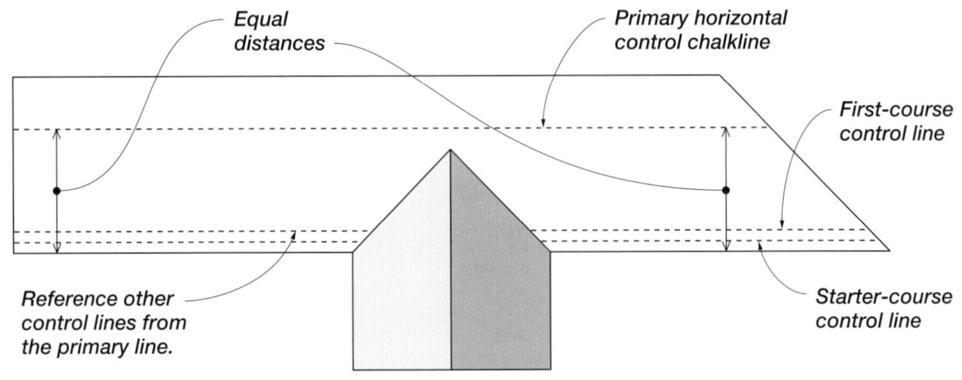

Laying Out Vertical Control Lines around an Obstacle

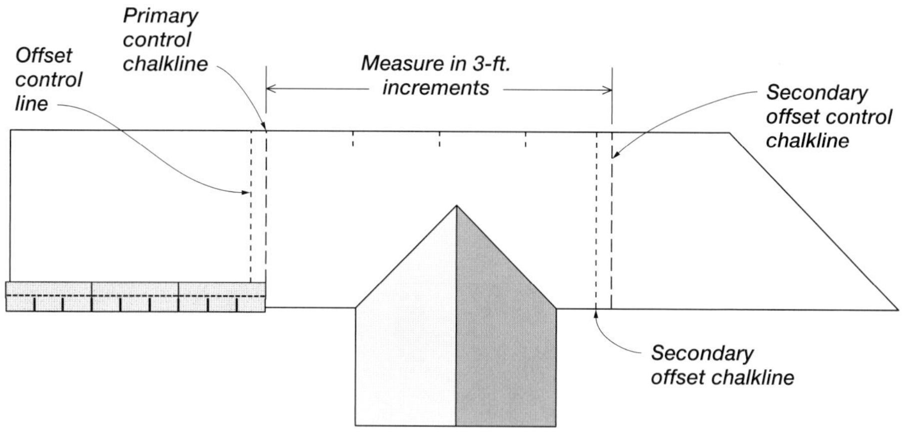

closest to the eaves edge. These will match the 7-in. starter-course line and 12-in. first-course lines you would make if measuring directly from the drip edge. You'll need to measure down at two points at each side of the obstacle so you will have two points to snap from on both sides of the obstacle.

3. **Check for correct shingle overhang.** Measure from the drip edge to the starter-course line at several points; the measurement should be 6¼ in. to 6¾ in., which allows for a ¼-in. to ¾-in. shingle overhang beyond the drip edge. If it is less or more than the target range, adjust the primary control line above the obstacle to make the correction.
4. **Establish additional control lines.** You can raise or lower one end of the line or both ends depending on how the drip edge measures up from one side of the obstacle to the other. After you adjust the primary control line, remeasure and resnap the pair of chalklines along the eaves, then check the measurements to the drip edge. When you are satisfied with the measurement range, mark and snap the rest of the control chalklines up the roof.

Establishing vertical control lines around an obstacle

To keep the cutout slots on both sides of an obstacle aligned, you'll need to snap two sets of vertical control lines; one set at each side. Select points and snap a primary vertical control chalkline and the offset lines on one side of the obstacle in the same fashion as described on p. 125. Most of your shingles will be guided by these primary lines.

Measure from your primary control line to the other side of the obstacle along the eaves edge and the ridge (or two points above or below the obstacle when it blocks the eaves edge or ridge). Make marks at 3-ft. increments so the ends of full shingles will land on the primary control lines as well as the secondary lines around the obstacles. Snap the secondary control chalkline and offset chalklines (see the illustration above).

Establishing Parallel Vertical Control Lines on Jogs in a Roof

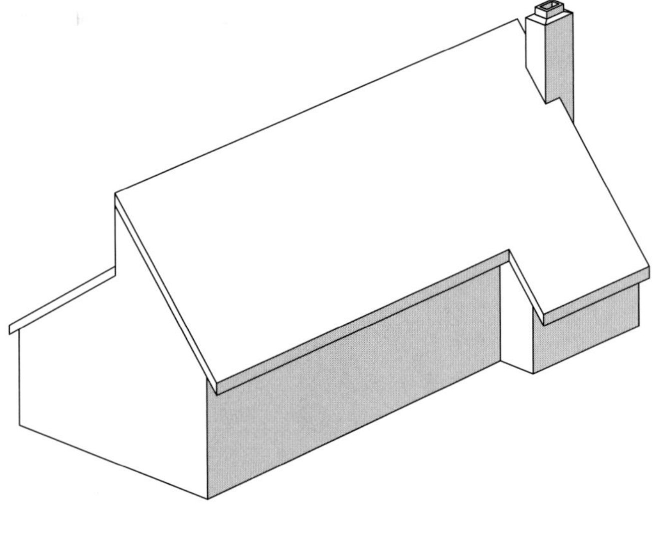

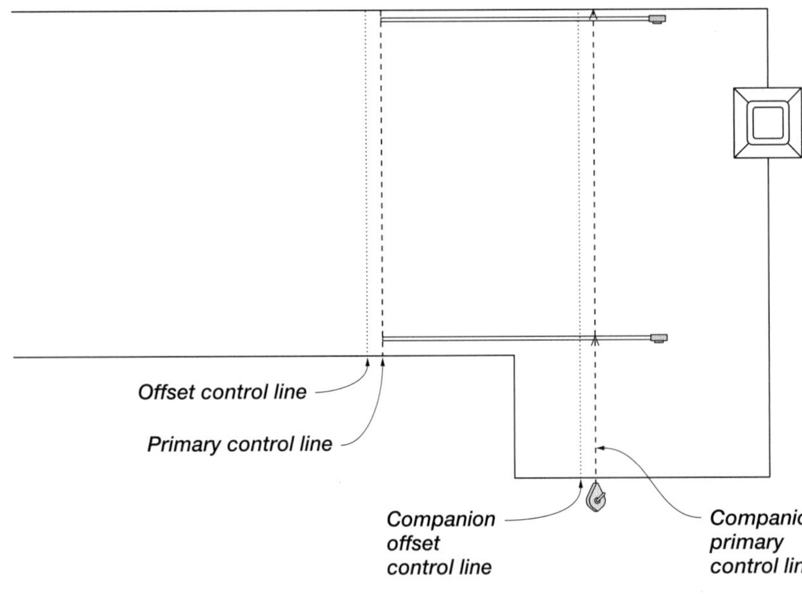

Establishing control lines on roof planes with jogs

Roof planes with jogs will have more than two rake edges and will have multiple eaves edges. This occurs when a portion of a roof plane continues past the eaves of the main part of the roof as is often the case with contemporary-style homes. This complicates the layout of vertical and horizontal control lines by forcing you to consider more variables.

Here's how to lay out first the vertical control lines and then the horizontal control lines on the jog (see the illustration at left).

ESTABLISH PRIMARY VERTICAL CONTROL LINES Again, the vertical control lines are needed only for three-tabbed shingles. Lay out for the primary vertical control line using the method described on p. 125. Measure to each of the rake edges from the control line to see that you'll end with a shingle piece longer than 6 in. and that the last tab will be 1½ in. wide or greater. Try to shift the vertical control line so the shingles will end within the 6-in. and 1½-in. minimums. Sometimes you won't be able to meet this standard on every rake, usually breaking the 1½-in. tab rule. When you can't avoid tabs narrower than 1½ in., plan to seal them down with a dab of asphalt cement.

ESTABLISH COMPANION VERTICAL CONTROL LINES ON THE JOG Where a roof section jogs below or above the main part of the roof, you'll need to snap a companion set of vertical control chalklines for the shingles to follow until you reach the main roof. The process is similar to marking a secondary vertical control line on the opposite side of an obstacle as described on p. 135.

Starting from the primary vertical control line, measure out an equal distance along the ridge and along the eaves. Mark two points that are over the jog and are at a 3-ft. increment from the primary line. Place the chalkline on the ridge point and pull it down to the eaves. Adjust the chalk string until it is exactly over the lower point and snap the line.

ESTABLISHING HORIZONTAL CONTROL LINES ON THE JOG If a roof plane jogs down, it's unlikely that the horizontal spacing for the main part of the roof will give you full shingles along the jog's eaves, so you have two choices. You can continue the horizontal alignment of the main roof and trim the butts at the jog eaves, or you can reduce the exposures on the jog to result in a full-shingle first course.

TRIMMING THE BUTTS If you decide to trim the first-course butts, mark and snap horizontal control chalklines for the starter and first course of shingles along the longest eaves edge. Extend the chalklines through the jog.

On the jog, measure down from the primary horizontal first-course line in 5-in. increments to mark and snap chalklines. Stop snapping chalklines when you reach the first exposure increment within 12 in. of the eaves edge. This will be the top of the first course of shingles. Mark for the 7-in.-tall starter shingles in the normal way, allowing for drip-edge overhang. After you install the starter shingles, measure from the bottom edge of the starters to the first control line, and trim the first-course shingles to this height.

REDUCING EXPOSURES ON THE JOG Here's a math-avoiding method to reduce the shingle exposures on the jog if you decide you want a full course at the jog's eaves. Again, start by continuing the starter- and first-course horizontal lines from the main roof across to the jog (see the illustration at right).

At the eaves of the jog, mark control lines for the starter and first course exactly as you would for a main roof. Before you snap lines between the marks, measure up to make sure these lines will be parallel to the lines you extended across the main roof. If they aren't, make minor adjustments up or down until the marks are parallel and the resulting shingle overhang is ¼ in. to ¾ in. By making this adjustment, the shingle overhang won't be equal beyond the drip edge, but the shingle courses will be parallel. Now snap the starter and first-course lines at the jog eaves.

Measure from the 12-in. line along the jog eaves up to the line extended from the 12-in. line for the main roof. Most likely the measurement won't be divisible by 5-in. increments, so you'll need to reduce each course by an equal amount. Here's the math-avoiding trick: Drive a nail into the jog's 12-in. line with the head protruding enough to hook your tape. You don't need to measure the position of the nail—just put it near one rake. Hook the tape and pull it past the main roof's 12-in. line, then tilt the tape until the next 5-in. increment crosses the line. Have someone mark every 5-in. increment along the tilted tape. Repeat the process near the other rake, then snap control lines between all these marks.

■ WORK SAFE
■ WORK SMART
■ THINKING AHEAD

When trimming first-course shingles, always cut from the butt of the shingles so the self-seal strip will be in the correct location to seal the tabs of the shingle above.

Adjusting Course Exposure (Height) on Jogs in a Roof

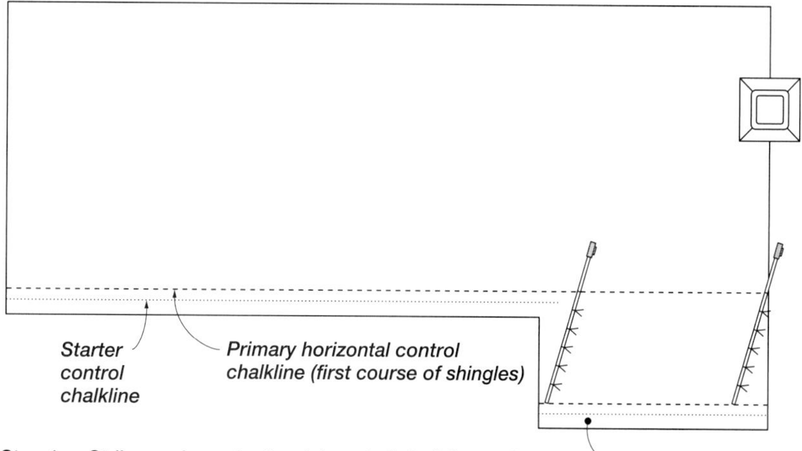

Step 1: Strike a primary horizontal control chalkline and control chalkline for the first course on the eaves edge of a jog.

Step 2: Hold the end of the tape measure at the control line on the jog. Tilt the tape across the primary control line, and index the first 5-in. increment.

Step 3: Mark for control lines at each 5-in. mark and snap chalklines.

Adjusting for Problem Roof Alignment

You've learned simple solutions for eaves and ridges that are slightly out of parallel and solutions for crooked edges. These adjustments enabled you to hide errors by adjusting the drip edges (see p. 102) and varying the shingle overhang. When roof edges are very crooked or if the roof is significantly out of square, corrections are harder to make. But there are some tricks you can use to make errors less obvious.

Hiding misaligned rakes

Rakes that are crooked or out of parallel by more than 1½ in. can't be adjusted by using the shingle overhang to conceal the error. The problem is highlighted by the straight, uniform pattern of vertical cutout slots in three-tab shingles (see the photo below). The best solution is to shingle the roof with random-pattern shingles such as laminated or multi-cutout. Trim the shingles to roughly match the curve in a badly misaligned rake, and use the shingle overhang to soften the error. Where there's a bulge out, let the shingles overhang the edge by only ¼ in.; where there's a curve inward, let the shingles overhang an inch or so. Without cutout slots, the variation will only be evident along the rake.

Tab shingles highlight how crooked the gable end of this 275-year-old house is. You can disguise the problem by installing random-pattern multi-cutout or laminated shingles.

Hiding crooked eaves

Crooked eaves are a problem no matter what style of shingle you use because the shingle butts will be out of alignment. However, the problem will be a bit less obvious with some laminated shingles that have tabs of different lengths to mimic shakes. As with rakes, if the variation is more than 1½ in., you can't correct it solely by adjusting the shingle overhang.

Ordinarily you'd start the horizontal control-line layout by marking and snapping straight chalklines for the starter and first full course of shingles. To veil a significantly uneven edge, you can break the control line into short segments that approximate the curve of the eaves edge, then mark the successive control lines with diminishing "curves" until you can snap a straight control line and continue up the roof.

1. **Snap a straight reference line.** Start by snapping a chalkline about an inch up from the ends of the drip edge as a reference for where the eaves curves up and down. Measure between this line and the eaves, and mark where the difference is greatest and where it is smallest.
2. **Lay out and install the starter course and first course.** Measure and mark for the starter and first course of shingles (7 in. and 12 in.) at points about every 10 ft. along the eaves edge. Let the tape measure overhang the drip edge by 1 in. where the edge curves upward the most and ¼ in. where it curves down the most; this

will vary the shingle overhang to take up some of the error. Connect the marks with chalklines and install the starter and first course of shingles (see the illustration below).

3. **Adjust additional courses in ¼-in. increments.** Strike a chalkline along the top of the shingle course to highlight the remaining error. Hold the string flush with the top of the course at the lowest points so the rest of the chalkline will strike across the shingles themselves and not the underlayment. Mark 4¾ in. up from the points along the shingle edge where the chalkline is the closest to the top of the shingles, and mark 5 in. up where the chalkline is the lowest on the shingles.

   Snap lines between the points and install the next course of shingles. Continue snapping a straight chalkline across the top of the shingles and making ¼-in. corrections until you can snap a straight 5-in. line for a course of shingles. From there, lay out the rest of the shingle courses in straight 5-in. increments.

Hiding crooked ridges

Masking crooked ridges is done in the exact opposite fashion as correcting the eaves-edge error. Mark out and install shingle courses with straight 5-in. exposures until you get within 3 ft. of the ridge. Measure down off the ridge to the top of the last shingle course to see how crooked the ridge is, then mark and snap the control lines in segments to create progressively greater curves in the shingle courses. Increase the curve by ¼ in. with each course until the control line roughly matches the ridge.

Although you don't have to make this ridge correction, without it the cap shingles will follow the curve of the ridge and be highlighted by the straight lines of the shingle courses.

Significantly out-of-square roof planes (3 in. or greater) are best covered with random-pattern shingles. Provided that the opposite edges of the roof are fairly parallel and that the predominant error is the square, random-pattern shingles will hide the problem. Avoid tabbed shingles; the cutout slots will look askew as you sight up a vertical column. If you must use tabbed shingles, then follow a 5-in. shingle-offset pattern (described in chapter 7) so the vertical cues that highlight the cockeyed slots will be too far apart to notice.

Adjusting Shingle Exposure to Hide a Crooked Eaves Edge

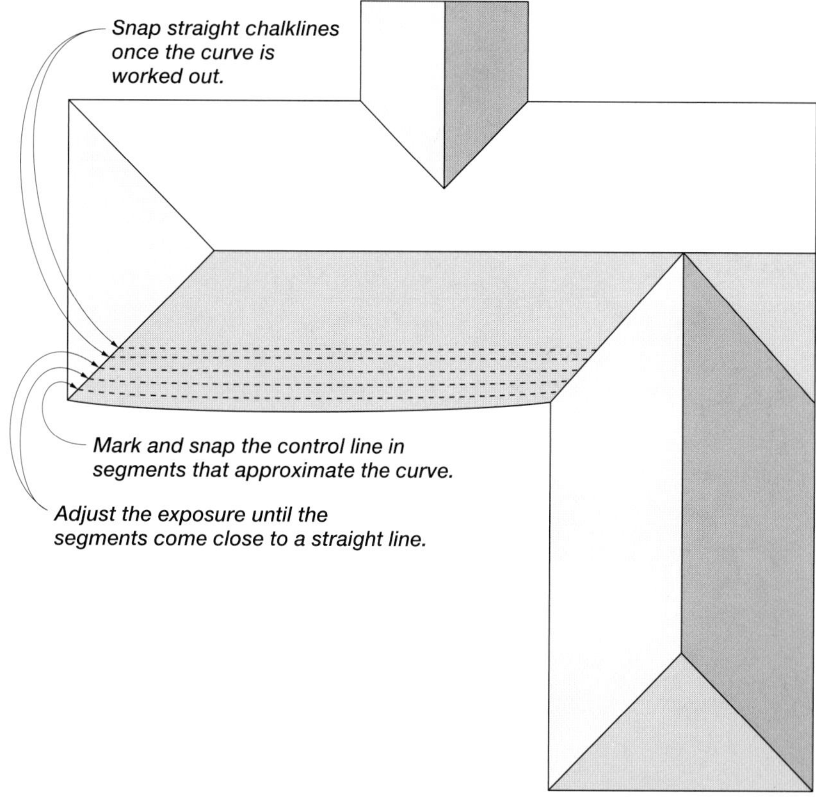

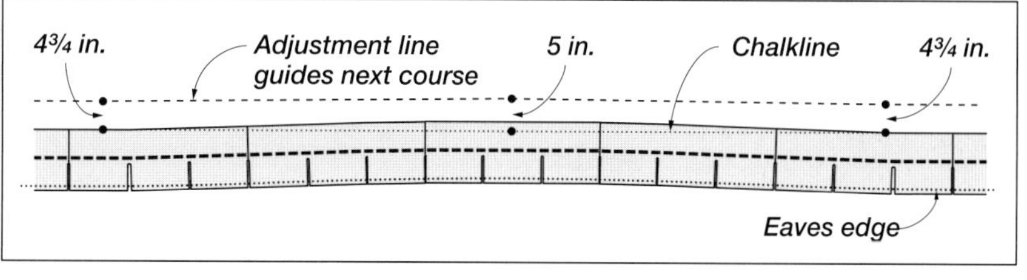

CHAPTER 7

Installing Roof Shingles

IF YOU'RE AS IMPATIENT as I am, you skipped the first six chapters and started here. That's fine, but you will need to refer back to sections of previous chapters for several important things. I recommend scanning roof ventilation in chapter 4, roof preparation in chapter 5, and shingle layout in chapter 6. Since the book is linear, this chapter presumes that you've already assessed the roof-ventilation situation and made a plan to incorporate vents as needed. I also presume that you've installed drip edge and underlayment and have begun striking control chalklines to guide shingle installation.

Applying shingles goes quickly if you spend the time to lay out and snap precise control chalklines.

If you already have the roof prepared for shingling, then you've already done most of the work. Installing roof shingles is a fairly quick, methodical, and easy process. Shingling is satisfying because in just a short time you can turn around and see some real progress; not just metal drip edge, tarpaper, and chalklines. The time-consuming part of shingling (installing flashing, valley shingling, cutting shingles into obstacles, capping hips and ridges, and so on) will be covered in chapter 8.

I'll start with some seemingly mundane but extremely important information about fasteners and fastening shingles. Roof failures can often be traced to improperly located and improperly driven fasteners. I'll move on to cutting and installing starter shingles, then actually installing roof shingles and using staging to work your way up the roof.

Fasteners and Fastening

You can use roofing nails or wide-crown staples to fasten asphalt shingles to a roof. Either will do the job provided you drive them properly. Properly driven fasteners penetrate the roof sheathing adequately, are located accurately on the shingles, and are flush to the surface without crushing it. See chapter 1 for a complete description of the different types of fasteners used to install asphalt-roof shingles.

Penetration of roof sheathing

Roof-shingle fasteners are commonly available in lengths from ⅞ in. to 1¾ in. Building codes and shingle manufacturers have standards for how deeply the fasteners must penetrate the sheathing to prevent them from pulling out. You may find that your local building code doesn't agree with the shingle manufacturer's printed instructions. When there's a discrepancy, follow the more stringent requirement.

In general, the requirements are as follows: For sheathing ¾ in. or thicker, the fastener must penetrate a minimum of ¾ in. into the sheathing. For sheathing thinner than ¾ in., the fasteners must penetrate the sheathing and protrude through the underside at least ⅛ in.

Remember that the fasteners must pass through the shingle you're applying, the top lap of the shingle beneath, the head lap of the one beneath that, then the underlayment and the sheathing. A ⅞-in. fastener may be fine when you are installing lightweight three-tab shingles over ½-in. plywood, but change the shingles to a heavyweight laminated style and you may need 1¼-in. fasteners to penetrate the same ½-in. sheathing. When in doubt about how long fasteners should be, either test the penetration or use a longer fastener you're sure will penetrate adequately.

A 1¼-in.-long roofing nail penetrates the ½-in.-thick sheathing on the left side but won't make it through the ¾-in. sheathing on the right.

The length of the fasteners needed to install new shingles over an existing layer is always a question. I like to do a test to make sure the nails I'm using are long enough. I lay a couple of shingles in place near the ridge after I tear off the cap shingles and drive a nail to see that it penetrates the sheathing enough.

Fastener placement

It is critical to locate the fasteners at the proper height on the shingle. If you drive them too high, they may blow off. If you drive them too low, the heads will be exposed, making the shingles prone to leaks. Fasteners also have to be located in the correct positions across the shingles. If they are not, the head may be exposed in the cutout slot of the shingle above. Standard shingle installation requires four fasteners per shingle, but in areas prone to high winds, six fasteners are necessary.

■ WORK SAFE
■ WORK SMART
■ THINKING AHEAD

A note of caution: On roof pitches greater than 21, self-seal strips don't do a good job of bonding shingle courses, so you'll have to hand-seal them after you've completed shingling the roof.

Orienting Fasteners

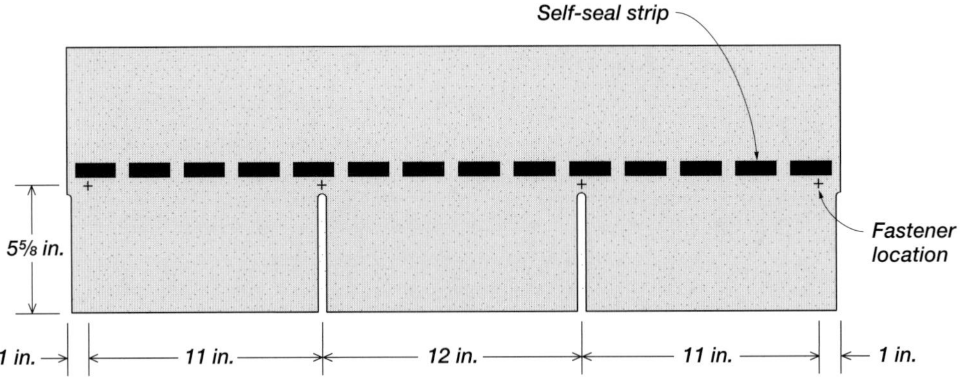

Standard four-fastener pattern

5⅝ in.
1 in. 10 in. 10 in. 10 in. 1 in.
2 in. 2 in.

Wind-resistant, six-fastener pattern

ORIENT FASTENERS VERTICALLY

The target area for fasteners is only ⅜ in. high. On standard-size shingles, these center points are 5⅝ in. from the butt edge (see the illustration above). On metric shingles, it's at 6⅛ in. above the butt. If you are using tabbed shingles, the target points are centered between the cutout and the self-seal strip. Some manufacturers print a target line on their shingles but most don't.

Some roofers incorrectly use the self-seal strip as a target, and sometimes they even nail above the self-seal strip. If the shingles blow off, the manufacturer will check how the shingles were fastened. If they were nailed too high, the warranty will be void and the installer will be held responsible.

Targeting such a narrow line with pneumatic nailers and staplers is difficult, especially when using the bounce-fire method. Some municipalities have banned the use of pneumatic tools for installing roof shingles because of this problem. Hand-nailing is slower but easier to do accurately.

ORIENT FASTENERS HORIZONTALLY

There are two nailing patterns for the location of fasteners along the horizontal target line: the standard four-fastener pattern and the six-fastener pattern used for roofs in high-wind areas (see the illustration above).

For the four-fastener pattern, place nails at 1 in. and at 1 ft. in from each end if you are using standard shingles, or at

Here are good examples of how *not* to nail shingles. Rather than nailing above the self-seal strip as shown here, locate the nails ½ in. above the cutout slots. (Photo by Kevin Ireton, courtesy *Fine Homebuilding* magazine, © The Taunton Press.)

1 in. and at 13⅛ in. in if the shingles are metric size. On three-tab shingles, the two inner targets are easy to locate because they are directly above the cutouts. For laminated and no-cutout shingles, you'll have to develop a good sense of where to place nails because measuring isn't practical. Fasteners driven within ¼ in. left or right of the target are acceptable.

The six-fastener wind-resistant pattern doubles fasteners at the middle positions and places them 1 in. to the left and right of center of the cutouts. When using staples, center them on the target locations to the left and right of both cutouts. For the staples at the ends of the shingle, position the outer leg of the staples at the 1-in. target points. See p. 229 for more about shingling in areas subject to high winds.

Properly driven fasteners

If hitting a fastener target smaller than a dime wasn't difficult enough, you also have to make sure nails and staples are installed straight and flush with the surface of the shingles. To avoid problems, fasteners must not break through the surface of the shingle nor be left sticking up. Hand-nailing roof shingles is probably the most accurate way to ensure that fasteners are driven properly. Pneumatic nailers and staplers are affected by many variables that make accurate driving more difficult.

FIX CROOKED FASTENERS Nails that go in crooked will either leave part of the head sticking above the surface of the shingle or part buried into the shingle. Likewise, crooked staples leave one side of the crown either buried or not in contact with the shingle.

When part of a fastener is left above the surface of a shingle, it can eventually wear through the shingle above, inviting leaks. And when part of a fastener cuts into a shingle, it fractures the fiberglass or felt mat and weakens the attachment point. During windy conditions the shingles can pull completely through the weak points and blow off the roof.

Hammer down crooked fasteners so the head or crown lies flat. If part of the head or crown breaks the surface, drive

Nails that stick up or were driven crooked can easily cut through the surface of the shingle above.

another fastener 1 in. away and apply a dab of asphalt cement to cover the head of the first fastener.

FIX UNDERDRIVEN OR OVERDRIVEN FASTENERS When you don't drive a fastener flush to the surface, it may not penetrate the sheathing deep enough to hold. Over time it may work its way out and leave the shingle loose. The shingle above the underdriven fastener won't sit flat and will look bubbled. In warm weather when shingles soften or when shingles are stepped on, the protruding fastener will break the surface of the shingle covering it (see the photo at left).

Fasteners that are set too deeply and break the surface of the shingle will rupture the fiberglass or felt-fiber mat that gives shingles their tear resistance. One overdriven fastener here or there probably won't result in a wholesale roof failure, but if you overdrive a lot of fasteners, the roof shingles are susceptible to blowing off because the fasteners are likely to tear through.

You should seal overdriven fasteners with asphalt cement and drive another fastener about 1 in. away. Use a hammer to set underdriven fasteners flush with the surface of the shingle.

There are two ways to seal errant nails that won't be covered by a shingle above. The first, shown above, is to coat the head of the nail with roof cement and then sprinkle it with granules. The second is to remove the nail and slip a cement-coated piece of aluminum beneath the shingle where the hole penetrates as shown at left.

Pneumatic Tools Cautions

There are some pneumatic nailers that have specially designed nose assemblies that automatically correct crooked nailer orientation and drive every nail perpendicular. But with most pneumatic nailers, the fastener won't enter straight and flush unless the tool is perpendicular to the roof when fired. This takes some practice to do if you use the tool in the bounce-firing mode. To bounce-fire, you keep the trigger depressed and fire the tool by bouncing it against the shingle. Even if the nailer automatically drives the nails perpendicular, it's still tricky to get the nails in the right spots when bounce-firing.

If you are new to pneumatic tools, it's a good idea to trigger-fire the nailer until you get more comfortable with the tool. In trigger-fire mode, which is a little slower than bounce-firing, you place the nose of the nailer where you want it and pull the trigger to fire each fastener.

It's also difficult to adjust pneumatic tools so that they consistently drive fasteners to exactly the right depth. Conditions change from one roof job to the next or even on the same job. The temperature of the shingles, shingle thickness, fastener length, and roof-sheathing density all affect how much energy it takes to drive a fastener. The air pressure, length of hoses, and number of tools being used also affect how well a tool drives fasteners.

Newer nailers and staplers have noses that can be adjusted for driving depth. You can also use inline air-pressure regulators to adjust how far fasteners are driven. Even after you adjust a tool, it may still occasionally drive a fastener to the wrong depth.

Because of these problems, some municipalities have banned the use of pneumatic tools for installing roof shingles. Hand-nailing is slower but easier to do accurately.

With pneumatic tools, it's easy to (left to right in each photo) overdrive, drive crooked, or underdrive nails or staples. Only when the nail head or staple crown lies flush with the shingle surface is it installed properly (far right in each photo).

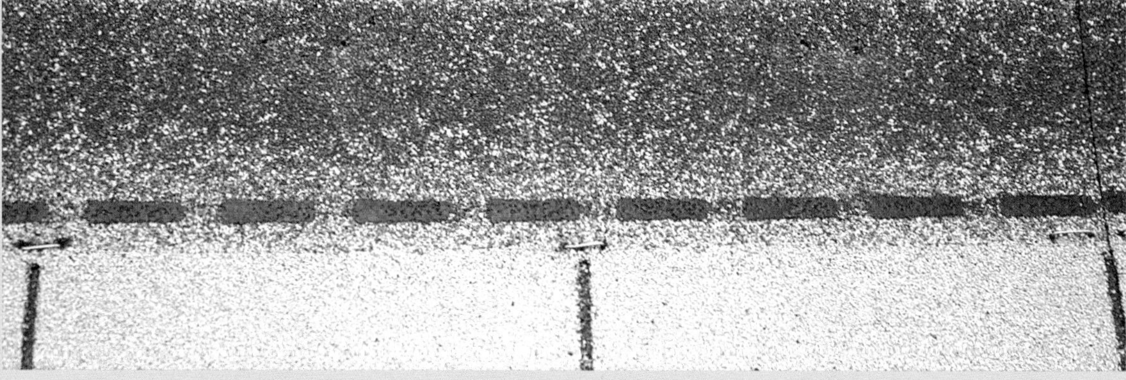

FIX FASTENERS NOT COVERED BY THE SHINGLE ABOVE Even when you are careful, you are bound to drive a few fasteners that aren't covered by the shingle above. You could remove and replace the shingle but that interrupts production. There are two fixes you can use to repair the problem. When you do notice a low fastener, flag it with a piece of shingle or bundle wrapper. After completing the bulk of shingle installation, you can make the repair.

The simplest solution is to dab the fastener head with roof cement. You can sprinkle color granules scraped from waste shingles to blend in the dab.

A better solution is to remove the nail and insert a metal flashing card beneath the hole. Be careful removing the nail so you don't damage the surface of the shingle. Cover both sides of the top end of a 5-in. by 7-in. flashing card with a medium layer of roof cement. Lift the butt edge of the shingle, slip the card beneath the hole, and press the shingle down. The cement will hold the flashing in place and any water that does get in will be directed out. A little cement should ooze through the hole in the surface of the top shingle. Sprinkle some color granules over the cement to hide it.

WORK SAFE ▪ WORK SMART ▪ THINKING AHEAD

Sometimes the edges of shingle bundles are damaged by forklifts or during delivery. Bruised butt edges are unsightly, so check your bundles and try to use up any damaged shingles in the starter course.

Installing Starter Strips

Starter strips are placed under the first full course of shingles along eaves and sometimes rakes. They are ordinary strip shingles with the exposure portion trimmed off, leaving the top lap and self-sealing strip. Normally, you don't want to use full shingles turned upside down because this will put the self-seal strip in the wrong place. The exception is some laminated shingles that have the self-seal strip on the underside of the shingles. With these laminated shingles, you can use full strip shingles as a starter course.

As an alternative to strip shingles, you can buy a specialty starter strip product that comes in a 7-in. roll. The product is granule-coated fiberglass-shingle material with a self-seal strip along one edge.

Starter strips help to weatherproof the eaves. They channel off the roof any water that passes through shingle joints and cutout slots of the first full course of shingles. The self-sealing strip or dots of tar seal down the exposure portion of the first full shingle course. The starter shingles also thicken the bottom edge of the roof and give additional support to the shingles where they extend past the drip edge in the event they are bruised by ladders or tree branches.

Starter strips used along rakes help support the overhanging shingles and provide a crisp, straight line to trim along. The starters also leave a clean appearance when the edge is viewed from beneath rather than the lapping shingles seen along edges without starters. The extra thickness that the starter shingles add along rake edges slightly elevates the ends of the roof shingles. This pitches the shingles back toward the body of the roof slightly so rainwater flowing down the roof is less likely to roll off the rakes. Rake-edge starters aren't required, but the benefits make them worth installing.

WORK SAFE ▪ WORK SMART ▪ THINKING AHEAD

If you are forced to make starters from laminated shingles because you don't have three-tab shingles on hand, save the exposure portions. If you are installing ridge vent, you won't need to lap shingles over the ridge, so you may be able to use the laminated exposures for the last course along the ridge.

Cutting starter shingles

The easiest way to cut starter shingles is right off an inverted bundle of shingles. You can cut starters from laminated shingles, but ordinary three-tab shingles are cheaper and will do the job just as well. Measure 7 in. down from the top edge of the uppermost shingle in the inverted bundle, and make a line across the shingle. Holding either a metal straightedge or the top of another

Starter Strips

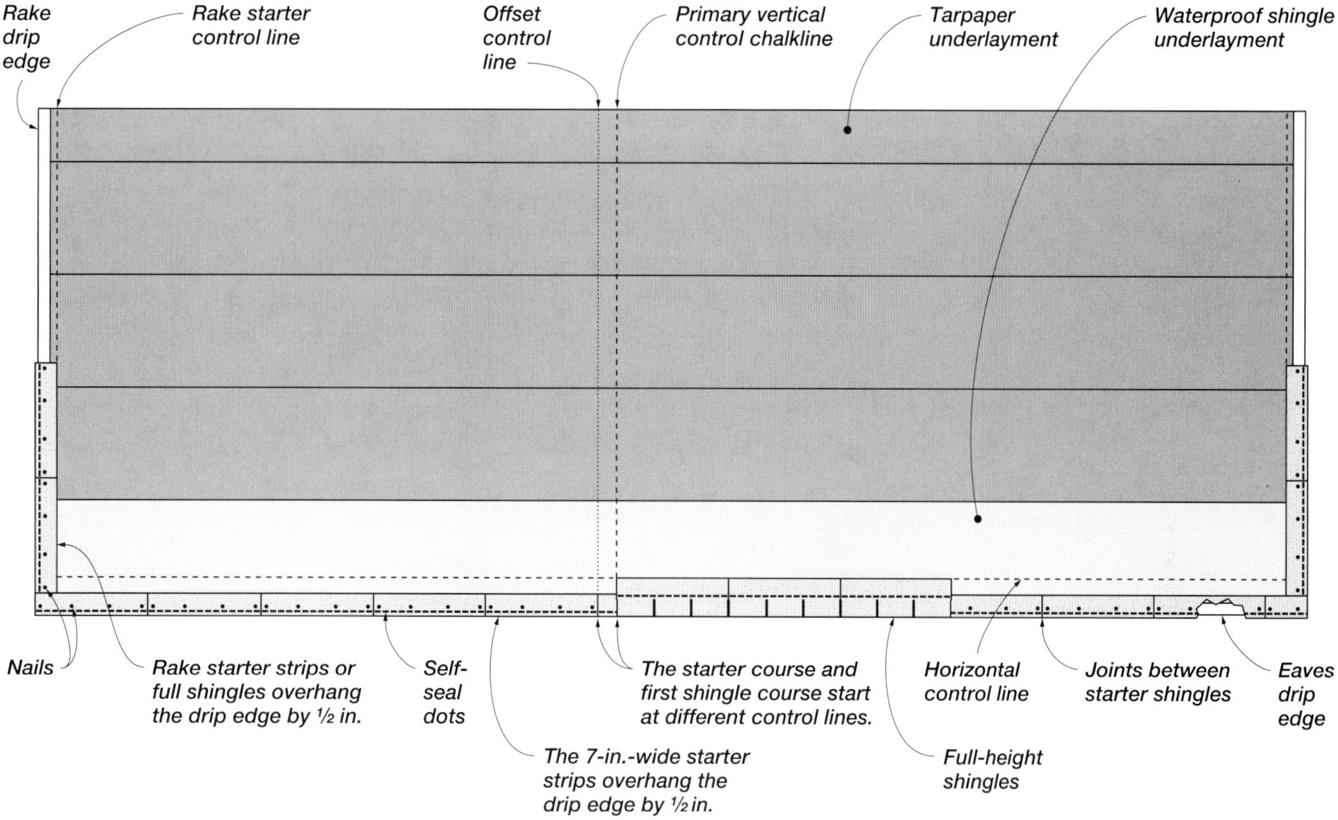

Rake drip edge

Rake starter control line

Offset control line

Primary vertical control chalkline

Tarpaper underlayment

Waterproof shingle underlayment

Nails

Rake starter strips or full shingles overhang the drip edge by ½ in.

Self-seal dots

The starter course and first shingle course start at different control lines.

Horizontal control line

Joints between starter shingles

Eaves drip edge

The 7-in.-wide starter strips overhang the drip edge by ½ in.

Full-height shingles

asphalt shingle along the line to guide your utility knife, draw the knife firmly once along the line and snap off the shingle tabs. Reverse the starter you just cut, and line its cut edge along the top edge of the shingle beneath. Using the top edge of the starter as a measurement guide to run a knife along, cut the rest of the 7-in.-wide starters. Another way to get precise starter strips is to use a 7-in.-wide rip of ½-in. sheathing as a knife guide.

By cutting the shingles from the back and only scribing once with the knife, you won't cut through to the granular surface of the shingle. This will extend the life of the knife blade, and the knife is easier to control on the smooth back of the shingle than on the rougher face.

Cut starter strips by trimming the tabs off roof shingles.

Making a Cutting Table

You can make a simple cutting table that holds half a bundle of shingles and will make cutting faster and more accurate. Simply nail a 1×4 strip of wood to the long bottom edge of a 2-ft. by 4-ft. piece of ⅝-in. or ¾-in. sheathing to serve as a stop. Nail a 2×4 on the bottom near the top edge as a leg so the table will angle downward when set on a flat surface or hook over the ridge when used on the roof. Rest the shingles upside down on the table against the stop and use a 12-in. triangular or framing square to guide square cuts.

A simple cutting table made of scrap plywood or OSB makes cutting shingles to length easy and precise.

Establishing control lines for rake starters

In chapter 6, you learned how to make horizontal control lines for starter shingles along the eaves. That was the first line you snapped, located 7 in. up from the outside edge of the drip edge less the overhang distance.

You can snap a chalkline as a guide to install starter shingles along a rake too. First install (or temporarily tack on) the rake drip edge over the underlayment, then plan out how much overhang you will use along the rake edge. It may not be equal up the rake if you are using the overhang to adjust a crooked or unparallel edge (see p. 102). Holding your tape measure out beyond the drip edge to account for the shingle overhang, measure in 7 in. if you are using trimmed starters or 12 in. if you plan to invert a shingle as a starter. Make marks at the top and bottom of the rake, then snap a chalkline between the marks.

Fastening starter shingles

Align the end of the first eaves starter shingle with one of your vertical control lines (if you are using them). When you install the first full shingle later, you'll alternate to your next vertical control line so the joints will be offset. This ensures that joints from the first shingle course will not fall over joints in the starter course.

Face the cut edge of the starters down over the drip edge, and align the top edge with the control line. This will leave the self-seal strip along the bottom edge so it can bond the underside of the first full shingle course. Fasten starter strips along the eaves with nails or staples just above the self-seal strip (see the top left photo on the facing page). This is the only time you'll install fasteners above the self-seal strip; if you fastened lower you might go through the drip edge but miss the sheathing.

Locate fasteners 1 in. and 12 in. from both ends of the shingle. This corresponds to the top of the tab cutouts on three-tab shingles.

Installing rake starter shingles

Once the eaves starter-shingle row is installed, you can install the rake starters. Rest the end of the first rake starter shingle against the top of the first eaves starter shingle. Align the inside edge of the rake starter with the rake control line, and drive fasteners about 1 in. to 2 in. in

Align the starter shingles to the first horizontal control line and drive fasteners *above* the self-seal strip.

Snap a chalkline from the eaves to the ridge to guide installation of rake starters.

from the rake board. If you're using full-width shingles as starters, drive additional fasteners at the two inside corners to prevent the wind from blowing the starters off before you get a chance to shingle over them. Continue installing starters up the rake edge as far as you have underlayment placed. When you reach the ridge of the roof, lap the last shingle over the ridge rather than ending the shingle at the ridge. This will help the shingles to resist blowoff at the end of the ridge.

Face the self-seal strip toward the edge of the roof and drive nails about 1 in. in from the self-seal strip.

Getting Started Shingling

Installing the first seven to ten courses of shingles along the eaves can be the easiest courses on the roof or they can be the most awkward. It depends on how you approach installation. Working from staging set up at a comfortable height is the easiest position in which to start shingling a roof. But sometimes when a site doesn't permit you to set up staging or if you think you can save time by not setting it up, you might consider working backward up the roof.

Starting from staging

As discussed in chapter 5, set up staging that is appropriate for the job site. Adjust the staging planks to give you a level

Hand-Nailing Shingles

It wasn't that long ago that all asphalt roof shingles were fastened by hand-nailing. Today, pneumatic nailers and staplers predominate, but some roofers still prefer the consistency they get by driving nails by hand. And there are municipalities that prohibit shingles from being pneumatically fastened.

Nailing shingles by hand takes a little getting used to because you need three hands to do three things at once every time you lay down a shingle. You need to place and hold a shingle in position, then hold a nail and drive it in. Since you need one hand to hold the nails and the other to swing the hammer, you're forced to hold the shingle in place some other way.

There are a few techniques you can use to hold the shingle once you line it up with the horizontal control line and butt in against the last shingle. You can use your toe if you're standing or your knee if kneeling. That frees both hands so you can drive the nails in any sequence you like: left to right, right to left, or middle out. But standing or kneeling involves a lot of bending and can lead to backaches, especially if you do it all the time.

Roofers who hand-nail all the time typically find sitting on one hip the most comfortable position, which leaves only your forearm to hold the shingle in place. Using the forearm of the same hand that holds the nails works best. It sets your hand in one of the middle two nail positions to drive your first nail. For someone who usually fastens shingles working in a straight line with a pneumatic nailer, it may seem awkward to start nailing in the middle, but it makes sense. The shingle is more balanced when nailed at one of the middle locations rather than at the end. After the first is set, you can release your forearm and ready another nail for driving without the shingle moving off the horizontal control line.

Holding the nail when hand-nailing is a trick in itself. Carpenters ordinarily hold framing and finish nails between their thumbs and index fingers, but roofing nails are short. If you overdrive a roofing nail on the first whack or miss a little, you'll smash your fingers and keel over in pain. Roofers squeeze the roofing-nail shanks between their index and middle fingers with the heads facing their palm side. This positions the fleshy part of your fingers up and your fingernails down. Your fingers are also thinner in this position, allowing you to drive a nail farther without squishing your fingers. And if you do whack yourself, it doesn't hurt as much.

When hand-nailing, you need to hold the shingle in place and still have both hands free to hold the nail and to swing the hammer. You can hold the shingle with your foot as shown at right or you can use your forearm as shown above.

A nail stripper holds a pound of nails and sorts them into slots at the base with a quick shake.

This hand position works great if you use a nail stripper (see p. 38). You just slide your fingers around a row of nail shanks dropping out of the bottom of the nail stripper and draw the heads out the side "door." Grab four nails at a time and you're ready to fasten a shingle without reloading.

With practice, you should be able to drive nails with two hammer blows. The first is a light tap to punch the nail through the shingle and maybe slightly into the roof sheathing so it stands upright on its own. The second blow, after you move your hand out of the way, drives the nail home flush with the surface of the shingle.

work platform that places the eaves edge at about waist height. This will let you comfortably install shingles to about 3 ft. to 4 ft. up the roof. The nice thing about working off staging is you don't have to bend over or sit and slide to install shingles. Enjoy working off the staging because it won't last for long.

Load the staging planks with a few bundles of shingles, and, if you are using the pyramid pattern, load some precut starter-kit shingles (see p. 159). Also, load up a box with the hand tools and fasteners you'll need, and set up air hoses for pneumatic tools. This will save you time hopping up and down to gather equipment and materials so you can focus on shingling.

Align the end of the first shingle with the primary vertical control chalkline, then fasten it down. Apply four or five shingles on top of one another matched to the horizontal control lines. Alternate aligning the shingles to the control lines for the racking pattern, or step the shingles back to meet the pyramid-pattern control lines (see "Shingling Up the Roof"

Start installing shingles by aligning them to vertical control lines, then grow the column (or pyramid) up toward the ridge. After several shingles are installed to the vertical lines, you can apply horizontal courses of shingles in groups of four or five by working off the staging until you hit the limit of your reach.

Installing Shingles Using a Pneumatic Nailer

Heeding the warnings in "Pneumatic Tools Cautions" on p. 145, you can accurately fasten roof shingles using nailers or staplers. You just have to practice how to position and fire the tool.

I've found the easiest way to position and fasten a shingle is to hold the shingle in the center of the top edge or bottom edge with my free hand and slide it in position. Then I place the nose of the nailer at one of the end-fastener positions and squeeze the trigger. I don't bounce-fire this first nail because the shingle can slip during the instant the nose of the tool hits it and before the nail drives home. With one end fastened, I slide my hand along the edge of the shingle to the loose end and adjust the height if necessary, then I bounce-fire the remaining nails in a straight line.

Accuracy comes with practice. Don't expect to be able to bounce-fire a roof nailer and hit that ⅜-in.-high target right away. Start by using the place-and-shoot technique to drive every nail until you have a feel for the tool. When you do try bounce-firing, make sure your arm moves in a straight line and avoid forming an arc. Keep the nailer perpendicular to the surface of the shingle. This straight and perpendicular action will feel awkward at first but will become natural after shingling several roofs.

When using a pneumatic nailer, hold the shingle in the center from either the bottom or top. Align the shingle and drive a nail at one end, then move your hand to the loose end of the shingle and bounce the nailer to drive fasteners at the two middle positions. Move your hand out of the way and drive the last fastener.

Don't forget to visually check every nail to make sure it's set flush with the surface of the shingle and is not crooked. Drive any underdriven nails with your hammer.

On roof pitches less than 6, you can save time by working backward to install the first several courses.

on the facing page). This sets up a series of shingle courses to run out horizontally.

Install the shingles along the four or five courses to the left and right until you reach the rake edge, wall, or hip, then return to the vertical control lines and apply four or five more shingles, running the courses out horizontally. Continue installing shingles as far as you can comfortably reach up the roof.

Starting backward from atop the roof

Shingling backward while standing on the roof is an option to consider under certain circumstances. Rather than setting up staging, you can stand on the roof and face the eaves edge. Then holding the top of the shingles, align them to the control lines and fasten (see the bottom photo on the facing page). After installing about six or seven horizontal shingle courses, you can turn around and, standing on the shingles you installed, work the rest of the way up the roof. Of course, leaning downhill looking at a 10-ft. to 30-ft. drop doesn't give you the safest feeling.

Working backward can only be done on roofs with pitches less than 6; steeper roofs require staging. Although working backward is awkward and slower than shingling from staging, it will save you the time of setting up and taking down equipment. I find it practical on short eaves and along eaves where it's difficult to set up staging.

Shingling Up the Roof

In chapter 6, I described the two shingling patterns (racking and pyramid) and how to lay out control chalklines for the shingles to follow. This section presumes you've already snapped vertical control lines (if you need them) and horizontal control lines. Following either the racking pattern or the pyramid pattern, there are several installation techniques you can use to work the shingle courses up the roof. The one you choose is just a matter of personal preference.

Try several of the techniques to see which suits your roofing style and production speed. You'll probably use different techniques at different times depending on the size of your crew and the roof you're working on. I'll focus here on the general shingle-application techniques that you'll use to cover a bulk of the roof area. In the next chapter, you'll see how to handle the details like rake edges, valleys, and obstacles.

Racking pattern

The racking pattern is typically used to install three-tab shingles. You can easily maintain the minimum offset between shingles in successive courses and keep the cutout slots lined up accurately. Many laminated shingle instructions

Gauge Notches

Some manufacturers of three-tab shingles stamp small cuts or notches in the top and side edges of shingles to use as gauges for horizontal exposure and vertical offset. The horizontal-exposure alignment notches are set so you can match the 5-in. exposure for each shingle as you place it. The vertical-offset notches are generally set at 6-in. increments for referencing successive courses so the cutout slots will alternate up the roof.

I don't recommend relying on these gauge notches for aligning shingles. To keep the shingles precisely aligned using them, you have to be extremely consistent. Because each shingle is referenced to the one beneath or to the side of it, one wrong placement will cause a shift in the next shingle above or to the side. Each subsequent error, however small, accumulates until you have a noticeable problem. Also, the notches themselves can be incorrectly placed on the shingles. The layout sequence for establishing vertical and horizontal control lines described in chapter 6 offers the most accurate method for aligning shingles for a precise installation.

Some shingles come with small gauge notches cut into the top edge. These notches can be used to align 6-in. offsets between courses but aren't as accurate as vertical control chalklines.

recommend *against* using this technique though, so read instructions carefully.

There are a couple of ways to work off the vertical control lines when installing shingles and then run courses out along the horizontal lines. One way is to run a column of shingles straight up the roof from eaves to ridge and then install courses horizontally or vertically from that first column. The other way is just to work up the vertical control lines a couple of shingle courses at a time, running out courses horizontally as you go.

As you will see, the manner you choose will depend on how much underlayment you want to install at once and the pitch of the roof.

INSTALL THE CONTROL COLUMN FIRST I prefer to install a control column from eaves to ridge along the vertical chalklines as a starting point for shingle courses. I concentrate on precisely orienting the side edge of each shingle with the vertical control lines.

Control Column with Skipped Fasteners

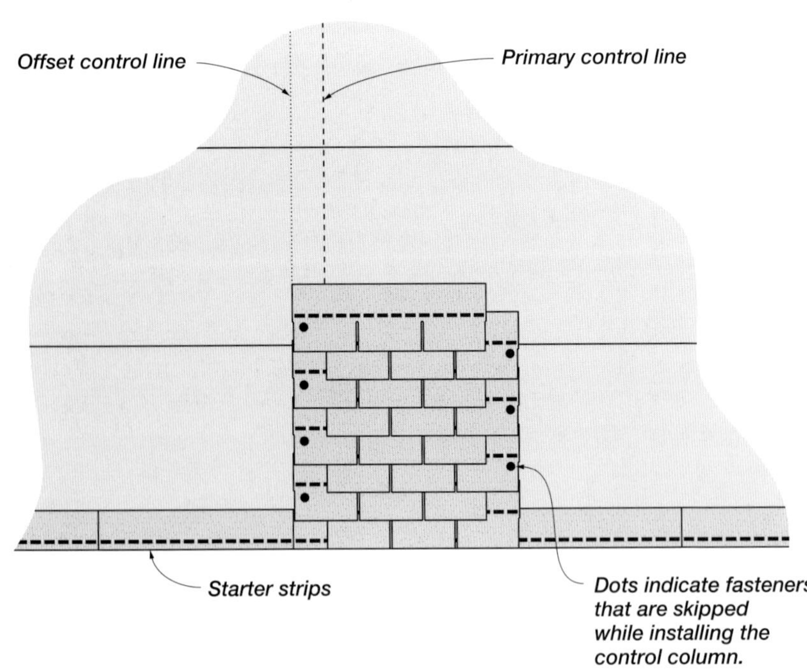

With this first set of shingles positioned accurately, I can focus on installing shingles. The cutout slots on the rest of the roof will line up automatically.

You can either install the whole column from eaves to ridge before running out horizontal courses left and right, or you can install the column in sections of 5 to 15 shingles. On roof pitches of 8 or less, it's easy to walk up and down without roof staging, so you can do it either way. For roof pitches greater than 8, you'll be better off installing the shingle column in stages.

To run a whole column of shingles from eaves to ridge up the vertical control lines, you need to install two sheets of underlayment vertically from eaves to ridge, or you need to tarpaper the entire roof plane. This provides a place to snap the vertical control lines.

If installing underlayment on the whole roof or running two vertical sheets is a problem, snap vertical control lines on the sheathing. Then, as you work your way up the roof, snap control lines onto tarpaper as you roll it out using the lines on the sheathing and the tarpaper below as a guide.

Begin by installing the eaves starter course along the entire length of the building. Align the shingles to the vertical control line that will offset the joint from the starter-course joints.

Now work your way up the column, alternating vertical control lines with each course. In each course, don't install the end fastener on the side of the shingle that extends past the shingle beneath. You'll install the missing fasteners later when you lift these shingles to slip in a shingle below.

If you have a long reach, you can install two shingles in each column course the first time up the control lines. If you have to step left and right all the time, it's not worth it.

Modified Pyramid

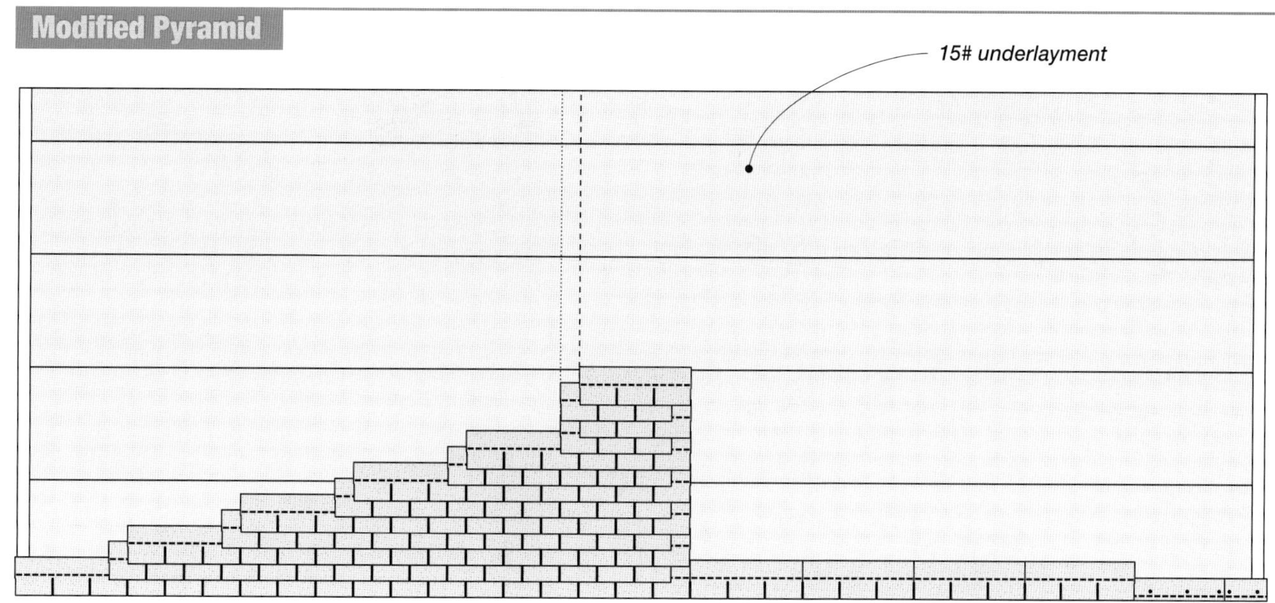

A modified pyramid of full shingles applied in pairs against a racking column avoids the lift-and-slip-beneath operation ordinarily needed when shingling up along side columns.

With the control column or part of the control column installed, you can continue shingling horizontally in groups of courses or you can continue vertically in columns. It's purely a matter of preference, and you may find certain roofs lend themselves to one method or the other.

RUNNING OUT COURSES HORIZONTALLY I favor installing the shingles horizontally following the horizontal control lines in groups of four to six courses from the control column; it feels more comfortable than working vertically. You can do this in two ways. The first way is to install all four or six shingles one atop the next then move sideways to the next set, sort of like mini columns. The drawback to this system is you'll have to lift the unfastened end of every other installed shingle in order to slip the end of the next one beneath.

The illustration above shows a way to avoid skipping shingle fasteners and lifting shingles. To do this, you create a modified pyramid by working two courses of shingles across the roof at one time. In each pair of courses, the shingle-offset overlap is stepped back to avoid lifting shingles.

In a stepped pyramid, you apply shingles in pairs against the primary shingle column.

Starting with the first two courses, fasten two shingles in each row. Move back to the vertical control column, and install one shingle each for the next two horizontal courses. Then go back to the lower pair of courses, and install two

In the racking pattern, every other shingle has to be slipped beneath the loose end of the shingle above it, as shown at left above. Drive a nail 1 ft. in from the opposite end of the shingle, as shown at right above, then the rest of the nails toward the column. Finally, fasten the loose end of the shingle in the course above, as shown at left.

shingles along the horizontal course line, one for each course. Step back to the second pair of courses and install two shingles, then return once again to the vertical control column to install shingles on the next pair of horizontal courses. This sets up a pyramid of six horizontal courses.

Continue installing shingles along the horizontal control lines, working up the pyramid until you reach the end of the roof plane. Although it may seem awkward at first to work in a diagonal fashion with 30-in. offsets, it can be more productive than lifting the end of every other shingle.

You could, of course, install a single course of shingles and work your way laterally. You'll avoid lifting and lapping the ends of the shingles, but it takes a lot of walking and may not be time efficient.

RUNNING OUT COURSES VERTICALLY

On lower-pitch roofs that don't require roof staging, you can install the shingles from eaves to ridge just as you installed the initial control column. To do this, you'll have to lift the loose end of every other shingle to slip in the shingle below. Drive a fastener at the end of the new shingle while you still have the end of the shingle above lifted, then install the rest of the fasteners. Drive the fastener in the loose end of the shingle above before moving on (see the photos above).

You'll develop your own system for lifting the loose shingle end, driving fasteners into the new shingle, and fasten-

Gauging Courses

You may have chosen not to snap horizontal control lines to follow or may have only snapped chalklines for every fourth or fifth shingle course. To keep the shingles in neat straight rows, you have to gauge the intermediate courses between control lines. There are four different ways to do this depending on the equipment you have at hand.

- Cutout slots. You can judge the exposure by eye by referencing the top of the cutout slots in three-tab shingles. This is pretty effective but won't work for random-pattern shingles.
- Hatchet gauge. If you like using a hatchet to drive nails by hand, you can set the gauge pin into the blade and gauge the forward end of every shingle. The aft end merely needs to be matched to the previous shingle.
- Stapler or nailer gauge. Most roofing staplers and some nailers have adjustable spacing-gauge stops on the base of the tool. You can preset the exposure for 5 in. or another measurement. The stop registers to the butt edge of the previous shingle course, and the nose of the tool sets the butt of the one you are applying. It takes a little while to get used to the routine of gauging the forward end of the shingle and then lifting up the tool to drive a fastener. Like the hatchet-gauge system, match the aft of the shingle to the previous one you applied.
- Shingle notches. The last and least reliable way to gauge the shingle courses is to use the notches stamped into the ends of the shingle if they are present. As I noted in the sidebar on gauge notches (see p. 153), this is an unreliable and time-consuming process, and most shingle manufacturers don't stamp the notches anyway.

If you don't snap any horizontal-course chalklines, you can really only use a gauging method for five courses before the shingles will begin to drift up or down. Because each method relies on the precise gauging and application of the previous course, any slightly misaligned shingle will throw off the shingles above it, and the problem will get worse as you progress to additional courses.

After every fourth or fifth free-gauged course, you should snap a horizontal-adjustment chalkline. Snap the line across the face of the last row of shingles at the proper exposure distance (typically 5 in. up). Align the butt edges of the shingles in the next course to the chalkline. You may have to actually drop the line a bit narrower than the standard course exposure if some of the shingles in the previous course were gauged too low; otherwise some nail heads may be left exposed.

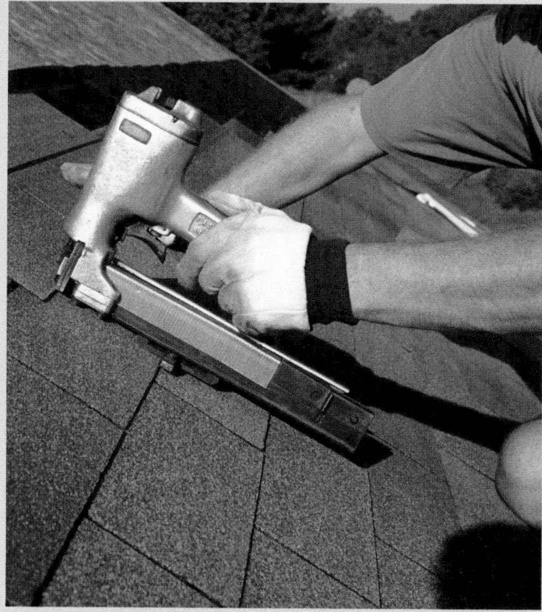

Roofing staplers and some nailers have gauge stops on their bases that you can use to set the height of shingle courses.

ing the shingle end. Some roofers don't actually lift the loose end of the shingle; rather, they pop the end up with the new shingle and slide it beneath. Others give the loose end a flick with their finger, just enough to slip the new shingle under.

You can also vary the fastener sequence. After you slide the end beneath the shingle above, you can fasten the opposite end and work your way toward the control column or start fastening at one of the middle positions. The important thing is to lift the end of

If your reach is long, you can avoid slipping some shingles under others in the racking pattern by installing a double column of shingles.

Apply full shingles up the diagonal pyramid until the rake edge is reached, then align another starter kit of shingles to the vertical control lines. The process will begin again from the bottom of the pyramid.

the shingle above and drive the last fastener, then fasten the end of the shingle you lifted. Your sequence will also depend on whether you hand-nail or use pneumatic tools.

Be careful lifting the shingle in cold weather when shingles aren't flexible. If you find shingles cracking when you lift them, switch to a different installation method such as the pyramid (described below) or modified pyramid (described on p. 155).

Installing the shingle in the next course doesn't require the lifting step; simply butt the end of the new shingle to the end of the column shingle that you just fastened and drive three fasteners. Remember to skip the last fastener at the end where it extends beyond the shingle in the course beneath.

If you have a long reach, you can build columns that are two shingles across instead of one. Since you only have to lift shingles to weave columns together, this will save you time because you'll have half as many shingles to lift (see the photo at left above). As you apply each shingle butted against the previous column, just move one more shingle to the side and apply it also. This brings two columns of full shingles up the roof rather than one.

Pyramid pattern for three-tab shingles

You'll probably find that shingling a roof using the pyramid pattern is faster and easier than the racking pattern in most instances. You don't have to lift the loose end of every other shingle to slip a new one beneath. There are a couple of installation techniques you can use.

As I discussed in chapter 6, the main drawback to using the pyramid pattern with three-tab shingles is cutout-slot control. Although the pyramid pattern

Cutting Pyramid Starter Kits

Before you can start installing shingles along a rake using the pyramid pattern, you must cut a series of shingles to length that will form this pattern's diagonal steps. I call these groups of shingles starter kits. You need to cut starter kits whether or not you are using vertical control lines when you are starting along a rake edge. There are slight differences when cutting the kits for three-tab shingle roofs using vertical control lines and for random-shingle roofs without control lines.

For a three-tab shingle starter kit, begin with a full uncut shingle, then trim a shingle 6 in. or 4 in. shorter (depending on the offset you are using) for each successive horizontal course up the roof. Trim off from the end of the shingle that will hang over the rake, and leave uncut the factory end that will butt the control line. Therefore, for a starter kit along the left rake edge, you would trim from the left edge of the shingles. For 6-in. offsets, you would start with a full shingle, then cut one each at 30 in., 24 in., 18 in., and 12 in. I recommend skipping the last piece in the sequence that would be 6 in. long; this is too narrow to use along a rake and would be prone to blowing off.

If you shifted the control lines following the steps in chapter 6 to eliminate narrow shingle tabs at the opposite rake edge, then the control lines may not start you off with a full 3-ft. shingle. In this case, trim the first shingle to length, matching the distance from the rake edge (plus the overhang) to the control line. Cut the rest of the shingles in the starter kit with offsets reduced from the first shingle. For instance, if the first shingle needs to be trimmed to 35 in., then the next shingle will be 29 in. for a 6-in. offset.

Since you're only using one piece of each shingle you cut, you're creating a lot of waste. Save the cutoff pieces; you may be able to use them at the opposite side of the roof to cut in a rake edge, valley, or hip.

Cutting starter kits when you don't need vertical control lines, as with random-cutout or laminated-style shingles, is easier. You can pick the offset between horizontal shingle courses that you want and keep it equal or vary it. Check the manufacturer's instructions because they may recommend lengths for starter shingles to randomize their particular model of shingle.

With this in mind, trim shingles to create a starter kit with successively shorter shingles by 6 in. to 9 in. You can reduce the offset down to 4 in., but such a narrow offset may be obvious and unsightly on the finished roof. You can cut random-style shingle starters from both ends of a shingle to yield two pieces for the starter kit. For a random kit, I usually cut two shingles to form a five-piece kit with a full shingle as the first one. One shingle is cut at 7 in. and 29 in. and the other is cut at 14 in. and 22 in. This sequence results in generous 7-in. and 8-in. offsets.

You can also use scrap shingles left over from trimming courses into other rake edges, walls, hips, or valleys. Sort the pieces to form kits with reasonable offsets or trim them to fit the offset you'd like. You may have to incorporate additional shingles trimmed from full shingles into these freeform kits, but it's a good way to use up shingle material that may otherwise end up as waste.

Whether you're following pyramid control lines or not, you'll need more than one starter kit to keep reforming the pyramid along the rake edge as you work your way up the roof. Cut several kits before you start shingling. Use the shingles you trim off the opposite rake edge to make additional starter kits as you get further along.

To start a pyramid, precut a series of shingles that get progressively shorter by the offset dimension. After cutting several shingles of each size, group the shingles into kits so they're ready to use (top of photo).

is the preferred method for installing random-style laminated shingles, it isn't as precise for controlling the slots in three-tab shingles.

If you are using three-tab shingles, review the control-line layout instructions in chapter 6 and follow the steps below.

1. **Establish control lines.** If you are using three-tab shingles, snap a primary control chalkline just inside of a rake edge for the end of a 3-ft. shingle and additional offset control lines for the 6-in. or 4-in. course offsets. (I'll describe the procedure for 5-in. offsets in the section on pyramids without control lines).
2. **Install the first starter kit.** Install the longest shingle in your starter kit

Starting a Pyramid

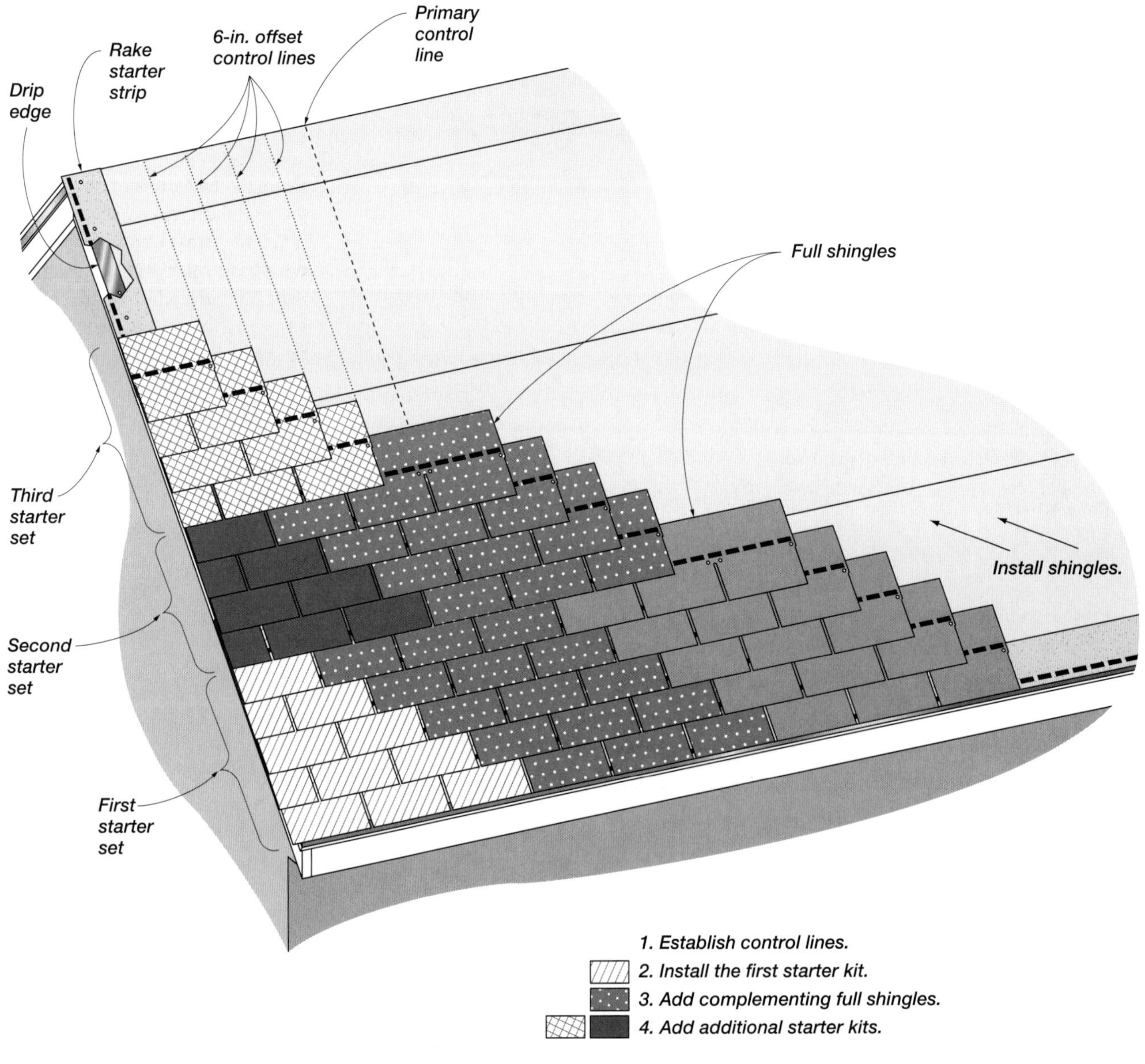

with the top edge aligned to a horizontal control line and the factory edge flush to the vertical control line. For the first kit in a 6-in. offset pattern, this will be a full shingle. Then install the next-longest shingle in the kit to its vertical and horizontal control lines and so on until you've exhausted your first set of starter shingles. As you are fastening each shingle along the rake edge, remember that about ¾ in. to 1½ in. of the shingle extends beyond the inside edge of the rake board. Hold back the end fastener at least ¾ in. inside the edge of the rake board to prevent it from breaking through the surface of the trim.

3. **Add full shingles.** When you reach the top of the first starter kit, install a full shingle against the end of each starter shingle.
4. **Add additional starter kits.** Return back to the eaves and apply the longest shingle in your next starter kit against the appropriate control line. In the case of a 6-in. offset pattern, this shingle will be 30 in. long. When you finish the second kit, add the full shingles against them and continue up the roof. You can see in the illustration on the facing page how the pyramid develops and extends diagonally across the roof as you continue installing shingles.

There are a couple of systems you can use to continue installing the shingles across the roof plane. See "Running out the pyramid" on p. 165 for a description of each.

Starting pyramids for random-style shingles

You don't need vertical control lines when you install random-cutout or laminated shingles. Also, variations in the trim length of the starter shingles won't affect the appearance of the roof. This is where the pyramid pattern for installing shingles excels. Cut several shingle starter kits and start along the eaves with a full shingle. Align the end of the shingle flush to the rake starter strip or extend it ½ in. beyond the rake edge if you aren't using a starter strip along the rake. Once you fasten the first shingle, align the edge of the next shingle in the kit with the rake starter strip, fasten, and continue up the rake with the rest of the starter shingle kit.

Random-style shingles, such as these laminated ones, make it easy to start and follow a pyramid-application sequence. Note how the shingle offsets vary an inch or two between courses; since there are no cutout slots to keep lined up between courses, equal offsets aren't necessary. (Photo by Andy Engel, courtesy *Fine Homebuilding* magazine, © The Taunton Press.)

Establishing pyramids without rake edges

Sometimes you have to establish a pyramid without the aid of a rake edge to follow. This occurs most often on roofs with hips and valleys. First, I'll look at pyramids for random-cutout or laminated shingles, then I'll describe how to work from control lines in the middle of the roof for tabbed shingles.

You'll learn more about shingling valleys and hips in chapter 8, but here's what

Using a 5-In. Shingle Offset

You may think that 5 in. is an odd measurement for shingle offset, but this pattern has an advantage. The odd number offset establishes a pattern that appears random by only repeating every twelfth shingle course. Since a viewer's eye probably won't pick up any deviation with such a distance between repeating slots, there's no need to follow control lines. Just following a rake edge will keep the slots lined up close enough.

Begin by cutting a starter kit with each shingle 5 in. shorter than the previous one. Since standard shingles are 36 in. long, there will be one course that will end up with a 6-in. offset unless you actually trim back the shingles in 5⁹⁄₆₄-in. increments. There's no trouble if you just use 5 in. because your eye won't pick up the discrepancy between the courses. Remember to stop when you trim a 10-in. starter shingle; a 5-in. starter is too narrow.

Install the pyramid of starter shingles in the same fashion as you would random-cutout or laminated shingles, following the rake edge as a guide. Continue adding full shingles as you typically would working up a pyramid.

To install random-pattern shingles out of a valley using the pyramid pattern, step the shingles back 6 in. to 8 in. (Photo by Andy Engel, courtesy *Fine Homebuilding* magazine, © The Taunton Press.)

you need to keep in mind for now: The offset pattern never continues through the change in roof plane. You'll follow the horizontal control lines on one plane and let the ends of courses fall into the valley or over the hip to be cut off later or in the case of some valleys to be woven with shingles from the other roof plane.

RANDOM-CUTOUT OR LAMINATED SHINGLES Since you don't need to follow vertical control lines for random-cutout or laminated shingles, you don't need to cut starter kits. Instead you can just offset full shingles about 6 in. to 8 in. coming out of one side of the hip or valley. The illustration on the facing page shows a 6-in. offset being established on the left roof plane.

If you will be making an open valley or are shingling the second plane of a closed-cut valley, you'll cut off the shingles before they pass through the valley crease, so place the first shingle in your pyramid with one end just touching the crease. Then add shingles on top, stepping each one 6 in. to 8 in. further into the valley. When you get to the point where most of a shingle is on the other side of the crease, stop building the pyramid, go back to the eaves, and add a shingle in each horizontal course. Then you can go back to the top and build the pyramid again with a shingle just touching the crease.

The only difference for the first plane of a closed-cut valley and for a woven valley is that you have to let at least one-third of the shingles run through the valley as shown in the illustration on the facing page. This means that the starting shingle in each stage of the pyramid must be placed with 1 ft. of its length crossing the crease.

With hips, all of the shingles on the first plane will be folded over the hip and cut off 4 in. from the hip, then the shingles on the second plane will be cut off

Shingling out of a Valley Using a Pyramid Type of System with Laminated or Random-Cut Shingles

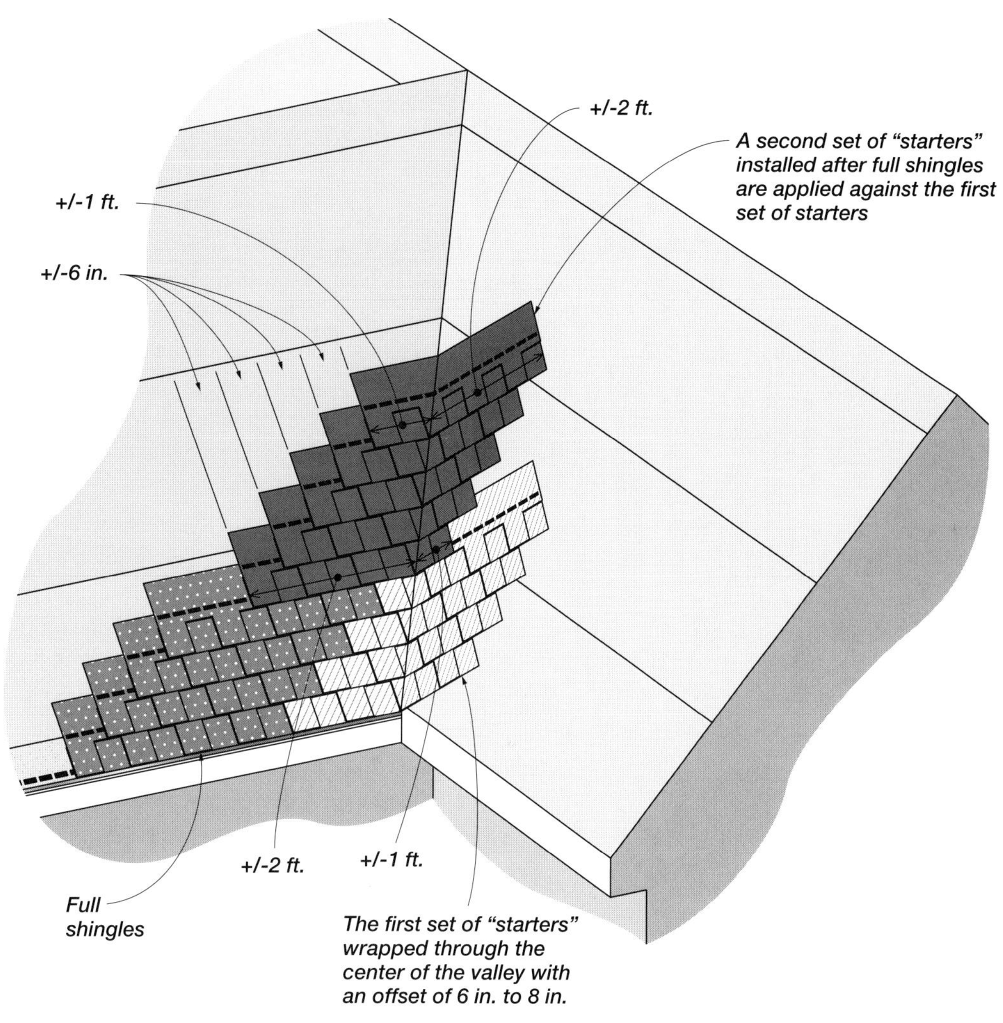

right at the hip line. Hips present a problem because the diagonal direction is opposite to the pyramid you're creating (see the illustration on p. 164). To overcome this, you must start with a wide base of shingles along the eaves edge. Install two or three full shingles along the eaves edge, starting the first one with its end overlapping the hip by about 4 in. Continue building the pyramid, stepping each course 6 in. to 8 in. further into the hip as shown. Stop building the pyramid when two-thirds of a shingle overlap the hip. Go back down to the eaves and add a shingle or two to each course. When you reach the top, start another pyramid with the first shingle overlapping the hip 4 in.

Whether you are doing a hip or a valley, you can run the courses diagonally up the pyramid or horizontally across the roof (see "Running out the pyramid" on p. 165). As the courses reach the hip, valley, or rake at the opposite end of the roof, consider trimming the portion of the shingles overhanging the hip you started the pyramid along to use as end fillers.

THREE-TAB SHINGLES You'll need vertical control lines to install tabbed shingles in a pyramid in situations such as a hip roof where you don't have a rake to follow. Following the instructions on p. 132, establish a primary control line in the middle of the roof and snap an offset control line at 18 in. (for 6-in. cutout slots), 15 in. (for 5-in. cutout slots), or 16 in. (for 4-in. cutout slots). Starting at the eaves, install two shingles butted at the primary control line, then center a single shingle in the next course atop the first pair and line it up to the second control line. This forms the beginning of a pyramid.

Working from one side and then the other, add shingles to each course. Cap off the top with a single shingle, registering its end precisely to one of the control lines. The pyramid will form inward with low-angle sides because of the wide offsets, but that's okay. The installation process will still be the same.

Once you have a short pyramid started in the middle of a roof plane, two workers can each tackle one side of the pyramid and grow it up and out at the same time.

Pyramid vs. Hip Direction

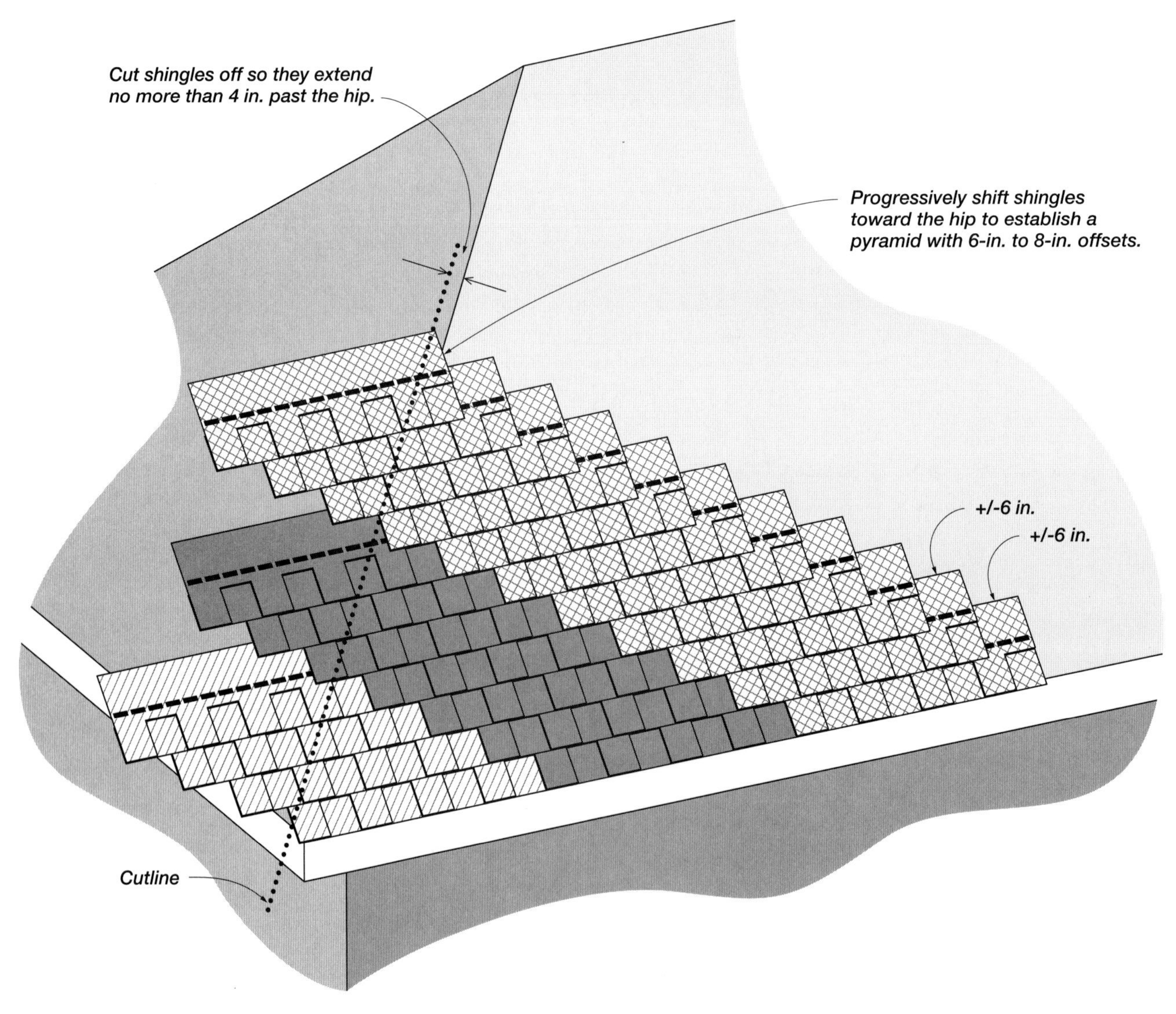

Running out the pyramid

Just as you could use a couple of methods to install shingles using the racking pattern, you have a couple of choices with the pyramid pattern too. Try variations to see what works best for you.

You can continue installing shingles diagonally up the stepped pyramid as it forms up a rake, hip, or valley. Each time you reach the top, install another series of starter shingles and return back to the eaves to start with a diagonal run of full shingles. When you reach the ridge, you'll no longer be installing starter kits and can focus on installing full shingles up the pyramid until you reach the opposite rake edge, valley, hip, or wall.

Many roofers install shingles in this diagonal pattern, walking up the roof as they go, sort of like working a racking column up vertically. But of course, there's no need to lift the ends of shingles; just place the shingle, fasten, and go.

If the roof pitch is steep enough to require staging or you prefer to work laterally, you can run shingle courses out along the horizontal control lines rather than diagonally up the pyramid. Work four to ten courses across so that with each sideways step you can install a whole series of shingles up the abbreviated pyramid. Once you've run the horizontal courses all the way to the opposite side of the roof plane, return to the primary edge to install another starter kit and run that group of shingles across the roof. You can install additional levels of roof staging as you work shingle courses up the roof (see the photo on p.166).

If you have a long reach, you can speed production by installing double shingles, much as I described in racking shingles. Starting at the eaves edge, install the first starter shingle in a kit

Pyramids with 18-in. offsets are easy to start in the middle of a roof. The layout process only requires two vertical control lines.

You can work both sides of a pyramid started in the middle of a roof.

to the rake edge (or control lines), then immediately place and fasten a full shingle to the side of it. Continue installing starters in tandem with complementary full shingles until you reach the end of the first starter kit. Rather than moving back down to the eaves, install the longest starter in your next kit (30 in. for a 6-in. offset pattern. Continue installing starters, but don't install complementary full shingles because in this case shingles would have to be installed under them. This technique doubles your upward diagonal motion without breaking your pace (see the illustration on the facing page).

Adjusting courses

As you shingle your way up the roof and reach a course about 3 ft. from the ridge, take a moment to check how parallel the horizontal courses are to the ridge. You can slightly adjust successive horizontal control lines near the ridge to make up for discrepancies in parallelism so that the last course is parallel and doesn't appear to get narrower along the ridge.

You may already have measured, made adjustments, and marked off horizontal control lines to accommodate an out-of-parallel ridge. If not, do so now. Measure the distance between the ridge and the top of the last shingle course you've installed at several points along the length. If the distance varies by more than ½ in. from one end of the ridge to the other, consider making adjustments.

Since you shouldn't expose more of the shingle than the manufacturer instructs (5 in. generally), you'll have to reduce the exposure width at one end. At the end of the ridge that measures the shortest distance, reduce successive horizontal control lines by ⅛ in. to 4⅞ in. each until the lines are parallel (see the photo on the facing page). Continue marking the layout for equal exposures, all the while keeping the exposure at the wide end of the roof consistently at 5 in.

Aligning the top courses

When you reach the ridge, you will run out of horizontal control lines to which to match the top of the shingles, but you

You can use the pyramid method even on steep roof pitches that require staging.

will still need one or two courses of shingles to finish the roof. The easiest way to keep these final courses straight is to snap chalklines on the face of the shingles beneath. Measure 5 in. up from the butt edge at each end of the last installed course of shingles, and snap a chalkline between the marks with blue or white chalk. These colors will wash off during the next rain but red, orange, and yellow chalk may remain visible for a long time.

Match the bottom of the shingles to the line and fasten them in place. If you'll be installing a ridge vent, you can precut the shingle height for these last courses so the top lap doesn't cover the vent slot or you can use a hook-blade knife to trim the overhang later. When no ridge vent is planned, just overlap the shingles over the ridge.

When you get within 3 ft. of the ridge, check to see how parallel the last horizontal shingle course is to the ridge. You can make adjustments to the last few courses.

Installing Double Shingles Using the Pyramid Pattern

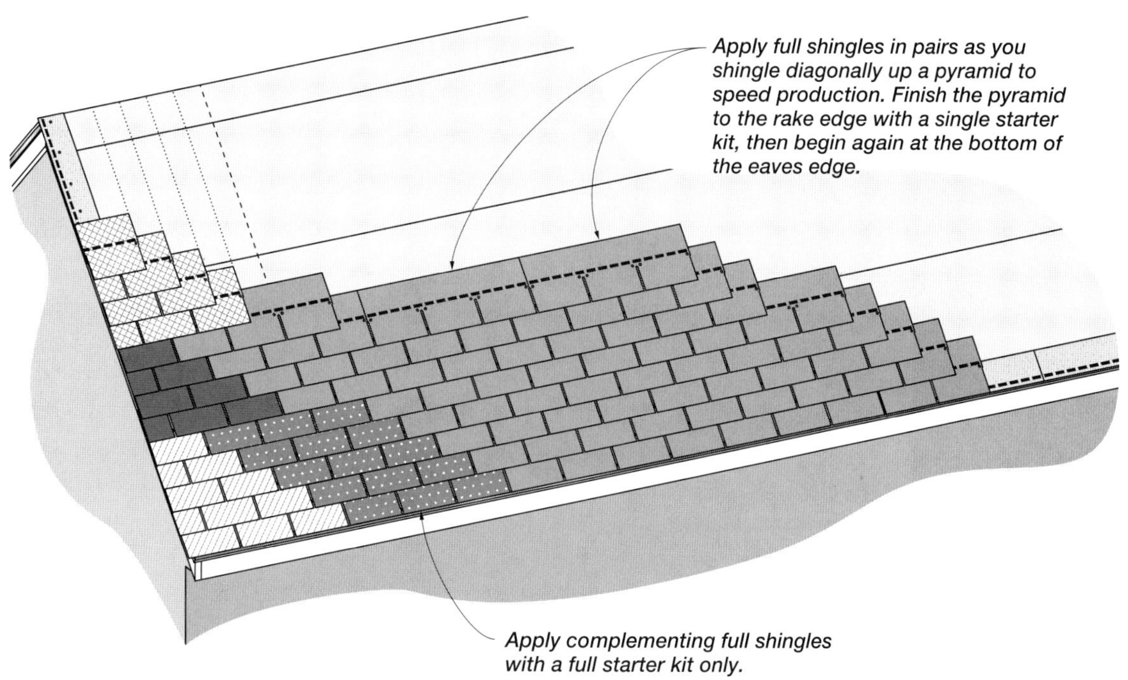

Setting Up Supplies

You're in constant need of a ready supply of fresh shingles as you move along installing shingles. It's important to have shingles close at hand to minimize wasted motion. You can set up your shingle supply several different ways depending on whether you're working from staging or on a low-slope roof pitch you can walk on easily.

Working Off Roof Staging

- Have open bundles stacked on the staging planks spaced 6 ft. to 8 ft. apart within quick reach.
- Drive 12d or 16d common nails into the roof about 5 ft. above the staging plank. Space the nails about 6 ft. to 8 ft. apart, and make sure they go through the sheathing into the roof framing about 1 in. Rest a stack of shingles above each nail. The nails keep the shingles from sliding down the roof so you can easily peel off the shingles as needed. This saves you the trouble of bending to pick shingles off the staging planks.

Walking Up the Roof

- Use the same technique of driving nails to hold stacks of shingles if you are running out shingles horizontally.
- Drive nails and stack shingles along a diagonal line above a pyramid so you can run up shingles diagonally.
- Tuck precounted shingles beneath the top of every third or fourth step up a pyramid. Draw the shingles out and install them on the courses below the tuck point.
- Rest a small stack of shingles on the tops of your feet and shuffle as you roof your way up a column or pyramid (see the bottom photo at right). Draw the shingles off your stack and resupply from bundles supported by nails on the roof.
- Rest a small stack of shingles on your thigh if you like to sit while roofing.

Two-Person Installation

This is not my favorite method of installing shingles, but I see roofers using the technique from time to time. Rather than one roofer holding and fastening his own shingles, you can have two workers split the task. One worker, typically a laborer, holds a stack of shingles and places each one in position, butt against the previous shingle to the side and aligned to the horizontal control line along the top. The skilled worker wields a pneumatic tool or swings a hammer to fasten each shingle.

The only way this system makes sense is if the laborer releases the shingle after the person fastening drives the first nail and has another shingle placed and ready by the time the first shingle is nailed off; otherwise someone is left waiting. Even with two fast workers, the two-person team seems a little unproductive to me, but if you find it works for you, by all means use it. The one advantage is that the laborer can quickly break away from his shingle-placement duties to resupply with shingles without the other worker breaking pace fastening.

To keep shingles within easy reach, drive spikes into the roof above your working level to hold half-bundles.

On roof pitches that don't require staging, you can carry half a bundle on your foot.

Working from Roof Staging

Most roofers feel comfortable working on roof pitches of less than 8 without roof staging. You may still be able to walk on roof pitches up to 12, but your footing isn't as sure; you move more cautiously and your productivity diminishes. Roof staging takes time to set up and dismantle, but it's time well spent for safety and production.

Set up roof jacks and staging planks as you shingle your way up the roof. Whether you're using the racking pattern or pyramid pattern to orient the shingles vertically, run the courses out horizontally as I noted in the descriptions of both methods. After you run out horizontal courses as far up the roof as you can from the wall staging along the eaves, install a row of roof jacks and planks. Work from that row of staging until you're close to your reach limit, then install the next set of roof jacks and planks. I usually space the staging 5 ft. to 7 ft. apart up the roof plane. Keep in mind that you'll have to scurry up and down the staging levels to bring materials and equipment up to your working level, so don't space them so far that you limit your mobility.

Buy or borrow enough roof jacks and staging planks to stage an entire roof plane. Don't remove the staging at lower levels and reinstall it at the upper portions of the roof. You will need the staging at every level in order to stack materials and move yourself up and down the roof. You'll also need the lower staging to stand on when you remove the row above it when breaking down. In addition, the lower staging levels give you extra safety stops in the event of a fall; remove them and you're off the edge of the roof before you can blink your eyes.

WORK SAFE
WORK SMART
THINKING AHEAD

Don't overload the planks or jacks. You will need to lay bundles of shingles on the staging from which to resupply, but stack excess bundles on the staging level below your work level or on the ridge above.

To horizontally align the last two courses, snap a chalkline 5 in. from the butt of the course below.

Roof staging gives you more secure footing on pitches 8 and greater. This will speed production despite the time the staging takes to set up.

WORK SAFE
WORK SMART
THINKING AHEAD

It's foolish to set up ladders that rest on the top of roof-jack staging. If you need the extra reach you get from a ladder, set up another row of roof jacks.

Roof jacks generally don't come with installation and use instructions when you purchase them but instructions are available. Contact the manufacturer (its phone number and address are normally printed on each jack) and request instructions; the company will gladly furnish them. The use description I've included here is general, so keep in mind that each style of roof jack may require special procedures to properly erect and use staging.

Setting up roof jacks

Roof jacks attach to the roof with nails, but don't use roofing nails; although the heads are broad, roofing nails are short, their shank diameters are small, and their heads pop off easily. Use 10d to 16d common nails and drive them through the roof sheathing and into the framing (see the photo above). Don't rely on nails driven just into the roof sheathing because they're likely to pull out.

Space the jacks about 6 ft. to 8 ft. apart horizontally. Plan the jack positions so that one falls within 1 ft. of the ends of your staging planks. Also think ahead to avoid placing jacks where the joints between shingles and cutout slots will occur in the course immediately above.

Roof jacks have a long attachment strap with three or four teardrop-shaped holes or diagonal slots to drive nails into. The shape of the holes or slots permits you to remove the jacks later without removing the nails: Just tap the jack upward and the nail heads will be released. To permit the jacks to slide upward during removal, be sure to let them hang low enough when you install them; otherwise the plank support leg will bruise the butt edge of the shingle.

The backs of the triangular-shaped jacks will rest on the exposure portion of the shingle course beneath. With all the motion the jacks will absorb as you walk on the planks set on them, the backs can dig into or scuff the granules on the shingle surface, or worse they can cut through the shingles. For protection, place a piece of scrap shingle between the back of each roof jack and the roof shingle. You can also use pieces of wood-siding shingles as a cushion.

Once you have a row of roof jacks in place and two courses of shingles applied above them, carefully lay staging planks, not dimensional lumber, across the roof jacks. Full-cut 2×8 or 2×10 planks fit roof-jack support arms pretty well. As you lay the planks, be sure you don't slam them in place because you may pull the nails out of the jacks. Overlap the ends of the planks by 1 ft. to 2 ft., making sure the lap occurs over a roof jack. To hold the planks fast, drive nails through the holes in the turned-up ends of the support arms and into the edges of the staging planks.

Install the roof bracket by driving 10d to 16d nails through the holes in the bottom strap of the bracket, through the top lap of the shingle, and into the solid roof framing beneath the sheathing.

WORK SAFE
WORK SMART
THINKING AHEAD

Roof-jack staging isn't a substitute for safety harnesses or other fall-protection systems. The staging is there to give you a work platform to increase your shingling production.

WORK SAFE
WORK SMART
THINKING AHEAD

As you feel yourself getting close to your vertical reach limit when shingling, install a row of roof jacks and apply two more courses of shingles above the jacks. This way you won't have to bend into an awkward position when you start working on the next level above. You'll start working 1 ft. above the plank.

Organizing a Work Crew

So far in describing processes, I've focused on one installer. Now let's look at how to use a crew most efficiently.

With even a small crew of workers, you can organize the installation sequences and other tasks to keep individuals focused on a single aspect of the roofing process. This will increase production because the crew can work together with assembly-line speed; each person can focus without the distraction of breaking pace to cut starter shingles or carry up more shingles.

I'll describe the task roles separately, but several of them can be going on at the same time so everyone on the crew is working. Some tasks such as cutting in don't need a worker dedicated to them throughout a project but rather can be done by someone left "jobless" as the progress compresses the workspace and workers begin to crowd each other out.

Lead Installer

This is an experienced person who understands the layout process and how to make adjustments to control lines for any number of wacky roof configurations. Have this worker set the control column of shingles if you're using the racking pattern or set the starter kits of the pyramid pattern. Having one person responsible to set the shingles to vertical control lines helps ensure courses and exposures will be accurately aligned. Once the control column or pyramid is installed, the lead installer can move on to another facet of the roof to mark the layout and snap control chalklines or he can jump in with the other installers and focus on production.

Installers

After the lead installer lays several shingles up the vertical control lines, installers can follow on his heels, running out several courses of shingles along the horizontal control lines or right up the column or pyramid.

When you start a racking control column or pyramid in the middle of the roof, you have two sides that installers can work away from or up along. Find out who works strongest right to left and left to right, and have each work in his best direction.

These are the workers who install most of the shingles. It's important to keep them concentrated on production. Use laborers to manage the materials and supplies that the installers need so installers don't have to break their momentum.

Cutting-In Tasks

There are several cut-in tasks you'll encounter on roofs. Cut-ins occur when you reach the opposite rake edge, hips, valleys, walls, and obstacles (I'll describe the cut-in process for each in chapter 8). Although you could have any installer who encounters a cut-in situation handle the task at hand, it's sometimes more productive to terminate a column or pyramid when you reach a cut-in point and assign one worker to focus on just cutting in shingles and finishing off the roof. Or you can save all the cut-in work until the end of the project and share the task between all installers. Cutting in takes a fair amount of skill and shouldn't be left to unskilled labor.

Laborers

There are always plenty of tasks for an unskilled or semiskilled laborer on a roof job. These include:

- Carrying shingle bundles up to the roof
- Spreading out stacks of shingles for installers
- Supplying installers with shingles, fasteners, and whatever else they need
- Setting up and breaking down roof staging
- Holding the end of chalklines
- Cutting shingles
- Rolling out underlayment
- Feeding shingles to an installer (two-person installation)
- Gathering up waste materials
- Unpacking and packing tools
- Making coffee runs

A lot of times I'll take on the task of laborer and feed supplies to a crew of installers. This gives me a chance to watch the progress and give tips to installers to increase their production.

■ WORK SAFE ■ WORK SMART ■ THINKING AHEAD

Be aware that your toes, tools, and materials stacked on the staging planks can easily bruise the surface of the shingles directly behind the planks. As you walk along the planks, they will flex. Anything touching the shingle surface can abrade it as the planks move up and down. The problem is worse in warm weather when shingles soften.

Apply two courses of shingles above the roof brackets before laying staging planks across them.

Protect the shingle surface beneath the roof bracket by slipping a scrap piece of shingle between the bracket and the roof.

SETTING UP JACKS AROUND SHINGLES Sometimes you'll realize that you forgot to install a row of roof jacks and you've exceeded your reach limit. You can still install the jacks below shingles that are already installed. Do this by lifting the exposure portion of the shingle where you want a jack, sliding the leg beneath, and carefully driving nails through the holes. It may take an extra set of hands to hold the shingle up while you hold the jack and drive the nails. Be careful not to hit the upturned shingle butt when swinging the hammer.

In cold weather, shingles won't bend up without cracking. In this case, you may be forced to drive nails through the face of shingles to attach roof jacks. Before doing this, place shingle scrap below the jack-nailing holes to protect the shingle beneath. When you remove the roof jacks, pull the nails and slide a piece of metal flashing coated with roof cement beneath the shingle under the holes. Apply small dabs of cement to each hole on the shingle exposure, then scrape off color granules from a scrap shingle and press them into the cement. This will seal and hide the damage the roof-jack nails caused.

Working from the Top Down

Although it may sound counterintuitive, working from the top down makes sense in certain circumstances. When I say top down, I don't mean applying each course in reverse direction starting at the ridge. Although it can be done, that would be a time-consuming pain in the neck. Top-down roofing is done in "lifts" or groups of horizontal courses from 4 ft. to 7 ft. tall. The lifts are installed working from the top down, but the individual courses within each lift are done from the bottom up.

But why bother at all? I consider top-down roofing in two instances: during hot weather and on steep roofs when roof staging is necessary. In the summer when the sun beats down on the roof unrelentingly, the asphalt in the shingles softens considerably. Even light traffic on the shingles, which is unavoidable using the bottom-up approach, can scuff and bruise the surface granules (see the photo at right). And while the damage may only be cosmetic initially, the disturbed and missing granules no longer protect the bodies of the shingles, causing premature deterioration.

Even on cool days when shingles can withstand more abuse, roof staging poses a threat. First, the jacks and planks can damage the course of shingles at the staging level. As you walk on the planks, they continually flex, and the motion rubs surface granules off the shingles. The legs of the jacks are points of concentrated abrasion. Even with a scrap-shingle cushion, the shingle beneath the leg can suffer. And of course, your toes, tools, and shingle bundles scuff the shingles just above the plank. Add a hot day to a steep roof and the damage can be substantial. Here's how to install shingles from the top down.

1. **Prepare the roof.** The process for top-down roofing is pretty simple. You use all the same layout and installation techniques as you would on a bottom-up job. Start by installing the eaves drip edge and sticking down waterproof shingle underlayment at critical areas such as the eaves, wall and roof intersections, and valleys. For three-tab shingles, lay out and snap vertical control chalklines to keep cutout slots straight. Snap the lines in two different colors, alternating the colors if you lay out multiple lines to guide a pyramid; I'll explain why later. Mark out for horizontal control lines to keep shingle courses straight, but hold off on snapping the chalklines for now.
2. **Set up staging.** Set up roof-jack staging at comfortable levels up the face of the roof if necessary; I like them about 6 ft. to 7 ft. apart. Keep the top level no more than 5 ft. from the ridge so you're at a comfortable level to install cap shingles before moving down.

Shingles damage easily on sunny days when they become hot and soften up. Scuffs like these can be seen from the ground and detract from the roof's appearance.

Top-down roofing is done in lifts. The first lift is begun about 5 ft. to 7 ft. down from the ridge.

When roofing from top down, snap every other horizontal and vertical control line in different colors to ensure that shingle cutouts will be properly aligned between lifts.

3. **Install underlayment and rake edge.** Working off the top level, roll out two courses of shingle underlayment, being sure to lap the upper course over the bottom one. Keep the staples along the bottom edge of the lower sheet up 4 in. so you can slip the next lift of underlayment beneath it later. Nail metal rake edge over the underlayment, but just tack the bottom of the strips.

4. **Snap control lines on the underlayment.** Resnap the vertical control chalklines over the underlayment, and snap the horizontal lines to guide the courses. I suggest snapping every other course line in a different color (red and blue, for instance) if you are installing three-tab shingles with a 6-in. offset. (This step isn't necessary when installing laminated or other random-pattern shingles). And although you don't have to snap a chalkline for each course, I find it does help when top-down roofing (see the bottom photo at left).

   When you begin shingling, you'll start at a horizontal control line that will place shingle butts at least 6 in. above the highest staging plank. Match the end of the first starter shingle to a matching set of colored vertical and horizontal lines; blue and blue, for instance. The next starter above will match to a red set of lines.

   Although the benefit of the colored control lines may not be obvious when you shingle the uppermost lift, it will become evident when you shingle the lift below. The color-coordinated lines help you keep the cutout slots in sequence so you don't end up with a pair of courses with slots in the same line when you shingle up the next lift from below. Without the color system, you would have to count out and keep track of each course so you don't make an error. The last thing you want is to reach the lift above only to find out you made a mistake and the slots line up in two courses, in which case you'd have to strip off all your work to correct the problem.

5. **Install the lowest course in the top lift.** Locating the nails on the first

course of shingles in each lift is critical. Instead of driving the fasteners in their normal positions, nail the shingles in the head-lap section (the top 2 in. of the shingle). Nailing high will permit you to slide in the top lap of the top course of shingles you install in the next lift beneath. Drive only two fasteners per shingle to hold it temporarily (see the photos below). Later, when you install the next lift of shingles, you'll nail off the course properly.

6. **Complete the lift.** Once the first course is installed, you can apply the rest of the lift as you would the field shingles during a regular bottom-up application. When you reach the ridge, prepare the top for a ridge vent if you'll be installing it, or just nail the top lap over the other side if you aren't.

   If you've already shingled the roof on the opposite side of the ridge, cap it off. If not, then you can tackle the job later when you're set up and shingling the other roof. Now you can break down the top level of roof-jack staging and prepare to shingle the next lift of courses.

7. **Start the next lift.** Install two more courses of underlayment, and snap the horizontal control lines, continuing the same color-alternating sequence you started with the first lift. Pick up the butt edge of the bottom course of the lift of shingles above to see which color chalkline you aligned the top to, then check which vertical control line the starting shingle is matched to. This is your key to which vertical line you need to align the first shingle of the first course in your next lift. Just match blue to blue and red to red and you'll always match the lift above correctly.

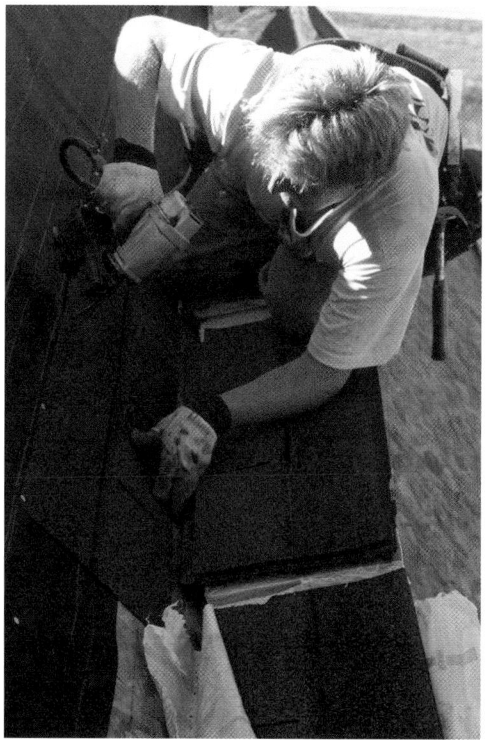

The first row of shingles in each lift must be aligned to a horizontal control line, as shown at left, and then held in place by two or three nails along the top edge at right.

Raise the shingles of the bottom row of the lift above to slide the top lap of the shingles beneath.

The final step in mating two lifts of shingles is to lift the tabs of the second row of shingles installed in each lift and drive fasteners to properly attach the first row, which you only top-nailed when you began the lift.

8. **Continue the lifts.** Fasten the first row of shingles the same way as you did in the first lift, then apply the rest of the shingles in the ordinary way until you reach the bottom of the shingles above. Slipping in and nailing the last course of shingles is the only time-consuming step in top-down roofing. Lift the tabs of the course above so you can slide the head lap of the last course in the lift you're installing beneath. While holding the tabs up, drive nails into the last course of shingles, then lift the tabs of the next course of shingles so you can nail off the first course of the previous lift, the ones you temporarily nailed when you started. This completes the transition between two lifts.

During cold weather, you may have a difficult time lifting the shingles to drive the last row of fasteners. Be careful; don't bend the shingles too far or you may crack them along the fastener line.

You apply additional lifts using the same steps until you find yourself at the eaves. Be sure to install step flashing, vertical wall flashing, vent-boot flashing, and roof vents as you work your way down the roof so you don't have to crawl back up later after you've removed the staging.

CHAPTER 8

Tending to the Details

SHINGLING a wide-open roof plane is fast because it's methodical. But once you fill in the field of shingles, you are left with the details including cutting in or trimming the shingles along a rake edge, cutting valley shingles, installing flashing, and capping hips or ridges. Sometimes you might choose or find it necessary to handle the details as you do the bulk of the roofing; other times you can leave them to later.

I find that the more you can focus on one roofing task at a time, the less time it takes. You can work with the tools in your hands and gather your materials nearby when you concentrate on a single task or related tasks rather than changing tools and jumping around. You lose your roofing momentum when you put down the nailer and find a secure spot for the stack of shingles you have on your toes just to snap a chalkline in a valley and trim the shingles. Whenever you can, leave the detail tasks until later and tackle them all at once. You could also assign one person to follow up on the details while others on a crew concentrate on shingling.

Although the roof looks nearly complete with the main body of the roof shingled, filling in the details can be time-consuming.

All the various detail jobs you're likely to encounter when shingling a roof are covered in this chapter. It's likely you'll have to tackle some while you're in the middle of installing roof shingles.

Detail jobs need to be done at various times depending on the job, so they aren't presented here in any particular order. Use your best judgment when deciding what to take care of immediately and what can wait.

I'll start with trimming shingles along rakes and into walls, then look at installing various flashing and roof vents. Next, you'll see how to shingle valleys and cap ridges and hips. Finally, I'll discuss special weather-related precautions and installations.

Trimming Shingles

When you reach the edge of a roof, whether it's at a hip, a rake, or a wall, the last shingle in each course will need trimming. Trimming shingles along hips is easy since hips will be covered by cap shingles; you can take a rough swipe with your utility knife either as you're bringing along courses or when you are done. Trimming along rakes and cutting into walls should be done more carefully because both will be visible. You can typically install full shingles in each horizontal course until you reach either a rake or a wall. Rather than breaking pace to cut and install the last shingle, leave it for later and continue roofing.

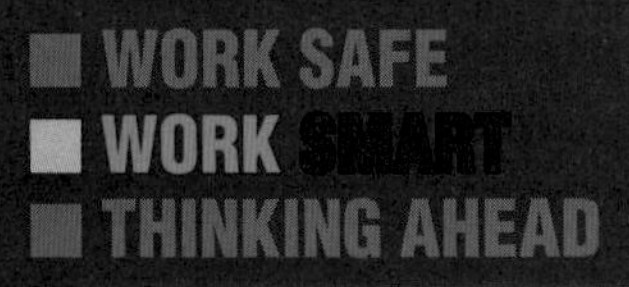

Whenever you trim shingles before installing them, it's best to scribe the shingles from the back before bending them apart. The back is smoother than the face, so your cutting line will be straighter.

Wrapping up the rakes

There are three methods for cutting and installing the last shingle in each course: You can precut shingle finishing kits, you can cut each shingle to length as you install it, or you can trim shingles after they are installed.

Precutting shingle finishing kits is the most efficient method but only works on roofs with straight, parallel edges. The length of the last series of shingles will repeat either every two to three courses (when following the 6-in. or 4-in. racking pattern) or every five to seven courses (when following the pyramid pattern). You can precut all the final shingles needed to fill in a rake edge in batches just like you did when making starter kits as described on p. 159.

If the roof isn't square or the edge is crooked, you have to resort to cutting each shingle to length, but there are even ways to speed this process using measuring tricks.

The third way to trim rake shingles is to install a full-length shingle at the end of each course and let it overhang the edge. After the roof is completely shingled, you can return to trim off all the overhanging portions. Although many roofers use this method, I rarely do. On warm days, the overhanging portions of the shingles droop, making it hard to mark and cut a neat, straight line. Also, rake shingles left untrimmed for several days can leave the edge deformed.

CUTTING RAKE FINISHING KITS

Start a finishing kit by measuring and cutting a pattern shingle for each shingle length you'll need. The lengths will vary depending on the roof width, but there will be only two lengths on a 6-in. offset racking pattern. If you used a 4-in. pyramid pattern, you'll have a lot more. To be sure precut shingles will work, you should measure one set of courses at the eaves and one near the ridge; on tall roofs check the middle too. You can measure the lengths directly and mark your patterns by holding the shingles in position as a gauge. If the lengths are within ¼ in., the finished edge will look consistent provided you used rake starters. The straight line of the starter shingles will conceal the slight deviation.

Count the number of shingles needed for each pattern length, then cut one pattern shingle for each length using a square or straightedge to ensure a crisp cut. Lay a pattern shingle on top of an inverted bundle of shingles, and align it precisely with the shingle beneath. Always orient the pattern shingle the same as the ones beneath and trim from the same edge. This will prevent you from cutting a stack of shingles backwards.

Draw your utility knife along the edge of the pattern shingle, and scribe about halfway through the shingle beneath. Lift both shingles in one motion; with one hand draw the pattern away and place it back on the bundle, then fold back the waste piece from the scribed shingle until it snaps. You'll develop a rhythm after cutting a few shingles. Keep count as you're stacking the trimmed shingles, remembering to include the pattern into your total count.

To make finishing kits, make a pattern for each different length of end shingle and use it to cut duplicates.

INSTALLING RAKE FINISHING KITS

After you've cut all the shingles for an edge, bundle up finishing kits with one shingle of each length (from two to seven shingles per kit depending on the shingle offset and pattern), then stack several kits together and head up to the roof to install them.

Installing the shingles up a rake when the racking pattern was used is fast work. The system is just like installing an ordinary column of shingles except you can fasten all the ends. Be cautious of where you place the last fastener however. You must keep it back far enough to avoid penetrating the overhanging portion of the shingles or drip edge. Normally, 1½ in. to 2 in. is a good setback.

Wrapping up a pyramid-pattern roof takes a little more time because you'll have to fill in full shingles along the way. When the eaves course ended at the rake edge, you stepped back all the shingle courses above it to form a diagonal. Now, as you fill in each kit of ending shingles, you'll have to follow up the diagonal with full shingles to ready the lower courses for the next finishing kit. Having help from another worker will speed the process.

After you fill in each finishing kit to the rake edge, have your helper fill in the full shingles up the pyramid while you install the next kit. At some point, the helper will return too quickly for you to ready the next kit, so send him off to work on something else while you finish the last few courses alone.

You can use this precutting system provided you followed precise vertical control lines to orient the starting shingle in each course. It's likely you didn't if you used random-cut shingles installed in a pyramid fashion. The final shingle in "equal"-length courses will differ slightly because the starter shingles were slightly different. In this case, you'll have to resort to the next method of trimming shingles.

TRIMMING INDIVIDUAL SHINGLES

Cutting the last shingle in each course to fit is much slower than gang-cutting kits of equal shingles. But if a rake edge drifts

Installing Rake Finishing Kits

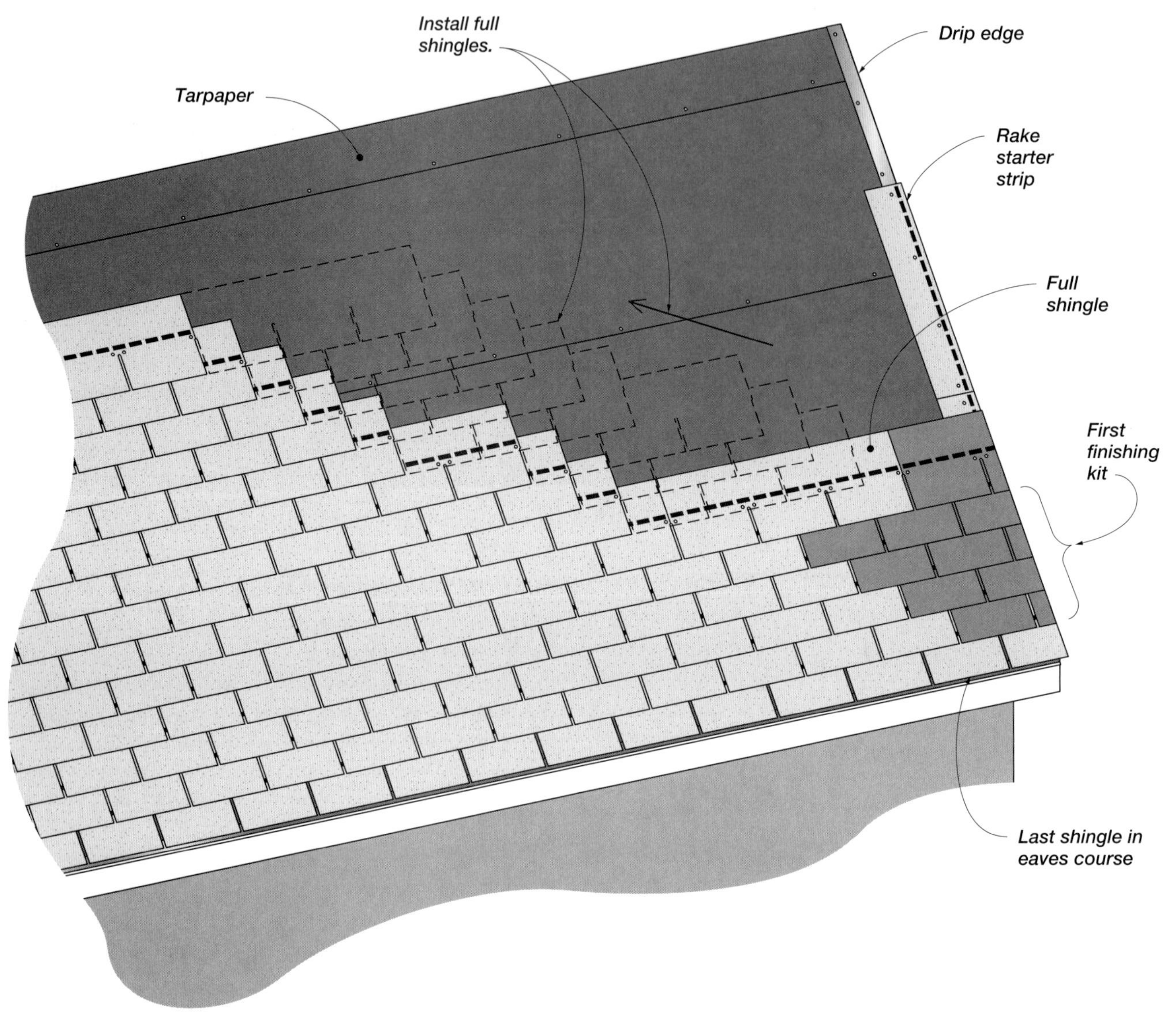

out of square or is crooked, you'll have to use this method. You'll also have to use it if you followed a random pyramid pattern to start your shingle courses.

To trim the shingles, start at the eaves with a pile of shingles oriented face down with the butt edge facing the ridge. Slide an upside-down shingle into place against the last full shingle and use your utility knife to nick the shingle where it meets the outside edge of the rake starter shingle below (see the top left photo on the facing page).

Pull the shingle in front of you rather than cutting near the edge of the roof. Using a square, scribe a knife cut halfway through the shingle. Snap off the waste piece, flip the shingle face up, then position and fasten it (see the top right photo on the facing page).

To mark the final shingle in each course to be cut flush with the rake starter shingle, turn the shingle upside down and butt it to the previous shingle, as shown at far left. Make a knife nick in the shingle to mark it for length, and use a square to guide a straight cut (near left).

CUTTING SHINGLES IN PLACE
If you decided to let the excess shingle length hang over the edge of the rake when you installed the field, you should trim them back as soon as possible. As soon as you shingle your way to the ridge, snap a chalkline matching the overhang of the starter shingles. Using a utility knife outfitted with a hook blade, draw it along the line. Only cut through one shingle at a time from the top down. After each waste piece falls free, bring the knife up to hook the top lap of the shingle beneath. Since there won't be a chalkline on the upper portion of the shingle, follow the edge of the shingle you just trimmed until you reach the chalkline again. Hook blades will dull quickly so change them frequently.

Fitting shingles against a sidewall or chimney

The process for trimming shingles to fit against a sidewall or chimney is the same. I recommend, if possible, shingling the bulk of the roof plane and returning to do the cut-ins. Although similar to the processes described in "Cutting Rake Finishing Kits" on p. 178 and in "Installing Rake Finishing Kits" on p. 179, you have to flip the shingles around a little more during the marking, cutting, and installing steps.

TRIMMING THE SHINGLES If the edge of the sidewall or chimney is straight and parallel to your vertical control lines, you can precut fill-in kits using pattern shingles as you did along the rakes. If the edges aren't parallel, you have to mark and cut each one individually.

Start with an upside-down stack of shingles in front of you with the butt edges facing down. Line up a shingle with

An alternative to precutting the final shingle in each course is to let all the shingles overhang the rake edge and cut them off flush using a hook blade.

Marking and cutting the final shingle against a sidewall is similar to cutting shingles ending at a rake edge except that you rotate the shingle end for end in addition to turning it upside down, as shown above. The photo below shows the installation of the shingle.

the course you're filling in, and press it against the wall or side of the chimney. It's okay if the step flashing is in place already; just press the shingle to the flashing. Next, back the shingle off about ¼ in. from the wall or chimney. This is important because it leaves room for expansion of the shingles and the flashing. If you left the shingle pressed tight, it may buckle up on a hot, sunny day.

Using your knife, make a nick at either the top or bottom edge of the shingle at the point where it meets the last installed shingle in the course. If you're gauging to the edge of a tabbed shingle, remember to account for the width of the cutout slot. Scribe and snap the shingle, then flip the shingle upright. The edge you trimmed will now face the wall or chimney and the factory edge will mate to the shingle course.

Check the length of the shingle at the top of the wall or chimney to see if the measurements are the same. If they are, you can use the shingle as a pattern and precut fill-in kit. If not, mark and cut all the shingles individually.

INSTALLING THE SHINGLES To install the shingles, butt the factory edge against the last shingle in the course and line up the horizontal control line. Layer the shingle properly into the step flashing if it's already installed, then fasten it down. Don't drive a nail within 3 in. of the end of the shingle because it's likely to leak (see the bottom photo at left). Move the last fastener back, making sure it won't fall within 1 in. of a cutout slot in the course above. Once you've installed all the shingles, move on to installing the step flashing.

Installing Basic Flashing

Flashing is installed at all critical transitions where water can penetrate, primarily along wall and roof intersections, and around roof penetrations such as pipes and skylights (chimneys and skylights require a special series of flashing pieces, which are covered in the next section). Step flashing is used when a roof meets a sidewall running perpendicular to the shingle courses, whereas roll flashing or flashing vents are used where the top edge of a roof plane such as a shed roof terminates at a vertical wall. Special molded flashing is used to seal around plumbing vent pipes, and many roof accessories such as vents come with their own integral flashing.

The most important principles to be aware of when installing flashing are that water moves downhill and sometimes uphill. With that in mind, make sure all your flashing is layered so that it sheds water down-roof and has sufficient overlap between layers to resist leaking during a windblown rain and due to debris or ice backups.

Step flashing at a sidewall

Step flashing consists of thin cards of metal, typically copper, aluminum, or lead, that are bent at 90 degrees in the center. One leg of the flashing attaches flat to the sidewall and is covered by the housewrap or siding underlayment and then by the siding; the other leg laps between the layers of roof shingles.

You can install step flashing during or after you fill in the last vertical course of trimmed shingles along the wall. I find it easier to install the step flashings after I've finished shingling.

Whichever way you choose, the first piece to go on is the bottom piece. There are two details you can use for the first piece of flashing depending on whether the wall continues beyond the eaves of the roof or if the roof wraps down and around a corner.

Flashing an eaves-to-sidewall intersection

Where a sidewall extends beyond an eaves, the bottom piece of step flashing has to prevent the water from getting into the wall behind the siding. To do this, the sidewall leg of the step flashing has to overlap the housewrap and the top edge of the siding to direct the water outward. Accomplishing the detail effectively can be tricky because you're counting on another person, the siding installer, to layer the siding properly into your step flashing. One way to help the siding installer get it right is to double up the bottom step flashing. Here's how to do that.

Installing the First Piece of Step Flashing

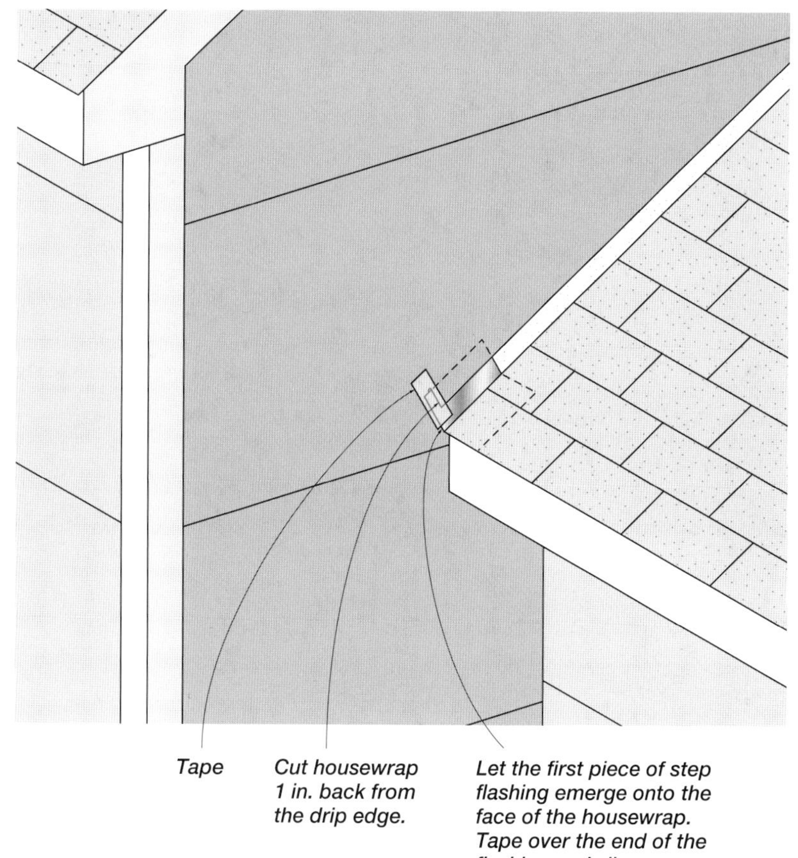

Tape

Cut housewrap 1 in. back from the drip edge.

Let the first piece of step flashing emerge onto the face of the housewrap. Tape over the end of the flashing and slice.

1. **Install the first piece of step flashing.** Layer the first piece of flashing beneath the starter shingle and beneath the housewrap on the wall. About an inch back from the eaves edge, slice the housewrap vertically, enough to let the step flashing emerge onto the face as shown in the illustration above. Slide the step flashing down until the end is flush with the drip edge, then tape over the slice in the housewrap and over the step flashing using housewrap tape. By doing this, even if the siding installer incorrectly layers the

Pattern for the Second Piece of Step Flashing When the First Piece is 10 in. × 10 in.

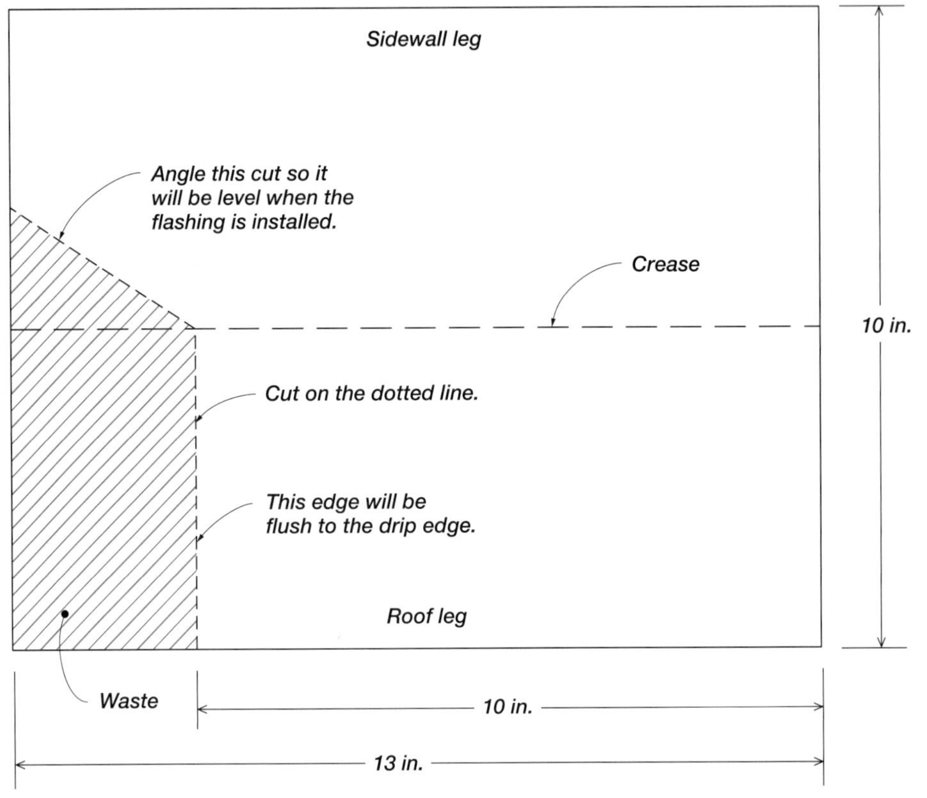

next step flashing you install, the water that reaches the lower step flashing will be directed to the outside face of the housewrap.

2. **Cut the second bottom flashing piece.** The second bottom flashing piece will be installed over the first piece. Its shingle leg will end flush to the drip edge, while its sidewall leg will extend 3 in. past the edge of the roof. To make this piece, you need a flashing card that's the same width as the other pieces but 3 in. longer. For example, if you have been using 10-in. by 10-in. cards, make one that is 10 in. by 13 in. Fold and crease the card to make the two legs, then cut 3 in. of the bottom of the roof leg. Put the card in place on the roof, and scribe a cut that will trim the sidewall leg to follow the horizontal line of the siding (see the illustration above).
3. **Install the second bottom flashing piece.** Bring the roof leg edge of the second bottom flashing piece flush to the drip edge. Make a slice about 4 in. back in the housewrap to let the sidewall leg of the flashing slip behind (see the illustration on the facing page).
4. **Install step flashing up the wall.** Interlace the step flashing between the roof shingles and slip the sidewall legs under the housewrap. When all the flashing is in place, tape the slit you made to let the second bottom piece protrude. The siding installer can slip the top of a course of siding shingles or lap siding beneath the wall leg of the second piece of step flashing. Using lead or soft copper

Install two layers of step flashing at the end of the eaves edge. The first emerges from behind the housewrap about 1 in. back from the eaves edge, as shown at far left. The second piece has an extended leg to tuck the top edge of siding under, as shown at near left.

flashing will make it easier for the siding installer to bend the extended wall leg over the siding.

MAKING A KICKOUT If a gutter won't be installed along the eaves, the detail described above will direct water onto the sidewall siding. Dumping a lot of water onto one point of the siding can cause discoloration and increase the likelihood of rot taking hold.

An alternative way to step-flash the bottom at the eaves edge may help get the water away from the siding altogether and is a preferred method of flashing for stucco and synthetic stucco, also called exterior insulation and finishing system (EIFS) siding. Start by installing the same first lower step-flashing piece as in the previous example. But rather than installing the second piece to lap just over the top edge of the siding, install a specially formed piece that aggressively directs the water away from the wall. This flashing is sometimes called a kickout (see the illustration on p. 186).

Installing the Second Bottom Flashing Piece

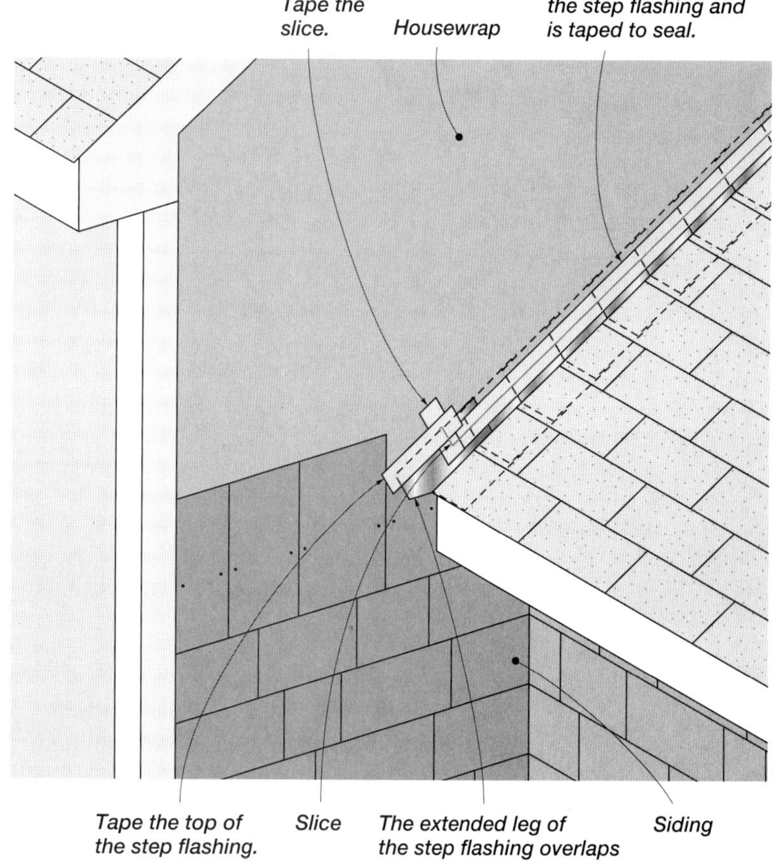

Making a Kickout

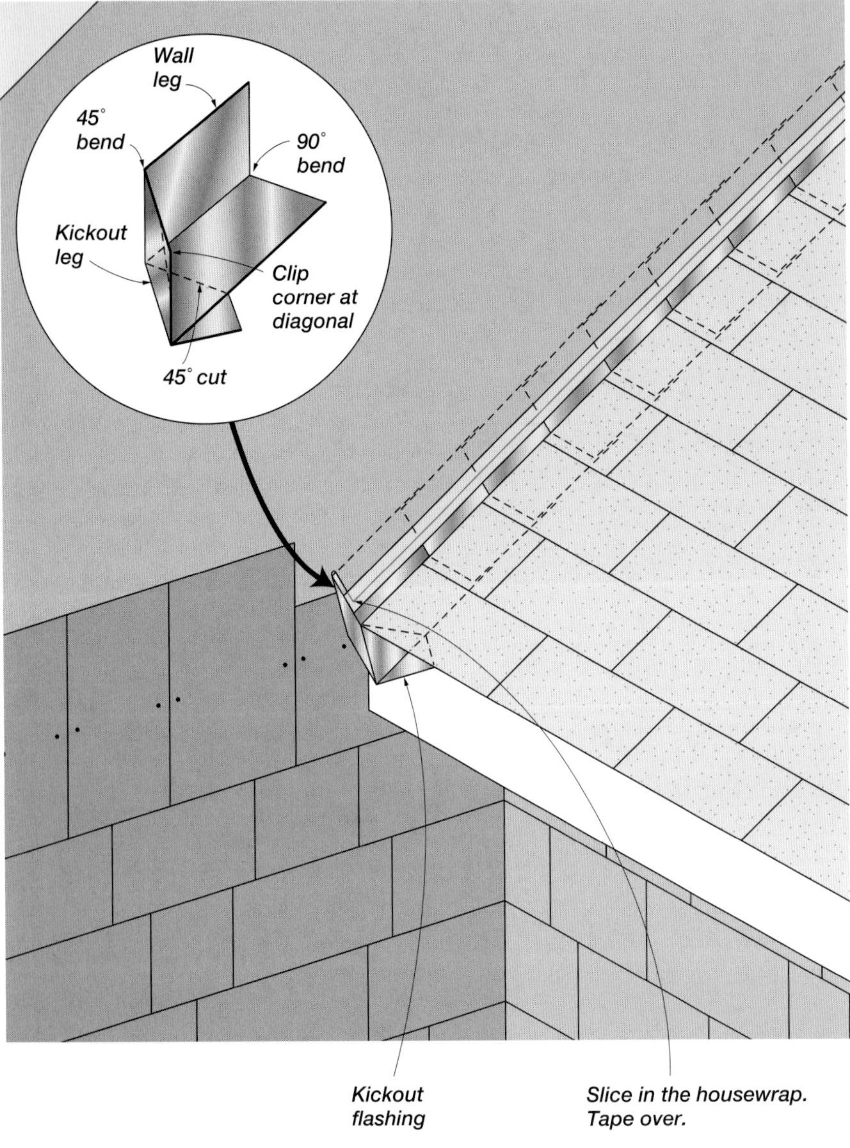

Form a kickout flashing from a large piece of step flashing, about 7 in. by 10 in. Start by creasing it along its length to form the two legs, then make a 45-degree angle cut in the roof leg of the flashing, starting at a point about 1 in. to 2 in. from the bottom and cutting to the center crease. Bend the sidewall leg of the flashing up at the point where the cut meets the center crease. As you're bending, slide the smaller lower piece of the roof leg beneath the larger upper portion; this forms the kickout. Seal the lap in the roof leg with roof cement or urethane caulk, and connect the lap together with a pop-rivet before installing. To make the installed kickout less obvious from the ground, snip a diagonal piece off the top corner of the kickout portion.

FLASHING AN OUTSIDE CORNER

You'll often have to start step flashing along a sidewall with a roof that wraps around a corner. This occurs where a single-story portion of the house meets a two-story section and a porch wraps around the wall corner or at the bottom of a dormer. The first step flashing is critical at this point. In addition to making the transition between the wall and the roof, it has to make the transition between the step flashing and the vertical wall-base flashing along the wall parallel to the shingle courses.

You can buy or form your own flashing to fit the corner. Preformed flashing pieces are usually small; the legs don't permit much overlap by the siding or roof shingles. Also, the roof leg of the flashing is corrugated, which makes the flashing thick and can be a problem.

The alternative is to hand-form or solder your own piece of flashing. Whichever method you use, it's a good idea to install a piece of waterproof shingle membrane around the corner of the wall and out onto the roof shingles before installing flashing. Any water that gets past the corner flashing will be directed out onto the shingle surface by the membrane.

Hand-forming a flashing from lead is easier than using copper or aluminum because lead is much more malleable. Start by folding creases in the upper portion against the corner of the wall, then hammer the lower leg down to the roof

A specially bent kickout flashing diverts water away from the wall.

Small, corrugated corner flashings are available to make the transition from sidewall flashing to vertical wall flashing around the corner.

to stretch the lead. Hammering will stretch and fan out the roof leg so the flashing will wrap around the corner (see the top right photo on p. 188). I admit that making an outside-corner flashing this way doesn't result in the prettiest detail, but it's fast and watertight because it's one piece.

MAKING SOLDERED CORNERS

Another alternative is to solder a piece of copper or lead flashing to wrap the corner. Soldered joints resist water much longer than joints sealed with caulk or roof cement. Crease a 12-in.-square flashing card in half, then place the crease along the intersection of the roof and sidewall. Slide the card down so half of it extends past the sidewall, and make a diagonal cut from the bottom outside corner of the card to the point where the crease meets the corner of the building. Fold the flashing around the vertical wall, making sure the flashing is flat against the roof and both walls.

Using a 7-in.-square flashing card, fill in the missing corner of the roof flange. Make a 1⅜-in.-deep diagonal cut in from one corner of the smaller flashing and bend up two short ears. Put the smaller card on the roof with one ear against the sidewall and one against the vertical wall, then solder the ears to the back corner of the main flashing piece and solder the main flashing piece onto the infill piece (see the photos at left on p. 188).

Soldered flashing takes longer to make but looks better than a preformed corrugated or hand-formed lead flashing and is nice and wide to shed water. If you have several such corners for which to make flashing on a roof, prep the pieces for all of them and solder the whole batch at one time.

Some roofers use a similar method using multiple pieces to form an outside-corner flashing but they seal the small, 1-in. overlaps with caulk rather than solder. This is risky because the sealant

Lead is soft enough to hammer-form around the corner intersection. Tap softly to stretch the lead without puncturing it.

To make a soldered flashing, cut a piece of lead or copper to fold over the corner of the wall and onto the roof. A smaller piece fills in the void of the larger piece, as shown above. Solder the joints with an iron affixed to a small torch (right).

can crack over time, leaving gaps for water to penetrate.

Installing step flashing up the wall

Once you have the lowest flashing on the roof fit at the eaves edge or outside wall corner, you can install the rest of the step flashing along the sidewall. Lacing the step flashing up the sidewall is fairly easy. Starting at the bottom, work your way up the roof so each flashing overlaps the one beneath it.

If housewrap is already installed, fold it up so the sidewall leg of the step flashing is tight against the wall. Preferably, you installed a folded piece of tarpaper underlayment or waterproof shingle underlayment against the sidewall before you shingled the roof. The sidewall leg of the step flashings will go over the underlayment.

Slide the roof leg of the flashing beneath the exposure portion of each shingle. Push the lower edge of the step

Step-flashing cards slip between shingle courses and lap over one another to shed water traveling down the roof along a sidewall, as shown at left. After the step-flashing cards are installed, the housewrap can be draped and taped over the wall leg (right).

flashing up about 1 in. past the shingle butt so that it won't be seen and won't prevent the self-seal strips from bonding the shingles together. Since most shingle manufacturers use self-seal dots rather than continuous strips of sealant, any water that the step flashing channels downward will drain through the self-seal voids.

The industry-approved method for attaching step flashing is to drive a single fastener into the top corner of the roof leg and through the shingle beneath. The flashing isn't fastened to the sidewall at all. The next shingle and step flashing will cover the nail, so the chance of leaking is minimal.

The primary reason the roofing industry recommends fastening the flashing to the roof is to allow the wall edge to slide down if the roof settles. This prevents wall-attached flashing from lifting off the roof when the roof settles. However, with today's framing techniques, it's unlikely there will be any settling along the intersection of a roof and sidewall, and older homes have probably finished settling by the time they are ready for a new roof. Another reason not to nail the flashing to the sidewall is to allow a future roofer to slide the step flashing from beneath the siding.

I prefer to fasten the upper corner of the step flashing to the sidewall rather than the roof, where the wall fastener will be covered by the next successive step flashing and again by the housewrap (see the photos above). There are several reasons to avoid fastening step flashing to the roof. First, it's difficult to drive a fastener into the roof because you have to lift the shingle up rather high, which slows progress and increases the likelihood the shingle will split. Also, a fastener driven into the roof will be difficult to remove without damaging the flashing when it comes time to reroof the house (if you use good-quality flashing, it will outlive the roof shingles and can be reused by the next roofer). This method

Flashing a Shed Dormer

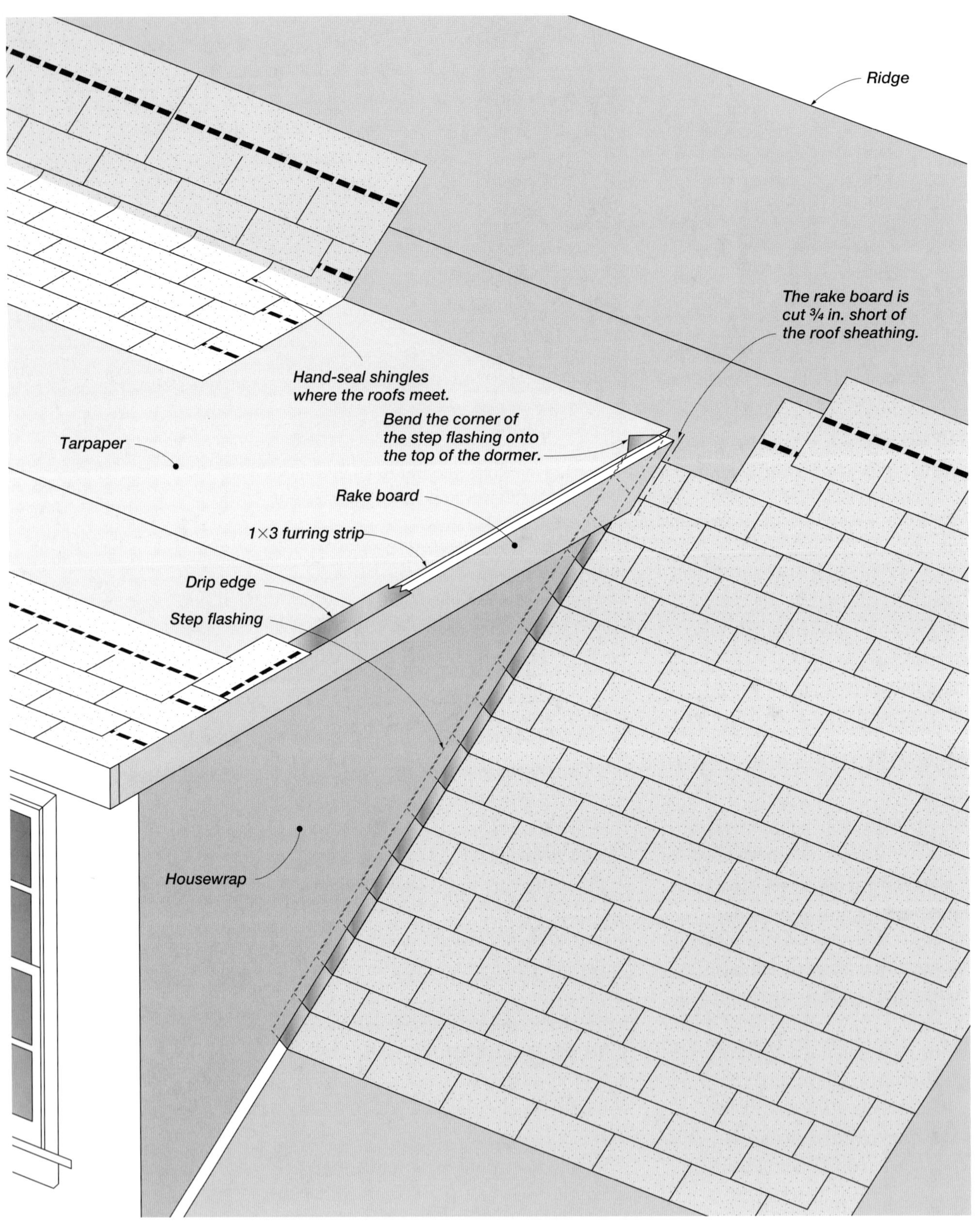

also minimizes damage to the siding when new step flashing does have to be installed. Think about which method suits each project you encounter.

Flashing the top of a shed-roofed dormer

When you reach the top of the roof/sidewall intersection, you'll encounter either a rake board or a soffit and fascia. You'll need to incorporate special flashing details for each. If you hit a rake board, the situation is pretty straightforward. Basically, you install step flashing all the way up the sidewall including behind the rake trim board. The process described here will work where the rake boards are applied directly to the sidewall or on spacer blocking of 1 in. or less. (For dormers with rake overhangs, follow the steps described in the next section on gable-roofed dormers.) The whole process is best done before applying the shingles to the roof of the dormer.

Unless the trim carpenter left you enough space between the end of the rake board and the roof sheathing, you'll have to cut it back. This isn't so much a concern for slipping in flashing as it is for installing the shingles. Cut the board back about ¾ in. from the roof sheathing to allow a ⅜-in. to ½-in. space between the rake board and the roof shingles.

It's important to leave the space even though many people consider it poor workmanship. The space prevents water from being wicked into the end grain of the rake board and promoting rot. The space also leaves enough room for a painter to properly prime and paint the end grain, further protecting the trim. And the space makes it easier for you to slide the roof shingles beneath.

Remove or cut any nails fastening the rake board to the sidewall within 5 in. of the main roof plane so you can slip step flashing behind it. You won't

Leave Space between Siding and Shingles

When siding a house, it's important to keep the bottom of the first siding course ⅜ in. to ¾ in. above the roof shingles. If you aren't doing the siding, remind the installer.

There are several reasons to leave the space. Wood siding will wick up moisture that clings in tight spaces, which is likely to result in paint peeling and rot. The space acts as a capillary break to prevent the wicking. A wide gap is also less likely to trap debris that can lead to siding decay.

In addition, the space makes it easier for the next roofer to disengage shingles from step flashing. Or, if a second layer is installed over the existing one, the space makes it easier to slip new step flashings under the siding. If you use colored flashing, the gap won't be noticeable.

Siding along roof edges must be kept ⅜ in. from the roof surface to prevent water from wicking into wood and debris from collecting.

When wood siding or trim is installed too close to the roof shingles, the wood is likely to rot and paint will continue to peel on the lower course.

Use a piece of ⅝-in. sheathing as a saw guide to cut back the fascia, subfascia, and the soffit, creating a ¾-in. space for the top lap of the roof shingles.

be able to nail the flashings to the wall behind the rake, so you'll have to resort to nailing it to the roof.

As you get closer to the point where the dormer roof meets the main roof, the top corner of the wall legs of the step flashing cards will stick up above the dormer roof. Where they do, bend the corners down onto the roof sheathing of the dormer (see the illustration on p. 190). Consider using lead step flashing for the last few pieces because it bends more easily. The top half of the last piece of flashing should extend above the point where the dormer roof meets the main roof.

Flashing a Dormer Valley

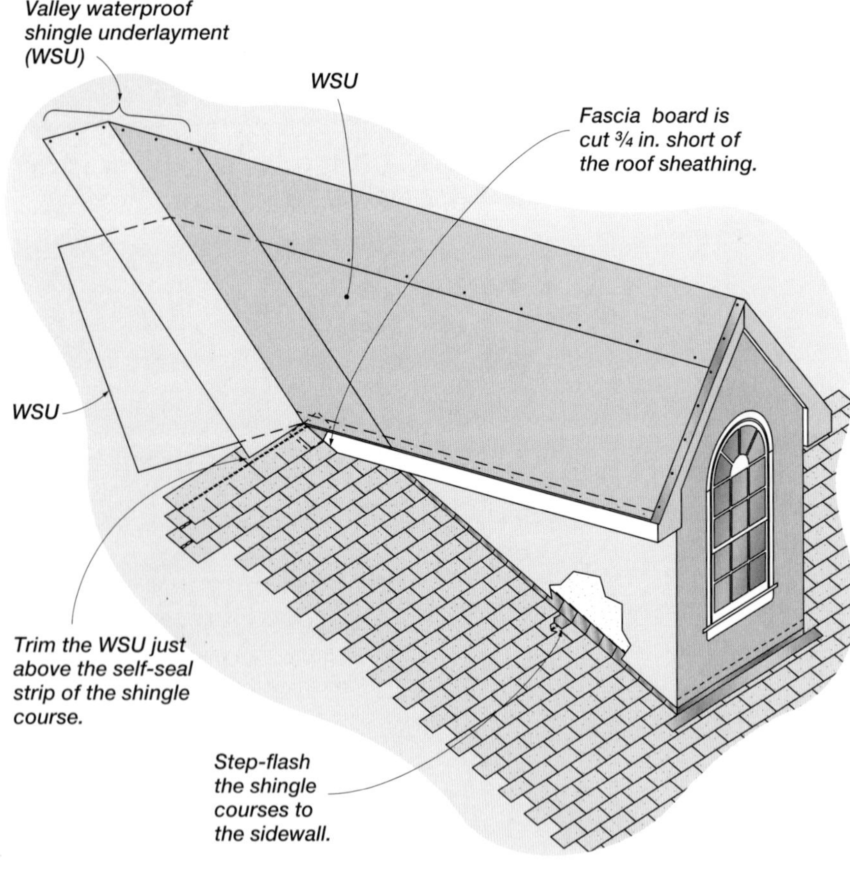

Flashing along a gable-roofed dormer

The process for flashing the transition area where the roof of a gable dormer meets the main roof is different from a shed dormer with a simple rake board. The soffit and fascia present additional obstacles to work around.

Ideally, the framers left about ¾ in. of space between the trim and the sheathing of the main roof. If not, cut back the soffit and fascia. Cutting the fascia and sub-fascia, if there is one, shouldn't be a problem, but it may be difficult to trim a soffit board that's already in place. Try using a handsaw riding on a ⅝-in.-thick board placed on the roof to make one cut through the fascia, subfascia, and soffit board (see the photo above).

Install step flashing and shingles along the sidewall until you reach the point where the soffit meets the roof. If there's enough space to slide the top lap of the shingles beneath the soffit and fascia, do so. You won't be able to nail the portion of the shingle beneath the soffit, so end each row with shingles at least 1 ft. (or a full tab) longer than the soffit is deep. This will allow you to drive a minimum of two fasteners into each shingle before it extends beneath the soffit to prevent the unfastened end from drooping.

You may not be able to get step flashing under the entire area where the soffit meets the wall, which is okay as long as the uppermost piece of flashing is tucked under the point where the soffit meets the roof. But if you're roofing in an area prone to wind-driven rain, then by all means install as many flashing pieces as you can. Using extra-long step flashing will make it easier to slide the flashing in place beneath the soffit. You won't be able to nail the top corner of the step flashing beneath the soffit, so nail the bottom corner and seal the head with roof cement.

When the top lap of a shingle course reaches the bottom of the dormer roof valley, you'll have to cut the shingle to end at the fascia and step-flash it to the subfascia or just behind the fascia. Bend the top corner of the step flashing onto the dormer roof, and cover it with the drip edge later.

This transition will be exposed to a lot of water because the valley channels all the water collected from above. The

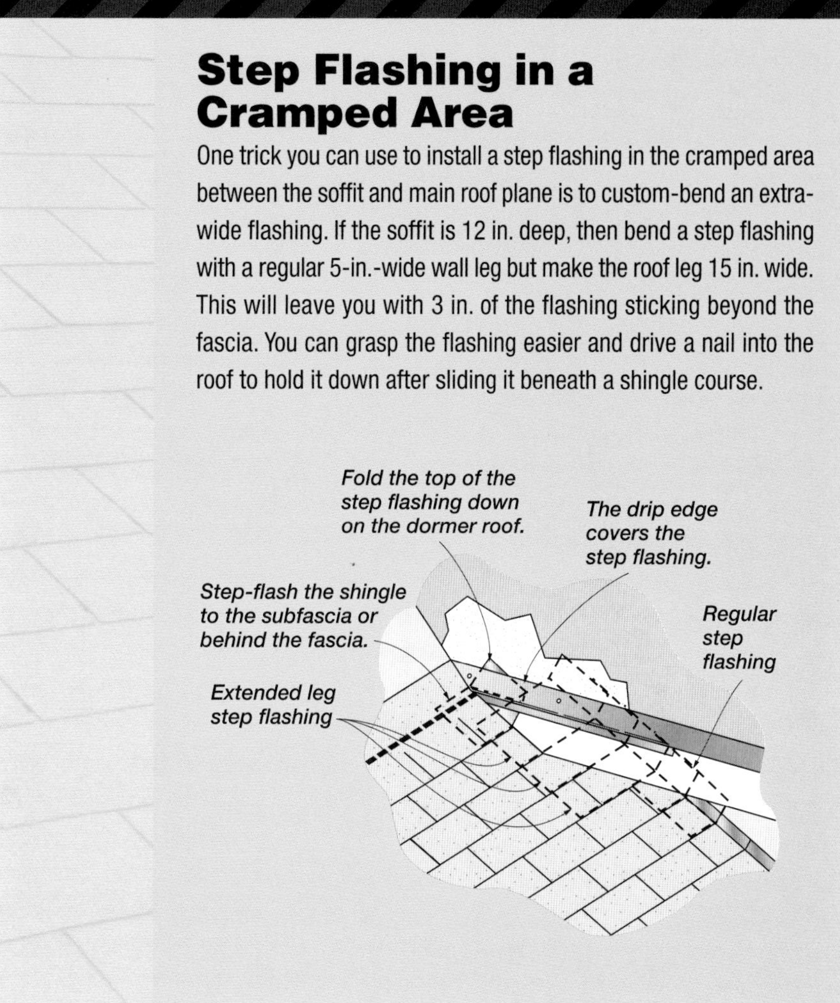

Step Flashing in a Cramped Area

One trick you can use to install a step flashing in the cramped area between the soffit and main roof plane is to custom-bend an extra-wide flashing. If the soffit is 12 in. deep, then bend a step flashing with a regular 5-in.-wide wall leg but make the roof leg 15 in. wide. This will leave you with 3 in. of the flashing sticking beyond the fascia. You can grasp the flashing easier and drive a nail into the roof to hold it down after sliding it beneath a shingle course.

Where the valley of a gable dormer roof ends, you'll have to step-flash one or two shingle courses behind the fascia or to the subfascia. (Photo © Susan Aitcheson.)

When installing waterproof shingle underlayment into a valley, lap the main roof side of the sheet (left) over the head lap of a shingle course and trim it just above the self-seal strip. (Photo © Susan Aitcheson.)

Flashing a Vertical Wall

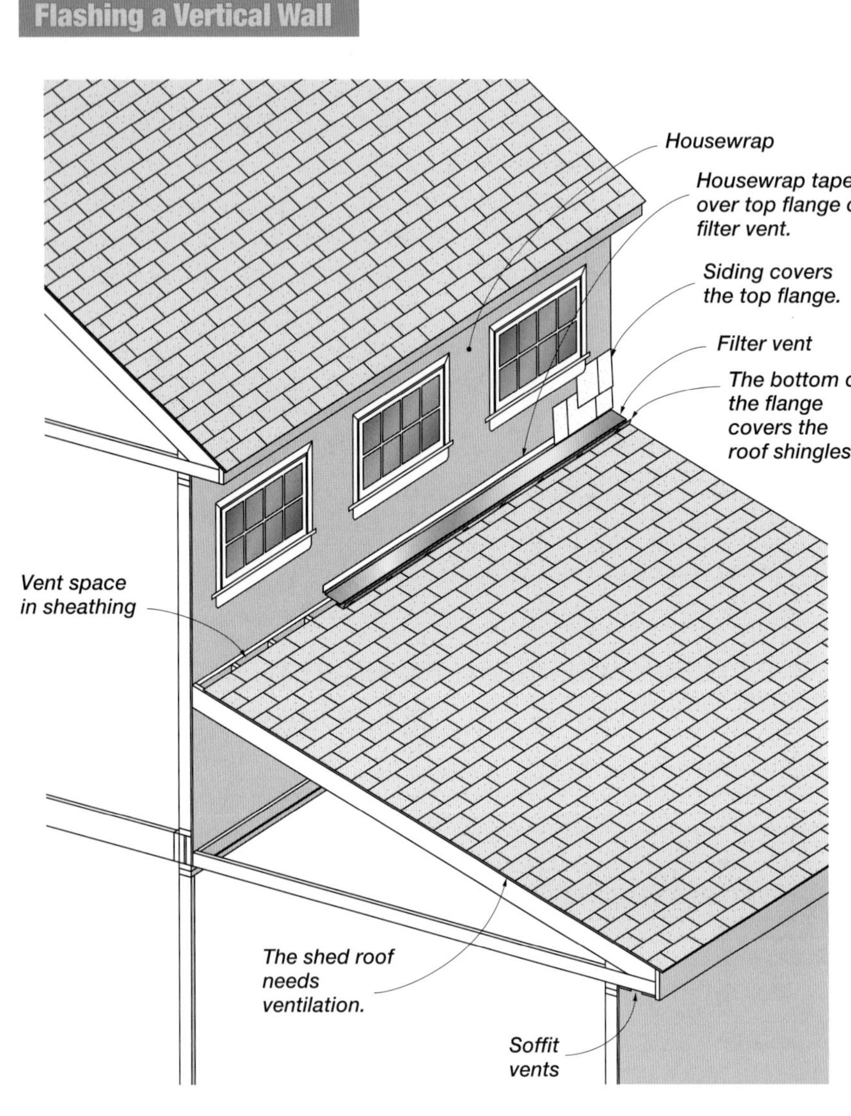

extra effort spent making it watertight is worth it. I like to overlap the waterproof shingle underlayment I lay into the valley over the top lap of the shingle course that matches close to the top of the fascia. Any water that penetrates the valley down to the waterproof membrane will be directed out onto the surface of the shingles of the main roof here rather than just traveling beneath them on the underlayment. Trim the bottom edge of the waterproof shingle underlayment just above the self-seal strip of the shingle on the main roof so the shingle above will bond (see the photo at right on p. 193).

Overlay the waterproof underlayment with metal valley flashing (for exposed valleys) or run the shingle courses through and up onto the dormer roof (for closed valleys). When you are shingling through a valley and the butt edge of a shingle course on the main roof doesn't closely meet the drip edge on the dormer fascia, install a piece of metal to cover the lower end of the waterproof underlayment (see "Shingling Valleys" on p. 210).

Flashing a vertical wall

When the top of a roof plane meets a vertical wall, you have to flash the connection to shed water rolling off the siding and direct it onto the roof shingles. The flashing here serves the same function as step flashing, but it can be formed and installed as one long piece rather than numerous small pieces because it runs parallel to the shingle courses.

The most common flashing used here is often called roll flashing because the metal it's formed from typically comes in a roll. The metal is creased lengthwise on site and bent at an angle to match the pitch of the roof. The wall leg of the flashing is covered by the housewrap and siding, and the roof leg sits on top of the roof shingles.

If the roof covers living space, it will need to be vented. Instead of unsightly roof vents, you can use a preformed metal flashing that incorporates a vent (see the bottom photo on p. 196).

BENDING AND INSTALLING ROLL FLASHING It's best to install the flashing after the roof shingles have been installed up to the wall. Lead, aluminum, and copper are common metals used to form flashings for vertical walls. Cut the top lap of the last course or two of shingles as needed so the top edge butts the wall, then install trimmed-down shingle courses until the fasteners of the last row are within 4 in. of the wall (see the top photo below).

The first task is to bend the metal to form the flashing. I often use lead for vertical-wall flashing because it's easy to form in place and its dull gray color suits most color schemes. Use metal that is at least 10 in. wide (12 in. is better).

To form lead in place, first roll out and cut a piece to the length of the vertical wall you are flashing. Lift the housewrap to expose the underlayment you installed and wrapped up the wall when preparing for shingling. To guide the installation, snap a chalkline 5 in. up the wall (higher for wider flashing material). Starting at one end of the flashing, lift and nail it to the line, driving the nails within the top ½ in. of the metal. As you work your way along the wall, drive nails about 2 ft. to 3 ft. apart. Having a helper lift the flashing to the line while you nail it off will speed production and diminish the chance of kinking the metal.

Once the lead flashing is attached to the wall, use a 2× board at least 6 ft. long to press the lead into the junction of wall and roof. Plan to make two passes along the flashing with the 2×. The first time, bend the flashing one-half to two-thirds of the way down. On the next pass, press it tight to the joint, then strike the board with a hammer to seat the lead for a crisp bend. Don't try to form the lead with only one pass along its length or you'll kink it at the end of the board and possibly pull out some nails. If the lead doesn't lie perfectly flat to the roof or the wall, use the 2× board as a cushion and tap along its length to even out the flashing.

Aluminum, copper, and galvanized steel flashing must be prebent using a metal brake. If you try to bend them in place using the same method as I described for lead, you'll end up with lots of unsightly kinks in the metal and they won't lie flat on the roof. Chances are your brake won't be long enough to make long flashing in one piece, so plan to overlap multiple pieces by at least 6 in. when you're measuring and cutting.

Use a bevel square to gauge the angle where the roof meets the wall and to guide your bend. Clamp a length of metal in the brake so that you'll have at least 5 in. on the wall and roof legs. Be sure to underbend the angle by 2 or 3 degrees so the leading edge of the roof leg will press firmly against the shingles. If you overbend the flashing, the bottom edge will have an unsightly gap and permit windblown rain to enter more easily.

Next, make a second chamfer bend about 1 in. in from the bottom roof edge at a 2- to 3-degree downward angle. This

Run horizontal shingle courses up to a vertical wall until the self-seal strip is within 4 in. of the wall. The wall flashing will cover the strip and shingle fasteners.

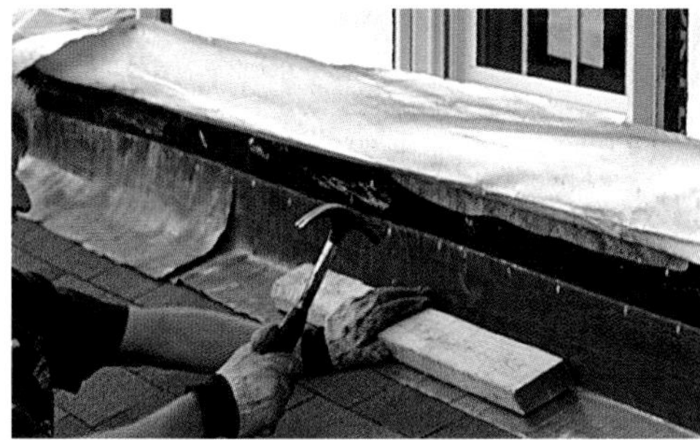

It's easy to flash the transition between a vertical wall and a roof using a roll of lead. First nail the lead to the wall, then tap on a 2× block to crease the lead into the corner until it lies flat.

Vertical walls can also be flashed with aluminum-coil stock. The extra chamfer bend along the bottom minimizes wrinkling due to expansion in the summer.

A flashing vent ventilates space below a roof that rises to end at a wall. It also flashes the intersection of wall and roof, as shown above. Although the hood and vent portion of the flashing vent protrudes several inches from the wall, it doesn't detract from the appearance of the building.

bend will help keep the flashing from fishmouthing when the material expands and help keep the edge tight to the shingles (see the photo at left). Nail the prebent pieces to the wall along the top edge, and cover the wall leg with the housewrap.

You'll find instructions in other roofing guides that recommend nailing vertical-wall flashing to the roof rather than the wall for the same reasons I outlined for step flashing. I think you're inviting leaks using this method. The leaks may not occur right away, but the potential increases as the roofing cement you dab on the nail heads deteriorates.

Some roofers like to cover the roof leg of vertical-wall flashing with the exposure portion of shingles so the flashing isn't visible. You can use the shingle tabs you trimmed off to make eaves starters or cut some new ones. Apply roof cement to the back of the tabs, and press them onto the flashing. I'm not a fan of this practice because the shingles can droop in hot weather when the cement softens. You could drive a couple of nails through the shingles to hold them in place, but every nail through the flashing is a potential leak point. I prefer to use lead, copper, or colored aluminum to match or complement the color of the shingles and leave the metal roof leg exposed.

FLASH-VENTING A WALL TO THE ROOF Many builders and roofers ignore the need to vent roof sections that terminate at a vertical wall. Although venting is unnecessary for roofs over porches, it is recommended when the roof covers living space. And since many people enclose porches and decks at some point, installing vents up front avoids labor later. Commercially available flashing vents are the best solution. They're easy to install and don't detract from the roof like ordinary mushroomlike roof vents do.

Flashing vents have preformed wall and roof legs to cover the joint where the wall meets the roof, and they are formed to allow air to flow from a slot in the roof sheathing through slots beneath an extended cap portion.

Flashing vents are typically prebent to match a 12-pitch roof and can be adjusted to work on pitches down to 3. Of course, this means you'll have to press the bottom leg down to the roof plane to match the pitch. The roof leg is upturned along the edge to keep the edge straight and to provide a baffle that helps keep wind-driven rain from blowing up into the vent perforations.

Before you install the roof underlayment in preparation for shingling, cut the roof sheathing back 1 in. from the point where it meets the vertical wall. Install the underlayment and roof shingles up to the edge of the slot but don't cover it. Air needs to flow through the slot to permit ventilation of the roof cavity beneath.

Using sheet-metal shears, cut the flashing vent pieces to length for the section at hand. Use a short, cut-off piece of flashing vent to mark out the height to snap a chalkline along the wall. Press the piece down to the roof plane until the lower leg lies flat to the shingles. Making sure the wall leg is flat against the wall, mark the top, then measure the distance up to the mark, transfer the point at the other end of the wall, and snap a chalkline between them.

Next, nail the flashing along the wall, and cover the wall flange with the housewrap. Because flash vent is rather large and the metal is thick, you may have to drive some nails down through the roof leg to keep it in place. Although I'm reluctant to do this, it's the only way I've found to keep the bottom flange from lifting up, especially on lower-pitch roofs. I drive nails about 1 in. up from the bottom edge spaced about 4 ft. apart. Before you drive each nail, put a dab of roof cement between the flashing flange and the shingles. Cover the heads of the nails with roof cement too.

When you need more than one length of vent flashing for a wall, join the two pieces together using a coupling piece supplied by the manufacturer, being sure to spread sealant into the grooves of the coupling first. Fill the ends of the vent with end plugs. Flashing vents are typically sold by the carton

To install vent boot flashing, make a slice in the underlayment to slip the top of the flashing beneath, as shown at far left. Nail the two top corners of the flashing through the underlayment (near left).

Cut an inverted U in the shingle exposure of the next two courses that cover the flange of the vent boot flashing.

with the accessories included. Although the vent does project about 4 in. beyond the face of the wall, it doesn't detract from the appearance of the building.

Vent flashing

Wherever a plumbing vent pipe, heating system- or fireplace-exhaust vent, or other ventilation-exhaust vent penetrates the roof, you'll need a special preformed flashing. Install these flashing pieces while you're shingling a roof. If you wait until the shingling is complete, you'll have to remove several shingles and nails to slip the flashing in place and then reroof around the flashing.

INSTALLING PLUMBING VENT BOOT FLASHING Plumbing vent flashing has a supple rubber or plastic collar to seal around the pipe and a broad metal or plastic flange to layer into the shingles. Most boot-flashing pieces are sold by the diameter of the pipe each will fit, but some have concentric rings stamped into the rubber collar you can use to trim to fit, making them universal.

New-construction roofs typically don't have the plumbing vent pipes installed at the time when roof shingles are installed, but you can still install the flashing. I like to have the plumber locate where he's planning to install the vent pipe, so I can cut a hole through the roof sheathing and install the flashing. Later, the plumber can cut and install his vent pipe through the installed flashing without climbing to install the flashing himself. On existing roofs, the vent pipe will already be sticking through the roof, so there'll be no question where the flashing goes.

Run out courses of shingles until you reach the row where the hole or vent pipe is cut through the roof sheathing. Install one or two more courses, then cut a U into the top-lap portion of the shingles around the hole or pipe. Stop installing courses when you reach the point where you'll have to cut more than halfway into the exposure portion of the shingle to clear the hole or pipe.

At this point, hold the boot flashing over the hole or slide it over the pipe. Pressing it down flat to the roof, draw a line around the top edge and down the sides about 3 in. Lift the flashing back up, and make a cut in the underlayment parallel to the top line but about 3 in. lower between the two side lines. This cut will enable you to slip the top edge of the flashing beneath the underlayment and help shed any water that does reach the underlayment layer over the flashing. Replace the boot flashing over the hole or pipe, but this time slip the top edge into the slice in the underlayment (see the photo at left on p. 197). To hold the flashing in place, drive two nails in the upper corners.

If you are installing the boot flashing over a pipe, make sure that the rubber boot seals with the upper rim pointing toward the top of the pipe. Sometimes if you move the flashing up and down the rim can pop down, forming a concave pool around the pipe where water can collect. If the rubber boot grips the pipe very tightly when you're installing it, the bottom edge can pull away from the bell of the flashing portion. Help the boot slip over the pipe easier by spreading some liquid soap on the pipe. Don't use petroleum oil or grease, which may deteriorate the rubber.

With the flashing in place, run out one course at a time and cut inverted U shapes out from the exposure portion of the shingle, leaving as much of the top lap intact as possible. The flashing flange will have a bell shape formed into it where the rubber collar attaches. Trim the shingles to match the curve of the bell as well as you can (see the photos on the facing page).

Continue trimming shingles in each successive course around the bell in the boot flashing until a row of shingles clears the penetration altogether. Lift each lap of shingle that covers the boot flashing, and apply a bead of roof cement from a tube. This will keep water from running sideways beneath the shingles. Do not, however, seal the bottom edges of the shingle courses or the bottom of the flashing flange; leave them open to permit any water that gets beneath to drain.

If the vent flange tends to rise at the bottom, you can install two nails along the edges just beneath the lower edge of the first row of shingles to cover the flange. At times I've decided to face-nail the bottom edge of the flashing, although I try to avoid it. If you do, dab roof cement beneath the flange where you'll set the nail and cover the head with sealant.

INSTALLING METAL CHIMNEY FLASHING Flashing is available for a variety of metal exhaust pipes and metal chimneys. Gas furnaces and boilers typically use single-walled galvanized or stainless steel B vents. The diameters of these pipes are pretty standard (5 in., 6 in., 8 in., and so on), and preformed flashings are available for each size. Some metal fireplace chimneys have proprietary flashing you'll have to purchase from a fireplace supplier. Both types are similar in design and installation to plumbing vent boot flashing except that they don't have a rubber portion to seal to the exhaust pipe. Rather than a bell shape formed in the metal roof flange, the flashing is made from two separate pieces. A flat, metal flange is specially

Metal fireplace and furnace-exhaust chimneys have special roof flashings. Although larger, they are similar to plumbing boot flashings and are installed the same way.

WORK SAFE
WORK SMART
THINKING AHEAD

A veneered chimney needs to be step-flashed against the wooden box before the veneer is applied. The optimal situation is to apply the roof shingles before the mason covers the wooden box. That way, you can install the step flashings, and the mason only has to cover them with his veneer.

crimp-sealed to a conical metal riser. The top of the riser tapers down in diameter to just a bit larger than the diameter of the exhaust pipe it's sized to flash. Instead of the rubber to seal the joint between the riser and the exhaust pipe, a separate adjustable storm collar fits tightly to the exhaust pipe just above the top of the vent.

Install the exhaust-vent flashing in the same fashion as I described for plumbing boot flashings and shingle around the flange, then install the collar to the exhaust vent and slide it about ½ in. above the top of the flashing riser. For a weathertight seal, apply some high-temperature silicone sealant that includes a UV inhibitor for long-term service.

INSTALLING EXHAUST-VENT FLASHING This flashing looks similar to the mushroom-shaped roof vents. It is used to exhaust some ducted ventilation systems within the house. Typical uses are clothes dryer vents, bathroom fan vents, and central ventilation exhausts. The hood on top of the vent flashing protects a duct collar that the exhaust ductwork connects to. A wide flange at the base forms the integral flashing.

Install exhaust-vent flashing in the same way described in "Installing Roof Vents" on p. 208. Just remember to point the exhaust face of the vent downward on the roof to prevent water from entering.

Flashing Chimneys

Weatherproofing around chimneys involves a series of properly configured and installed flashing components. Some, like step flashing, are similar to those used in general roofing. Other components you'll have to make. The base flashing is installed first along the bottom (down-slope) edge of a chimney and wraps a little up the sides. Step flashing is used along the sides and is installed in much the same manner as when a roof meets a sidewall. At the top (up-slope) edge of a chimney, you need a cricket to shed the water. You have a couple of options to flash the area depending on the cricket's size. The pieces around the cricket will be the last flashing installed around the chimney.

A key element for all flashing components to work properly is the counterflashing. On masonry chimneys, counterflashing is installed by the mason during construction. The mason layers pieces of lead, copper, or other metal flashing into the mortar joints about 6 in. to 12 in. above the roof plane. All the flashing you install will be covered by the counterflashing for a weathertight assembly.

Sometimes chimneys are made of wood (which can have a veneer of brick or stone) rather than masonry, which changes the flashing details slightly. You should still treat the flashing around newer wooden chimneys with the same care and in a similar fashion as flashing around traditional masonry chimneys; the only real difference is that there will be no counterflashing fitted into a wooden chimney. Instead, make sure the housewrap and siding cover the wall legs of the flashing to help shed water.

Base flashing

Flashing the base of a chimney is essentially the same as flashing the front of a dormer as described earlier. The only difference is the base flashing for a chimney is typically done in one piece that wraps up both corners by a couple of inches.

You can encounter a couple of different flashing arrangements depending on how the mason set up the chimney. He may have installed a wide counterflashing that folds out onto the roof several inches. In this case, you won't have to install additional flashing of your own; just raise the existing counterflashing/base flashing and slide your underlayment and shingles beneath. Make sure that the flashing will cover the fastener heads before you press it back down over the shingles. I usually dab the heads of the fasteners with roof cement as an added precaution.

Sometimes the mason installs a counterflashing that just reaches the roof plane but doesn't cover the shingles. In this case, you'll need to form and install a base flashing that slips beneath the counterflashing. Bend the flashing at an L shape so that the bottom leg extends out 4 in. to 6 in. onto the roof to cover the top of a shingle course. You can make the flashing from one piece of lead, hammering the roof leg to spread it around the corner, or you can make it with an insert soldered end to flash around the corner. Always use the same metal as the counterflashing to avoid a galvanic reaction.

Chimney side flashing

Use step flashing along the sides of a chimney just as you would along a sidewall. Run the lowest piece to the bottom corner of the chimney to cover the short return piece of the base flashing. Instead of overlapping the wall leg of the flashing with the housewrap and siding, fold the counterflashing over it (see the right photo below). Depending on how the mason arranged the counterflashing, several pieces of step flashing may be covered by a single piece of counterflashing.

As a secondary precaution, install waterproof shingle membrane to the side of the chimney beneath the counterflashing and out onto the roof sheathing before you begin.

The bottom edges of masonry chimneys are flashed with a base flashing that's similar to vertical wall flashing. The mason typically inserts lead or copper flashing into a mortar joint when building the chimney.

On the sides of a chimney, the mason installs counterflashing. The roofer lifts the counterflashing, installs step flashing against the chimney, then folds the counterflashing back down.

Cutting in New Counterflashing

On reroof projects, it always saves time if you can reuse the old counterflashing rather than install new pieces. But eventually, old flashing pieces deteriorate or they may break when you're stripping off the old roof shingles. The easiest way to install new counterflashing is to cut slots into the mortar joints of the chimney.

To cut the slots, use a circular saw, preferably outfitted with a dry-cut diamond blade, although a masonry blade will also work. Set the blade depth at 1 in. to 1½ in., then cut along the lower edge of the mortar joint with one side of the blade running against the brick. This will preserve most of the mortar in the joint and leave a slot wide enough to slip the new flashing into.

Make one cut 4 in. to 6 in. from the bottom of the chimney, from corner to corner, and continue the cut 2 in. to 3 in. around both sides. Along the sides of the chimney, make stepped cuts about 8 in. long in successive mortar joints. Overlap the slots by 3 in. so the installed flashing pieces will overlap one another. Using a compressed-air blower, clean dust out of the slots. You can also flush out the dust with water as long as you let the slots dry before installing flashing.

I find copper is easier to work with than lead for these new flashing pieces. Copper is a little stiffer and thinner, so it slides into the slots better. Start by fabricating the base flashing. Bend a flange along the top edge of the flashing to insert into the slot, making the flange a tiny bit shorter than the slot is deep so you don't have trouble fitting it in.

Squirt some urethane or butyl sealant that's compatible with masonry construction into the slot, then insert the flashing flange and fill any gap left between the flashing and the slot with more sealant. Don't use roof cement to seal the flashing in place; it's likely to ooze out when it gets hot and may fail to maintain a leakproof seal.

Next, form and install counterflashing for step flashing along the sides of the chimney. Cut the bottom edge of each piece to match the roof pitch, and keep them about ¼ in. above the roof shingles to make installing the step flashing easier.

A diamond circular sawblade cuts a groove in a mortar joint wide enough to insert new flashing.

A specially formed and soldered base flashing is inserted into the saw kerf in the chimney.

Copper is easier than lead to work with and install into the narrow grooves cut into the masonry chimney.

Chimney crickets and flashing

Crickets are designed to channel away water, snow, and ice that can accumulate at the up-slope side of a mid-roof chimney. Depending on its size, a cricket can be covered entirely with metal flashing or a combination of flashing and shingles.

COVERING A CRICKET WITH FLASHING Small crickets can be covered and flashed with one piece of formed metal or a couple of pieces layered together. Copper solders easily to form a flashing with wide legs to lie on the roof sheathing and up the sides of the chimney. Counterflashing or siding covers the chimney leg, and the underlayment and shingles cover the roof leg.

If you aren't handy at soldering copper sheets, you can layer a couple of wide sheets of lead to cover the cricket. Use one piece of lead to form the chimney leg, and cover a substantial portion of the cricket. Overlapping a second piece of lead over the first by at least 6 in., bend flanges out onto the roof sheathing. Tap the lead gently with a hammer to form flares and creases so it lies flat against the roof and chimney (see the illustration on p. 204).

The cricket behind a chimney (or wooden chimney box in this case) can be covered with a formed metal flashing. (Photo © Scott McBride.)

Since a lot of water will flow off the main roof above the cricket, always apply the flashing sections closest to the body of the main roof on top of those closest to the chimney. This will keep rushing water from washing beneath the overlap seams.

Before you attach the cricket flashing you've fabricated, cover the cricket with waterproof shingle underlayment. Wrap the edge of the waterproof underlayment up the side of the chimney about 4 in. and out onto the main roof sheathing, then wrap it around the corners of the chimney and over the step flashing installed along the sides and out onto the top lap of the roof shingles. Underlayment applied to the roof sheathing above the cricket should overlap the roof flanges of the cricket flashing.

SHINGLING A CRICKET You won't be able to use a single piece of flashing to cover a large cricket behind a wide chimney, so handle these crickets as you would a small gable roof and apply roof shingles to them. Treat the small valleys

WORK SAFE
WORK SMART
THINKING AHEAD

The fumes that spew out of a chimney can be dangerous to breathe, and while they probably won't kill you, they can cause headaches, nausea, and dizziness—not a good thing, particularly on a roof. Never stuff rags in the flue as a solution. Instead, have any fume-producing equipment turned off while you're working.

Crickets can be shingled like small gable dormer roofs. Prepare the entire cricket and valleys by covering with waterproof shingle underlayment before roofing.

Covering a Cricket with Flashing

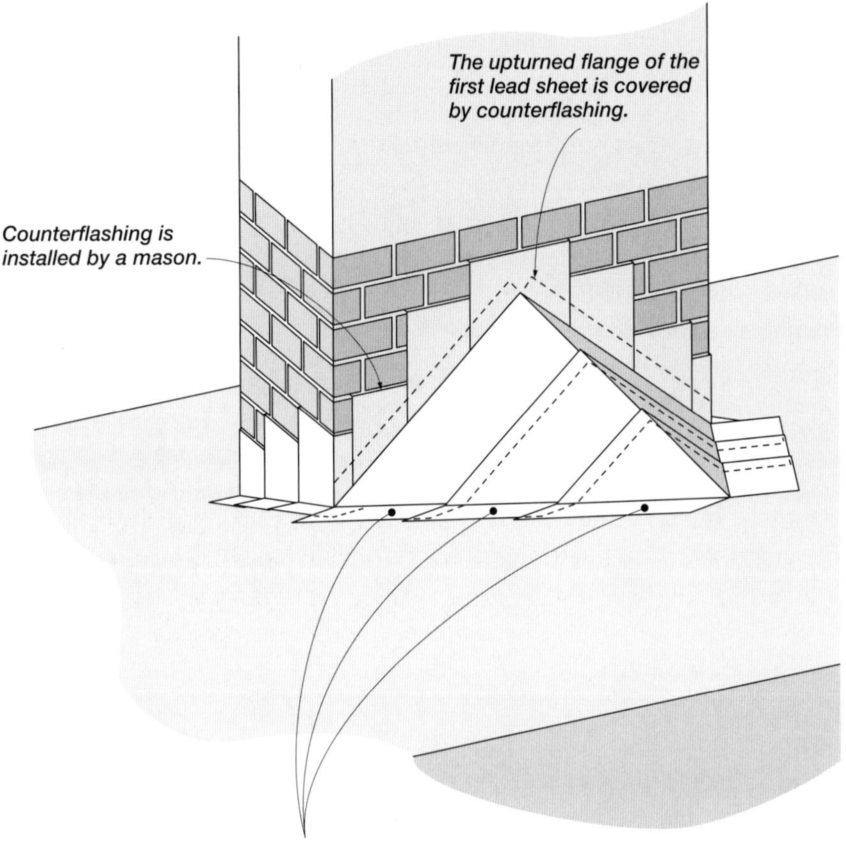

The lead sheets folded over the cricket and onto the main roof.

The sheets are overlapped starting at the chimney. Joints are soldered or sealed with roof cement.

The sheet closest to the chimney has an upturned flange to go against the chimney and is covered by counterflashing.

created from the ridge of the cricket to the corners of the chimney either as an open valley with metal valley flashing or wrap shingles through the valley. Install step flashing along the chimney for each shingle course, and cover the side flange with counterflashing or siding (see the photo at right on p. 203). As a precaution before you begin shingling, cover the entire cricket with waterproof shingle underlayment.

Always shingle the cricket and wrap the ends of the shingles through the valleys (unless you are installing an open-valley system) before shingling the main roof. The shingles applied to the main roof deck will be cut along the valley line (see "Shingling Valleys" on p. 210 for a more complete description).

Flashing Skylights

There are two basic flashing systems used on commercially available skylights. The simplest is used on the less-expensive models, which have integral flanges similar to those on roof vents (see the photo on the facing page). I've found this arrangement more prone to leaking than the other type of flashing, which consists of a separate multiple-piece flashing *system*. These flashing systems, used on good-quality skylights, are similar to those around chimneys and are the type I'll describe here. For skylights with integral flashing flanges, follow the directions described in "Installing Roof Vents" on p. 208.

Parts of skylight flashing

The frame of a skylight raises the glass panel off the surface of the roof plane and is often called the curb. A plastic or rubber gasket rims the top of the curb. It forms an airtight, water-resistant seal for the glass panel to seat into and folds over the side edges of the curb by 1 in. to 2 in. All of the pieces of metal flashing that layer into the roof shingles will slip beneath this gasket so water rolling off the glass panel will be shed on top of the flashing.

Skylight manufacturers usually offer preformed flashing kits for use with their products. These kits are convenient because they include a base flashing and a head flashing (used at the top of the skylight) sized to fit the curb. Also included are large step-flashing pieces for the sides with legs tall enough to fit perfectly beneath the edge of the gasket. The flashing pieces are colored to match the skylight sash. They are also nicely formed so when completely installed, the skylight and flashing appear integrated rather than a jumble of parts.

Installing the flashing

Normally, the glass panel of the skylight can be removed. This is the case with both stationary and operating panels. Removing the panel makes it much easier to roll back the gasket to slide the top edges of the flashing pieces tightly against the curb.

1. **Shingle up to the skylight.** Shingle the roof until you reach the last course that will give you a full-width

Simple skylights have an integral flange around the perimeter (exposed here at the bottom edge). These skylights are installed the same way as a roof vent.

Framing a Cricket

Chances are when you arrive to shingle a new house roof, you'll find a cricket already behind each chimney. The same goes for reroof projects. But if a cricket was never installed, you should consider framing one before you roof.

You'll need some 2× lumber for rafters and plywood or OSB for sheathing. Start by finding the center of the chimney and marking the height for the ridge of the cricket. Plan to make the pitch of the cricket from 8 to 12 to effectively shed water and reduce snow and ice buildup. Cut the first pair of rafters to go close to the chimney; plan for a 1-in. air space between the rafter and the chimney brick to minimize fire hazard. Keep the bottom of the rafters about 1 in. shy of the corners of the chimney so once the sheathing is placed, it will meet the corners.

Prop the rafters in place and tack-nail the bottom edges to the roof sheathing. Using a level, find the point where the ridge of the cricket will meet the main roof. At this point, install a ridge board between the rafters and the main roof. Cut and install rafters 16 in. to 24 in. apart, then cover the rafters with sheathing.

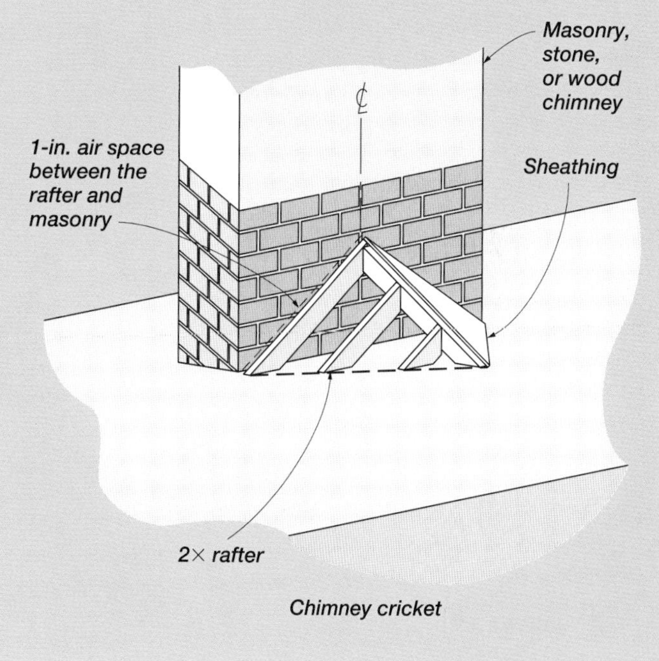

Chimney cricket

More expensive curbed skylights come with special preformed flashing kits that include a base flashing, step flashings, and a head flashing.

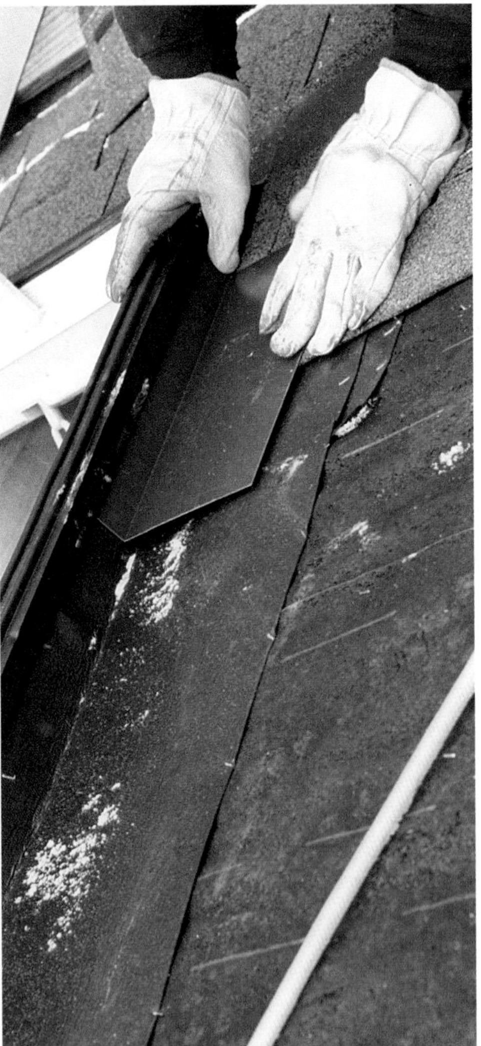

The curb leg of the skylight step flashing slips beneath a rubber gasket that also seals the window to the curb. (Photo by Andy Engel, courtesy *Fine Homebuilding* magazine, © The Taunton Press.)

shingle below the skylight curb. In the next course, notch the head lap of a shingle to fit directly beneath the curb and around both sides of the curb. Depending on where shingle joints fall and the width of the skylight, you may have to cut two shingles to fit around the curb.

Check to make sure that the edge of the base flashing will land somewhere on the exposure portion of this shingle or shingles. If not, cut another course to fit around the curb and up the sides. Drive the fasteners in the shingles about 1 in. below the skylight curb; the base flashing will cover them.

2. **Install the base flashing.** Fold the gasket up, lay the flashing on the shingles beneath the curb, then slide it up snug against the bottom of the curb. You'll need a helper to install base-flashing pieces on wide skylights so both sides will slide up together. If you struggle alone and force a base flashing up crooked, you might kink the metal or break the roll-formed corners.
3. **Install the side step flashing.** Shingle the courses all the way up to the top of the skylight. You can either install each step flashing piece as you go, or you can slip in the flashing pieces later. Either way, cut the shingles ¼ in. short of the curb. Slip the side leg of the flashing under the rubber gasket, and press the roof flange down until it sits firmly against the shingle (see the bottom photo at left). There's usually enough friction between the gasket and the curb to hold the step flashing in place without nails, but assess the product you're working with to decide if fastening the step flashing is necessary. If nails seem necessary to hold the step flashings

Extra Protection for Skylights

As an extra precaution against leakage around a skylight curb, I like to install strips of waterproof shingle underlayment around the sides. To do this, cut 36-in.-wide membrane down the middle, then cut these 18-in.-wide pieces into strips for the top, bottom, and sides. Make the pieces long enough to extend 9 in. past each edge. Install regular underlayment on the roof sheathing and up to the edge of the skylight. Shingle up to the last full course of shingles that pass beneath the base of the skylight without needing the head lap cut.

Next, apply the bottom piece of waterproof underlayment. Lifting the gasket, stick the top edge of the underlayment flush with the top of the curb. Bend a crisp crease at the base of the curb, and fold the bottom over the head lap of the shingles. If the underlayment extends below the self-seal tabs on the shingles, trim it off. Make diagonal cuts in the underlayment at the corners of the skylight, and fold the top ears along the sides of the curb and the bottom ears down to the roof.

Apply the side pieces of waterproof underlayment about 2 in. higher than the top of the curb. Make diagonal cuts at the top and bottom corners, then fold the ears around the ends of the curb and onto the roof.

Finally, apply the top piece of waterproof underlayment. After making the diagonal cuts at the corners, fold the top ears over the side pieces of underlayment and the roof ears over the top of the lower pieces.

Using silicone or butyl caulking, seal the corners where you made the diagonal cuts and folded the ears around each corner. Don't use asphalt roof cement because it may deteriorate the waterproof shingle underlayment.

Make the skylight curb more water-resistant by wrapping waterproof shingle underlayment up the sides and onto the roof. (Photo by Andy Engel, courtesy *Fine Homebuilding* magazine, © The Taunton Press.)

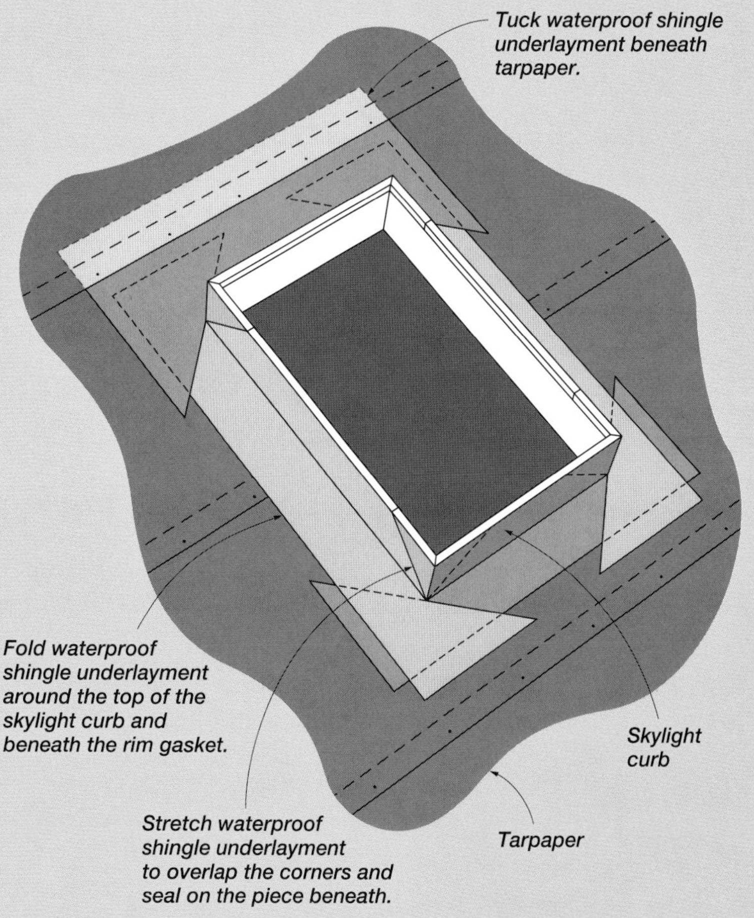

The preformed skylight head flashing extends around the corner and down the sides to interlace with the step flashing. The rubber gasket seals the top edge. (Photo by Andy Engel, courtesy *Fine Homebuilding* magazine, © The Taunton Press.)

in place, I'd recommend driving them through the top corner of the step flashing into the roof sheathing rather than into the curb. Curbs are only about an inch thick, and you don't want to drive a nail through to the inside finish face.

4. **Shingle the top of the skylight.** As you did for the curb, cut a shingle to fit around the top of the skylight before installing the head flashing. Again you might have to cut two shingles.
5. **Install the head flashing.** Once the shingle is cut and fastened, you can slide the head flashing down around the top of the curb. Using the same caution as with the base flashing, move it down evenly. Fasten the top edge of the head flashing with nails every 12 in. and continue installing shingle courses. Finally, fold the gasket over all the flashing edges to complete the seal.

The butt edge of the first shingle over the head flashing will need to be trimmed to fit around it, but the second course will continue straight through.

Installing Roof Vents

Roof vents are very easy to install. Although they may be second best to ridge vents for ventilating the upper portion of a roof, they may be the only choice in instances where ridge vents aren't practical. Other roof products including large, flanged metal chimney flashing and flanged skylights can be installed using the same technique I'll describe here.

Locating and cutting the hole

The higher you can position the roof vents on the roof, the better. This will increase the stack effect and naturally draw more air into the soffit vents or vented drip edge. Of course, you want to keep the roof vents at least 8 in. below the ridge so you can install cap shingles or below a vertical wall so you can install wall flashing.

From the ventilation calculations you made in chapter 4, you determined how many roof vents you'll need to vent the attic. Plan to space the vents equally along the length of the roof to maximize air movement. The lines of nails in the sheathing will tell you where the rafters are located beneath. Position the vents between rafters rather than over them, even if you have to shift the even spacing. Placing them over rafters would reduce their effectiveness.

Measure the opening in the bottom of the roof vent to determine how large to cut the holes in the sheathing. Be sure to measure the vent opening, not the outside flange. To keep the vents lined up horizontally with one another, snap a straight chalkline parallel to the shingle courses. Use the eaves edge or the top of a course of shingles as a reference. I like to position the top of the vent hole along the bottom edge of a shingle course. This saves time because I don't have to trim the shingles above the vent. It also looks neater, although you can't really tell from the ground.

Mark and cut the holes about ¼ in. larger than the opening in the roof vents. A battery-operated circular or reciprocating saw is great for working on the roof. Be careful of the sawdust: It makes the roof slippery, and it can collect in lumps beneath the top edge of underlayment or shingles you've already installed. Sweep it up or blow it off the roof right away.

Installing the vent

As soon as you roll underlayment over the vent holes, cut out the fabric; otherwise the concealed holes become dangerous to an unwary roofer. Continue shingling the roof up to the bottom of the vent holes without covering them, then install another course of shingles so the top lap covers the holes. After nailing off the course, cut the shingle material out of the vent holes. Position a roof vent over one of the holes to see if the bottom edge of the flange covers down to and over the fastener line of the shingle. If so, you can install the roof vents. If not, install another course of shingles and trim out the material overlaying the holes.

Because roof-vent flanges are only about 2 in. wide, you may want to spread roofing cement around the hole to prevent leaks from wind-driven rain. When you spread the cement, keep it about ½ in. from the edge of the flange so it won't ooze out. Install the vent with the flange covering the shingle below the hole and the underlayment around the sides. It's good to have the underlayment along the top flange overlap onto it to help shed water. Make two horizontal slits in the underlayment out from the top corners of the hole just long enough for the flanges to slide under.

A Trick for Vent Installation

If you don't want to go to the trouble of slicing the underlayment along the top edge and slipping the flange beneath, you have another option. Apply the vent flange over the underlayment and then add a second layer of underlayment to overlap the top of the roof-vent flange. Since the vents are located near the top of the roof, you'll only need narrow strips about 4 in. to 8 in. wide. Fold the top edge of the underlayment over the ridge or up the vertical wall, then overlap the vent flange with the bottom edge. Seal the lap with roof cement. Any water that makes its way down to the underlayment will be shed on top of the roof-vent flanges rather than beneath.

In cases where the roof vents are several feet from the ridge or wall, you can still use this trick. Just cut a strip of underlayment wide enough to reach from the top of the vent hole to the next underlayment course overlap above. This will be no more than 3 ft. Cut the strip wide enough to lap beneath the underlayment above by 5 in. or more.

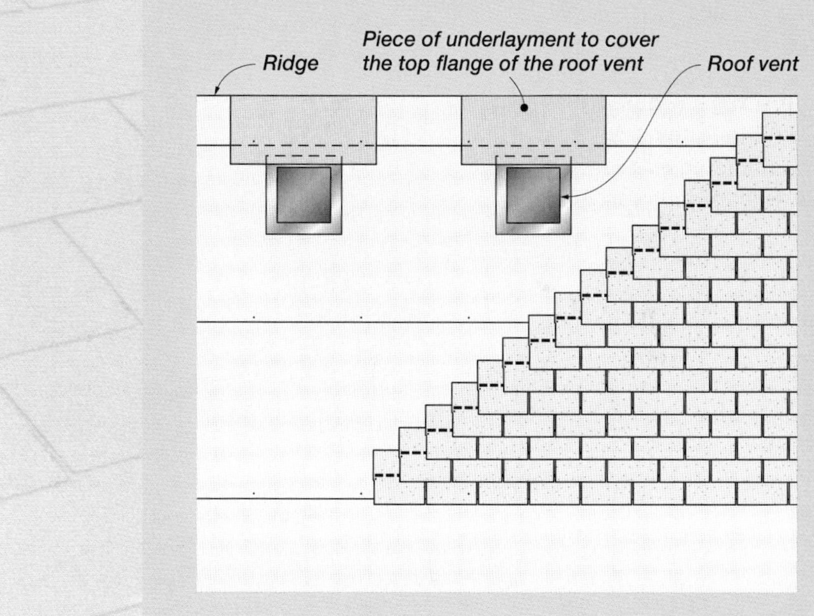

Lift up the bottom of the vent as you slide the top flange beneath the underlayment, and line up the top with the chalkline you snapped earlier. Then press the roof vent down into the cement. Lift the underlayment along the top edge, apply a line of cement to the top flange of the vent, and press the underlayment back down.

Shingle up to the point where the self-seal strip is within 3 in. of the bottom of the roof-vent hole. Slide the top flange of the roof vent beneath the underlayment and position it over the hole.

Cut the next one or two shingle courses to overlap the roof-vent side flanges, and cover the top flange with a final shingle that's cut to fit around the vent.

Drive four nails into the flanges to hold the vent in place: two in the upper corners and two on the side flanges just above the point where the butt edge of the next course of shingles will cover.

Shingling around the vent

With the roof vents fastened, you can shingle around them. Cut shingles in each course about G in. from the sides of the roof vent to allow for expansion. The vents, which are often made of plastic, can expand quite a bit on a hot day. I like to run a bead of roof cement from a tube over the vent flange before installing each shingle that overlaps it. You could go back later to seal the shingles, but it can be next to impossible to get the nose of a caulking tube beneath the hood of the roof vent and under the shingle.

You'll only need to install one or two courses of shingles before you reach the top of the roof vents. When the top lap of a course extends above the vent, you'll need to cut it to fit around the roof vent. Cut the exposure part of each shingle that fits above the roof vent and leave the top lap intact. Slide the shingle over the flange and down.

The next course of shingles should clear the top edge of the roof vent if you positioned the hole as described above. There's no need to apply any roof cement under either of the shingles over the top flange of the roof vent provided the underlayment laps the flange. In fact, it's better to leave them unsealed so any moisture caught by the underlayment will drain.

Shingling Valleys

Many of today's new-home designs include multiple gable and hip-roof configurations. When various roof planes meet at an angle, valleys are created. Because valleys collect and channel a greater volume of water than an ordinary roof plane, you need to pay special attention to water-resistant design and construction.

There are two basic ways to configure a valley: an open valley where the valley flashing is exposed and lines the channel to carry away water, and a closed valley where the shingles wrap through the valley and line the channel.

In chapter 5, I described how to install underlayment for valleys and how to assemble metal valley flashing or roll roofing for open valleys. In this section, I'll explain how to end shingles along open valleys and to cut them in a straight line. You'll also see how to use the shingles to form closed valleys using both the weaving and cutting techniques.

Shingling an open valley

Whether you're using a mineral-surface (roll-roofing) valley or a metal valley, the process for shingling up to and cutting the shingles along a straight line at the valley is the same. Follow the instructions in "Preparing Valleys" on p. 103 to apply the valley flashing.

There are two ways you can cut in the shingles. The most common way is to let the ends of the shingles run into the valley and cut them off later. The other way, which I prefer, is to cut the shingles as you install each course.

In either case, you should prepare the valley the same way. To form a leak-resistant joint between the shingles and valley flashing (and comply with most manufacturers' instructions), apply a 3-in.-wide band of asphalt roof cement along the sides of the valley flashing into which to bed the end of the shingles. You can either spread the cement before you apply the shingles, or you can squirt cement from a tube beneath the edge of the cut shingles after you've completed the valley. If you choose to apply roof cement before installing the shingles, snap chalklines to guide the application so you don't spread cement into the exposed portion of the valley.

The shingles should end along a line at least 3 in. out of the center of the valley, so snap this line to use as a guide for both the cement and shingles. Measure and mark the top and bottom of the valley on both sides, then snap chalklines between them. Spread the roof cement about 1 in. away from the line so the shingles will cover it completely.

You may find that some shingle manufacturers' instructions recommend the space between the shingles and the center line of the valley be wider at the bottom than at the top. Some recommend that the shingle cutlines should each diverge from the center of the valley by ⅛ in. per foot. On a large roof, you may encounter valleys 20 ft. or longer. Starting with the minimum spacing of 3 in. at the top of the valley, you'd have 7½ in. of spacing at the bottom of a 20-ft. valley. This is fine as long as your valley flashing is wide enough to leave at least 8 in. of flashing overlapped by shingles.

In the snow belt, there may be a benefit to exposing more of the valley at the bottom than at the top in that it may help the snow slide out and minimize ice dams. Also, the bottom of the valley carries more water than the upper portion so more width at the bottom may be beneficial.

CUTTING VALLEY SHINGLES AFTER ROOFING The most common way to trim the shingles along the valley line is after you've installed them. Just run the shingles of each course into the valley and

> **■ WORK SAFE ■ WORK SMART ■ THINKING AHEAD**
>
> **When shingling an open valley, spread only 2 ft. to 3 ft. of roof cement ahead of you. Any more may begin to dry, collect blowing leaves, or worse, get all over you and your tools. When you quit for the day, scrape off any excess cement applied to the valley and reapply when you return.**

An open valley is wrapped with a metal (shown here) or mineral-surface valley flashing. The shingles end about 4 in. to 6 in. from the valley center and the water flows down the flashing.

Avoiding Joints between Shingles

It's best to avoid joints between shingles within 12 in. of a valley center, especially on open valleys. You can make a simple adjustment when applying shingles to avoid the problem as you bring a course of shingles across and up to a valley.

As you place the last full shingle in each course working toward the valley, notice how close its end is to the valley center. When you're installing shingles for a closed valley, look for the shingle to end 1 ft. to 2 ft. from the valley center. If it does, go ahead and nail the shingle in place. The last full shingle approaching an open valley (or the second layer in a closed-cut valley) cannot end from 2 in. to 12 in. from the center, but those that fall more than 12 in. away or wrap through the valley center are fine and can be nailed. Don't nail down shingles that fall within the danger zone for the type of valley you're shingling. Instead, insert a short section of shingle in the course first and then apply the full shingle. The piece must be long enough so the full shingle you apply next to it will extend all the way into an open valley for trimming or through the valley a minimum of 12 in. for woven valleys or the first layer of closed-cut valleys.

With three-tab shingles, the piece you insert will have to be either a 1-ft. or 2-ft. section to maintain the cutout-slot arrangement. With random-pattern laminated shingles, you can insert any size you need. In fact, this is a good place to use pieces cut off the ends of courses.

The last shingle ending each course at the valley must be at least 16 in. long to avoid nailing too close to the valley center. If necessary, slide a long shingle into the valley, leaving a space between it and its neighbor, as shown at left, then nail. Fill the space between the two shingles with a piece later (right). (Photos by Andy Engel, courtesy *Fine Homebuilding* magazine, © The Taunton Press.)

leave them long. After shingling an entire section of the roof, measure and snap a chalkline to guide your cut. Using a hook blade in a utility knife, draw it toward you, cutting through only one shingle at a time. Be careful not to penetrate too deeply and cut into the valley flashing; a metal valley is pretty tough but a mineral-surface valley will puncture easily.

Instead of a knife, you can use shears to cut through one layer of shingles at a time. Handled correctly, shears are less likely than a knife to puncture the valley flashing. Cutting shingles will dull shears quickly, but even somewhat dull shears will cut through shingles. Just don't count on them to cut anything else, such as sheet metal, afterwards.

CUTTING VALLEY SHINGLES AS YOU GO I prefer to cut the shingles into the valley as I go. It doesn't necessarily save time, but you get cleaner cuts than you would trimming the shingles later. It also minimizes the danger of puncturing the valley flashing.

You can use two methods to guide the shingle cutting. You can follow the chalkline you snapped earlier to guide the roof-cement application, or you can set up a string between the top and bottom of the valley. I follow the chalkline to cut along mineral-surface-covered valleys, but chalk smudges easily from exposed metal valleys, so on those I use the string as a guide.

Once you have a guide, run the shingle courses across the roof towards the valley. When you reach the last shingle in a course, put it in place but don't nail it. Use the blade of your knife to press small marks at the points where the chalkline or string crosses the top and bottom edges of the shingle. Flip the shingle over, then use a straightedge to run the knife blade along between the marks. Snap the shingle and install it in position (see the top photo on the facing page).

Shingling closed valleys

In closed valleys, the shingles wrap through the bottom of the valley. Closed valleys are by far the most common type used on asphalt roofs because there's no need for valley flashing and there's less shingle cutting involved.

There are two ways in which the shingles from the opposite roof planes can meet in a closed valley. The older, and now less common, method is called a woven, or laced, valley. The simpler method is called a cut valley, which is also referred to as a California valley, western weave, or half-laced valley (see the photos on below).

The technique you choose is a matter of preference and local norm. Both shed water with equal effectiveness, although some roofers claim that you get a double-coverage effect from woven valleys because the shingles from both roof planes wrap through the center of the

Cut the shingles ending at the valleys as you go to avoid damaging the valley flashing when cutting after they are installed. Make knife nicks where the shingle crosses the string (or chalkline), then flip and cut. (Photo by Andy Engel, courtesy *Fine Homebuilding* magazine, © The Taunton Press.)

WORK SAFE
WORK SMART
THINKING AHEAD

Never drive fasteners within 8 in. of the center of a valley no matter which methods or materials you use to shingle and flash them. Rain will eventually get between the shingles and the valley flashing (or between shingles of a closed valley). Holding fasteners back a little will minimize the chance of a leak developing.

There are two types of closed valleys. In a woven-closed valley, shown at left, the shingles of adjoining courses are interlaced. In a closed-cut valley, shown at right, shingles from one roof plane cover over the ends of the ones from the other roof.

Woven valleys are assembled by overlapping the last shingle in every other course from the two roof planes meeting at a valley.

valley. On the other hand, the shingles in woven valleys are more likely to split and cause leaks if they aren't installed with precision. The problems are most likely to occur in climates with wide seasonal temperature changes.

Always prepare the valley for the worst-case condition—a leak—so that any water that does penetrate through the shingles will be collected and diverted off the roof by the valley flashing or underlayment beneath (see "Preparing Valleys" on p. 103).

Woven valleys are inconvenient to install. You have to bring the shingles up both roof planes simultaneously a few courses at a time so you can weave the valley shingles together. This means moving back and forth between the roof planes, unless you have two roofers working toward the valley at the same pace. There are ways you can weave the shingles into the valley after you shingle the roof planes, but they are tedious and time consuming.

INSTALLING A WOVEN VALLEY To install a woven valley, run three or four horizontal courses toward the valley from one roof plane but stop about one shingle short of the valley. Do the same from the opposite roof plane, then gather your tools and some shingles at the valley to weave the ends of the courses together.

Starting with the bottom right-hand course, run the final shingle through the valley. Follow the horizontal control line until the shingle reaches the center of the valley. Press the shingle snugly into the valley crease but don't fold or crack it. The end of the shingle will splay slightly upward on the opposite roof plane. Nail the shingle in place along both the course line and the free end, but omit nails within 8 in. of the valley center.

Next, apply the last shingle to the bottom course from the left-hand roof plane, run it through the valley, and fasten it the same way. Return to the right side and bring the second course across, then the course from the left side (see the photo above).

Installing a woven valley is really no more complicated than lacing up your boots, but switching gears between production shingle application and weaving the valley slows you down. One way to speed the production is to have three roofers working in unison. Two can each shingle a roof plane, while the third focuses on weaving the valley where the planes meet.

Every few courses you'll find that a shingle joint will end within 12 in. of the valley center (either before or after the shingle wraps through the valley). Use the same technique I describe in the sidebar on p. 212 to insert pieces of shingle to avoid the joints.

INSTALLING A CUT VALLEY Before you begin shingling a cut valley, determine which roof shingles will wrap through the valley and which ones will be cut. The rule of thumb is to have the shingles of the smallest roof or the one shedding the least water wrap through the bottom of the valley and to cut the shingles of the larger roof. This will direct the heaviest flow of rainwater out over the surface of the shingles. Overlapping and cutting the valley in the opposite fashion can cause problems; water rushing down the larger roof will slam into the cut-shingle edge and may be forced under the shingles.

The first course of shingles in a cut valley will shed water better if it's woven with the first course of the opposite roof. Once you've overlapped the first courses, install shingle courses of the first (smaller) roof plane through the valley and wrap the shingles onto the opposite roof plane (see the top photo at right). Make sure the shingles extend onto the other roof by 1 ft. to 2 ft. before fastening. If one's too short, insert a piece of shingle in the course before applying the last full one. Remember to avoid fasteners within 8 in. of the valley center.

After the first roof plane is shingled, you can shingle the larger, opposite roof. Start by snapping a chalkline on this roof plane 2 in. from the center of the valley; you'll trim the shingles along this line. Lay the last shingle in each course over the shingles that wrapped through the valley from the first roof plane. The bottom of each shingle must cross the top of the cutoff line, but the top of the shingles can be up to 2 in. short of the line because you'll be clipping the tops of the shingles later. It's okay if the shingles fold into the valley or extend beyond because the ends will be cut later. Remember to omit fasteners within 8 in. of the valley center and not to nail the ends of any shingle that extends onto the opposite side of the valley.

The last step is to trim the shingles of the second roof plane. Even though there's already a chalkline under the shin-

Closed-cut valleys don't require that you shingle the two roof planes simultaneously. The ends of the shingles from the first roof plane are wrapped through and up onto the opposite roof plane at least 1 ft.

The shingles of the second roof plane meeting at a closed-cut valley are cut in a straight line about 2 in. from the valley center.

Clipping Shingles

Some manufacturers' instructions recommend clipping the top 2-in. corner off the top lap of the shingles ending at open valleys or the trimmed edge of a closed-cut valley. Clipping (sometimes called dubbing) the corners is said to prevent water rushing down the valley from being diverted beneath the shingles by an uncut corner. Others claim it prevents the sharp end from digging into the valley flashing and puncturing it. In any case, the process is simple: Just clip the top corner at a 45-degree to 90-degree angle.

Trim about 2 in. off the upper corner of the top lap with a 45-degree or 90-degree cut. Called dubbing, this helps keep rushing water from being directed beneath the shingles by the shingle tip. (Photo by Andy Engel, courtesy *Fine Homebuilding* magazine, © The Taunton Press.)

Sealing Valleys

If you've cut shingles along an open valley or a closed-cut valley, you need to seal the edges with roof cement. Earlier I described how to apply roof cement before installing shingles along the valley, but that may not be practical on a windy day when leaves are blowing around. I find it easier to cement the valley shingles after they are installed.

One way is to spread a 2-in. to 3-in. ribbon of roof cement between the shingles of the first roof plane and the cut edge of the second roof plane using a trowel. Try to keep the cement back ½ in. to 1 in. from the edge so it won't ooze out and be noticeable. For more control, you can squirt two beads of cement from a tube.

The ends of shingles along open valleys or the one cut edge on closed-cut valleys must be sealed with roof cement. (Photo by Andy Engel, courtesy *Fine Homebuilding* magazine, © The Taunton Press.)

gles, measure and snap another chalkline on the surface 2 in. from the valley center as a guide. Using a utility knife with a hook blade or a pair of shears, cut the shingles, being careful not to puncture the shingles beneath. Clip off the top corner of each shingle by 2 in. by lifting the shingle above it slightly.

An alternative method to install and trim the last shingle in each course is to follow the description for cutting shingles into an open valley. Using the 2-in. chalkline or setting up a string as a guide, cut each shingle before you lay it in place. You can spread a band of roof cement and trim the top corner of each shingle before placing it too.

Installing Cap Shingles

Roof-cap shingles cover ridges and hips where the shingles from two roof planes meet at a high point. About 12 in. square, cap shingles are installed in an overlapping fashion just as regular shingles to shed water and protect fastener heads. There are only a couple of points where you will need to face-nail the shingles where the fasteners are left exposed and then cover the fasteners with roof cement.

You can make your own cap shingles by cutting them from three-tab strip shingles (see the sidebar on p. 218), or you can buy premade cap shingles. Typically the premade cap shingles are intended for use with laminated and specialty shingles.

In this section, I'll describe how to prepare a ridge or hip for covering. You'll see how to install cap shingles directly over a ridge and how to install them over a ridge vent. And I'll cover special situations such as installing a metal ridge vent and blending caps into a roof plane.

Shingling up to an unvented ridge

The preparation for unvented ridges is straightforward. Fold the top lap of the last two or three courses of shingles up and over the ridge, then fasten them down over the roof underlayment on the other side. Shingle the opposite side of the roof up to the ridge. Fold the top laps of the last courses over the first roof, but trim them off along a line no more than 4 in. beyond the ridge before nailing down. The third from the last course may roll a little over the ridge, the second to the last will need an inch or two trim, and the last course will need a substantial trim; it all depends on how the horizontal courses lay out. However they lay out, the last course on both sides will be the one where the self-seal strip falls within 5 in. of the ridge.

You can improve the water tightness of the ridge by interlocking the last two or three shingle courses between the two sides of the ridge. Rather than folding all three of the top laps from one side over onto the other, only fold the top of one course. Shingle the other side of the roof up to the ridge, then fold the top lap over onto the first side. Return to the initial side of the ridge and install another course folded over, then go back to the second side. By doing it this way, you'll only have to trim the last course of shingles that overlaps the ridge.

Cutting an air slot for the ridge vent

A ridge that will receive a vent needs a slot along its length that allows at least 1 in. of air space on each side of the ridge. Hopefully, in a new house, the framers left the gap, but you'll have to cut the gap if you are retrofitting ridge vent on an older home. If there is a 2× ridge board present, snap chalklines on both sides of the ridge 1¾ in. down. If there is no ridge board, snap the line 1 in. down.

Cut back the roof sheathing along the ridge to leave a 2-in.-wide gap for air to escape when installing ridge vent.

Set the bevel on a circular saw so the cut will be plumb instead of square to the roof sheathing. Also adjust the depth of the blade so it just cuts through the sheathing and not more than 1⁄16 in. into the framing. I prefer to use an old carbide-tipped sawblade knowing full well that I'll hit a few nails.

Clean off the sawdust as soon as possible after cutting so no one slips on it and it doesn't blow beneath the underlayment or shingles. Remove the strips of sheathing you cut out, then drive new nails along the top edge of the remaining sheathing.

Now you can install the shingles up to the edge of the air slot. Cut the top lap off the upper courses of shingles as needed so the air slot stays clear. Continue installing courses until the self-seal strip is within 3 in. of the slot. You need the strip to be within 3 in.; otherwise the cap shingles won't be wide enough to cover the self-seal strip and the fasteners. If the strip falls between 3 in. and 6 in. away, you'll need to apply one more row of shingles. The self-seal strip of these shingles will be trimmed off but that's okay.

WORK SAFE
WORK SMART
THINKING AHEAD

Don't install ridge vents on hips. Vents are best installed high and low on roofs because they can short-circuit airflow when installed in the middle. They can also be prone to leaking.

You can precut narrow strips (those less than 6 in. or the width between the butt and seal strip) from laminated and no-cutout shingles before nailing them down. But if you cut three-tab shingles this narrow, you'll end up with a bunch of loose tabs. The tabs will be difficult to register into position, and the slots you leave to mimic the cutouts may vary. To avoid the problem, install three-tab shingles before cutting. Drive one fastener at each side of the cutout, then knife the top of the shingle off along the edge of the vent slot.

PREPARING A HIP You have to be careful when overlapping shingles over a hip. Unlike ridges, where the shingles run parallel and only the top laps cross the peak, the ends of shingles cross over along hips. If you overlap shingles in both directions, you can end up with a heavy lump, especially with laminated shingles. There are two methods to limit the excess thickness of double overlaps along hips.

The easiest is to trim all the shingles off right at the hip. The only precaution is to make sure you don't have any joints between shingles falling within 12 in. of the hip. This avoids having any small pieces that may come loose or blow off. The drawback of cutting the shingles from both sides of the hip is that there's no protection beyond the underlayment to limit water from penetrating if the cap shingles blow off in a storm.

As a tradeoff between the problems associated with double overlaps and no overlap, use a single overlap. Cut the shingles flush along one side of the hip. Let the shingles from the other side overlap about 4 in. or 5 in., then nail securely. Even if the caps blow off, the hip is reasonably protected.

Another way to make hips watertight is to trim the shingles off at the hip and cover the joint with a 6-in. to 8-in. strip of waterproof shingle underlayment. The cap shingles will cover the strip.

Cutting Cap Shingles

Cutting cap shingles from regular three-tab shingles is quick and easy. Turn a bundle of shingles upside down and face the top lap toward you, then draw a utility knife with a straight blade toward you to cut partway through the shingle. You want the top laps of the cap shingles to be tapered a little. To accomplish this, make two cuts at a diagonal of 10 degrees to 15 degrees starting from each of the two slots and one cut in at each end of the shingle from the half slot. The cuts don't have to be perfect or straight; the top lap will be covered by the exposure of the shingle above. Lift the shingle and bend slightly; the pieces will break off.

Stack the cap and discard the small triangles. One bundle of shingles will make almost 90 cap shingles or enough to cover 36 ft. Don't forget to gather up all the shingle cutoffs from gable ends, valleys, and hips. Any pieces longer than 1 ft. will yield at least one piece of cap.

Cap shingles are cut from regular three-tab shingles. Diagonal cuts from the top of the cutout slots across the top lap result in three caps per shingle.

Installing regular cap shingles

The process for snapping a chalkline and installing cap shingles is the same for ridges and hips. Cap shingles are about 12 in. wide so when they are folded over a ridge or hip, they will overlap each side by 6 in. You can "cheat" the caps toward one side or the other if necessary to cover completely the top lap of the last course of shingles, but don't shift them more than 1 in.

Measure down one roof plane from the peak equal distances at both ends of a ridge or hip. Using nonpermanent chalk (white or blue), snap a chalkline between the marks. On hips, always start installing cap shingles from the eaves. Begin capping ridges at the opposite end from the prevailing wind or the direction that the most severe storms blow from. This gives the wind less purchase on the cap shingles, since the butt edges will be facing away from the worst weather.

Align the edge of the first shingle with the chalkline, and drive one fastener 1 in. in and just to the exposure side of the self-seal strip. Fold the shingle over the ridge, making sure it lies as smooth as possible. Drive the second fastener on the opposite side to hold the end down. Register the next cap shingle with the chalkline, then slide it over the previous shingle so the fasteners are covered by ½ in., leaving 5 in. of the exposure showing on the shingle beneath. Continue the simple process until you reach the other end of the hip or ridge.

Sometimes I line up and fasten only one edge of the cap shingles to the chalkline and move on to the next until I reach the end of the roof. Then I go back and fold and fasten the other side down. See which way works faster for you.

Align cap shingles along the ridge to a chalkline, and drive nails about 1½ in. to 2 in. up from the edge just below the self-seal strip, as shown in the top photo. After nailing several caps along the chalkline, go to the opposite side to fold and nail the other side of the caps (bottom).

TERMINATING A ROW OF CAP SHINGLES AT A GABLE END OR WALL

A ridge can end at a gable end or a wall or die into a roof. Hips typically end at a ridge but can meet a wall too. Some of the termination details are easy and others are a little complicated.

Ending at a gable end or wall is the easiest to treat. The top lap of the cap shingles will be the first edge to encounter the end point. Trim off just enough of the top lap from the last two or three shingles to maintain the 5-in. exposure as you get close to the end. Cut the last piece as wide as the exposure (about 5 in.), and put a dab of roof cement on the underside of each corner. Press the last piece over the ridge and drive a nail in each corner, then cover each head with another dab of roof cement (see the photo at right on p. 220).

If the cap shingles end at a wall, attach a piece of metal flashing to the wall and fold it over the last cap. Lead works well because you can form it to the curve of the cap shingles and keep it flat to the wall where it will be covered by the housewrap and siding.

When a hip ends at a ridge, you will have to complete capping the hips before starting on the ridge. Overlap the top laps of the last couple of hip cap shingles onto the ridge, then nail the top edges of each cap in addition to the regular location to keep them from sticking up. Start the first (or end the last) cap shingle on the ridge so it overlaps down the hips about 3 in. To get the ends of the shingle

Cap Shingle Cautions

Choose your cap fasteners carefully. Depending on how may layers of shingles you overlapped across a hip or ridge, you may need longer fasteners than you used to install the shingles. I typically use 1¾-in. nails to be sure they penetrate the roof sheathing and hold the cap shingles securely.

Be careful when using pneumatic nailers to drive nails into cap shingles. The built-up layers of shingles beneath may have air pockets between them, and the nailer can overdrive the nail heads easily. Even though the head may not pull through the cap shingle, it can dimple it a little. Over time the nail head can cut through the cap and it will come loose. When nailing, set the depth of drive on your nailer or lower the air pressure to limit how deep the nails set. It's okay to leave the nails a little above the shingle surface and set them flush with a hammer blow. It takes a little longer but it will give you peace of mind during the next windstorm.

With several layers of shingles built up along the ridge, choose nails long enough to penetrate the sheathing. A 1¼-in. nail will just work for the ½-in. sheathing on the left, but 1¾-in. nails are needed for the ¾-in.-thick sheathing on the right.

to fold over and stay in place, make a 3-in. slice in the center of the cap. Press each wing down to the roof and the inside edges will overlap. Lifting the wings, spread some roof cement beneath the overlap and at the bottom outside corners. Drive three fasteners (one in the center and one at each corner) in addition to the two regular ones just below the seal strip. Dab the exposed fastener heads with roof cement.

BLENDING CAP SHINGLES INTO THE ROOF Where the ridge of a gable dormer or other smaller intersecting roof terminates into the main body of the roof, you'll have to blend the cap shingles beneath the roof shingles. Start capping the ridge at the gable end and work toward the main roof. When you reach the main roof, lift the first shingle that crosses over the ridge of the dormer. You may have to remove a couple of fasteners on the shingle so you can slip the caps beneath (just remember to refasten when you're done capping). Gently slide the top laps of the next two cap shingles beneath the shingle. To make the transition, you'll have to make a slit in the top lap of the cap shingles. The slit will spread open and allow the caps to fold over the ridge.

The last cap on a ridge must be fastened with nails through its surface. Seal the nail heads with a dab of roof cement.

To prevent leaking at the vulnerable spot where the caps are split, I often stick a 16-in. square of waterproof shingle underlayment over the transition before installing the caps (see the photo on the facing page). The cap shingles on the main roof covering the underlayment membrane will protect it from exposure, and any water that gets past the caps will be stopped by the membrane and be directed into the valleys. After you slip the caps beneath the main roof shingles, you can apply a second square of waterproof underlayment over the slit in the caps.

As an added precaution, you can also apply a 10-in.-wide by 16-in.-long piece of

Shingling the Hip and Ridge Intersection

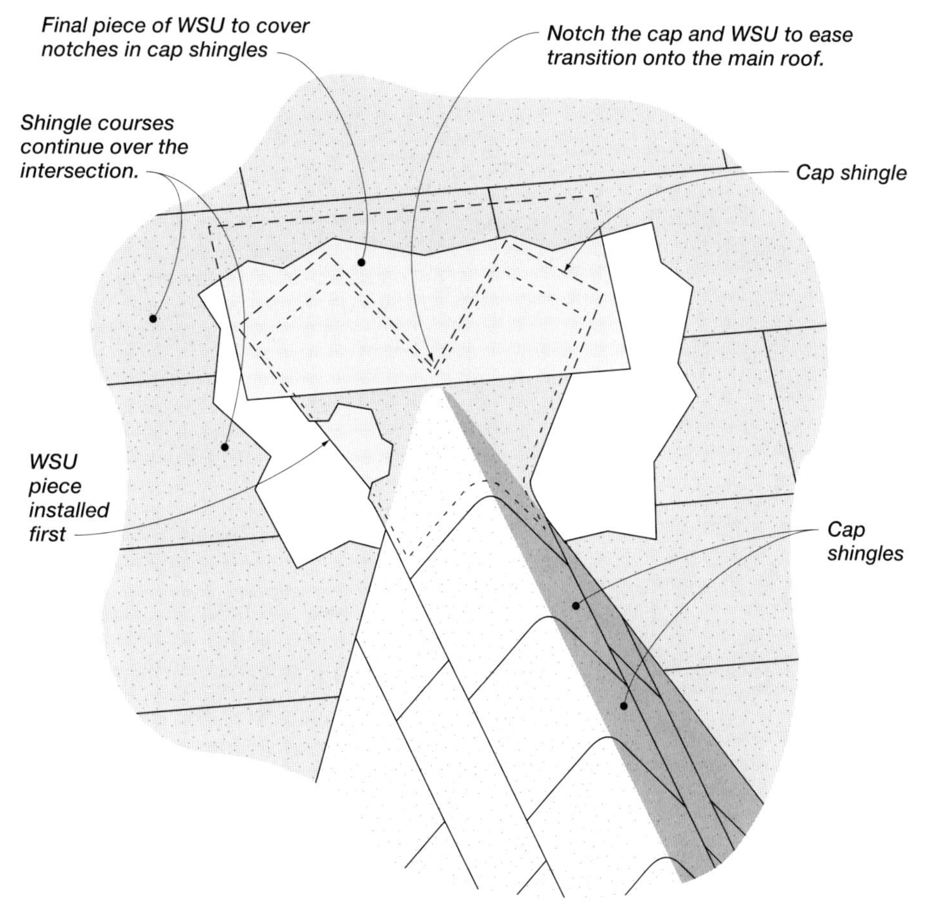

waterproof shingle underlayment over the ridge and up under the main roof shingles before you install the last two or three cap shingles. By making the piece only 10 in. wide, the edges will be completely covered by the cap shingles. Plastic-coated shingle underlayment is easier to form than the fiberglass-reinforced type.

Installing ridge vent that will be capped

Installing ridge vent and covering it with cap shingles add just a few steps to the usual process of capping a ridge. Start with a control chalkline along the ridge

When the ridge of a gable dormer ends at the roof plane of the main house, prepare the intersection by covering the end of the next-to-the-last cap with a piece of waterproof shingle membrane. (Photo by Andy Engel, courtesy *Fine Homebuilding* magazine, ©The Taunton Press.)

WORK SAFE
WORK SMART
THINKING AHEAD

The dabs of roof cement you use to cover nail heads can be visible from the ground, especially on light-colored roofs. Colored granules hide these spots and extend the life of the cement—just scrape the granules off the exposure portion of shingle scraps.

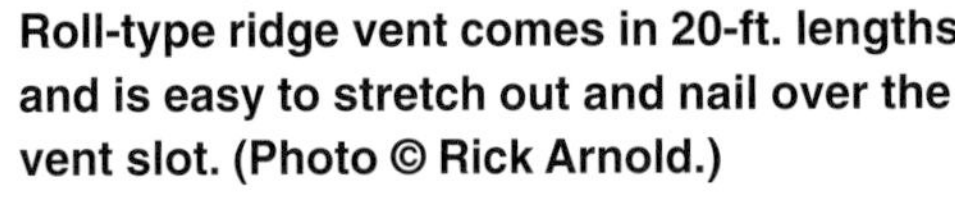

Roll-type ridge vent comes in 20-ft. lengths and is easy to stretch out and nail over the vent slot. (Photo © Rick Arnold.)

Rigid-plastic ridge vents come in 4-ft. lengths. Snap a chalkline to keep the vents lined up along the ridge.

It's easy to align cap shingles to rigid ridge vents, as shown at top, but shingles overhang the soft roll-type vent material (bottom) so take more care to line up shingles by eye when installing shingles over them. (Photo © Rick Arnold.)

to guide the installation (center a piece of vent on both ends of the ridge to mark for the line).

Follow the manufacturer's instructions for the location to begin applying the vent. Typically the vent is held back from the end of the ridge by 1 ft. to 3 ft. Lining up one edge of the vent with the chalkline, drive a fastener into each roof rafter or truss (16 in. to 24 in. apart) along the side. Don't drive the nails so far that you crush the vent. If you do, the airflow will be impeded and the ridge will look wavy. Hand-nailing is better than using pneumatic tools, which can easily overdrive nails.

Gently fold the vent over the ridge and nail down the other side. The job is easier and neater if you have a helper fold and hold the vent down ahead of you a couple of feet. Installation requirements vary slightly from brand to brand, so follow the manufacturer's instructions and be sure to use long nails (2 in. may be necessary to penetrate the sheathing).

Nailing caps over ridge vent

Use the ridge vent to orient the cap shingles. With some vents this will be easy because the shingle meets up flush with the edges of the vent. On others, the cap shingles overhang a little, so you'll have to adjust them side to side to keep a straight line. Drive the nails by hand, just bringing the head snugly to the surface of the vent. Don't overdrive the nail or you may crush the vent and deform the shingle. Be extra gentle when installing the cap shingles over the softer roll-type vents because they deform more easily than the rigid-plastic vents.

Overlap and nail the caps as you would on an unvented ridge. Many vent manufacturers include extra-long (2-in. to 2½-in.) roofing nails with which to fasten the cap shingles. This is really helpful because a lot of suppliers don't stock extra-long roofing nails. Some of the nails supplied by manufacturers even have a short plastic sleeve on the shank that automatically registers the proper depth to drive the nails.

I've tried using pneumatic nailers to attach shingles over ridge vent numerous times with mixed results. I don't recommend it but you may have better luck than I. Nailers tend to overdrive the fasteners and either crush the vent beneath or puncture the shingle surface. The nailing is also inconsistent due to oscillating air pressure and differences in sheathing density; some nails drive too deeply and others not deeply enough.

The beauty of shingle-over-type ridge vents is that their low profile makes them nearly disappear into the roof (see the top photo at right).

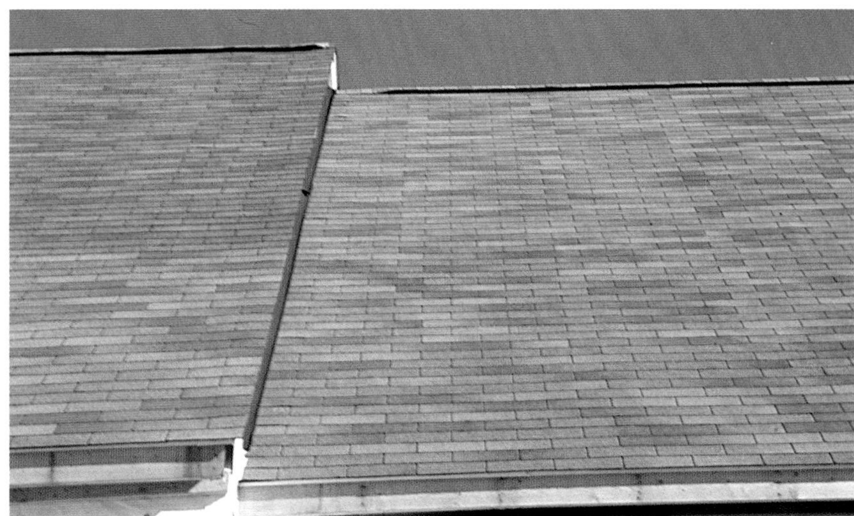

Capped ridge vent has a low profile that blends in nicely with the body of the roof.

Starting and terminating ridge-vent capping

Most types of ridge vents shouldn't be run all the way to the ends of the ridge, so read the instructions to see what the manufacturers recommend. I like to start the vent back from the ends by about 2 ft. to protect it from being lifted by the wind. There are two methods I use to transition from cap shingles at the ends of a ridge.

The easiest method is to gently transition the cap shingles at the end of the ridge up and over the end of the vent material. This method works best with the softer roll-type vents. Squash the first few inches of the vent material to form a ramp, then work the cap shingles up and over the end of the vent, driving the nails on the first two cap shingles tighter to hold the vent compressed at the transition as shown in the bottom photo on the facing page. Once you're past the transition, install the caps as usual. When you reach the other end of the vent, reverse the process to ramp the shingles down off the ridge-vent material to the roof level.

When the cap shingles are terminated abruptly on a ridge vent 2 ft. or 3 ft. from gable ends, a distinct step is noticeable. You can avoid this by blending the caps over the vent and down onto the ridge, as shown in the bottom photo on the facing page.

If you try this method with rigid-plastic vents, the transition point will be more abrupt and form an undesirable hollow. If you have some roll-type vent on hand, you can insert a 6-in. piece at the end of the rigid vent to form a ramp.

The other method is to terminate the vent abruptly and step down to ordinary cap shingles over the ridge. Before you install the ridge vent, apply the first couple of feet of cap shingles at each

Metal ridge vent isn't covered by cap shingles. It is both the vent and the cap, but it doesn't blend in as well with the roof as shingle-over vents do.

end of the ridge. Run each short section of cap shingles toward the center of the ridge rather than following my earlier instructions to orient them to the prevailing storms. Apply the ridge vent over the last cap shingle at each end of the ridge. The overlap covers the nail heads and helps keep the termination water-resistant.

Some brands of ridge vent have special rigid end plugs to apply before capping with shingles and others have integral ones. Overhang the butt edge of the first shingle about 1 in. beyond the end of the ridge vent and fasten, then install all the other cap shingles as you ordinarily would. At the other end, cut off the top laps that overhang beyond the end of the vent. Finish with a piece of exposure dabbed with roof cement at the nail locations.

Installing metal ridge vent

You can avoid the trouble of shingling over the ridge vent by installing a metal one that works both as the vent and weather protection. For this convenience, you give up the low-profile integral look of the shingle-over ridge vents. Metal vents can fit a range of roof pitches, typically 3 to 12.

Installation is simple. You can run the vent all the way to the end of the ridge or install a couple of feet of regular cap shingles over the ridge at each end, then set the metal vent on top. Even though the metal is straight and rigid, I like to snap a chalkline to keep it lined up.

Plan to drive the nails into the roof framing beneath the sheathing. You can see the framing through the vent slot, but once you place the vent the framing will be hidden. Using chalk marks, indicate the locations at each rafter/truss below the chalkline you snapped to align

Pyramid cones are composed of flat facets, which make them easy to shingle. Treat each facet as its own roof section and cap the hips between them.

the vent. Since the nails will be driven through the foot of the vent just inside of an upright baffle, the heads will be exposed to the weather. As a precaution to leaks, I dab a spot of roof cement at each nail location before placing the vent over the ridge.

A helper will make installing the metal ridge vent easier and keep the dabs of roof cement from smearing. First, you'll have to bend the vent slightly to conform to the roof pitch. A gentle squeeze or spread should do the trick. Cover the first cap shingle with the end of the vent, and drive a nail on each side. Use the nails that are supplied with the vent or purchase nails made of the same metal. Most metal ridge vents are made of painted aluminum—be sure to use aluminum nails or you risk dielectric corrosion.

If couplings are supplied by the manufacturer, insert them to join vent sections before installing additional lengths. Apply end plugs (also supplied) at the ends of the vent. Finally, dab the nail heads with a sealant. Most roofers use roof cement because they have it on hand, but I recommend a butyl or urethane caulk used to seal gutters or motor-home roofs since it will last a lot longer than roof cement.

Shingling Cones

There are two types of cone roofs: multisided and round. Multisided cones are like pyramids in that they have a steep pitch and each face is flat with small hips occurring where faces meet (see the bottom photos on the facing page). There's nothing unusual about shingling multi-sided cones; treat them like hip roofs and hand-seal the tabs as you would on any very steep-pitch roof.

Round-sided cones are the most challenging roofs to shingle. The challenge,

It's impossible to line up the vertical slots of tabbed shingles on a round cone. Use laminated or other random-style shingles to avoid the problem.

of course, is that each horizontal course is curved. And since shingles are 3-ft. by 1-ft. rectangles, you need to make adjustments to both the control-line system and the shingles themselves.

Since the circumference of each circular course becomes less as you roof up a cone, there's no way to keep the cutout slots of tabbed shingles vertically aligned. The best way to avoid this problem is to use random-cutout shingles. For consistency, that means using the same shingles on the entire roof. The following outlines the installation process.

Preparing the roof

You won't be able to use metal drip edge along the curved eaves edge of the cone. Instead, use the old method of installing a wood-shingle undercourse to support the asphalt-shingle overhang. Narrow shingles will follow the curve more closely than wider shingles, so use wood shingles from 3 in. to 8 in. wide. Let the wood shingles overhang the fascia by ½ in. To help you register each shingle's overhang, use a small gauge block of ½-in. OSB or plywood. It's best to use preprimed wood

When a cone roof blends into a flat roof, you'll need to extend the horizontal control lines around the cone.

shingles to keep them from absorbing moisture that can cause them to rot.

Apply the wood shingles over an 18-in.-wide strip of tarpaper. Then, when the wood starter shingles are in place, cover them with a 36-in.-wide course of waterproof shingle underlayment. The asphalt shingles will go over the underlayment.

You won't be able to wrap one length of underlayment flatly around the cone. Instead, cut the underlayment into lengths of 3 ft. or 4 ft. For the underlayment course that goes under the wood shingles, lay each piece so the center of the lower edge just meets the bottom edge of the eaves and the ends of the piece overhang the eaves edge. Overlap the ends of the underlayment by 6 in., and trim off the underlayment that overhangs the eaves edge. Do the same for the waterproof shingle underlayment, but this time trim along the butts of the wood shingles.

As an extra precaution, I cover the entire cone with waterproof underlayment, overlapping each course about 2 in. and overlapping the ends 6 in. Alternately, you can run courses vertically, overlapping them 6 in. at the bottom and letting the overlap increase as the roof rises toward the peak.

Laying out horizontal control lines

You can't snap chalklines to keep courses straight; instead you will have to draw horizontal lines around the circumference of the cone using a reel-type tape measure and a piece of chalk. I'll describe the process as if you were marking all the courses at once, but because of the steep roof pitch on most cones, you will probably mark the courses as you set up staging.

Start by driving a long nail into the peak of the cone and hooking the end loop of a reel tape measure over it. These tape measures have narrower blades and are more pliable than the self-retracting tape measure you carry in your pouch. By holding a piece of chalk at layout points along the tape measure, you can rotate it around the cone to make horizontal control lines.

Measure up and mark points on the underlayment at 6½ in. and 11½ in. from the end of the undercourse of wood shingles. These locate the starter and first courses of asphalt shingles, allowing for a ½-in. shingle overhang along the eaves edge. Next, hold the chalk alongside the tape measure hooked at the peak at each point you marked, and draw a horizontal line around the circumference of the cone.

Use the same process to mark out every other horizontal course all the way to the peak. You can either make marks at 5 in. from the top of the first full course of shingles or subtract 5 in. along the tape measure. The process of walking around the roof to mark each control line is time consuming, but it's necessary to keep the courses lined up.

Sometimes a flat roof blends right into a curved roof and back to a flat roof (see the photo above). Lay out the horizontal control lines on the flat portions of the roof first. Treating the curved portion of the roof as a cone, drive a nail at the top on which to hook the tape measure. Hold a piece of chalk to the tape measure, and register it to the level of each horizontal control line on the flat roof. Swing the arc around the curved portion of the roof to continue the control line.

Laying out vertical gauge lines

Unlike vertical *control* lines used to keep cutout slots aligned on a flat roof, these vertical *gauge* lines are used to mark and cut the shingles. Because of the curve of the roof, you'll need to trim the ends of the shingles at an angle so they are flush against one another. Also, as the circumferences of the horizontal courses become smaller as you go up, you'll need to make the shingles shorter so they'll lie flat as you wrap them around the roof.

Start by holding the shingle along the 11½-in. control line and making marks at the bottoms of both ends of the shingle. Snap chalklines between each mark and the peak. This will give you two converging lines up the roof (see the illustration at right).

Cutting the shingles

Cut the shingles for every course to match precisely the width and angle of the vertical gauge lines. The width of the shingle you begin with at the base will depend on the diameter of the cone. Here's my rule of thumb: Greater than 16 ft., use a full 3-ft. shingle; between 12 ft. and 16 ft., use a 2-ft. shingle; and on cones less than 12 ft. in diameter, use a 1-ft. shingle.

To determine the cut size, hold a shingle face down between the vertical control lines at each horizontal course line. Make nicks in the shingle where the vertical lines meet the top edge and butt edge of the shingle, then cut straight lines between the marks (note that these lines won't be square to the long edges of the shingle because the vertical lines aren't parallel).

You will generate a fair amount of waste in the process of trimming shingles. There's no getting around this, but as you get farther up the roof, the waste pieces will become larger. Save any waste pieces that are 6 in. or longer to use closer to the peak.

When you reach the course where the vertical control lines are closer than 6 in., stop cutting narrower shingles and

Laying Out a Cone Roof

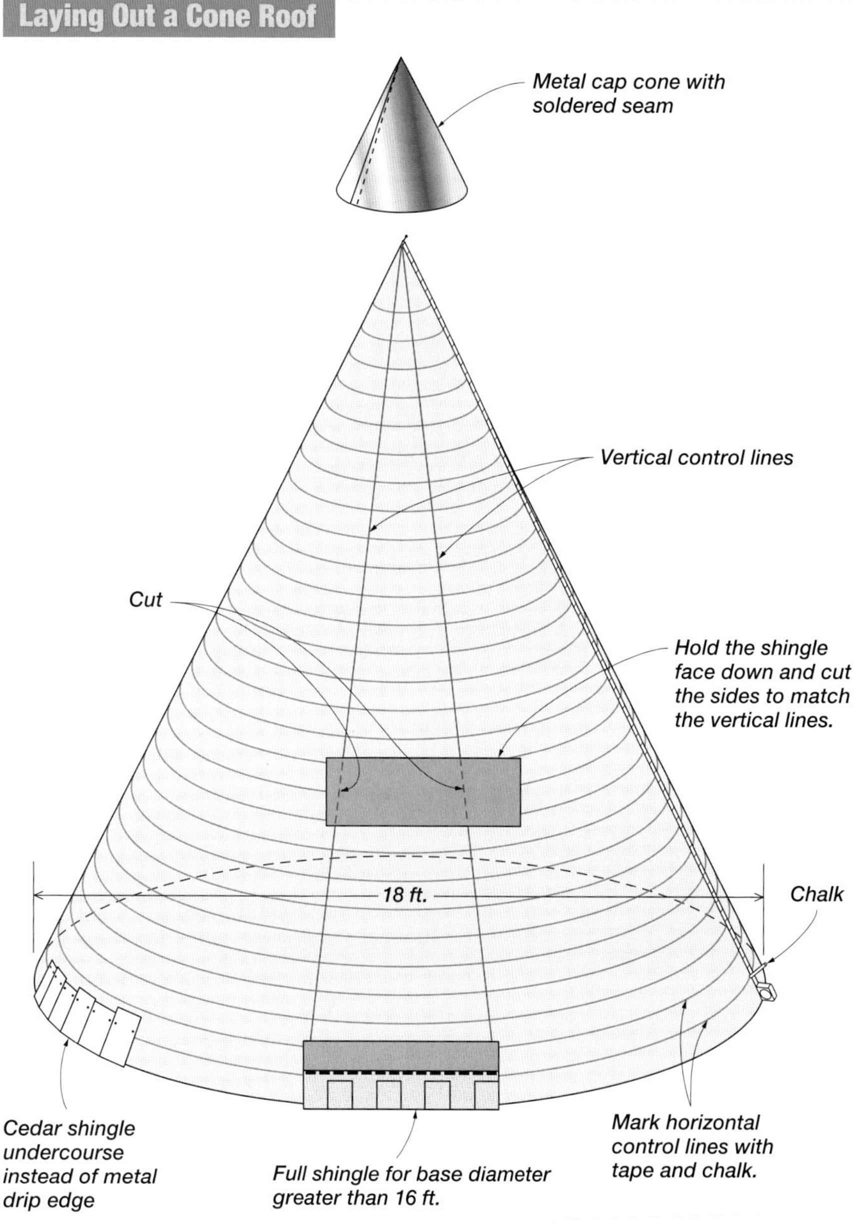

The Effects of Weather

Unless you live in Eden, you're lucky to get 20 good roofing weather days each year. Every other day you're making adjustments to prevent damage to the shingles or yourself. Temperature is probably the biggest factor to consider and adjust for.

Cold-Weather Considerations

In temperatures below 40°F, shingles are stiffer and can break when you fold them into valleys or over a ridge. One way to overcome the problem is to warm the shingles. There's an off chance you can store them inside somewhere, but it's unlikely you or your client will enjoy a living room full of shingles. Another way to warm them is to put them in a sunny spot protected from any wind. And on the very coldest days, shingle flat roof planes in the early morning and wait until it warms up before you do jobs that require bending shingles.

Nails don't penetrate the shingles as easily when they're cold and stiff. You may have to increase the air pressure in pneumatic nailers or set the depth-of-drive adjustment lower. I find I spend more time driving fasteners home by hand in the winter than in the summer. The problem is worse with thick, laminated shingles.

The biggest problem with cold-weather roofing is that the self-seal strips that bond the exposure portion of each shingle to the one beneath don't get warm enough to activate. On some cold days, the sun may warm the roof planes that face south and west enough to activate the strips but not enough to activate them on the north and east planes. Unsealed shingles can blow off on a windy day.

During cold weather, the self-seal strips won't get warm enough to activate and seal down the shingle tabs above. To avoid shingle blowoffs, apply two half-dollar-sized spots of roof cement beneath each shingle tab.

The only remedy is time consuming but necessary. Lift each shingle tab (on three-tab shingles) and apply a half-dollar-sized dab of roof cement 1 in. from each corner, then press the tab down. On laminated shingles and no-cutout-type shingles, apply four dabs of cement.

Hot-Weather Considerations

Hot weather presents its own set of problems. A sunny 85°F day is pleasant on the ground but it can be 100°F on a roof. Shingles get soft and fastener heads can easily break the

continue using 6-in. shingles the rest of the way.

Installing the shingles

There are only a few notable differences in installing shingles on a cone roof versus a flat roof.

- When you align the top of a shingle to the horizontal control line, the curve of the roof makes it impossible to get it to match along the entire length. Just match the two ends of the shingle to the line and let the middle fall where it may. Make sure the body of the shingle lies flat against the roof before you nail.
- As the shingles get shorter, you'll need to compress the usual nailing pattern. For shingles from 26 in. to 36 in., use four nails (or six for windy conditions); for shingles from 16 in. to 26 in., use three (or four with double nails at the middle location); and for shingles less than 16 in., use two nails.
- Start the end of the first shingle in each course halfway between the

surface when you drive them. Adjust the air pressure down and depth of drive up on pneumatic tools.

Be careful when walking on hot shingles because the softened surface can easily scuff. Light-colored roofs, while a little cooler to work on, will show scuff marks the most. Walk with your feet flat on the roof and don't twist the ball of your foot when your shoe is planted. Plan your roofing day around the direction of the sun. Shingle the side that will become the hottest in the afternoon early in the morning and move to shady areas in the heat of the day.

You won't have to worry about shingles sealing in hot weather, but don't let any shingles or pieces of shingles lie face down on completed sections of the roof. The self-seal strip will bond the shingles to the exposed surface. When you lift up the shingles, you can tear the shingle beneath or be left with black spots. Keep shingles stacked in bundles until you're ready to use them. If loose shingles are stacked haphazardly, the release tape on the underside of some shingles may not be directly over the seal strip of shingles beneath; when this happens, you end up with a stuck-together mess.

Shingling in High-Wind Areas

You have to take extra precautions when installing asphalt roof shingles in areas subject to high wind. I've mentioned some of these precautions throughout the book, but I want to reiterate the information here. The first thing you can do is choose a model of shingle designed for high-wind speed. More manufacturers offer models with higher wind resistance than ever before. Look for a shingle with a wind rating that meets or exceeds the wind speed for your area.

Before you even begin shingling, you can prepare for the worst. Cover the entire roof with waterproof shingle underlayment instead of regular felt underlayment. If water gets blown beneath the shingles or flashing, the waterproof underlayment will give you better protection than ordinary tarpaper. And if shingles actually blow off, the membrane will probably stay in place because it's self-adhering.

When installing shingles in wind-prone areas, there are two things you can do to help them stay in place. First, use six fasteners to install each shingle. Drive one at each end of the shingle and two fasteners at each of the 1-ft. and 2-ft. mid-shingle positions (see the illustration on p. 142). Space the paired nails apart by about 1 in. Second, use dabs of cement beneath the roof shingles as you would for cold-weather installation.

Light-colored roofs show scuff marks more than do dark-colored roofs like the one shown here. Scuffing is especially a problem in warm weather.

joints of the shingles in the course beneath. This will give you the greatest offset distance. However, keep a close watch where the joints between shingles fall relative to the course beneath. Each horizontal course is slightly shorter than the one beneath, so there is the chance that joints will get close to one another. When the joints get close to 4 in., insert a narrower shingle to jump over the joint below and reestablish a wider offset.

Capping a cone

Stop installing shingles when you get within 16 in. of the peak because there's no way you'll be able to wrap shingles around the top of a cone and have it look good. Instead, bend a sheet of 24-in.-wide lead or copper around the peak to form a cone. Cut the metal to form a straight butt joint and solder it. Slip the cone cap over the top, and fasten with screws along the bottom edge. You can also purchase decorative weather vanes to cap a cone.

CHAPTER 9

Low-Pitch, Layover, and Roll Roofing

In many cases, a layover roof can be installed, which will save you a lot of work and your client a lot of money.

IN THIS CHAPTER, I'll discuss the special application techniques you'll need for low-pitch roofs. I'll also describe the techniques you'll need if you install a new roof over old—called a layover. Finally, I'll cover asphalt roll roofing, a product that is often used instead of or in conjunction with asphalt shingles, particularly on low-pitched roofs.

When covered with asphalt shingles, roofs with pitches from 2 to 4 are more prone to leaking than steeper roofs. Water doesn't flow off low-pitch roofs as rapidly, and snow builds up easier. Leaves and pine needles can collect and cause water to back up, and snow buildup can lead to ice dams. Although most of the procedures for installing shingles on low-pitch roofs are the same as those described in chapters 7 and 8, you'll need to take a few precautions and make a few modifications in the way you prepare the roof and install the shingles.

Most shingle manufacturers and model building codes permit a second layer of shingles to be installed over the original. I used to be a big fan of layovers because I could avoid the messy work of stripping off the old shingles. I'm not so sure it was in my clients' best interests. Although layovers save money, second layers of shingles never last as long as they are supposed to. And after a couple of years, the thinner three-tab shingles look shabby as the old shingles beneath telegraph their problems through the new surface.

Here, I'll describe the steps in evaluating whether a roof is suitable for another layer of shingles, the process for doing a proper layover, and ways to minimize telegraphing problems.

Roll roofing is primarily used instead of shingles on roof pitches from 1 to 4. It can also be used on medium-pitch roofs to save money. The installation methods are different from those for shingles, but you will use many of the same tools and materials.

Specialty Shingles

There are literally dozens of unique shingle designs available. Some are old, regionally popular styles like T-lock interlocking shingles available from several manufacturers, while others are proprietary designs by individual manufacturers.

Evaluate these shingles for their appropriateness on specific projects. High-end homes typically deserve distinctive roof shingles to complement the exterior detailing. Homes in hurricane-prone areas may benefit from the better wind resistance of interlocking or high-speed-wind-resistant shingles.

Unique shingles often have specialized installation instructions. Although the ventilation, roof-deck preparation, and underlayment requirements are normally the same as for ordinary asphalt shingles, the layout and installation patterns frequently differ from those described in this book.

When I'm asked to cover a roof with an unfamiliar shingle, I gather as much installation information from the manufacturer as possible. The manufacturer may publish this information on the shingle bundle wrappers or in brochures distributed by the local supplier. Another good source for installation instructions is the company's website. And don't be afraid to call the manufacturer for technical assistance on installation details that aren't described in its instructions. I've had good service from the companies I've contacted for assistance in the past. It's in the company's best interest to support you so the installation goes smoothly.

Shingling Low-Pitch Roofs

Because low-pitch roofs are more prone to leaking, you have to rely on the underlayment to provide a very leak-resistant barrier. It also helps to reduce the exposure when you install the shingle, so there is greater overlap of the top laps and head laps. Reducing the exposure positions the self-seal strip higher on the shingle above, so you need extra sealing to prevent shingles from blowing off.

Underlayment options

There are two ways to give the shingles some back-up protection in the event water gets beneath them. The old standard is to install regular 15# tarpaper underlayment in a double-overlap fashion. To do this, cut a strip of underlayment 19 in. wide as a starter to install along the eaves instead of using a full 36-in. sheet. Then roll out a full-width sheet to cover over the starter sheet to begin the overlap pattern. Overlap the full course with a third course by 19 in., leaving 17 in. of the full course exposed. Continue rolling out full-width courses and overlapping the previous one by 19 in. until you get close to the ridge. As the final strip, you can use the 17-in. strip left over from the first eaves-edge strip you cut (see the illustration on p. 232). Overlap any vertical joints in underlayment sheets by a minimum of 12 in.

Since ice dams are more likely on low-pitch roofs in the snow belt, you should take extra precautions preparing

Shingles can be applied to a low pitch when special application steps are taken. Here, the shingle exposure has been reduced to 4 in. and the shingles sealed with roof cement. Beneath, the underlayment is overlapped 19 in. rather than 2 in.

the underlayment. Spread asphalt roof cement or lap cement over the 19-in. top lap of the starter and first two or three courses of underlayment. The 17-in. exposure of the overlapping sheet will cover the tar. Continue the process until you are at least 2 ft. beyond the inside edge of the exterior wall. The rest of the sheets need only to be overlapped, but for added leak protection, you can cement all the underlayment on the roof together.

The other way to provide a very leak-resistant barrier is to install waterproof shingle underlayment instead of tarpaper over the whole roof. Since waterproof shingle underlayment is self-healing and self-adhering, there's no need to overlap the courses by 19 in.; just overlap layers the typical 2 in. or 3 in. recommended by

Low Roof Slope Underlayment Application

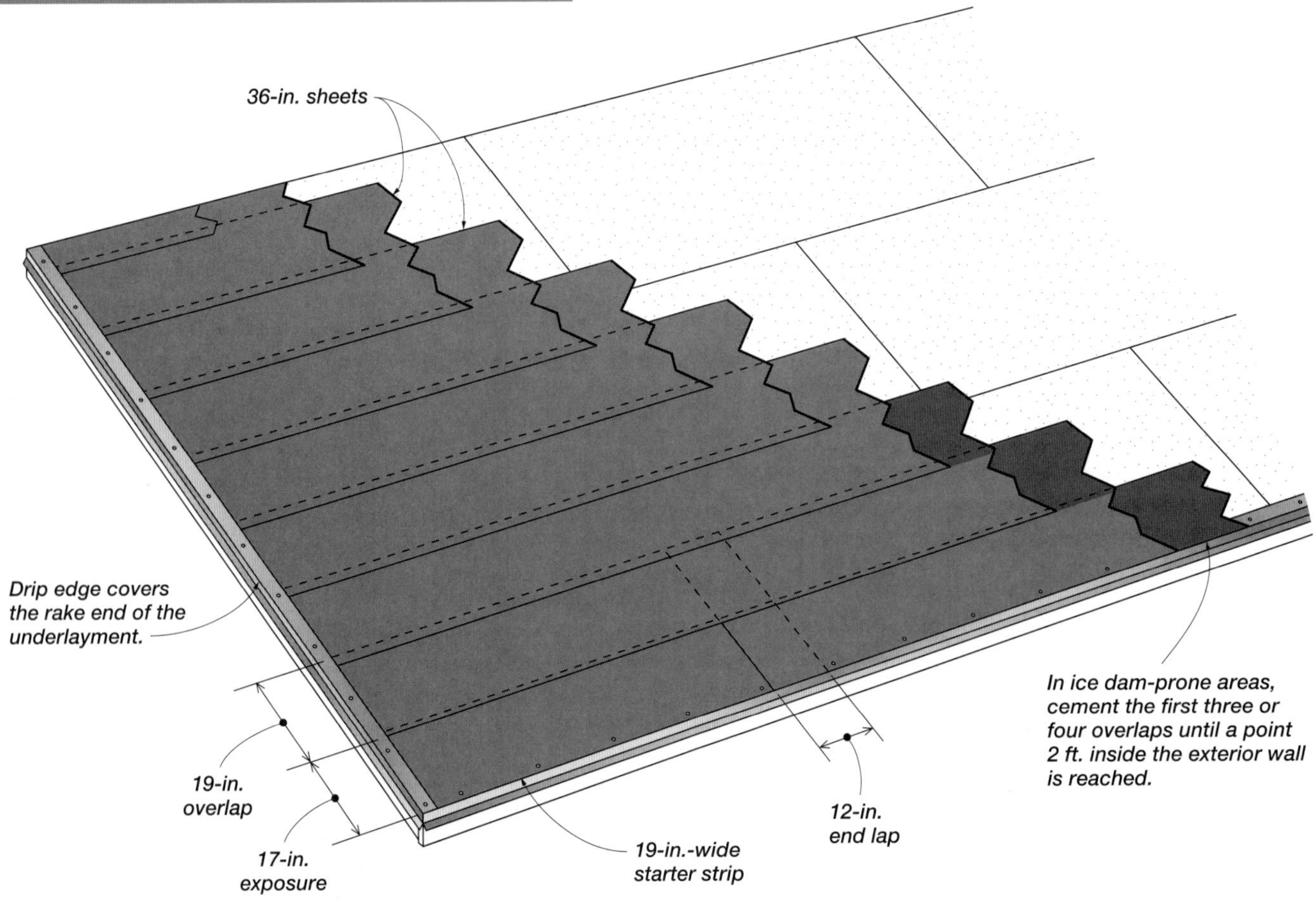

36-in. sheets

Drip edge covers the rake end of the underlayment.

19-in. overlap

17-in. exposure

19-in.-wide starter strip

12-in. end lap

In ice dam-prone areas, cement the first three or four overlaps until a point 2 ft. inside the exterior wall is reached.

the product manufacturer. Covering the entire roof with waterproof shingle underlayment will cost more than doubling up tarpaper, but you will save a fair amount of labor, particularly if you planned to cement the tarpaper together.

Make sure that the attic space is adequately ventilated if you do choose to install waterproof shingle underlayment; it's a vapor barrier and moisture can condense beneath it. Good ventilation will move excess moisture out to the atmosphere where it will do no harm to the roof assembly.

Shingle exposure

Read the shingle manufacturers' instructions before applying asphalt shingles to low-slope roofs. Some will instruct you to reduce the shingle exposure to 4 in. rather than the standard 5 in. Other instructions won't include this precaution. Be sure to follow the instructions to preserve the shingle warranty.

If the instructions do call for the reduced exposure, follow the same procedures discussed in chapters 6 and 7 for layout and application, but just change the horizontal-course layout to 4 in.

As an extra precaution against shingles blowing off, apply a half-dollar-sized dab of roof cement under the lower corners of each shingle tab or four dabs beneath no-cutout and laminated shingles.

Installing a Layover Roof

You can save your client a lot of money and yourself a lot of work by doing a layover instead of stripping off the old shingles. It takes me about 50 percent to 75 percent of the time I spend installing new shingles just to get the old ones off and to clean up. Plus you have to pay to have the old shingles hauled away to a landfill or recycling facility.

■ WORK SAFE ■ WORK SMART ■ THINKING AHEAD

When spreading the cement for underlayment, try not to get it on the roof sheathing. When someone eventually has to strip and reroof the house, the underlayment will be nearly impossible to remove if it's bonded to the sheathing by the cement.

A second layer of shingles can be applied over existing shingles. (Photo by David Ericson, courtesy *Fine Homebuilding* magazine, © The Taunton Press.)

WORK SAFE
WORK SMART
THINKING AHEAD

Don't try to put shingles over an old roof covered with plant life. You may spend more time cleaning moss and lichens off the old layer than it would take to strip the entire roof.

Installing shingles over an existing layer is pretty simple and quick. A lot of the preparation and layout work is already done, although there's some preparation unique to reroofs that you'll have to attend to. Before you strap on your tool belt, you have to evaluate if the existing roof framing can handle the weight of a second layer of shingles and how the existing shingles will affect the appearance of the new roof.

Shown from the top are three roof situations that are not suitable for a layover roof: moss growth, large patches of missing shingles, and shingles with clawing or curling edges. It is better to strip roofs like these before applying a new roof.

Evaluating the roof and shingles

Today's asphalt roof shingles weigh from 2 psf to 3 psf. That adds up to an additional 1½ to 2½ tons on the roof a small 1,300-sq.-ft. ranch house.

Houses built since the late 1970s were probably constructed following one of the model building codes and should have adequate roof framing to support the extra load. But unless you know for sure that a building code was enforced, you should check the capacity of the roof framing. You can look over the engineering documentation or have a professional engineer (or architect adequately trained in engineering principles) evaluate the framing for you.

If a roof is framed using roof trusses, you can check the truss-design engineering paperwork if you have it. The truss design will note the dead-load capacity of the roof and the live-load capacity. The dead load is the total weight, expressed per square foot, of materials that the roof is made of (truss, sheathing, underlayment, and shingles) and the truss is engineered to support.

A common capacity is 10 psf. Rule-of-thumb weights I use are 1½ psf for roof sheathing, 1 psf for the truss, 2½ psf for the underlayment, and one layer of three-tab shingles. For laminated shingles plus underlayment, I use 3½ psf, so adding a layer of laminated shingles to a roof covered with laminated shingles would be: 1½ + 1 + 2½ + 3½ = 8½ psf, which is just getting close to the maximum allowable dead load of a 10-psf roof.

Without the truss documentation or if the house is stick-framed, you should have a professional evaluate the roof. Unless you feel qualified to size up the framing members, determine the species, and calculate the capacity, leave it to someone who is. Red flags should go up if you notice any rafter sag from eaves to ridge or if the ridge appears to sag in the middle. These roofs may already be overloaded and you surely don't want to add the last straw. Chances are such a roof won't collapse when you shingle it but very well might after the next heavy snowfall.

If the framing passes muster, look in the attic for two things—adequate ventilation and any evidence of decay in the roof framing or sheathing. Replacing damaged framing or sheathing is next to impossible without stripping off the existing layer of shingles. Deteriorated sheathing may be too weak to hold the nails of new shingles, so it needs to be replaced.

Finally, look at the condition of the existing layer of shingles. People often wait to replace shingles until they are long overdue. Shingles that are basically sound but show signs of age such as loose surface granules and thermal splitting are good candidates for a layover. But if the shingles are seriously deteriorated or show signs of serious defects, you should think about stripping them off. Look for curling edges, bear-clawing, loose tabs, and shingle brittleness. Anything that sticks up or is missing on the existing roof probably will telegraph through the new layer.

A good option to consider for covering a questionable first layer of shingles is to use heavy laminated shingles. Their extra thickness and random appearance will hide minor problems with the roof beneath.

The hip and ridge-cap shingles must be removed before applying a second layer of shingles.

Preparing the roof

If you decide to leave the old shingles in place, there are only a few major steps you have to do to prepare the old roof. These include removing the cap shingles, dealing with old flashing, and installing new drip edge if necessary. Minor but important steps include hammering in raised nails and sweeping the surface clean of debris such as leaves and broken shingle pieces.

REMOVING CAP SHINGLES The first step is to remove the old cap shingles from the ridge and hips. They are so thick that adding another layer over them is impractical. You can use a regular stripping shovel

A Note of Caution about Old Flashing

Some roofers avoid labor by leaving the old roof shingles interlaced with the old flashing, running the new shingles over the top of everything, and then bedding the end of the new shingles in roof cement. I've been called out to repair this mistake when the shingles are just a few years old. The cement seal works for a while, but eventually water gets beneath the new shingles. The old layer, now punctured by the nails holding down the new shingles, leaks. And because the leaks are usually small and slow to start with, the roof sheathing begins to rot before anyone notices water stains on the ceilings beneath. Repairs can be extensive and costly.

Drip Edges for Layover Roofs

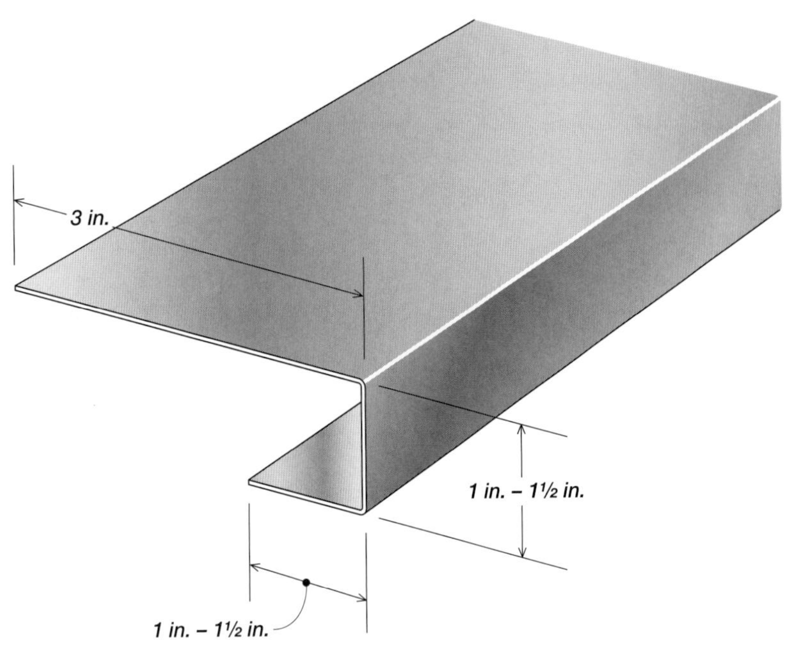

Standard style C drip edge

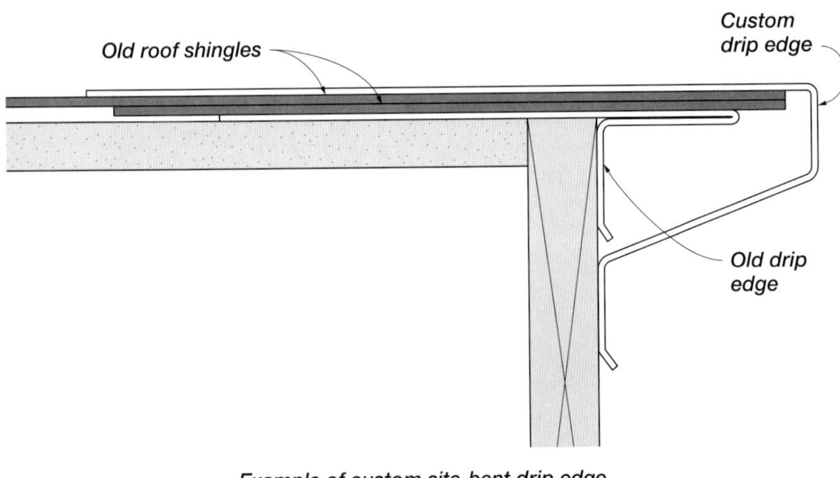

Example of custom site-bent drip edge

or just a flat bar to pop them off. Don't worry about damaging the top course of roof shingles; you'll be going over it anyway. If there's ridge vent beneath the caps, you may be able to save and reuse it if you take a little care removing it.

REMOVING OLD FLASHING Remove any roof vents and vent-pipe boot flashing. You'll need to install new ones (or reuse the old ones if they are still in good condition) with the new layer. If you break away any pieces of the old shingle layer when removing them, fill in the voids with pieces of new shingles.

Evaluate any step flashing, shed-roof roll flashing, chimney flashing, and skylight flashing. Unless someone has smeared roof cement along the transition, you can usually unlace the flashing from the old roof by stripping back just a few tabs of shingles.

If the sidewall and chimney step flashing and the skylight flashing is in good condition, recut the line of old shingles you broke back so it's straight. Install a strip of new shingle material on the roof sheathing up against the edge of the old shingles and beneath the old step flashing. This will shim up the new shingle layer so it doesn't dip.

If flashing is deteriorated or if you damaged it when removing the old shingles, it will have to be replaced. Chimney flashing and skylight step flashing are usually easy to replace. Just pull the old pieces out from behind the counterflashing or rubber gasket and insert new ones. Chimney counterflashing is sometimes deteriorated and needs replacing (follow the instructions in "Cutting In New Counterflashing" on p. 202).

Replacing sidewall step flashing can be difficult depending on how the house is sided. First, remove the old step flashing. If the pieces don't pull out, cut them along the bottom edge of the siding and snap off the roof legs. Then pull the lower edge of the siding away from the wall a little with your fingers or a flat bar. Slip the wall leg of a new step flashing beneath. Try to slip it behind the old flashing if it's there. If this doesn't work, you'll have to strip back some of the siding to install the new step flashing.

The roll flashing used where roofs meet vertical walls is typically easier to prepare than step flashing, provided it hasn't been covered by shingles or sealed with roof cement. Lift the bottom edge of the flashing with a flat bar or flat shovel. Carefully pop any nails without tearing the heads through the flashing, then bend the flashing up and strip off the last course or two of roof shingles that were installed under the flashing. This will give you enough space to slip in new shingles without raising the thickness beneath the flashing. Don't worry about seeing a dip in the new shingle layer where the old shingles were removed; because the shingles follow a horizontal line, the transition won't be noticeable from the ground.

Fill in missing shingle tabs with scrap pieces of new shingle material before laying the new roof over. Just drive nails right through the surface to hold the pieces in place; they'll be covered by the new layer. (Photo by David Ericson, courtesy *Fine Homebuilding* magazine, ©The Taunton Press.)

You don't need to install underlayment when doing a layover roof.

PREPARING THE EDGES The eaves and rake edges often need treatment. The shingles probably overhang the edges and may be curling. Snap off the curling or loose shingle edges, then install new drip edge to hide the tattered, old shingle layer and support the new shingles. Most suppliers carry preformed drip edge (often called style C) specifically for this purpose. This drip edge has a tall face and return bend to encase the old shingle layer and old drip edge, but it's a one-size-fits-all flashing that may not meet your exact need. You can also bend up your own drip-edge profile to suit unusual situations or to fit more tightly around the shingles.

Another approach is to cut back the overhang of the old shingle layer and install conventional drip edge. To do this, mount an old carbide blade in a circular saw, and set the depth to cut through the shingles and the drip-edge extension. Snap a chalkline on the old shingles to guide the cut, which will remove the bottom leg of the drip edge and make the shingles butt flush to the fascia and rakes. Starting from the ridge, cut down along the rakes so the saw doesn't bump into shingle butts. The new drip edge should cover any shallow scrapes the sawblade makes on the rake or fascia boards.

Nail the new drip edges right over the old layer of shingles. Along the rakes, be sure to nail ½ in. above the butt edge of the shingles about every 10 in. to 15 in. If you nail in the hollow below the butt edge, the drip edge will kink a little and look shabby. Nail the eaves edges anywhere except at cutout slots on three-tab shingles; on laminated shingles, nail into the raised portions of the exposure and not the low areas.

Nest the new layer of shingles into the old layer by meeting the top edge of the new shingles to the butt edge of the old ones.

Installing the layover shingles

There's no need to install underlayment over the old shingles before installing new shingles. In fact, underlayment may cause problems. The same goes for waterproof shingle underlayment. The old layer of shingles provides the same secondary backup to leaks that the underlayment ordinarily would.

The most important thing to remember when installing a layover is to "nest" the new shingles into the old ones. Nesting is a sensible process where you press the top edges of the new shingles up to the butt edges of the old ones. This keeps the new shingles lying as flat as possible with full support by the old shingles beneath. If you just started laying new shingles over the old ones without nesting, the new shingles would bridge over the butt edges of the old ones. The bridging leaves voids that the new shingles would sink into, eventually leaving the roof looking wavy. The wavy roof shingles will deteriorate much sooner than flat, nested shingles.

Metric Shingles

Always measure a couple of shingles on an old roof to see what size they are and at what exposure they were installed. You may come across a roof shingled with metric shingles, which have an exposure of about 5⅝ in. Don't order regular-sized 5-in. exposure shingles to lay over metric shingles because they won't work with the nesting technique.

The only solution is to purchase metric shingles to do the layover. Even if your roofing supplier doesn't stock metric shingles, it can probably order them. And in the event you're ordering metric-sized shingles to lay over a regular-sized shingle roof, order extra shingles. You can use metric shingles over a 5-in. exposure, but since the exposures will be reduced by ⅝ in., a square of shingles won't cover as much roof. Increase your shingle order by about 12 percent to make up for the shortage.

NESTING THE SHINGLES You'll start the nesting process the same way you would a new roof, with starter shingles along the eaves edge, but you'll need to cut each starter twice so it will nest up to the butt of the old shingle course without sticking too far past the drip edge. First, cut the tabs off the shingle so the self-seal strip is left along the bottom edge. This will leave a 7-in.-wide starter. The distance to the first butt edge is only 5 in. (or perhaps 6 in. if you installed extended drip edge). Trim 2 in. off the *top* edge of the starters to account for the narrow space. Press the starters up to the butt edge of the second shingle course, and nail in place just above the self-seal strip (see the photo at left).

The first full course of shingles also needs to be trimmed so it will nest to the next butt edge of the old shingles. The distance should be 10 in. (or 11 in. with extended drip edge), but measure to be sure. Now, cut the butt edge of the shingles to make the adjustment. If you cut the top edge, the self-seal strip would end up too high and would not bond well to the next course of shingles. Nest the trimmed shingles up to the butt of the third course of old shingles and nail them in place.

The rest of the shingle courses won't need cutting to nest properly. You can use either the pyramid or racking pattern to guide the installation. Lay out and snap vertical control lines as you would on a new installation; just have your chalkline full to snap bright lines across the rough shingle surface. There's no need to snap horizontal control lines; you can align the new shingles against the butts of the old.

Of course if the old roof was installed in a sloppy fashion, the new shingles will mimic the same horizontal defect. You can tweak the shingles a bit by snapping horizontal control lines on the surface of the old shingles up to ½ in. lower than the butts of the old courses. The small space between the top of the new shingles and the butt edge of the old ones won't cause a bridging problem. Again, this is where laminated shingles excel at layovers. Aesthetic problems caused by poor layout of an old three-tab roof are somewhat concealed by the randomness of laminated shingles.

The rest of the details, including finishing valleys, layering in roof vents, and installing cap shingles, follow the same procedures I described in chapters 7 and 8.

Roll Roofing

Asphalt roll roofing (also called mineral-surface roofing) can be used in conjunction with or instead of asphalt roof shingles on houses and utility buildings. Think of roll roofing as uncut shingle material. The composition is the same—stabilized asphalt over a base layer of fiberglass- or asphalt-saturated organic felt with granular surfacing and back coating on the outside faces.

However, on some roofs, roll roofing won't last as long as roof shingles. Because it is installed in large sheets, the cumulative effects of thermal cycling will deteriorate roll roofing faster. Shingles cope with shrinking and expanding much better than roll roofing. Roll roofing can bubble up as it expands in hot weather and crack when it shrinks in the cold. It's also more likely than shingles to blow off. Besides, on most roofs, it is less attractive than shingles.

Despite its deficiencies, there are some situations where it may make sense

Roll roofing is made of the same material as asphalt roof shingles. It's less expensive and faster to install than strip shingles, but it won't last as long.

Determining the Necessary Nail Length

Most manufacturers prohibit the use of staples when installing a second layer of shingles, so you'll have to use nails. Remember, the nails must penetrate the roof sheathing by ¾ in. or go all the way through it if the sheathing is less than ¾ in. thick. To determine the nail length, I usually measure through a roof-vent hole from the bottom of the sheathing to the thickest part of the existing shingles, or you can hammer a 2-in. nail through the roof and measure how much protrudes through the attic ceiling. Then I stack two new shingles together and add that measurement to the total. Sometimes 1½-in. nails will work. Usually 1¾-in. nails are a safe bet, but sometimes 2-in. nails are necessary.

There are two types of roll roofing: single coverage (bottom), which has a granular surface over the entire sheet, and double coverage (top), which is only coated halfway with a granular surface.

to use roll roofing. I'll look at some cases where it is typically used.

Roll roofing comes in 36-in.-wide rolls. Like shingles, roll-roofing courses are overlapped to shed water, but instead of self-seal strips, roll-roofing courses are bonded with roofing cement. Some roll roofing is designed for single coverage with an overlap of only 3 in. to 4 in. You can also get double-coverage roll roofing that is designed to be overlapped 19 in. with a 17-in. exposure. Double-coverage material has a 19-in. "selvage" edge that is designed to be overlapped and has no granules on the surface. This helps the cement bond better. Single-coverage material may have no selvage edge or a selvage edge of up to 3 in. wide.

I'll describe how to install each type of roll roofing using a couple of technique variations for each.

WORK SAFE ▪ WORK SMART ▪ THINKING AHEAD

To prevent the sheets from buckling when they warm up, don't install roll roofing in temperatures below 50°F. Conversely, to prevent splitting when temperatures get cooler, don't install roll roofing in temperatures above 85°F.

Where and when to use roll roofing

Roll roofing can be used on a full range of roof pitches on most buildings with the same requirements for roof sheathing and ventilation as apply to shingles. But steeper pitches make the roof more visible, so roll roofing is most often used on low-pitch roofs.

Single-coverage material can be used on pitches greater than 2, and double coverage can be used on pitches greater than 1. Roofs with pitches less than 1 won't shed water quickly enough to use roll roofing. For these roofs, use an ethylene propylene diene monomer (EPDM, also called rubber) roofing system or a heat-fused single-ply asphalt bitumen membrane (AKA torch-down). Check with your roofing-material supplier for product information and installation instructions for these roofing systems.

There are situations in which you may want to consider using roll roofing as a temporary roof on a home. If the construction schedule, labor force, and weather are such that you need to get the roof covered for an extended period but don't want to take the time to install roof shingles, roll roofing may be a quick and inexpensive preliminary roof. It will last longer than tarpaper and can be quickly removed in order to shingle. You could also shingle over the roll roofing, but I don't recommend it; wrinkles may telegraph through on hot days.

Budget may be another reason for a temporary roll roof. If a premium roofing material such as slate or wood is planned but not affordable during initial building construction, roll roofing can shed the elements until money is available.

Roll roofing also makes a good weather-tight barrier beneath metal or tile roofing where you want more substantial protection than tarpaper alone can provide.

Single-coverage installation

Single-coverage roll roofing can be installed with exposed nails or concealed nails. The rolls can be run parallel to the eaves or perpendicular to them. I'll describe each method and direction separately. But no matter which one you choose, there are a few details that are common to all single-coverage and double-coverage installations.

There's no need to apply tarpaper in preparation for roll roofing, but you should install metal eaves and rake drip edges. Follow the instructions on p. 99; the only change is that the rake edge is applied directly to the sheathing since there's no underlayment for it to go over.

To install, roll out and cut each course of roll roofing a little long. Spread out the sheets on the roof and allow them to relax for an hour or more. If you skip this step, the material may wrinkle after you nail it down. Once you've nailed the sheets, trim the excess off the rake edges.

Install all valleys as open valleys as described on p. 211. You can use either roll roofing or metal in the valley.

As a regular precaution after you install any roll roofing, check the roof regularly (or instruct the homeowner to) for splits or loose edges, especially before and after severe storms. If the roof is high, use binoculars rather than hauling out a ladder for the inspection.

Roll Roofing on Low-Slope Roofs

Roll roofing is sometimes used on low-slope roofs that will be covered with a rooftop deck. I think this is a bad idea. A well-built deck can last 30 to 50 years or even longer. Chances are the roll roofing will fail long before that, and you'll have to dismantle the deck to fix the roof. It's well worth spending a little extra money to install EPDM roofing because it will be more watertight and last far longer than roll roofing. Plus, with EPDM, the roof pitch of the framing beneath the deck can be as low as $\frac{1}{16}$ in. per ft.

EPDM rubber roofing is a better option than roll roofing to cover roofs beneath decks. (Photo by Roe A. Osborn, courtesy *Fine Homebuilding* magazine, © The Taunton Press.)

Applying horizontal single-coverage roll roofing with concealed nails

This method is called concealed (or blind) nailing because all of the fasteners are covered by the sheet above. One of the advantages of this method is that there are no exposed fasteners to leak. But in order for the system to work, you have to rely on a thin layer of roof cement to bond the bottom edge and sides to the sheet beneath.

1. **Install starter strips.** Cut 9-in.-wide starter strips of roll roofing to run along the eaves and rakes. Facing the

Horizontal Single Coverage with Concealed Nails

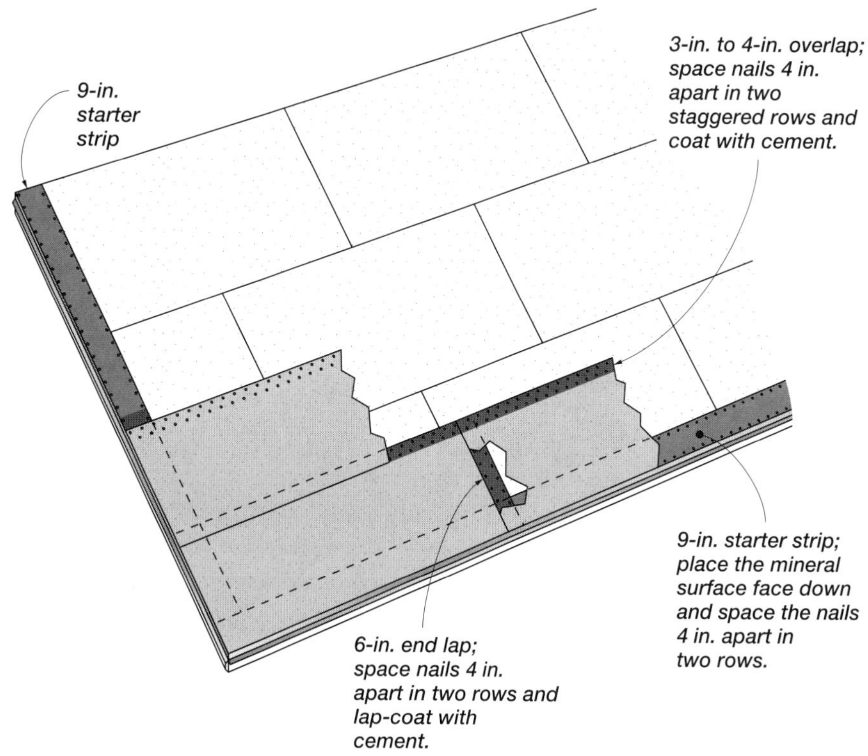

■ WORK SAFE
■ WORK SMART
■ THINKING AHEAD

One way to protect the sheathing when you're spreading roof cement is to slip strips of tarpaper under the top edge of the lap you're applying cement to. Any cement you slop over the edge will be caught by the paper. Slide the piece of tarpaper along as you go, and dispose of it when you're done.

mineral surface down, overhang the strips about ½ in. over the drip edges. Fasten the strips with two rows of roofing nails each 1 in. in from the edges. Space the nails 4 in. apart and stagger them between the two rows.

2. **Install the first course.** Roll the first course flush with the eaves overhang and nail the top edge. Starting the nails 12 in. from the rake edges, stagger an offset row along the top edge 4 in. apart. Keep the nails within 1 in. to 2 in. of the top edge so they will be covered by the next course overlap.

   Fold the bottom edge up halfway on itself to expose the starter strip. Be careful in cool weather not to step on the folded sheet or the material will crack at the fold. Apply an even coat of asphalt lap cement or roof cement to the entire surface of the starter strip, then fold the sheet back down and over the cement-covered strip. Press the edge into the cement. A heavy roller like the ones used for installing vinyl flooring is great for pressing a good lap. You can also push a stiff-bristle broom over the surface to embed the sheets, but this may disturb the surface granules.

   Roll the ends of the sheet back off the rake starter strips, and apply cement over the starter strips up to the point where the top of the sheet will cross. Fold the sheet over and press it down.

3. **Install subsequent courses.** Repeat the sequence again, but this time overlap the first sheet by 3 in. to 4 in. I usually snap a chalkline to keep the butt edge straight. If any sheet droops even a little, it may create a wrinkle that you may not see right away but will show up within a few days. Align the bottom edge with the chalkline and nail the top edge. Fold the bottom back and apply cement to the overlap, making sure you keep the cement back ½ in. from the chalkline. Flop the sheet down and roll-seal, then fold back the ends and cement the rake edges.

   Where a sheet is too short to reach the opposite end, you'll have to splice two sheets together. To do this, nail the end of the first sheet to the sheathing with two rows of nails positioned 1 in. and 4 in. from the end. Snap a chalkline 6 in. in from the edge as a guide, and spread roof cement over the lap up to the line. Fold the end of the balance sheet over the lap and press together firmly.

Lap and Roof Cement

You can bond roll-roofing overlaps with either liquid lap cement or trowel-consistency roof cement. Which one you use depends on preference, application location, and the temperature. Liquid lap cement is hard to control when spreading a narrow band, whereas trowel-consistency roof cement is easy. On wide-overlap areas, like those on double-coverage roofing, lap cement can be mopped or spread with a broom quickly.

Cold weather will turn roof cement almost completely solid, whereas lap cement will come close to trowel consistency. The converse is true on hot days. Having a pail of each on the job makes it easy to pick and choose the best for the conditions.

Old paintbrushes and hand brooms are good for spreading lap cement in small areas, whereas mops and full-sized push brooms work best for coating large sections. You'll need metal trowels to spread roof cement. I like to use a ⅛-in. V-notch trowel made for spreading synthetic tile mastic. It makes controlling the thickness of the roof cement easy. Permanently dedicate the tools to cement application; once coated, you'll never be able to get them completely clean. Rather than trying to clean them, store tools in tight plastic bags or in an airtight pail for use on the next job.

You'll undoubtedly get cement on you when you're spreading it, so wear old clothes you don't care about or cover yourself with a one-piece disposable coverall jumpsuit. Rubber gloves are a must to keep your hands clean. And have some solvent and rags on hand for cleaning up.

When working into a valley, apply a 3-in.-wide strip of cement to the edge of the valley, fold the roll roof in, then trim.

When you reach the ridge or hips, fold the roll roofing over the top, and nail down about 4 in. onto the other side. If you're installing ridge vent, cut the material flush with the air slot. Face-nail the top edge about 4 in. apart. I'll describe how to cover hips and ridges on p. 244.

Installing horizontal single-coverage roofing with exposed nails

The advantage of this method is that you are not relying on the roof cement to bond the sheets. Of course, the trade-off is that the exposed nails can leak and may detract from the appearance of the roof.

INSTALLING THE FIRST SHEET

There's no need to prepare the roof with starter strips; the roll-roof sheets will be edge-nailed so you'll only need full sheets. Overhang the first sheet over the drip edges by ½ in. Run a row of preliminary nails 1 in. down from the top edge about 16 in. to 24 in. apart, then drive a staggered row of nails around the rest of the perimeter of the sheet spaced 3 in. apart (see the illustration at right).

INSTALLING SUBSEQUENT COURSES

Snap a chalkline 3 in. down from the top edge of the first sheet, and spread a band of roof cement to within ½ in. of the line. Roll out the next course of roofing material, aligning it with the chalkline. Tack-nail the sheet along the top edge, then nail off the perimeter using the same spacing as the first sheet. By bedding the lower edge of each sheet into a band of cement, the shanks of the nails penetrating the overlap will be sealed from moisture to some extent.

Fold the top edge over the ridge or hips and install the valleys in the same way as for the concealed-nail application.

Applying roll roofing vertically

Some roofers prefer to run the sheets of roll roofing from eaves to ridge. There doesn't seem to be any advantage or disadvantage from a performance standpoint. The application is essentially a concealed-nail installation, so follow the same process as for a parallel installation.

Start by installing 9-in. starter strips along the rake and eaves edges. Run the first course from the ridge to the eaves edge, and overlap the drip edges by ½ in. Nail down the edge facing the opposite

■ WORK SAFE ■ WORK SMART ■ THINKING AHEAD

Don't apply the cement too thickly on any laps or it will ooze out of the bottom edge and make a mess. Excessive cement can also cause the roofing material to bubble when the solvents in the cement are absorbed by the roll roofing—try to keep the cement on the lap area and avoid getting it on the roof sheathing. Roll roofing should not be bonded to the sheathing or wrinkling can develop.

Horizontal Single Coverage with Exposed Nails

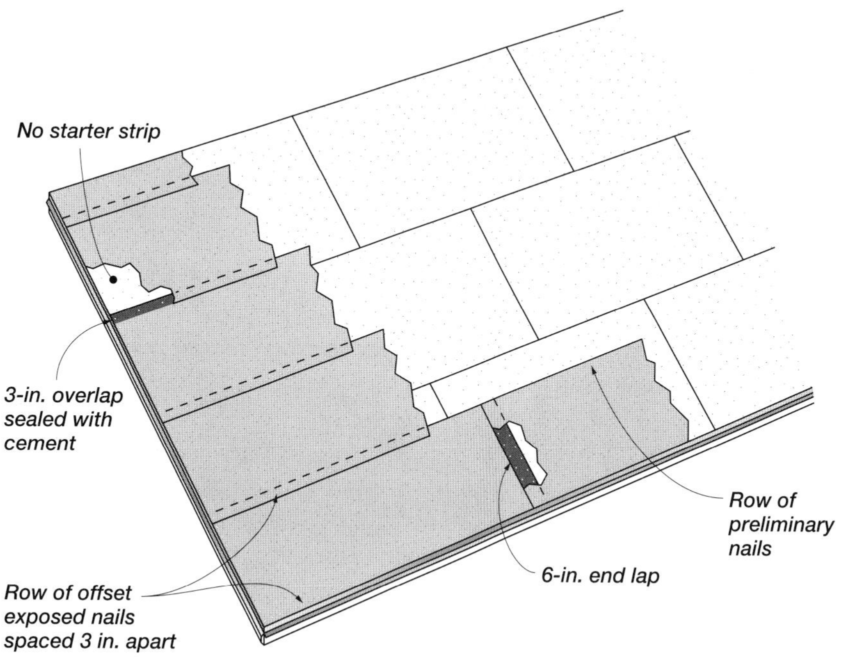

Covering Nails with Roof Cement

There's always a question of whether you should cover the exposed nail heads with a sealant. On one hand, it may help seal any small leaks around the shanks. On the other hand, the sealant may look ugly. Roof cement is typically the first choice for a sealant, but as I noted in chapter 7, it may not last. I prefer a urethane or butyl sealant rated for UV exposure. You can usually find colors similar to and compatible with the roll-roof color so the sealant won't show up too much.

Sealant isn't necessary to protect the galvanized coating on the nail heads, since you can only expect an exposed roll-roof installation to last from 10 to 15 years. The nails probably won't deteriorate too badly by then unless the roof is very close to salt water.

Vertical Single Coverage with Concealed Nails

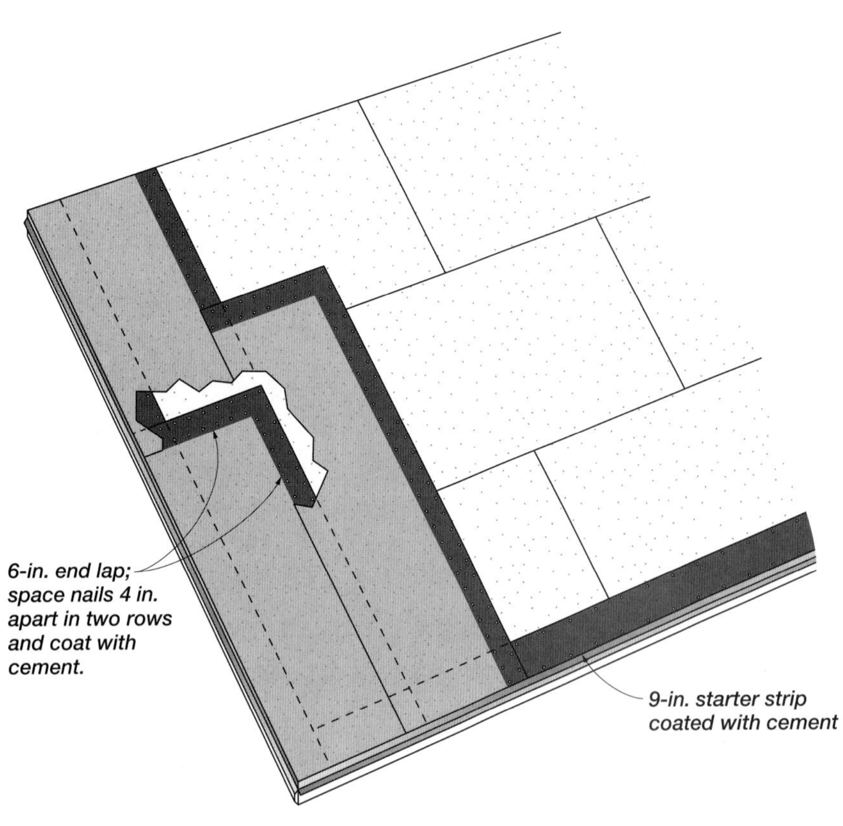

side of the roof, but hold back the nails 12 in. from the bottom edge (see the illustration below). Fold back the rake edge and the eaves edge to apply roof or lap cement to the starter strip, then roll the sheet back down and bed it into the cement. Continue installing courses from ridge to eaves edge until you reach the other end of the roof.

The last sheet will differ from the rest. You will only bond it to the roof with cement along the previous overlap and the starter strips along the rake and eaves.

Capping hips and ridges with roll roofing

Rather than covering hips and ridges with cap shingles, you'll use roll-roofing cap strips. There are methods for concealed nails and exposed nails.

INSTALLING A CAP WITH CONCEALED NAILS Start the concealed-nail cap-strip application by snapping two chalklines 6 in. to each side along the ridges and hips. Crosscut 12-in.-wide strips from a sheet of roll roofing so that you now have strips that are 12 in. wide and 36 in. long. Spread roof or lap cement over the hip and ridge between the chalklines to within ½ in.

If you are doing hips, do them before the ridge. Begin at the eaves edge of the hip, and apply the first strip so it extends past the corner (later, you'll trim off the corners flush with the edge of the main courses). Aligning the strip with the chalklines, press it into the cement. Drive two nails on each side of the hip, about 1 in. and 5 in. down from the top of the end of the strip, then apply roof cement over the top 6 in. Place the next strip overlapping the first by 6 in., and continue the process until you reach the top (see the top illustration on the facing page).

Install the ridge cap strips the same way. Let the end of the ridge cap extend over the hip cap by 8 in., then make a slice in the overhanging material in line with one of the hips. This will allow you to fold the overlap piece down onto the hip. Trim the material in a neat diamond shape, and bed the fold into a layer of roof cement applied to the top of the hip caps. Finally, drive three face nails to hold the folds down over the hips.

INSTALLING A CAP WITH EXPOSED NAILS The cap strips for exposed-nail hips and ridges can be cut lengthwise from the roll so a single piece covers the top. Cut the strips 12 in. wide and snap the same pair of 6-in. chalklines to guide installation as you would for the concealed method. Spread a 2-in. to 3-in. strip of roof or lap cement ½ in. inside of each chalkline.

Lay the cap strip over the hip and overhang the end for later trimming. Press the strip into the cement, then drive a line of nails along each edge about ¾ in. in spaced 3 in. apart. Along the ridge, carry the strip of cement over the top of any hip-cap strips and nail down the same way (see the illustration at right below).

Installing double-coverage roll roofing

Double-coverage roll roofing is installed almost exclusively in a concealed-nail fashion. It is much more resistant to leaking than single-coverage roofing, which is why it can be used on pitches as low as 1 in 12. Of course, it takes twice the material and three times as much cement plus some extra labor to install.

You can apply the sheets horizontally or vertically. I'll describe the process for horizontal application, and you'll be able to extrapolate the vertical process by applying the technique used in the single-coverage method. Start by cutting the strips of roofing to length in advance

Hip and Ridge Caps with Concealed Nails

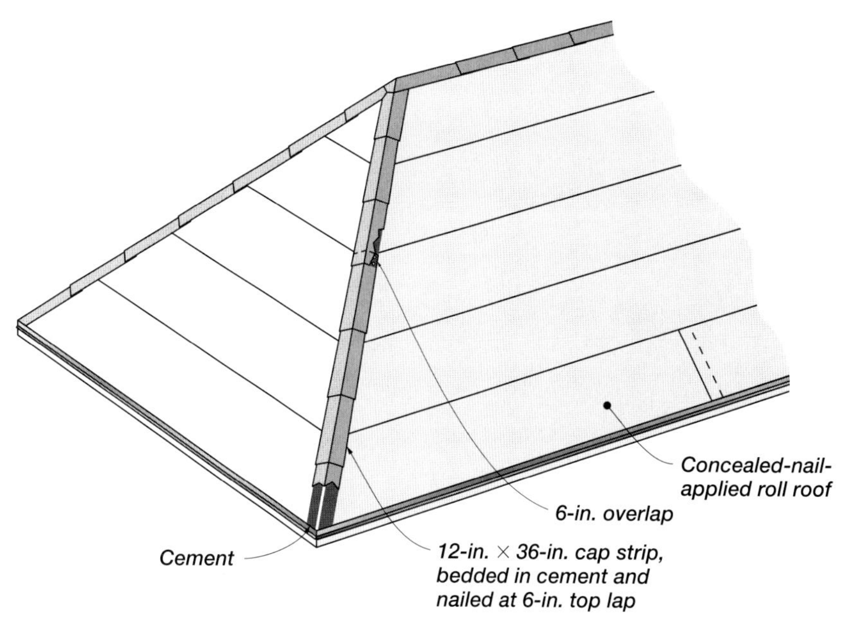

Hip and Ridge Caps with Exposed Nails

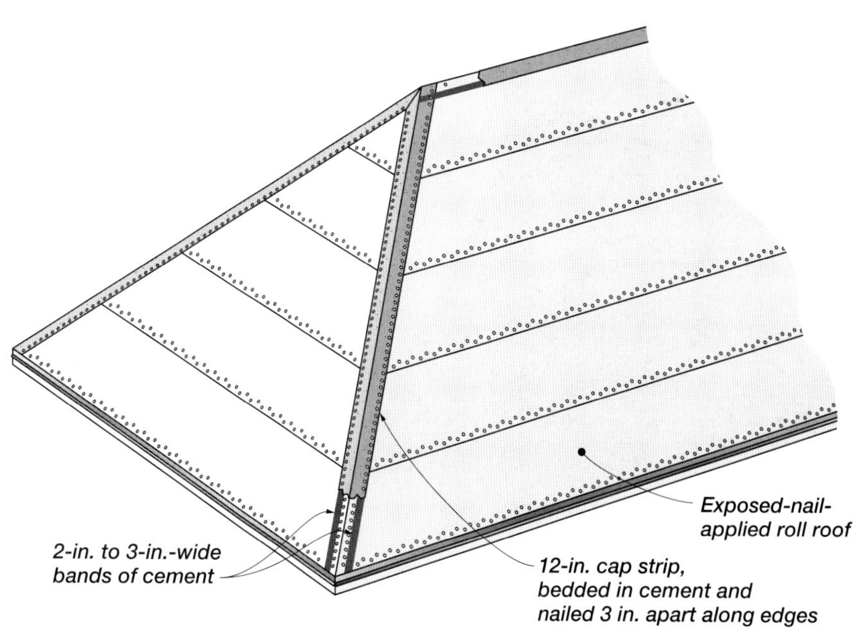

Horizontal Double Coverage

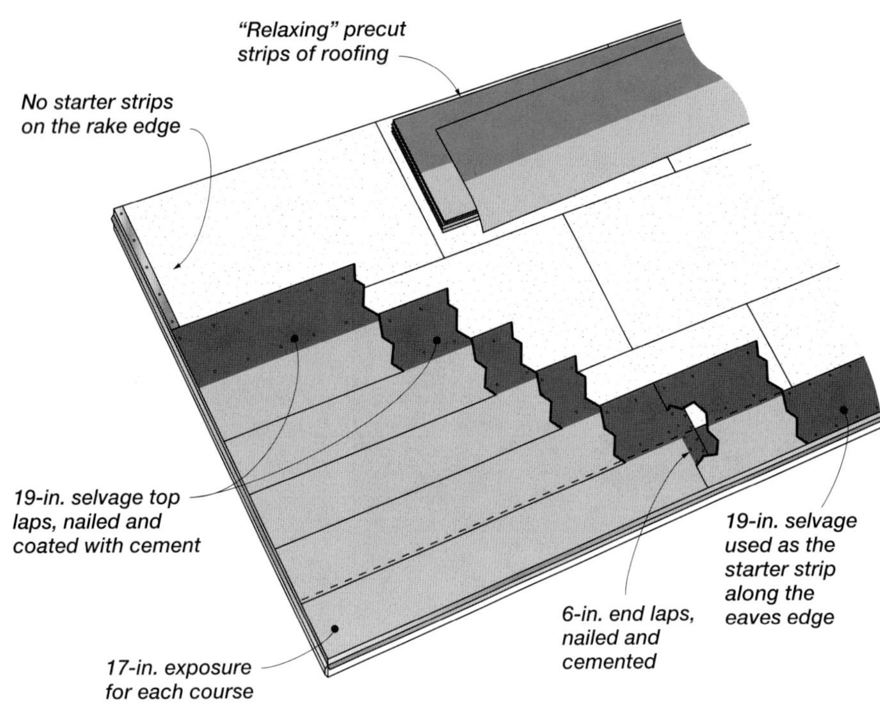

Vertical Double Coverage

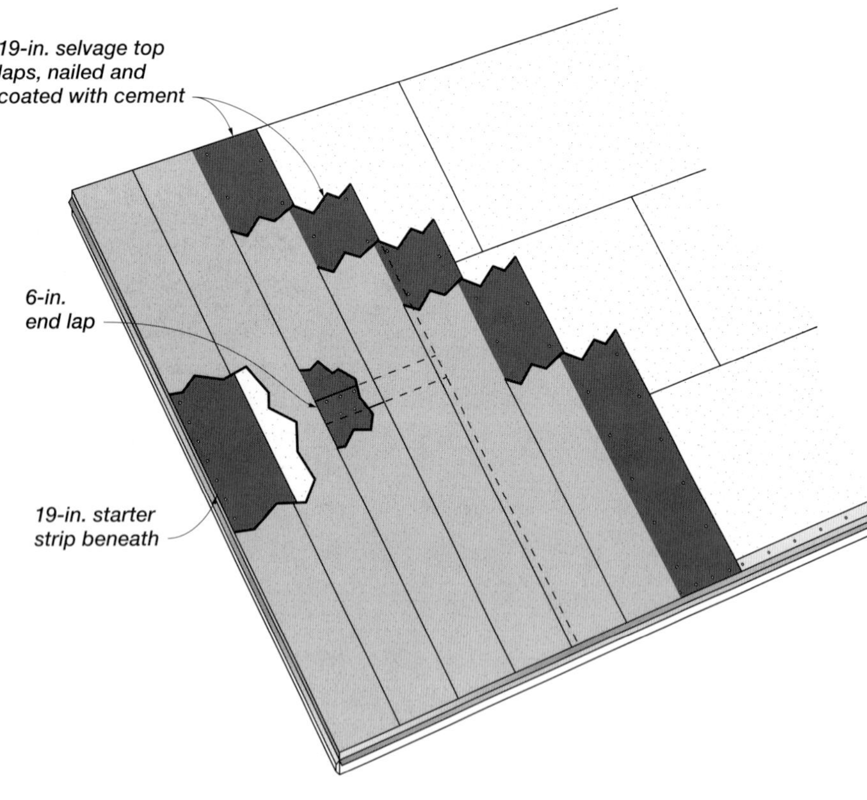

and stacking them on the roof to give the roofing a chance to relax and lie flat.

1. **Install eaves starters.** Cut the 19-in. selvage edge off a sheet of material to use as the starter strip along the eaves edge. Because the exposures of each course are cemented down to the top lap of the previous sheet that is nailed down, there's no need to run starter strips up rake edges.

   Overhang the eaves starter ½ in. beyond the drip edge and nail it down. Run one row of nails about 4 in. down from the top edge and a second row 2 in. up from the bottom edge and along the rake edges. Space the nails 8 in. to 12 in. apart.
2. **Install the first course.** Lay a full-width sheet of roll roofing completely over the starter. Align the eaves and rake edges, then drive a row of nails about 4 in. down from the top edge. Rolling back the lower portion, spread roof cement over the entire surface of the starter strip. Fold the lower portion of the full sheet over the starter and press it into the cement. Drive a second row of nails 14 in. to 15 in. down from the top of the sheet and 2 in. in along the rake.
3. **Install subsequent courses.** If the exposure granules on the selvage edge don't form a crisp line to follow, snap a chalkline 17 in. up from the butt edge. Lay another sheet of roll roofing over the selvage of the first full sheet. Using the granule edge or the chalkline, align the bottom of the sheet. Nail along the top (4 in. down), and fold the bottom of the sheet up to coat the selvage of the sheet beneath with cement. Use the granule edge or the chalkline as a guide to spread roof

cement over the top 19 in. of the sheet, keeping the cement ¼ in. to ½ in. back from the line.

Roll the bottom of the sheet over the cement-covered selvage, and press toward the bottom edge. For a good seal, force the cement until a little oozes out of the overlap. Continue installing additional courses until you reach the ridge, then finish the same as you would for single-coverage ridges.

Treat the end laps on double-coverage roll roofing the same way as for single-coverage concealed nailing. Nail down the edge of the first sheet and cover 6 in. with cement, then overlap the second sheet 6 in. to cover the cement and seal the sheet.

Finally, cut and install cap strips as described for the single-coverage concealed-nail method but with one important difference: Instead of overlapping the 12-in. by 36-in. strips by 6 in., overlap them 19 in. (see the illustration at right).

Hip and Ridge Cap Double Coverage

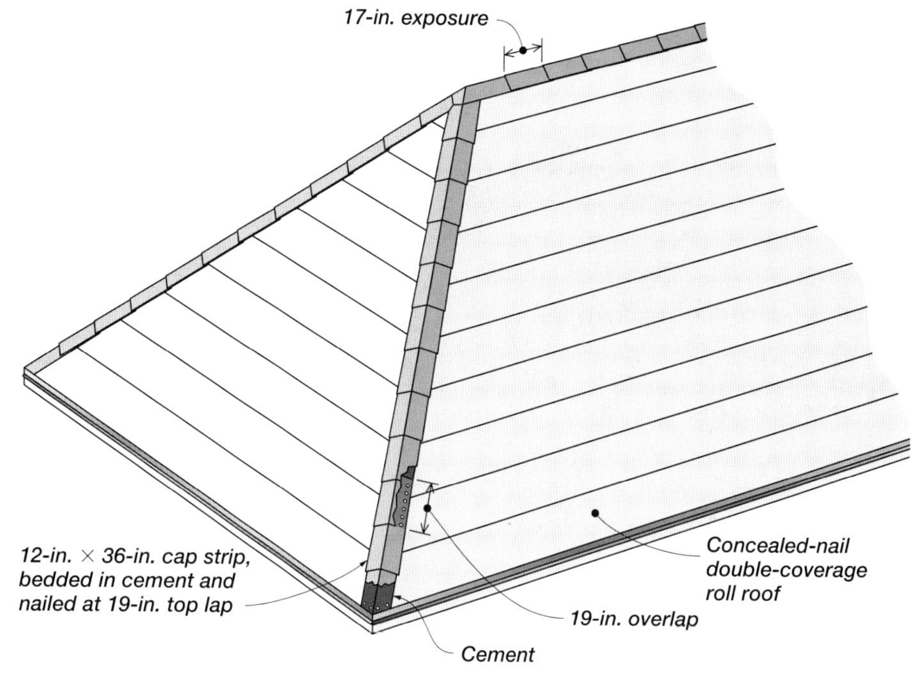

Time-Saving Tricks for Roll Roofing

You can speed the production of roll roofing by focusing your attention on one step and repeating it rather than jumping back and forth between aligning sheets and spreading cement.

After you nail on the top edge of a sheet, snap the chalkline for the bottom of the next course, then lay the next sheet in position. Don't pull out the roof cement or lap cement until you have all the courses positioned and nailed down along their top edges.

Starting at the ridge, flop the loose bottom of each sheet up over its top. Spread cement over the starter course along the eaves edge, and then roll the bottom half of the first full course down over it. Spread cement over the selvage of the first course and overlap the second course. Continue until you reach the top of the roof.

WORK SAFE
WORK SMART
THINKING AHEAD

Although you can install roll roofing alone, having an extra set of hands will make the process easier. A long sheet can be heavy to shift up and down to align accurately with the course beneath. And having someone to hold down a folded-back sheet while you spread lap cement will prevent the wind from prematurely placing the sheet.

Index